Unless Recalled Earlier
Date Due

D1116667

BRODART, INC.　　　　Cat. No. 23 233　　　　Printed in U.S.A.

The I.W.W. and the Paterson Silk Strike of 1913

The I.W.W. and the Paterson Silk Strike of 1913

Anne Huber Tripp

University of Illinois Press   Urbana and Chicago

© 1987 by the Board of Trustees of the University of Illinois
Manufactured in the United States of America
C 5 4 3 2 1

This book is printed on acid-free paper.

Library of Congress Cataloging-in-Publication Data

Tripp, Anne H. (Anne Huber), 1934–
   The I.W.W. and the Paterson silk strike of 1913.

   Bibliography: p.
   Includes index.
   1. Silk Workers' Strike, Paterson, N.J., 1913—History.
2. Industrial Workers of the World—History.   3. Social-
ist Party (U.S.)—History.   4. Paterson (N.J.)—
Economic conditions.   I. Title.
HD5325.T421913.P387   1987   331.89′287739′0974924   86-24989
ISBN 0-252-01382-4

To Robert Campbell Tripp

Contents

Preface

The Paterson silk strike of 1913 has been grist for many an historian's mill. In virtually all studies of the Industrial Workers of the World (I.W.W.), that anarcho-syndicalist labor organization which provoked panic in the hearts of the comfortable in the decade before the Great War, the struggle of the silk workers of New Jersey occupies a prominent position. Of those scholars who wrote about the I.W.W. in the 1960s, when interest in the revolutionary union was at a peak, Joseph R. Conlin, Melvyn Dubofsky, Philip S. Foner, and Patrick Renshaw all include a lengthy account of the struggle in Paterson.[1] That contest similarly is given full-chapter treatment in Graham Adams's study of the investigation of industrial violence by the 1914 Commission on Industrial Relations,[2] and in the anthology on the I.W.W. edited by Joyce L. Kornbluh.[3] The general strike in the silk industry of New Jersey also has been examined, in whole or in part, in numerous scholarly articles.[4]

Those individuals who played major or secondary roles during the strike have not lacked for biographers and, in many instances, have left their own reminiscences concerning their involvement in the Paterson struggle. William D. Haywood, the best-known figure in the I.W.W. and the most visible leader in the battle against the silk employers, is the subject of works by Conlin and Peter Carlson,[5] and is the author of a posthumously published account of his life and work in the I.W.W.[6] Elizabeth Gurley Flynn, the "Joan of Arc" or "Rebel Girl" of the labor movement and Haywood's feisty associate in Paterson, has to date found no biographer, but did relate the events of her early life in an autobiography published in 1955.[7] Less well-known leaders of the Paterson strike—Carlo Tresca, Patrick Quinlan, and local I.W.W. officers or members—were the subjects of contemporary pieces as well as authors of numerous accounts in the journals of the day.[8]

Others involved in the strike, albeit in less immediate roles, include men and women of the New York City area (loosely defined as liberal-minded intellectuals) who were I.W.W. sympathizers and contributed to the production of the artistically acclaimed Paterson Pageant. A number of these individuals, most notably Mabel Dodge, Hutchins Hapgood, and Max Eastman, have left lively accounts of their involvement in the Greenwich Village-based support system of the Paterson silk workers.[9] Additional observers/supporters of the I.W.W.-led struggle for whom the strike made a lasting-enough impression to be included in their memoirs are Upton Sinclair, Mary Heaton Vorse, Lincoln Steffens, and Margaret Sanger.[10]

One member of the New York circle, and the individual most closely associated with the production of the stunning pageant, unfortunately died before he could author his own full account of the strike and its Madison Square Garden reenactment. John Reed succumbed to typhus in Russia in 1920 leaving only a short autobiographical piece published years later; although his Paterson involvement is touched upon in that account, the complete story of this period in his short life comes from his biographers.[11]

The Paterson silk strike of 1913, then, has not been overlooked or left unexamined by either professional historians, biographers, I.W.W. field generals and publicists, approving writers and artists of the day, or contemporary journalists.[12] Even novelists of the period plumbed material and drew upon individuals associated with the struggle.[13] But there has not been a book-length account of the strike to detail all aspects of that event. If parts of the story have been done or even overdone, still a good portion of the struggle remains either unexplored or without appreciation of its full impact. The silk strike of 1913 deserves a book, and this study is an attempt to give the contest its due.

To the extent that one can call a strike dramatic, Paterson would qualify for such a description. At least as much as any other industrial struggle in our history, the I.W.W.-led contest contained all of the ingredients of a moving drama. This is so, first, because of the length of the strike and the number of workers who were directly involved in it: the labor confrontation in the silk industry, begun on February 25, 1913, lasted five full months and at its peak involved more than 25,000 workers.[14] As the strike wore on, and as the always meager relief sources virtually disappeared, the struggle between the strikers and their employers took on the tones of a grim fight for survival. When the battle of endurance finally came to an end—and in defeat for the workers—the curtain fell on a genuine tragedy for those who had withstood so much and gained so little.

There is drama also, or a dramatic quality, in the individuals who played the leading roles in the contest. The stars of the I.W.W. were in Paterson almost daily throughout the greater portion of the strike. "Big Bill" Haywood was a figure almost larger than life—a tall, one-eyed miner from the West, he captured national attention as he pleaded, promised, threatened and roared to keep the strike alive. By the time the contest ended, the physical toll on him was obvious: he literally sacrificed his health to the struggle. Elizabeth Gurley Flynn similarly attracted the attention of the public during the duration of the strike. Twenty-three years old in 1913, the "Rebel Girl" of the I.W.W. was already a seasoned veteran of the organization's battles; seen variously as a fearless fighter or a dangerous woman, she provided her own flair to the drama which unfolded.

Finally, the Paterson strike provided drama in the literal sense: the reenactment of the struggle before a New York City audience in early June. The artistic creation of Reed, given creative and financial support by the group of Greenwich Village intellectuals who identified with the struggle being fought across the Hudson River, the pageant makes the Paterson strike unique among the labor wars of the country.

The story of the Paterson strike thus deserves to be told in full because of its duration, the number of workers involved, the prominence of its leaders and supporters, and its melding on one night at least of art and revolution. But, more importantly, the prolonged contest demands attention for what it contributes to our understanding of the I.W.W., the labor union confrontations of the time, and the relationship between various left-looking organizations.

The Paterson strike tells us something about the intentions and the limitations of the industrial union which was formed in 1905 in reaction to the dominance and philosophy of the American Federation of Labor (A.F.L.). Launched less than one year after the I.W.W. had won a major victory for the textile workers of Lawrence, Massachusetts, the Paterson struggle was a crucial test of the durability and potential hegemony of the eight-year-old revolutionary body in the East. But unlike the Lawrence struggle, and the smaller contest fought among the textile workers in Little Falls, New York, prior to Paterson, the general strike of the silk workers ended in defeat. The question of why the New Jersey strike failed, particularly given the union's high hopes and recent victories in other branches of the textile industry, demands full attention.

The explanation of the failure is complex and includes the peculiar nature of the silk industry, the evident differences between Lawrence and Paterson, the varied responses of the city authorities in the two textile centers, and the way in which the two contests were perceived at the time. But part of the explanation can be found as well in the aims and tactics of the organization which orchestrated the strike and made it a center of national attention. If Lawrence demonstrated the I.W.W.'s strengths and potential, Paterson raises questions about its limitations.

The New Jersey silk strike also illuminates the struggle within the struggle of labor confrontations in the early twentieth century. Both the

A.F.L. and the Socialist Party of America (S.P.A.) played roles during the lengthy contest. Although this had also been true in Lawrence, the outcome of the I.W.W.-A.F.L. and I.W.W.-S.P.A. interrelationships are not identical. In both textile contests, the limited vision, self-interest, and conservative nature of the United Textile Workers' (U.T.W.) leaders is evident. In both Lawrence and Paterson the A.F.L. textile union was unable to attract the strikers to its standard; in each, after mounting an attempt to intervene and capture the leadership of the struggle, the A.F.L. withdrew with its reputation unenhanced if not badly tarnished. But in the relationship between the I.W.W. and the S.P.A., the outcome of the strike in Paterson differs substantially from that of Lawrence. In the Massachusetts woolen center, the S.P.A. played a role in the ultimate I.W.W. victory which suggested what might be accomplished if the two bodies could work together to improve the lot of the industrial workers of the country. Paterson tested the durability of that relationship and ended that promise. No sooner had the silk workers returned to the mills than a prolonged and heated war of words was launched between socialist and I.W.W. adherents. It is not an overstatement to contend that the Paterson strike had an important impact on the possibility of future joint efforts.

The lengthy contest in New Jersey also had a significant effect on the subsequent history of both Paterson and the I.W.W. For both the strike was crucial because the stakes were so high. Although "Silk City" was experiencing problems as a textile center well before 1913—the difficulties, in fact, played a part in precipitating the conflict—the strike contributed to and accelerated the further decline of the city. One of the ultimate victims, then, was Paterson itself. Whether it could have weathered its economic difficulties and remained a vibrant industrial center if the strike had never been launched is uncertain; but the 1913 battle had a deleterious effect on the city's future.

The same could be said for the organization which provided the leadership for the striking silk workers. What the future would have held for the I.W.W. if the Lawrence and Little Falls victories had been followed by a similar triumph in New Jersey can never be known, but the defeat in the silk center had a disastrous effect on the organization's campaign among eastern industrial workers. The months following the end of the struggle featured a self-examination of the union's goals, tactics, orientation, and organizational structure which can be described as anything but dispassionate. In attempting to find answers to explain the Paterson defeat, prominent I.W.W. leaders all too often engaged in heaping blame on one another. The I.W.W. changed in the years between 1913 and the advent of the government's war-inspired attack on the organization's leaders and the outcome of the Paterson battle provides part of the explanation for this change. Moreover, the defeat in the silk center of New Jersey marks the beginning of the end of the active involvement of many who had been most prominent in the union since its earliest days. The decline of Silk City and the decline or at least reorientation of the I.W.W. are thus part of the story of the Paterson strike.

Finally, although the Paterson strike of 1913 is a tale more than twice told by professional historians and interested parties, it remains an event with questions still unanswered. Not only is there a lack of agreement on why it failed, there is also no consensus on such matters as the degree of violence in the struggle, the role played by the I.W.W. in leading the strike, the impact of the pageant on the outcome, and whether part of the failure can be attributed to agent provocateurs within the I.W.W. ranks. One might argue whether history repeats itself —less arguable is whether historians repeat one another. Certainly, a close examination of the Paterson strike and its literature suggests that certain "facts" concerning it have been reiterated without close examination of the sources. Perhaps some of these errors can now be exposed and corrected.

A major problem for one who seeks to uncover what really happened and why concerns the number and nature of the sources available. The Paterson strike was a major chapter in the life of the I.W.W., and few members of that body could eschew the temptation to give their version of it. Moreover, since the contest took place less than twenty miles from New York City, it was given unusually complete media attention: the New York press and most of the best-known magazines of the day followed the progress of the strike fully from beginning to end. Paterson itself had four newspapers in 1913, and their front-page coverage and editorial comment continued throughout the battle.

In addition, the New Jersey silk strike was one of those industrial conflicts examined closely by the United States Commission on Industrial Relations, whose report runs to eleven volumes and includes the testimony of more than 700 witnesses.[15] As part of its investigation, the commission met for three and one-half days (June 15–18, 1914) in Paterson and heard testimony from twenty-one witnesses. Every voice possible was represented: I.W.W. local strike leaders, Paterson city authorities, socialist sympathizers, mill owners and managers, newspapermen, the business agents of the U.T.W.'s locals in the city, business leaders, and a Paterson clergyman. In all, their testimony fills 215 pages in the final report. The hearings provide a rich source of information for students of the Paterson strike and have been used in varying degrees by many of them, but the material presents the same difficulties as do

other accounts of the contest: how to determine the veracity and reliability of the witnesses.

The I.W.W. was from its inception an extraordinarily controversial
union, with dedicated members and supporters as well as equally determined detractors. Controversy followed it everywhere, and accounts
of its actions differ enormously. What one reads in the testimony before the Commission on Industrial Relations or in the press or autobiographical accounts too often is closer to propaganda, wishful thinking,
or self-serving remembrances than an accurate accounting of events or
motives. For example, if one follows the daily events of the strike in the
New York *Times*, the *American Federationist*, or the Paterson newspapers, none friendly to the I.W.W. and its role in Silk City, and com-
pares their accounts with those in the socialist New York *Call* or
Kansas-based *Appeal to Reason*, the I.W.W.'s *Solidarity*, Emma Goldman's *Mother Earth*, or the *International Socialist Review*, it is often
difficult to remember that all are discussing the same incidents or contest. Even within the two camps of friends and foes, there are evident
discrepancies dependent upon a particular orientation or purpose.[16] This
presents an enormous problem and challenge for the historian and in-
vites a variety of intepretations based on whose word or which account
is most fully utilized or deemed most credible.[17]

I am indebted to many people for their help and advice during the
preparation of this book. I am particularly grateful to my colleagues in
the history department and to the librarians and staff of Kresge Library
at Oakland University. The assistance given me at the Paterson Free
Library, the Labadie Collection of Labor Materials at the University
of Michigan, and the Archives of Labor History and Urban Affairs at
Wayne State University was of immeasurable help. My visits to New
Jersey were made enjoyable by the hospitality of Mary Lou and Walter
Boll.

I would like to thank Marjorie Hampton, Claire Smith, and Patricia
Tucker, who typed portions of the early draft of the manuscript; Rita
Edwards produced the final copy with exceptional speed, care, and good
humor; and Wendy Boschert, for her invaluable help with the index.
The errors that remain are my responsibility alone.

Finally, I wish to acknowledge my debt to Professor Sidney Fine,
who has been a friend and counselor to me, and to my late parents, who
supported me always in my endeavors. This book is dedicated to my
husband. Although he has never been to Paterson, he cared enough to
hear about the strike from beginning to end.

The I.W.W. and the Paterson Silk Strike of 1913

Chapter 1

The Industrial Workers of the World

The old form of pure and simple unionism has long since out-grown its usefulness; that it is now not only in the way of progress, but that it has become positively reactionary, a thing that is but an auxiliary of the capitalist class. . . . We are here for the purpose of uniting the working class, for the purpose of eliminating that form of unionism which is responsible for the conditions as they exist today.
—Eugene V. Debs's Speech Before the Founding Convention of the I.W.W., *Proceedings of the First Convention of Industrial Workers of the World* (New York, 1905), pp. 142–143.

The movement which eventually materialized in the formation of the I.W.W. had its roots in the western part of the United States. Although seen by some contemporaries as a manifestation of "the unbroken-colt spirit of the pioneers,"[1] its lineage might be more accurately traced to the A.F.L.'s disregard of western workers and its refusal to support industrial organization. The radical and often violent nature of the trans-Mississippi unions stemmed from peculiar characteristics of the area in which workers encountered employers in head-to-head contests unsoftened by the existence of a mitigating middle force.[2]

The guiding force behind the formation of the I.W.W. was the Western Federation of Miners (W.F.M.), a union of nonferrous metal workers established in 1893 after an unsuccessful strike at Coeur d'Alene, Idaho. Organized by Edward Boyce, who served as its first president, the W.F.M. sought to provide a measure of organizational strength to miners who, year after year, walked out of the mines in protest over their conditions only to be driven back in defeat. In 1897, in an effort to provide strength through unity, Boyce led the union into the A.F.L. But this marriage of convenience did not last. More prone to the frequent strike than the slow accumulation of a war chest to finance the well-timed walkout, organized on an industrywide basis rather than by craft, the W.F.M. disaffiliated when the A.F.L. did not provide the financial aid it sought. From that point in 1898, the W.F.M. set forth on its quest to establish a labor alliance which would be more amenable to the needs of the beleaguered miners.

The first step in this direction was taken in the same year that the W.F.M. returned its A.F.L. charter. At its annual convention in Salt Lake City, Boyce and his associates formed the Western Labor Union to unite those workers who shared the miners' problems—those in lumber camps, migrant agricultural laborers, and the like—and whose low economic status had led to their exploitation as strikebreakers in mining strikes of the past. In 1902 this organization was further broadened into the American Labor Union (A.L.U.), established in Denver to draw together all those who stood outside of the A.F.L.[3] This union proved to be a weak organization, with almost no support in the areas of A.F.L. strength and little more in the West.[4]

In 1903–1904, the W.F.M. led a number of strikes in the mining camps of Colorado. Despite the union's attempt to construct a sympathetic labor organization strong enough to assure victory in such confrontations, the strikes failed for lack of support. The W.F.M. considered reaffiliating with the A.F.L. as a result of its defeats, but, not in sympathy with the craft organization's policies, it finally decided to remain aloof and try again to establish a new industrial union. At its convention in the spring of 1904, sentiments for the creation of a broadly based industrial union crystalized, and the Executive Board was instructed "to take action necessary to bring organized labor together in one general organization."[5]

The next step toward the establishment of such an organization was taken in November 1904 when a group of six men met to explore the possibility in some depth. Those who gathered at this meeting in Chicago were William Trautmann, editor of the *Brauer Zeitung*, the official paper of the A.F.L.'s United Brewery Workers of America; George Estes and W. L. Hall, president and secretary-treasurer respectively of the United Brotherhood of Railway Employees; Clarence Smith, secretary-treasurer of the A.L.U.; Thomas J. Hagerty, editor of the A.L.U.'s *Voice of Labor*; and Isaac Cowen, the American representative of the Amalgamated Society of Engineers of Great Britain. These men, finding a sufficient area of agreement to proceed further, decided to extend an invitation to thirty-six others active in socialist or radical labor circles to attend a meeting the following January.

Those invited represented the whole spectrum of radical sentiment in the country and all, with the exception of Max Hayes and Victor Berger who declined to participate, accepted the call. In addition to those who had initiated it, the gathering included Algie M. Simons, a member of the S.P.A.; Charles Moyer and William D. Haywood, president and national secretary-treasurer respectively of the W.F.M.; Charles O. Sherman, general secretary of the United Metal Workers International Union; Frank Bohm, a member of the Socialist Labor Party (S.L.P.) and a lecturer in history at Columbia; and "Mother" Jones, the legendary septuagenarian organizer of the United Mine Workers.

The outcome of the January meeting was the issuance of a "manifesto" and call for a convention to establish a new industrial union. A critique of existing organizations and a blueprint for what should be constructed in their place, the manifesto read in part:

> Previous efforts for the betterment of the working class have proven abortive because limited in scope and disconnected in action. Universal economic evils can only be eradicated by a universal working class movement. Such a movement of the working class is impossible while separate craft and wage agreements are made favoring the employer against other crafts in the same industry, and while energies are wasted in the fruitless jurisdictional struggles, which serve only the personal aggrandizement of union officials.
>
> A movement to meet these conditions must consist of one great industrial union embracing all industries, providing for craft autonomy locally, industrial autonomy internationally, and working class unity generally. It should be founded on the class struggle, and its general administration should be conducted in harmony with the recognition of the irrepressible conflict between the capitalist class and the working class.
>
> It should be established as the economic organization of the working class without affiliation with any political party.
>
> All power should rest in the collective membership.

Those who agreed with these principles were invited to assemble in Chicago on June 27, 1905, "for the purpose of forming an economic organization of the working class along the lines marked out in the manifesto." The three-day January meeting ended with the appointment of a five-man committee to plan and promote the convention. Chaired by Haywood, the members were Trautmann, Simons, Hall, and Smith.[6]

Those who affixed their signatures to the manifesto were not the only individuals active during the interval between the issuance of the call and the opening of the convention.[7] The plan to establish a new all-encompassing industrial union predicated on the existence of class conflict, the appeal to existent trade unions to eschew organization by craft and join with the unorganized and unskilled industrial workers, demanded a response from individuals and groups within the socialist and union movements. For many, the period from January to June 1905 was one of soul-searching and a reexamination of long-held principles and commitments.

Samuel Gompers and his associates in the A.F.L. needed no time for reflection. Recognizing a direct frontal attack when they saw one, the federation's leaders acted quickly to make their views known. Every number of the *American Federationist* from March through June contained at least one vitriolic assault on the architects of the proposed revolutionary union. Gompers, employing the devices of ridicule and distortion, led the verbal charge. Assuming an attitude of déjà vu, the A.F.L. president chose to mock the new movement as just more "delectable work" by those who for years had tried to "divert, pervert, and disrupt the labor movement in the country." It was, he contended in dismissal, simply another socialist convention.[8]

For members of the S.P.A., a response to the January call proved difficult. Gompers could lump all socialists together, including even members of Daniel DeLeon's S.L.P., but the socialist movement in the United States was far from unified. In 1905 the S.P.A. was more a thin body with two pronounced wings—the radicals or "impossibilists" on one side, the moderates or "slow-cialists" on the other—than a monolithic party which spoke with one voice.

Although a number of issues divided the two factions, one of the more prominent concerned the relationship of the party to the labor movement, particularly to the A.F.L. The radical wing was disdainful of the "half-loaf materialism" of the A.F.L., despaired that its craft form of organization would ever be altered, and ridiculed its lack of class consciousness. Many of those in this wing of the party, including Debs, its titular head, had long advocated the establishment of an industrial union with socialist goals. The moderates of the party, men like Hayes and Berger, opposed such dual unionism. Although critical of many of the same A.F.L. policies that Debs opposed, they remained in the federation and sought to introduce change from within. At the 1904 convention of the S.P.A., the latter position was upheld by the delegates. Despite the urging of Debs and others, the members refused to issue a condemnation of A.F.L. policies and declined to put the party on record in support only of industrial unionism. The convention in fact passed a resolution urging workers to join the federation.[9]

The vote on the trade-union resolution in 1904 made evident a line of division within the party which tended to hold when the question of joining the new industrial organization was raised the following year. Those members of the S.P.A. who attended the June convention or later joined its creation came from the minority radical wing of the party and acted contrary to the official position it had taken. Of the prominent S.P.A. members, only Debs and Simons were present at the Chicago convention. Their support of the industrial movement, as individuals rather than as party representatives, was more than matched by the vocal opposition of other well-known members, particularly National Committeemen Berger and Hayes.[10]

The S.L.P.'s response to the January manifesto was in direct contrast to that of the S.P.A., but its membership of 1,400 was no equal to the 10,000 counted in the rival party. In addition, the early initiators of the revolutionary industrial union were something less than enthusiastic about forming an alliance with S.L.P. leader DeLeon. A domineering and divisive figure who sought to lead any group that he joined, the "socialist Pope" had not been invited to the January meeting; Simons, in fact, was concerned when he saw DeLeon's interest in the result. But DeLeon was a natural participant in such a venture. For over a decade, the brilliant but irascible DeLeon had attacked the policies and leadership of the A.F.L. Demonstrating his apt description as a "master of political invective," he had called the trade union "a cross between a windbag and a rope of sand," and had dismissed Gompers as a "labor fakir" and "a greasy tool of Wall Street."[11]

DeLeon's commitment to industrial unionism was well developed before the conception of the I.W.W. in 1905. Joining the S.L.P. in 1889, he soon urged the formation of an industrial union and, in 1895, he helped form the Socialist Trade and Labor Alliance (S.T.&L.A.). The S.T.&L.A. never reached the heights its founder hoped for it, but it still existed in 1905. DeLeon saw the Chicago convention as a way to revive the aim of his union and was not hesitant to voice his support. Writing in the *Daily People* on the day the convention was to begin, he hailed the event as "destined to make an important change in the history of Labor."[12] Simons might have been apprehensive about DeLeon's association with the new union he hoped to form, but the S.L.P. leader demanded a role.

On June 27, 1905, the long-anticipated Chicago convention opened in Brand's Hall. The 186 delegates, claiming to represent 50,000 workers, came from some thirty-four local, state, district, and national organizations. The number of groups, however, which sent official delegations distorts the true nature of the assemblage: the bulk of those said to be represented came from the W.F.M., with a membership of 27,000, and the A.L.U., with 16,000. There is considerable truth to the view that the convention was "simply the Western Federation plus a smattering of fellow-travelers." The absence of the broad vein of support which the founders had hoped to mine was particularly evident in the small representation from unions affiliated with the A.F.L. Of the organizations represented in Chicago, only sixteen held federation charters and even the socialist-led and industrially organized United Brewery Workers did not follow Trautmann into the new labor union.[13]

The three giants of the founding convention—Debs, DeLeon, and Haywood —personified the varied positions and ambitions of those present. Debs, representing only a wing of the S.P.A. but generally acknowledged as the most notable man present, sought the establishment of an organization which would serve as the "economic backbone of the political socialist movement" which he had helped found in 1901. DeLeon, with similar ambition, hoped to forge a dual union which would become the economic arm of his S.L.P. and assume the role which the S.T.&L.A. had been too weak to play. Haywood, a member of the W.F.M., A.L.U., and S.P.A., spoke on behalf of the unionist aspirations of western workers who had long been dissatisfied with the organizational structure and dues-paying mentality of the A.F.L. Many of the men Haywood represented were simple unionists who wanted a less conservative organization at their head. The western delegates of the W.F.M. and A.L.U., outnumbering the others in voting power, opposed political affiliation as vehemently as they derided the A.F.L. assumption of the community of interest between employer and employee. Their principal aim was to establish a class-conscious apolitical organization which would speak for the mass of unskilled workers.[14]

Haywood, chosen to chair the convention, presented this position in his opening comments. "This is the Continental Congress of the working class," he began after he had gavelled the delegates to order. "We are here to confederate the workers of this country into a working class movement that shall have for its purpose the emancipation of the working class from the slave bondage of capitalism." After establishing the thesis of class struggle as the common ground upon which the diverse representatives could unite, Haywood launched into an equally noncontroversial attack on the A.F.L. Dismissing it as an organization not of the working class, he warned that Gompers's union would be "the most ardent enemy" which the new body confronted.[15] Other speakers rushed to take up this theme and no address was complete without at least one impassioned blast against what Trautmann termed "the harmful actions of the officers of the A. F. of L."[16]

If condemnation was one thread in the oratorical tapestry of the convention, the appeal for unity was another. Recognizing the ideological gulfs which divided the delegates, leaders of the various factions preached conciliation. Debs could not forego a jab at the S.T.&L.A. and his old adversary DeLeon, but he emphasized that past divisions could be bridged. "I believe that there is a middle ground that can be occupied without the slightest concession of principle," he declared. "I believe it is possible for such an organization as the W.F.M. to be brought into harmonious relation with the Socialist Trade and Labor Alliance."[17]

Debs's appeal for harmony, directed primarily toward the S.L.P. contingent, was well received by DeLeon. For a time at least, the latter was willing to join forces with those in the convention who did not share his views.

The test of the protestations of unity and good will came over the question of the new organization's political orientation or affiliation. The major division on this issue was between those who envisioned a purely economic body and those who sought to include some statement of political purpose as well. David C. Coates, a representative of the A.L.U., voiced the unionist position, but his appeal was challenged by delegates who wanted the constitution of the new union to include a strong political plank.[18] The arguments of S.P.A. and S.L.P. loyalists aroused some suspicion that each of the two socialist parties intended to capture the I.W.W.

The point was finally resolved in a clause which disclaimed any political affiliation while including political as well as economic action: "Between these two classes [capital and labor] a struggle must go on until all the toilers come together on the political, as well as the industrial field, and take and hold that which they produce by their labor through an economic organization of the working class, without affiliation with any political party." The acceptance of this clause by a sizeable majority settled the matter for the moment, but the issue was papered over rather than firmly resolved.

The delegates to the founding convention found it less difficult to agree on other matters pertaining to the nature of the new organization. In large measure, they simply fashioned an industrial union which remedied the perceived faults of the A.F.L. In place of the relatively high initiation fee and dues of the federation, a policy which tended to place a heavy burden on the low-paid unskilled workers, the I.W.W. constitution set a limit of $.50 a month on dues and a maximum initiation fee of $5. The exact sum would be set by the individual industrial departments. (Later, dues of $.25 and initiation fees of $1 were common.) The A.F.L. policy of signing trade agreements for specified periods of time was also cashiered. Arguing that such contracts prevented workers from striking when the time might be best and also served to preclude sympathy strikes, the I.W.W. reserved the right to use the strike weapon when and where it chose. The new union, in fact, differed from the federation in its entire concept of the strike. Instead of seeing it as a last resort, called reluctantly and only when sufficient funds had been accumulated to sustain it, the I.W.W. preached the positive virtue of frequent and unexpected walkouts. The strike, and particularly the general strike, was seen as a device to educate the worker and as a weapon in the class warfare which would ultimately result in the workers' control and operation of industries.[19]

Following the framing of the Constitution of the I.W.W., the convention delegates rushed to complete business and adjourn. Their last task was the election of officers for the new union, a matter not given undue attention by an assemblage which emphasized grass-roots rather than centralized direction. When Coates and Haywood both refused to accept nomination for president, Sherman of the United Metal Workers was selected for that office. Trautmann was then chosen as the secretary-treasurer of the General Executive Board.[20]

The meeting adjourned on July 8, and the weary delegates scattered to await the reaction to their work. They could guess what would be forthcoming from Gompers, and he did not disappoint them. In an editorial in the first number of the *American Federationist* following the convention, the A.F.L. president was at his deprecating best: "The fame of the three tailors of Tooley Street, London, who issued a proclamation in the name of 'We, the people of England,' has lived for over three hundred years. Alas! they have now been outdone and will henceforth be supplanted by the ... gathering held at Chicago. . . . These later-day bombasts . . . needs speak in the name of the workers of the world.

"The mountain labored and brought forth a mouse, and a very silly little mouse at that." To Gompers, the new organization was simply an amalgamation of already proven failures: the "vulture-like" S.T.&L.A. and the "confessedly dying" A.L.U. He was confident that time would expose the Chicago "hodge-podge" as the "most vapid and ridiculous" meeting ever assembled and the delegates as "the most stupendous impossibles" in history.[21]

Gompers's reaction to their accomplishment might have prompted a smile from the I.W.W. founders since the A.F.L. was the prime target of the new organization and the yelp of its president suggested the barbs had found their mark. Besides, few of those whom the I.W.W. hoped to attract were readers of the *American Federationist*! More important was the response of the socialist press.

DeLeon's *People*, the organ of the S.L.P., not surprisingly greeted the new union with great enthusiasm and urged the party loyalists to give it their support.[22] In Chicago, the *International Socialist Review*, with a circulation of 4,000 and a readership which spanned the socialist spectrum, also offered its early editorial endorsement. Simons was its editor in 1905 and, as one of the earliest proponents of an industrial union movement under socialist leadership, he used the monthly to praise the work of the convention and to promote the fortunes of its creation.[23] The *Appeal to Reason*, published in Girard, Kansas, as the voice of radical causes in the Great Plains area, was somewhat less supportive.[24] But, despite its reservations, it at least tolerated the I.W.W. and, along with the *International Socialist Review*, was a conduit which carried news of it to those most likely to be interested.

In an August article in the Chicago socialist monthly, Debs had acknowledged that the organization's progress would be "beset with difficulties," but had expressed confidence that it could "sturdily face and successfully overcome them all."[25] The S.P.A. leader's recognition of the problems proved to be more prophetic than his assurance that they could be surmounted! The first years of the I.W.W. were so beset with internal wrangling and near ruinous defections and ousters that the organization seemed destined never to reach adolescence.

The rock upon which the I.W.W. foundered was the heterogeneous and often conflicting aspirations of its leaders. Visible at the founding convention, it was only a matter of time before the pledges of conciliation and compromise were broken. President Sherman, the United Metal Workers' leader and S.P.A. moderate, was the first to fall victim to the internecine squabbling. Almost as soon as the 1905 Convention disbanded, the luckless Sherman came under attack. Caught in the crossfire between those who wished to tie the I.W.W. to the Marxist orthodoxy of the S.L.P. and those who wished to delete the political clause from the constitution, and not helped by Trautmann's personal enmity nor his own financial incompetence, Sherman lasted only until the 1906 Convention. With the faction led by DeLeon and Vincent St. John dominating, the convention abolished the office of president, elected Trautmann secretary-treasurer, and chose a new General Executive Board.[26]

The second convention changed the nature and composition of the union in a significant way, but it did not put an end to the internal divisions. DeLeon and St. John had fashioned an alliance to oust Sherman, but little harmony could be expected as long as the politically oriented DeLeon and the nonpolitical "Saint" remained under the same banner. What the 1906 meeting did provide was a cleaning out of the most traditional unionists in the organization. The I.W.W. thus began its transformation from "a mass industrial union of workers fighting for limited economic demands [into] a revolutionary organization proclaiming an all-out fight against the capitalist system."[27]

The DeLeon-St. John victory provoked the defection of the most numerous faction within the organization, the W.F.M. The majority of the W.F.M. delegates to the second convention sided with the Sherman supporters and bolted the meeting. The following year the W.F.M. severed its affiliation with the I.W.W., taking with it the mass of workers the organization had claimed to represent. After its defection, the actual membership of the union fell to less than 6,000.[28] Only if revolutionary zeal is viewed as a worthy substitute for mass appeal can the result of the 1906 imbroglio be interpreted as an encouraging sign for the young organization.

Debs and Simons were also casualties of the Second Convention. Although Debs was not present to witness the events at first hand, the socialist leader was repelled by the outcome. He did not publicly disavow the organization he had praised so fulsomely the year before, in fact he often defended it in later years, but he did not renew his membership.[29] Simons was appalled by what had transpired and was not reticent in expressing his ire. Writing for the *International Socialist Review* while the convention was still in session, he held nothing back in attacking the work of the "bunch of half-crazed fanatics under the leadership of DeLeon."[30]

The disassociation of the W.F.M. and the withdrawal of Debs and Simons virtually ended the active connection between prominent members of the S.P.A. and the I.W.W. Although the party had never endorsed the dual union, a number of its members had joined; after the 1906 Convention, many of these quit the organization. For those who remained, of whom the most notable was Haywood, the dual allegiance became increasingly difficult.

From 1906 to 1908, the I.W.W. limped along in a semi-moribund state. Despite its widespread activities in leading strikes, the union made few organizational gains. The depression of these years was part of the difficulty, but internal faults were at least of equal importance. Even before the economy began its downward slide, it was evident that the recruitment of members was hampered by the inability of the I.W.W. to finance its organizational effort. Partly because of its low dues policy and partly because of its financial ineptitude, the union could not support its organizers in the field. By the end of 1907, only five organizers remained to cover the entire country. It was not surprising that the membership of the union grew little.[31]

The one bright spot for the I.W.W. in the interval between the Second (1906) and Third (1908) Conventions, although not evident at the time, were the 1907 trials of Haywood and Moyer in Idaho. Arrested along with George Pettibone more than a year before for the murder of former Idaho Governor Frank Steunenberg in December 1905, the W.F.M. leaders attracted the sympathy and support of virtually the entire radical and labor movement in the country. Haywood, the first of the accused to be tried, became a hero. Although long a well-known figure among the miners of the West, his reputation had been essentially regional. The trial changed this and the W.F.M. officer emerged as a symbol of radical and unionist protest in the country; the ordeal transformed him into a public figure with an international reputation.[32]

For the W.F.M., the initial beneficiary of the publicity attached to the trials, and for the I.W.W., which depleted its slim treasury to aid the defense fund, the event had particular significance. As one consequence of their long incarceration, the relationship between Haywood and Moyer became strained. After the two were acquitted, Moyer returned to the presidency of the W.F.M. and began to ease his fellow defendant from the organization. In 1908, partly because of personal animosity and partly because he was identified with a radical position which the more unionist-oriented Moyer did not share, Haywood was not reelected to his position in the W.F.M. His largest role thereafter would be within the S.P.A. and the I.W.W., the principal beneficiaries of his new-found notoriety.[33]

The S.P.A. was first to capitalize on Haywood's new acclaim. In 1906, although the W.F.M. leader was in prison awaiting the start of his trial, the party nominated him as its gubernatorial candidate in Colorado.[34] The following year the *Appeal to Reason* urged his nomination as the party's presidential candidate in 1908.[35] Haywood did not make a bid for the nomination—although he is said to have entertained the notion—but he did further build up his credits in the party when he actively supported Debs in the campaign. After the election he continued his work in the S.P.A., becoming a spokesman of the radical wing. In 1910, he was chosen as a delegate to the International Socialist Congress in Copenhagen and the following year he was elected to the General Executive Committee of the party.[36]

Haywood retained his membership in the I.W.W. during these years, but his involvement as a spokesman and rising figure in the Socialist party superseded his work in the union. This was just as well. He thus avoided the controversy which continued to fragment that body, particularly the conflict between St. John and DeLeon which marked the I.W.W.'s Third Convention.

The issue in 1908 was the political clause in the organization's constitution. St. John had been opposed from the beginning to the inclusion of the statement supporting political action and had voted against it in 1905. More than simply fearful that Debs and DeLeon sought to use the I.W.W. to advance the fortunes of their respective socialist parties, the Saint saw the class struggle as one in which political and parliamentary procedures were irrelevant. Coming from a western environment in which many of the workers were rootless transients for whom the ballot had no meaning, he believed only in direct economic action. In addition to differences over political action, although not wholly divorced from them, St. John and DeLeon disagreed on unionist tactics. The veteran of the western mining wars urged use of the most militant tactics (including sabotage and disregard of the law); DeLeon advocated fighting capitalism on a more "civilized" plane. When the Third Convention of the I.W.W. convened, therefore, the two remaining giants in the movement — one a political theorist and intellectual, the other schooled in the violent conflicts of the mining camps—stood ready to contend for supremacy.[37]

Although DeLeon cannot be taken as an impartial observer of what transpired at the 1908 convention in Chicago, his account captures the flavor of what occurred:

> Among the G.E.B. [General Executive Board] members and general officials, some desperate measures were ripening for fruition, augmented by a delegation from Spokane known to fame as the "Overall Brigade" and headed by J. Walsh.
> They proceeded to execute their plan, by any means. Depriving some of the delegates of their seats, under pressure from the "Hallelujah, I'm a Bum" outfit, the way was cleared for the end in view, the changing of the fundamental law of the I.W.W.
> Vincent St. John, who in the morning at headquarters, had given an exhibition of his concept of settling differences of opinion, by hitting a delegate with whom he differed, a vicious blow in the face ... became the hero in the plot to emasculate the Industrial Union movement.[38]

DeLeon was one of those denied a seat at the convention. With his ejection, the westerners were able to dominate the S.L.P. delegates and score a victory for the direct-action, nonpolitical faction. The transformation of the I.W.W. was then made more complete when the political clause was deleted from the constitution. St. John, clear victor over the "Socialist Pope," was elected to the position of general secretary and treasurer.

Joseph R. Conlin denies that the deletion of the political clause had much ideological importance,[39] but most students of the organization have seen the events of 1908 as significant in altering the direction of the industrial union.[40] Even if the change was more apparent than real, based more on expediency and personality than ideology, it did prompt a harmful and confusing division among the industrial unionists. DeLeon, unwilling to accept the defeat handed him in Chicago, rallied his supporters. The S.L.P. loyalists set up an industrial organization, also under the label I.W.W., and elected officers to guide it. Henceforth, until the DeLeon union changed its name to the Workers' International Industrial

Union in 1914, this organization continued to vie with the St. John-led body for recognition as *the* I.W.W. After it established its headquarters in Detroit, it was referred to as the Detroit I.W.W. to distinguish it from the antipolitical Chicago I.W.W. The Detroit faction never was numerically strong, but it did lead some strikes in the East and contributed its share to the labor confusions of the day.[41]

Following the 1908 Convention, the Chicago I.W.W. was led by direct-action militants, revolutionary in spirit and creative in tactics, who identified with the most powerless and ill-paid workers in the country. Their first source of membership was from among the migratory workers of the West, particularly those in agriculture and lumbering. The nonpolitical proponents of class warfare held an appeal to these rootless westerners who rarely cast ballots, were attracted by the revolutionary rhetoric of I.W.W. organizers, and had already experienced a form of economic warfare in their confrontations with employers. It was among this group, who drifted in and out of the union as their condition varied, that the St. John organization attracted national notice.[42]

The I.W.W. gained recognition as a militant revolutionary organization, rather than a somewhat eccentric band of warring antagonists, during a series of "free-speech" campaigns in the Northwest. Associated with its aim to organize and lead the migrant workers in that part of the country, the first of these battles began in 1909. In that year, in the city of Spokane, I.W.W. organizers began their drive to recruit members from among the restless and unorganized migrant workers. They set up their soapboxes near the hiring halls where the unemployed sought work, handed out their literature, and harangued those who stopped to listen to their indictment of the employing class and their promise that the workers would eventually control the means of production. Such talk frightened the local inhabitants. The police were sent in, the meetings broken up, and the organizers arrested. Thus did a practical effort to enlist worker support take on the overtones of a battle to uphold the constitutional rights of free speech and assembly. Once the local authorities began to arrest the speakers, I.W.W. members and sympathizers would pour into the city, court arrest as they filled the places of their already imprisoned comrades, and clog the jails to overflowing. The need to feed and house the men and women who sought rather than avoided arrest finally put such pressure on the city's treasury that the authorities would relent and release them all. The free-speech fight would thus end, and the soapbox orators and their rail-riding cohorts would move on to repeat the process elsewhere.[43]

The union's activities in a very different arena were of more lasting importance in the life of the organization than the some thirty free-speech fights waged prior to 1916. Coupled with the "hobo" or "bummery" element which the dual union attracted in the West was the vast number of more stationary unskilled workers in the industrial centers of the East. These workers had similarly been ignored by the craft orientation of the A.F.L. and were among the most poorly paid and powerless group within the American labor force. Shunned by the skilled workers in their own industries and exploited by their employers, this heavily immigrant mass seemed ripe for any organization which promised hope and offered direction. The I.W.W. policy of low dues and minimal initiation fees, its emphasis on rank-and-file direction, its willingness to strike, and its militant denunciation of the employers appealed to them.[44] Even before the tumultuous Third Convention, the I.W.W. had led a number of strikes among this group, most notably in the textile industry of New England. The first major strike in the East, however, occurred in 1909 at McKees Rocks, Pennsylvania. There, the I.W.W. captured a strike in progress and won a victory over the Pressed Steel Car Company, an affiliate of the United States Steel Corporation.[45]

Oddly, the I.W.W. did not follow up its success in Pennsylvania by a concerted organizing effort among the industrial workers of the East. The free-speech fights diverted the union's efforts westward, and until 1912 most of its attention focused there. Even the membership gains registered during the McKees Rocks struggle were lost.[46] But the strike, despite this, was a significant chapter in the early history of the I.W.W. It demonstrated that a heterogeneous mass of unskilled immigrant workers could be mobilized and led by a labor organization willing to make the effort. Further, it provided a first opportunity for the union to develop tactics which could be employed in future confrontations. The victory in Pennsylvania was truly "the harbinger of a new spirit among the unorganized workers in the Eastern manufacturing districts."[47] In 1912, the I.W.W. would build on the discontent of these workers and score its greatest victory.

Chapter 2

Lawrence

No strike ever "succeeded" that was not encouraged and directed by some measure of practical wisdom. A strike, like any other rude force, is so much power applied for a specific object. It does not "succeed" because it is a strike. If it succeeds, it is only by virtue of shrewd and skillful adaptation to time, to place, and to conditions. —John G. Brooks, *American Syndicalism: The I.W.W.* (New York, 1913), p. 149.

Here in Lawrence was the flame; that surging forward toward the light which is the distinction of mankind.—Mary Heaton Vorse, *A Footnote to Folly* (New York, 1935), p. 14.

Even during its unpromising first half-decade of existence, when personal and theoretical differences winnowed out many of the early leaders and the 1907 depression contributed to the decline in membership, the I.W.W. had been active in the textile industry. Haywood, at the founding convention, had singled out the textile workers as one group to which the new union could appeal and his statement proved prophetic. One characteristic of textile unionism at the time was its centrifugal tendency; few other industries experienced such a profusion of unions, each flourishing for a period before it withered away to be replaced by a new organization. In part, the explanation for this lay in the very nature of the industry. Plagued by cyclical depressions, marked by technological advances which reduced its dependence on craft skills, and increasingly manned by a heterogeneous mix of immigrants, the textile industry both generated frequent labor explosions and thwarted union longevity.[1]

The I.W.W., as ready and willing to challenge the A.F.L. in the textile industry as elsewhere, made its first show of strength against the U.T.W. in Skowhegan, Maine. During the summer of 1906 its organizers began to work among the operatives of the Marston Worsted Mills in that city. Exploiting long-standing grievances of low pay and poor conditions, an excessive fine system, and alleged brutality on the part of foremen, the I.W.W. organized Local 376 and began to enroll members. Soon after its formation, Local 376 sought a 10 percent wage increase and was able to obtain an immediate 5 percent raise with the remainder promised the following summer if business remained good. In January 1907, however, management began to move against those workers who had been active in pressing for the earlier increment, and the I.W.W. responded by demanding the additional 5 percent at once. When the company dismissed some forty of the union members, the rest struck. The I.W.W. later charged that U.T.W. President John Golden offered "scabs" to help break the strike, but if Golden did try to use his members in that way, his effort was not successful. In April the Marston Mills settled on terms which included reinstatement of the dismissed workers without discrimination, abolition of the fine system, and recognition of an elected shop committee to meet regularly with management.[2]

The success in Skowhegan was followed by organizing drives and strikes in other textile centers of the East. Within a year the I.W.W. had eight textile locals and had waged strikes in Rhode Island, Pennsylvania, and New Jersey. Although these strikes were not successful by Skowhegan standards, the interest in the I.W.W. manifested by the textile workers prompted General Organizer Trautmann to recommend that representatives of the existing locals be brought together to consider forming a national textile union within the I.W.W.

The General Executive Board responded by calling a convention in Paterson for May 1, 1908. On that date, twenty-two delegates—representing the locals in Paterson; Providence and Woonsocket, Rhode Island; and Lowell, New Bedford, and Lawrence, Massachusetts—began three days of deliberation. By the meeting's end, the National Industrial Union of Textile Workers (N.I.U.T.W.) had been established. This first industrial union formed by the I.W.W. was to be open to workers in every branch of the textile industry, with locals organized by language groups or by production unit.[3]

From its beginning in Paterson, the N.I.U.T.W. set forth to build up its organizational strength. Early in 1910, Secretary-Treasurer Francis Miller reported that there were eleven locals in good standing, that the I.W.W. was attracting the Italian and Armenian textile workers in New England, and that union prospects were particularly good in Lawrence, where Local 20 had recently opened a new headquarters and had a membership second only to that in New Bedford.[4] By the fall of the year, however, Miller had to admit that the union's condition was less bright. A depression had struck the textile industry (most severely in the silk, wool, and worsted branches) and an estimated one-half of the N.I.U.T.W. members were out of work and unable to pay the minimal dues.[5]

The N.I.U.T.W. managed to weather the economic doldrums, albeit in a weakened condition, and in 1911 mounted an ambitious organizing effort in the textile cities. Among the I.W.W. speakers who took part in a lecture tour for the union was Elizabeth Gurley Flynn, later to gain fame in the textile strikes of 1912–1913. Referring to the Flynn efforts, Miller wrote in July 1911: "From all reports, this is the most successful tour of an I.W.W. speaker in the East. Big meetings are reported from every place, and increasing interest in the idea of 'The One Big Union.'"[6] The I.W.W. was six months away from engaging in what would become its most successful activity in the textile industry, the strike in Lawrence.

In 1912 Lawrence had a factory investment of some $80 million, an annual payroll of approximately $13 million, and a total work force of 30,000; it stood second in the country as a producer of woolens and worsteds. The dominant employer was the giant American Woolen Company, which operated the Ayer, Prospect, Washington, and Wood mills in the city. The last of these, the largest facility of its kind in the country, had thirty acres of floor space under one roof. The Washington Mill, the original but largely rebuilt American Woolen plant, and the relatively new Ayer Mill adjoined the Wood on the south side of the Merrimack. Modern-appearing structures of six stories, the three mills together extended in length almost one-half mile and were connected to Lawrence proper by a bridge. The American Woolen Company employed 16,500 workers in 1912 with the remainder of the textile operatives employed in the Lawrence Dye Works, the Pacific Mills, the Arlington Mills, and a few other smaller mills.[7]

The textile industry in Lawrence prospered and grew steadily until 1907; it was a mecca for those seeking work, and skilled and unskilled alike found ready employment there. The detached observer would have found it difficult to understand the lure of Lawrence. The work was hard, the hours long, the pay low, and the conditions of life almost unspeakable. Full-time adult employees worked a fifty-six hour week for wages which the Massachusetts Bureau of Statistics termed in 1912 "entirely inadequate to maintain a family." Of the 21,922 workers for which the bureau had collected data, 7,275 earned less than $7 per week and 1,932 of these were adult males eighteen years or older. With an average family size of five, it seemed impossible that the men were able to provide the bare necessities.

That families were sustained is explained by further statistics. In 1912 females comprised 44.6 percent of the Lawrence work force and those under eighteen of both sexes represented 11.5 percent. These figures suggest that Lawrence's textile families were able to survive because the typical family unit supplied more than a single worker to the mills. For the others, as the bureau reported, "the condition of the head of the family in one of the poorer-paid occupations, with two or three children so young as to necessitate the mother remaining at home to care for them, is one of extreme hardship."[8]

A strong union and a successful strike were needed to assure the Lawrence workers of a better life. Unfortunately, they had neither until 1912. The National Labor Union and the Knights of Labor had both carried on organizing drives in Lawrence in the late nineteenth century, but both had disappeared before 1900 without having made a significant contribution to the city's workers. The S.T.&L.A., the economic arm of the S.L.P., established a strong local in 1899, but the split in the party the following year divided the members and reduced the union to insignificance.

Prior to the establishment of the U.T.W. union in 1901, the A.F.L. had been able to organize only a few craft locals and most did not survive long. Gompers joined U.T.W. President Golden in an organizing effort in the city in 1905, but after months of effort and the claimed expenditure of thousands of dollars, the federation had little to show for the attempt.[9] The U.T.W. did not abandon its efforts in the city, but the gains remained minimal. As one of its organizers reported on his six-months of work in 1911, "I started in Lawrence to try and get a Weavers' Union, but after a few days I found that the feeling was so strong against the U.T.W. that it would be a waste of time to stay there."[10]

The inadequacies of the craft unions, led by English-speaking men who tended to share the employers' social outlook and disdain for the unskilled foreigners, resulted in an organizational vacuum into which the I.W.W. was happy to move. In 1906, in the same organizing effort which brought success to the workers in Skowhegan, the union established its first local in Lawrence and attracted the remnants of the old S.T.&L.A. membership. Local 20 barely managed to survive the hard days of 1907, but it was brought to life by the creation of the N.I.U.T.W. By 1910 it had its own hall, which served as the site of the N.I.U.T.W.'s Third Convention.[11]

The year 1911 was an active one for the I.W.W. in Lawrence. As evidence of its growth, the Lawrence organization had seventeen delegates at the N.I.U.T.W. convention in that year. Organizers Joseph Ettor and Flynn spoke frequently in the city and by summer the union prospects there looked excellent. "If the boys in Lawrence keep up their work," Miller reported in *Solidarity*, "they will have one of the largest local unions in the I.W.W."[12]

Encouraged by its membership gains and the attention which it was receiving from the national organizers, Local 20 increased its activity. Late in August 1911, when the Lawrence mills began to change their production system—putting weavers to work on twelve looms at

$.49 per cut instead of the old arrangement of seven looms at $.79 per cut — the I.W.W. protested the reduction in piece rates and the potential displacement of workers if this change was allowed to stand. One hundred textile workers responded to the I.W.W. argument and struck the Atlantic Mills.

James P. Thompson spent two months in the city trying to keep the strike alive, and Flynn worked to get national support, but the strike was not a success.[13] The I.W.W. claimed that the action had increased the workers' revolutionary sentiment, and thus could be construed as a victory, but its professed optimism was unwarranted: Local 20 had been able to exploit a specific grievance to get some workers to join the I.W.W. for only a brief time. By the end of the year, although it claimed 1,300 members and prided itself on being the largest single union in Lawrence, Local 20 had a mere 300 textile workers in good standing. When the next instance of worker discontent erupted late in 1911, the state of disorganization was so complete that the active I.W.W. men opposed calling a strike.[14] As had been the case in McKees Rocks, the I.W.W. captured rather than initiated the successful strike which marked 1912 in Lawrence.

During the early years of the twentieth century, the Commonwealth of Massachusetts had been in the vanguard of those states which sought to legislate some measure of protection for workers employed in its industries. In 1911 the Commonwealth enacted a fifty-four-hour week for women and children, a two-hour reduction which followed earlier legislation which first had lowered the work week from sixty to fifty-eight hours and then from fifty-eight to fifty-six. The previous adjustments, which actually affected all workers because it was not feasible to have men work longer hours than the women and children whose tasks were so closely interrelated, had brought changes in piece rates so that the weekly pay of the workers had not been reduced by the shorter hours. The manufacturers, however, contended that the legislature's solicitude put them at a disadvantage in competing with firms in states which had not displayed similar concern. During the 1911 hearings on the proposed fifty-four-hour measure, the mill owners had testified that they were already at such a competitive disadvantage that they were unable to make a profit. The owners warned the legislature that they could not adjust piece rates as they had done in the past and that the fifty-four-hour week would result in a reduction in wages.[15]

Although it was later contended that the wage reduction had been announced in the mills, it is doubtful whether such notification was given in every establishment in Lawrence. The legislation provided only that notice had to be posted indicating the number of hours that were to be worked each day. This was done, but there was no mention of any change in piece rates, the system of pay under which the majority earned their wages. Many employees, as the State Bureau of Statistics later reported, remained uncertain about the impact of the new law on their pay. The employers, however, feigned surprise that there should have been confusion. Since the mills in 1910 had posted the new fifty-six-hour schedule along with new piece-rate scales, they argued that "the absence of such notice was itself notice that reduction in hours would automatically mean work at reduction in earnings." But the large number of foreign-speaking employees in Lawrence, unable to understand the nuances of notification by omission, apparently were not all aware that the protective legislation would mean an average of $.32 less per week. Up to January 1, as acknowledged by the bureau, there was "no official and direct statement . . . made public on the subject."[16]

The Lawrence textile owners underestimated the effect that a 3 percent wage cut would have on their workers. Late in December 1911, when one of the mill owners in Boston warned a counterpart in Lawrence that a reduction in pay would precipitate trouble, he was assured that the workers' response would be minimal, at most limited to a single mill.[17] So great was the gulf between the tenement-dwelling workers in the crowded city and the comfortable mill managers in the residences of Prospect Hill that the latter could not imagine that a pay cut of a few cents a week would cause a general explosion. For those already living at a bare subsistence level, however, the reduction meant a wage below the survival point; to them it was "the last straw in a string of injustices." As one of the workers later told A.F.L. organizer Mary Kenny O'Sullivan, "we were drowning men ready to grasp at a straw."[18]

There were a number of early indications that the Lawrence workers would not submit meekly to reduced pay. Employees in some of the mills, particularly I.W.W. members of Polish and Italian background, began holding meetings to discuss the situation. Although the English-speaking members of the industrial union advised the others not to strike until the workers were better organized, some were determined to walk out if the first pay envelopes of the year showed a cut. These meetings were well covered in the local newspapers, which should have been warning enough to the employers that trouble was imminent, but the whole matter was allowed to drift without any effort made by the owners to prevent a confrontation. Then, as the end of the first two-week pay period of 1912 approached, some 900 Italian workers met at Ford's Hall and voted to strike if their pay was reduced.[19]

The first Lawrence workers to act were some 500 weavers and spinners from the Everett, Arlington, and Duck Mills who quit their places on Thursday, January 11. The next day, when the pay envelopes were distributed, the strike began in earnest. The Italian workers in the Wood, Ayer, and Washington mills of the American Woolen Company demonstrated their fury against the "short pay" by going on a rampage through the mills, breaking windows and urging their fellows to join them in a strike.[20]

Gradually, as others received their wages, the demonstration spread to the other mills in the city. Fred E. Beal, in 1912 a sixteen-year-old worker at the Pacific Worsted Mill, later recalled what occurred that day:

> Just like any other Friday, the paymaster, with the usual armed guard, wheeled a truck containing hundreds of pay envelopes to the head of a long line of anxiously waiting people. . . . When the great moment came, the first nervously opened their envelopes and found that the company had deducted two hours' pay. They looked silly, embarrassed and uncertain what to do. Milling around, they waited for some one to start something. They didn't have long to wait, for one lively young Italian had his mind thoroughly made up and swung into action without even looking into his pay envelope. "Strike! Strike!" he yelled.
>
> There were cries: "All Out!"
>
> And then hell broke loose in the spinning room. The silent mute frames became an object of intense hatred, something against which to vent our stored-up feelings. Gears were smashed and belts cut. . . . It was a madhouse, a thrilling one, nevertheless.
>
> We piled out onto Canal Street, singing and shouting.[21]

Thus did the unled and essentially unorganized textile workers of Lawrence release their pent-up anger against employers who, one striker later told Reverend Harry Emerson Fosdick, treated them "like cattle."[22]

I.W.W. Local 20 had not planned a strike until the summer, an opportune time when the mills usually operated at peak capacity, but it immediately reacted to the first spontaneous walkouts and sent an urgent wire for help to Ettor. The I.W.W. organizer was reluctant to leave New York, but Haywood convinced him to answer the appeal. Accompanied by his equally hesitant friend Arturo Giovannitti and with the promise that Haywood, Thompson, and Flynn would soon follow, Ettor left for the Massachusetts city. The two men arrived at midnight on January 12, spent the next day walking around Lawrence to acquaint themselves with the situation, and then set to providing the organization and leadership which was so badly needed.[23]

Ettor and Giovannitti found a disorganized mob of idle workers, angered to undirected outbursts of violence, on strike to protest their reduction in pay. Confronting them, called out in response to the initial rampage in the shops, was the entire police force of the city and three militia companies which had been ordered into the city for use if necessary. No sooner did Ettor arrive on the scene than he began to organize the strikers into a disciplined force, preach the virtues of peaceful confrontation over mindless violence, and transform the issues in the strike. Under his direction the strike became a fight for a 15 percent wage increase, double pay for overtime, and the abolition of the bonus and premium system. On the first Monday of the strike, there was some violence—which the mill owners and authorities blamed on the I.W.W. organizers' oratory at the weekend meetings—but this was virtually the last of such outbursts. The mayor of the city used the incident to call out the militiamen to keep order and patrol the mills, but Ettor's coordination and direction was equally responsible for the peace.[24]

Soon after he arrived in Lawrence, drawing upon the successful model of McKees Rocks three years before, Ettor established a permanent strike organization to make policy, provide relief, direct publicity, and generally supervise the course of the movement. The Central Strike Committee, which met daily, was composed of three representatives from each ethnic group in the textile city. This body was not an I.W.W. committee and a number of its members remained unaffiliated with the union throughout the strike; Ettor served in an advisory capacity only, insisting that the workers themselves should determine policy. He and other I.W.W. organizers played a major role in devising tactics, but the manufacturers' claim that "outside agitators" were in control was not true.[25]

The owners' contention that the strike was only an uprising of radically inclined new immigrants, who had no appreciation of American institutions, was also incorrect. The degree of support and enthusiasm for the strike, however, did vary according to nationality, with the older immigrant groups the least involved. It was popular to attribute this to racial characteristics, but the manner in which the various ethnic groups responded was primarily the result of their positions in the work force.[26]

The ethnic representatives on the fifty-six-man committee marshaled the support of their communities and helped forge the heterogeneous body of workers into a well-disciplined and effective force. With Ettor devising the strike tactics, Giovannitti using his oratorical powers to enthuse the numerous Italian strikers and his organizational abilities to direct relief operations, and various other I.W.W. leaders soliciting funds from outside the city, the strike settled into a routine.

The strike tactics were well planned and posed a challenge which the city's authorities were ill-equipped to meet. The Central Strike Committee established picket lines, to keep workers from returning to the mills and also to maintain morale, and relied heavily on the participation of the working-class women of Lawrence. Nothing confused or angered the predominantly Irish police force of the city more than the role the women played. If the police moved against these women, the I.W.W. used the occasion to level charges of brutality and thus gained valuable publicity. When women were arrested—and they courted arrest—the city officials were soundly criticized.[27]

There were distortions about the strike from both sides: the daily press overemphasized the violence of the strikers, and the radical press greatly exaggerated the actions of the officials. It is true that militiamen patroled the streets and stood guard in front of the mills, but the *International Socialist Review*'s description of fourteen hundred soldiers initiating a "reign of terror" in Lawrence was as untrue as the stories of daily violence perpetrated by strikers. In a strike involving some 23,000 workers, the total arrested was 296, of whom only 54 were sentenced to prison.[28] That is not to suggest that the city officials were third parties who dealt with the conflict in an even-handed fashion. Most of the strikers who were arrested were fined and released, but some were given harsh sentences by decidedly hostile courts.[29]

The use of the militia also indicated the antistriker sentiment exhibited by the local authorities. One militiaman, who had spent two weeks on duty in Lawrence, stated flatly that there was "too much of the feeling that we were fighting on the side of the mill owners. . . . No one of us felt that he was like a policeman in the employ of the city to do justice to all its citizens." He labeled the newspaper reports of frequent riots and violent acts as "absolutely false" and concluded that "the militia ought not again to be placed at the service of the mill owners." A lieutenant in the Eighth Regiment disagreed with the enlisted man and wrote of the "small-sized Civil War" which raged in the city, but the officer's obvious disdain for what he called "the off-scourings of Southern Europe" seems to support the soldier's doubt that "any officer of the militia was particularly interested in protecting the strikers."[30]

The clearest indication of the Lawrence administration's stance, and the first of two major errors made by the newly installed city officials, concerned the treatment of Ettor and Giovannitti. Unable to dampen the workers' enthusiasm for the strike by urging the policy of mass arrests in the first days of the walkout, the mill owners apparently believed that they could defeat the workers by stripping them of their leaders. The opportunity for this came as a result of events which began on January 29.

Before daylight on that day, as the mills were beginning to receive those workers who had not joined the strike or had already returned to their places, an angry group of strikers threatened to attack the trolley cars carrying the "scabs" to work. The police had difficulty controlling the situation and the city was alarmed at the possibility of widespread violence. That night a large crowd of strikers congregated and attempted to parade through the streets. Although the procession was peaceful, the authorities decided to break up the march. Police were sent in, shots were fired, and a woman bystander, Anna LoPezzi, fell dead to the pavement. Two days later, Ettor and Giovannitti were arrested and arraigned in the Lawrence police court on the charge of being accessories to the murder of LoPezzi. The contention was that the inflammatory speeches of the two had provoked the still unknown assailant to violence. Not until the middle of April did the authorities arrest the alleged perpetrator, a young striker, Joseph Caruso. Meanwhile, the two strike leaders, who had been nowhere near the scene of the incident, were held in prison without bail.[31]

If the incarceration of Ettor and Giovannitti was an attempt to break the strike, as the workers and their sympathizers believed, the action was a tactical blunder. As I.W.W. publicist and editor Justus Ebert later wrote, the arrests actually benefited the strike and increased rather than diminished the strikers' allegiance to the union they represented. Those responsible for the arrests also miscalculated in attributing positions to Ettor and Giovannitti which could not be filled by others. The Central Strike Committee, which had never been under the dictation of the two outsiders, rallied to the occasion and carried on as before. The I.W.W.'s national organization, active from the start in raising funds and providing speakers, sent its most prominent and effective organizers to fill the places left vacant by the arrests. Haywood, who had encouraged Ettor and Giovannitti to go to Lawrence and had promised his help if needed, had visited the Massachusetts city only once since the strike began. But when the two leaders were jailed, he became the major I.W.W. figure in the strike. Other prominent industrial unionists also rushed to Lawrence, among them Flynn, Thompson, Trautmann, Miller, and Carlo Tresca. In arresting Ettor and Giovannitti, the mill owners had called forth the stars of the I.W.W.[32]

Haywood changed little in the strike organization which Ettor had created in the first days. He was careful to follow his predecessor's insistence on nonviolence, arranged frequent meetings to maintain morale, and appealed widely for the relief funds needed to sustain the strike. What he and the twenty-two-year-old Flynn provided most was expanded national attention. They were more than able to hold the hearts of the textile workers, which Ettor and Giovannitti had won. Nothing was lost by the change in leadership.[33]

One of the few forces in the labor movement which the leaders' appeals and the strikers' plight could not move was the U.T.W. More than one observer in Lawrence charged that Golden's union worked with the mill owners, militia, and police to defeat the strike.[34] The A.F.L. textile union, which had a membership in Lawrence of no more than 200 when the strike began, clearly saw the appearance of the I.W.W. as a direct threat to its own existence and responded accordingly: it supported the city's attempts to remove the I.W.W. influence, it sought separate agreement with management, and it tried to capitalize on the new militancy of the workers by attracting them into the craft union. This last intent involved sending organizers into Lawrence and establishing relief stations which would give the appearance of U.T.W. involvement in the strike.[35]

By March, the strike in Lawrence had assumed the character of a full clash between the U.T.W. and the I.W.W.; some even saw this as the "real significance" of the strike.[36] Golden came close to admitting that he was more interested in beating off the I.W.W. than he was in helping the mass of unskilled workers. On one occasion he stated that the U.T.W. could not "silently permit the pernicious doctrines of brute force further to be spread broad-cast by the would-be leaders of Lawrence without suffering injury" to itself.[37] This and similar comments attracted the criticism of some within the A.F.L. Kate O'Sullivan, for example, condemned the U.T.W. president's actions in Lawrence as "the first time in the history of the American Federation movement that a leader failed the people in his industry." And Gompers, although he defended the role of the U.T.W. in Lawrence and denied any complicity with the employers, felt compelled in his testimony before the House Rules Committee to correct the impression Golden had made earlier.[38]

Gompers realized that his colleague's derogatory comments about the immigrant workers of Lawrence and his obvious concern for protecting his own union—almost at any price—would not set well with those who sympathized with the plight of the mill workers. In fact, the damage done to the U.T.W. as a result of its actions in Lawrence was considerable.

The position of the U.T.W. and its parent organization was especially noteworthy and disappointing in contrast to the general treatment of the strike in the national magazines of the day. Haywood and the other leaders proved themselves to be skilled publicists, patiently explaining the issues to those writers from middle-class journals who swarmed into the city. Among those outside investigators who travelled to the textile center to see the situation at first hand were Lincoln Steffens, Walter Weyl, Ray Stannard Baker, Richard Washburn Child, and Mary Heaton Vorse. (Weyl spoke for most when he called the strike "a flaming appeal to the conscience and intelligence of the American people.") In all, more than eighty articles and reports about Lawrence were published by the sympathetic journalists and social workers of the country.[39]

The workers' most important allies came from the S.P.A., which deserved much of the credit for the eventual success of the strike. Even before he assumed the leadership in Lawrence, Haywood had appealed to the S.P.A. for help and the National Committee, at its January meeting, had unanimously adopted his resolution to provide financial assistance to the New England textile workers. Friction existed between the I.W.W. men and the moderate wing of the party, but the two factions joined in providing whatever aid they could. By the end of the strike, it has been estimated that the party had raised $40,000 to sustain the strikers.[40] Massachusetts party members held rallies, collected food and clothing for the strikers, and provided a considerable amount of money to the strike fund. Such financial assistance, even from socialist bodies fearful that an identification with the I.W.W. would be politically harmful, enabled the workers to hold out.[41]

A different sort of contribution concerned the socialists' participation in the most notable and imaginative tactic used by the I.W.W. in Lawrence: the evacuation of the strikers' children from the city to sympathetic homes elsewhere. By the second week of February, contributions of approximately $12,000 from socialists, trade-union locals, and others had enabled the Central Strike Committee to establish eighteen separate commissaries and a number of soup kitchens. But despite these facilities there was concern that the committee could not continue to provide for the strikers and their dependents, especially as individual savings were depleted and outside relief sources were exhausted. This fear helped prompt the suggestion that groups of children be sent from Lawrence to be cared for by supporters in other cities. The proposal, which followed a practice which had been used in European strikes, received widespread approval. The socialist New York *Call* printed the suggestion and within days offers poured in from people wishing to open their homes.[42] Shortly after the plan was announced, the first children, a total of 119, were escorted to temporary havens in New York City. This group was followed by smaller contingents to other cities in the East.[43]

The chairman of the Strikers' Vacation Committee, which supervised the so-called evacuations, steadfastly maintained that the purpose of these removals was only to "take the little ones out of such a place" as Lawrence and denied that the object was to stir sympathy or provoke a reaction from authorities.[44] But from the start, many in the city saw the action as a mere propaganda device. C. C. Carstens, general agent of the Society for the Prevention of Cruelty to Children (S.P.C.C.), believed that strike funds, augmented by assistance from churches and charity organizations, could meet the strikers' needs and saw the evacuation as a publicity tactic and nothing more. It was his contention also that some of the children were being sent from Lawrence without parental consent or, in some cases, with consent through "coercion and threat" by the strike leaders.[45]

The S.P.C.C. official probably overstated the aspect of coercion—that charge became a common one with the union's detractors—but the evacuation of children from the strike city was more a calculated tactic than an action prompted by a humane concern for the children's welfare. Haywood later acknowledged that the evacuations were "for the purpose of calling the attention of the world to the conditions existing in Lawrence."[46]

The evacuation of the children did more than anything else to involve the socialists actively in the strike. Party members organized the process by which the children were screened, found the homes which would receive them, and escorted them to the welcoming cities. Margaret Sanger, a nurse as well as a S.P.A. member, was one of the most active, serving as an escort for the first group sent to New York.[47]

To some in Lawrence, the ragged appearance of the children was a contrived bit of staging, a "sordid piece of advertising" designed to elicit support for the strikers and discredit the community. Even Sanger later admitted that the "main purpose" of the removals was to evoke sympathy.[46] If this was the aim, it was more than realized. But the use of the children also accomplished something more: it provoked the Lawrence authorities into their second blunder, one which resulted in victory for the textile workers.

The citizenry reacted strongly to the bad publicity generated by the I.W.W. maneuver; in Carstens's words, "the sending of children away from Lawrence seemed un-American and an unnecessary 'war measure' which hurt the community's pride." Proclaiming that the city's churches and charitable institutions had always stood ready to offer assistance to those in need, the defenders of the civic image began to protest to the city officials, urging them to stop the evacuations. The initial position of the local S.P.C.C. was that parental authority could not be challenged unless parents' actions were injurious to their children and that nothing could be done to stop the practice. However, in the last week of February, the local agency reported receiving complaints from parents who alleged that their children were being taken from them without their consent. It was at this point and at the urging of the local charitable agencies that the city decided to halt further relocations. Colonel E. Leroy Sweetser, the commander of the militia force in Lawrence, issued an order that no more evacuations would be allowed.[49]

In defiance of this dictum, early in the morning of February 24, some forty children ranging in age from two to twelve gathered at the North Station in Lawrence to await the train which would carry them to temporary homes in Philadelphia. As they stood with their parents and four Philadelphia socialists who were to act as escorts, Police Captain John O'Sullivan and twenty of his officers appeared on the scene. O'Sullivan had warned the Central Strike Committee the night before that the children would not be allowed to leave the city and, at the station, ordered those assembled to return home or face arrest. But they remained and, when the train arrived, made a rush to get the children aboard. At this point, in the words of a *Survey* article, the police "hustled the shrieking women and children aboard a big ordnance truck from the state arsenal." At the police station, a judge declared the youngsters "neglected children" and ordered them held at the City Home until the Juvenile Court could determine action.[50]

From across the country, in radical and moderate newspapers alike, the action of the Lawrence police was soundly condemned. Quite apart from the sympathy generated by the mental picture of women and children being clubbed by burly Irish cops, an account whose veracity was much debated, the incident at the railroad station provoked the outcry of those who saw it as an invasion of personal liberty.[51]

The socialist press had a field day covering the confrontation. Under a banner headline proclaiming "Remember Lawrence, the Lexington of Labor's Struggle for Liberty, on Election Day," the *Appeal to Reason* began its front-page story:

> The blackest page in all the four hundred years of American history was written February 24, 1912. Russia has its Bloody Sunday and the United States now has its Black Saturday.
> On that day the police under orders issued by a republican mayor and the soldiers under orders issued by a democratic governor, by command of the republican and democratic mill owners . . . assaulted the working class mothers . . . clubbed them until the blood flowed, tore their children from their arms, threw them shrieking with fright and terror into patrol wagons and carted them to the police station and jail for seeking to save their offspring from starvation.[52]

The Kansas paper made no mention of the I.W.W. in its stirring piece; in its account, it was a socialist struggle which only the election of S.P.A. candidates could remedy. The New York *Call* used the incident in a similar fashion. "We thrive and grow on the blunders of capitalism, and the more idiotic the opposition the better for us," it astutely stated in its editorial. "We can always depend on the local Dogberrys and Bumbles for assistance in such situations as that which prevail in Lawrence." [53]

Whether or not the fortunes of the S.P.A. would be enhanced by the incident, the party's role in the strike had just begun. And, paradoxically, it would be through the utilization of the political power which the I.W.W. shunned that the S.P.A. would help the union it later deplored to its single greatest victory.

The so-called Cossack carnival at the railroad station prompted politicians at the national level to take a greater interest in the industrial war in Lawrence.[54] Senator Miles Poindexter, a Republican from Washington, made a personal visit to the city and afterward issued a statement which denounced the mill-owners and local authorities.[55] Of even greater importance was the role played by Victor Berger, the socialist Congressman from Milwaukee. Although Berger had been since 1905 one of the party's most vociferous opponents of the I.W.W., considering the dual unionists as antisocial anarchists who would repel sympathy for the reformist socialists in the country, the first-term congressman was far from indifferent to the plight of the workers whom the union led. When Haywood asked Berger to launch an investigation of the strike, the congressman arranged for a hearing before the House Rules Committee.[56]

Meanwhile, other leaders of the S.P.A. pressed for action and John M. Work, the national secretary of the party, telegraphed President Taft asking him to use his influence with Mayor Scanlon and Governor Foss to halt the violations of the strikers' constitutional rights. By February 28, the *Call* could report four separate movements underway at the national level: an investigation by the Justice Department, to determine whether the strikers' rights had been violated; a resolution by Senator Poindexter, asking the Commerce Department to report to the Senate on wages and conditions in the textile industry of Lawrence; a resolution by Congressman William B. Wilson, a Democrat from Pennsylvania, to begin an investigation by the House Committee on Labor into allegations that the police and militia had denied the mill workers their constitutional rights; and Berger's call for a broad investigation by a special House Committee. When Republican Senator Henry Cabot Lodge of Massachusetts protested that the Commonwealth could manage the situation without Senate interference, Poindexter in response introduced a matter which provoked considerable alarm among the wool manufacturers. The Washington Republican, supported by Senator James Reed, a Missouri Democrat, argued that an investigation was necessary to obtain facts which ought to be examined before revision of the wool tariff was considered.[57]

The proposed investigations were heartening to the strike sympathizers. Only Emma Goldman opposed such political intervention, arguing that the workers should rely on direct action and the general strike. "Investigations!" the anarchist scoffed. "The country is overflooded with them. If the good people were not a mass of concentrated apathy and dullness, these thousand and one investigations would have long since been laughed out of existence."[58]

Goldman's objection was consistent with the anarchist philosophy, but she vastly underestimated the impact of the proposed congressional action. The mill owners did not even wait for the first of the investigations to begin before they offered to end the strike, but the mass of strikers, under instruction of the Central Strike Committee, preferred to await developments in Washington.

From March 2 to March 5 the House Rules Committee heard testimony concerning the situation in Lawrence. Those testifying included Golden and Gompers, representing the union establishment in the country; a score of Lawrence officials and civic leaders, who told of the conditions in the city and complained of the irresponsible tactics of the I.W.W.; and the socialist participants in the children's evacuation, including Sanger and the four Philadelphians who were at North Station. The most compelling testimony, however, came from the more than a dozen boys and girls, ranging in age from fourteen to sixteen, who had been sent by the Central Strike Committee to tell of conditions in the mills. Helen Taft and Alice Roosevelt Longworth were among the spectators who listened to their pitiful account of life and work in the Massachusetts textile center.[59]

Berger, in introducing his resolution for a special investigating committee, hammered home the point that the American Woolen Company had long been "the recipient of a Government subsidy in the form of a high tariff," and had argued for protection on the grounds that it would benefit the workers; yet, the Wisconsin congressman pointed out, it was "generally conceded that these operatives [were] among the lowest paid . . . in America." Again, the wool company saw the threat of tariff revision. If Berger and Poindexter on the tariff did not provoke sufficient alarm, others took up the cry. Boston Settlement House leader Robert A. Woods commented on "the anomaly of protection for commerce and free trade for labor," and *Survey's* observer at the hearings wrote that "bits of testimony gave interesting glimpses into the house-keeping which goes on in an industry protected by a prohibitive tariff." Even Governor Foss, allegedly eager for the Democratic presidential nomination, assumed his party's position vis-à-vis tariff revision and called for a state investigation of the strike to determine whether the workers derived any benefit from protectionist policies.[60]

On March 12, five days after the House Rules Committee had concluded its hearing, the American Woolen Company yielded. It offered its workers terms, later followed by other Lawrence mills, which included a flat 5 percent increase for all piece workers, with an additional scale increase which boosted the pay of the most poorly compensated workers 20 percent; one and one-fourth pay for overtime; payment of premiums every two weeks instead of monthly; and the promise that there would be no discrimination shown toward strike leaders. Although most observers attributed the capitulation to the congressional investigation and the weight of public opinion, the company maintained that improved conditions in the industry, with unfilled orders up more than four-fold, allowed "the rise in wages in March that was not possible in January."[61] Even if true, this face-saving explanation could not obscure the fact that the textile workers, under the leadership of the I.W.W., had scored a major victory.

On the afternoon of March 14, some 10,000 gathered on the Lawrence Common and brought the nine-week strike to an end. Haywood spoke to those gathered on the Common and Carl Hovey, who heard the I.W.W. leader, recalled the speech as "one of the most dignified and feeling" that he had ever heard. Hovey recorded Haywood's concluding words in an article for *Metropolitan Magazine*: "You, the strikers of Lawrence, have won the most signal victory of any body of organized working men in the world. . . . You have carried on the strike as no strike was ever carried on before. No one can point to any striker and say that he has committed any act of violence. You have carried on a noble fight. It is simply the first step in the progressive march toward industrial freedom."[62] *Solidarity*, in reporting the triumphant outcome, hailed the "greater significance" of the strike: "the moral effect . . . upon the working class in general and upon the revolutionary movement in particular."[63] The promise of all those associated with the union was the same—more would be heard of the I.W.W. in the future.

While industrial unionists exalted, others sought to determine the meaning of the Lawrence victory.[64] Many, whether with approval or opprobrium, saw the Lawrence strike as of major significance to the American labor movement. Even those who feared or hated what the I.W.W. represented had to admit that the union, by the brilliance of its tactics or the blunders of its adversaries, had won an impressive victory for the textile workers of New England. The craft unions, in contrast, had demonstrated weakness and had been soundly repudiated by the mass of workers. People after Lawrence began to speak of the "rise of a new labor movement."[65] The editor of Charles W. Post's ultraconservative *Square Deal*, for example, prophesized: "The real force in the labor history of 1913 . . . will undoubtedly be the I.W.W. . . . If they continue to increase in membership during the coming year they will become an organization which will have to be reckoned with when it comes to the settlement of labor disputes."[66]

The bright future predicted for the I.W.W. in 1913 did not materialize, however. By the end of that year the dual union had lost much of its allure. The immediate impact of Lawrence, as *Square Deal* predicted, was an impressive gain in I.W.W. membership; almost overnight the N.I.U.T.W. could count 18,000 members. But, even in Lawrence, the gains were only temporary. In October 1913 the I.W.W. had an estimated membership of only 700 in that city; a year later, a mere 400 members remained of the thousands enrolled in 1912.[67]

The later decline and disappointments, however, were in the future. For the moment Lawrence appeared to be only the beginning of "a new chapter" in labor-management relations in the country. This "greatest victory in American labor history" seemed a signal that a new and effective force was ready to assume dominance within the labor movement.[68] Few discounted the significance of the Massachusetts victory. From progressive journalist Baker to anarchist Goldman, from I.W.W. proponents in the *International Socialist Review* to antiunionist writers in the *Square Deal*, from lapsed union member Debs to I.W.W. enthusiast Ebert, the message was the same.[69] Almost all expected that the Lawrence struggle would be followed by other I.W.W. victories. Haywood, obviously buoyed by his success, made it clear that he intended to press forward. "The fight is on, on with the fight," the hero of Lawrence proclaimed late in 1912. "We are the Revolution."[70]

In the months following Lawrence, the I.W.W. fulfilled its promise of greater agitation and organization. In Lowell, 18,000 textile workers struck almost immediately after the Lawrence settlement for wage increases similar to those won in the neighboring city; in July some 15,000 in New Bedford responded to the I.W.W. call to strike. Throughout New England, mill workers received wage increments; in the case of Salem and Fall River the threat of a strike was sufficient to win the demands. The I.W.W. claimed that 300,000 workers in the textile mills of New England benefited from the Lawrence victory.[71]

In October 1912 some 1,500 textile workers in Little Falls, New

York, struck in protest of wage reductions ranging from $.75 to $2 per week and issued an appeal to the N.I.U.T.W. Organizers responded, welded the previously unorganized workers into an effective strike force, and provided leadership in the twelve-week struggle against the city's two textile mills.[72]

Haywood described the Little Falls struggle as "a miniature repetition of the great Lawrence strike," and this characterization is accurate. As in the Massachusetts city, the strike was begun as a spontaneous outcry by unorganized and largely unskilled immigrant workers over a wage reduction, the I.W.W. entered after the strike had begun, and the struggle attracted the sympathy and financial aid of socialists and progressive-minded citizens alike. Once again the confrontation between labor and management was confused by the interunion competition between the I.W.W. and the A.F.L., with both claiming credit for the outcome and each attacking the other for interference.[73] The wage increase of up to 12 percent was less an I.W.W. victory than the Lawrence result—the final settlement came through the intervention of the State Board of Mediation—but the industrial union was credited for holding the strikers together long enough to pressure the employers to terms.[74] When the N.I.U.T.W. met in convention the week following the New York strike, it could claim with some justification that the victories at Lawrence, Lowell, Salem, New Bedford, and Little Falls had proven the soundness of industrial organization in the textile industry.

The textile manufacturers were not the only employers to feel the I.W.W. sting in the aftermath of Lawrence. The union was active from coast to coast in 1912, leading free-speech fights (as in San Diego) and strikes in a variety of industries. One of the more publicized struggles in the latter category concerned the union's involvement in a strike waged in New York City against some of the most prominent hotels and restaurants in that metropolis.[75] The hotel strike did not result in victory—confronted by the intransigence of management and the hostility of the press, the I.W.W. leaders advised the strikers late in January 1913 to return to work—but the defeat was viewed at the time as only temporary.[76] The union organizers remained in New York City to prepare for the next encounter. It was while they were so engaged that Flynn and Tresca were called to New Jersey to take charge of the revolt of silk workers in Paterson. A titanic struggle, along the lines of Lawrence, began there on February 25, 1913.

Chapter 3

Unrest in the Silk Industry

> Strikes are taking place every season, and the workers as a rule get what they ask for, but they have not hitherto stuck to an organization, and consequently lose what they gained through organized effort.
>
> A strong industrial union embracing all the workers in and around the silk mills and dye houses is what the silk workers need to hold what they once gain.—"Conditions in the Silk Industry," *Solidarity*, August 13, 1910.

> In all these places where the I.W.W. (Detroit) is engaged in conducting bona fide strikes, that aggregation of slummists calling themselves I'm-a-Bummery and sailing under the colors of the I.W.W. have attempted to put in their dirty work and break up the strikes by engendering confusion, and trying to throw discredit upon the leaders of the strikes and the I.W.W.—"From the Strike Zone," *Industrial Union News*, May 1912.

When the Lawrence textile workers walked out of the mills in 1912, their counterparts in Paterson, New Jersey, had on numerous occasions demonstrated their dissatisfaction with conditions in the silk industry. To a greater degree than the men and women who abandoned their looms over a reduction in their pay envelopes, the workers in Paterson had shown their frustrations in a series of strikes. This willingness to walk off the job, however, did not mean that the status of union organization differed from that in the Massachusetts city; the majority of the silk workers in 1912 was essentially unorganized. But three separate labor organizations—the U.T.W., the Chicago I.W.W., and the Detroit I.W.W.—had locals in Paterson and had been active in providing leadership to one segment or another of the work force. Seemingly more antagonistic toward each other than to the silk manufacturers, the presence of the three gave the Paterson labor scene a complexity and sense of turmoil which Lawrence could not match.

In 1901, when the U.T.W. was formed within the A.F.L., Paterson had four rather well-established silk workers' unions: the Loomfixers' and Twisters' Benevolent and Protective Association, the Horizontal Warpers' Benevolent Association, the United Silk Ribbon Weavers of America, and the United Broad-Silk Workers' Union. At the First Convention of the U.T.W., the secretary of the Broad-Silk Workers' Union requested that his independent organization be given a separate charter from the A.F.L. rather than be linked to the federation through the textile national. This application was refused and the broad-silk weavers remained outside of the U.T.W. and the A.F.L. In 1902 and 1903, representatives of the other silk unions, then loosely bound together in the United Silk Workers of America, also sought affiliation with the federation, even petitioning Samuel Gompers to intercede in their behalf, but again no agreement could be reached with the U.T.W. leadership. As a last declaration on affiliation with the A.F.L. only on their own terms, the delegates to the 1903 Convention of the United Silk Workers of America voted to remain independent until the federation issued it a separate charter.[1]

When the United Silk Workers' Union issued its "either/or" ultimatum, however, it was already an organization which had seen its best days. (The following year it held its last convention and disappeared.) Aware that the local silk federation to which it belonged was little more than a paper organization, the Loomfixers' and Twisters' Association voted in July 1903 to join the U.T.W. Granted a charter as Local 439, this body of highly skilled English-speaking silk workers was the beginning of the U.T.W. presence in Paterson. The Broad-Silk Workers' Union joined the A.F.L. textile union in 1905, but that Paterson organization disbanded shortly thereafter. It was not until three years later that the U.T.W. admitted its next silk local in the city. At the U.T.W. Convention in 1907, the Executive Committee had instructed its general organizer, Charles A. Miles, to launch an organizing drive in Paterson. Miles, working closely with the leaders of Local 439, directed his attention to the Horizontal Warpers' Association, which had a membership of some 350 skilled operatives. At a meeting during which the U.T.W. organizer debated the merits of the A.F.L. union with DeLeon, representing the alternative I.W.W. brand of organization, the warpers voted to affiliate with the federation.[2]

The Loomfixers' and Twisters' local and the Horizontal Warpers' local would remain the backbone of the U.T.W. in Paterson from 1908 forward. It was around these two bodies of skilled craftsmen that Golden's union attempted to organize the mass of silk workers. The problems confronting the weavers were of a different nature than those of the twisters, loomfixers, and warpers—of more recent immigrant origin, even the ethnic backgrounds of many were dissimilar—but the U.T.W. nevertheless tried to model weavers' locals along lines identical to the already established affiliates. From 1905 through 1911, the U.T.W. made four separate attempts to form and maintain a local of weavers in

Paterson. As mentioned, the broad-silk union joined the U.T.W. in 1905 but disappeared soon after. In 1908, Miles was able to build on the remnants of that earlier weavers' local and organized U.T.W. Local 607 in Paterson, the Broad-Silk Weavers' Protective and Benevolent Association. The weavers in the three shops of Henry Doherty Silk Company soon joined the local, and by the end of the year Local 607 claimed 600 members in good standing. When the Ninth Convention of the U.T.W. met in October 1909, the three silk locals in Paterson were considered to be among the strongest in the textile union.[3]

Part of the progress of the U.T.W. in Paterson at this time could be attributed to its first successful strike late in 1908. As the industry emerged from the economic slump which had affected it for over a year, the loomfixers began to agitate for an increase in their wages. Members of Local 439 employed in the Doherty mill walked out when they were unable to obtain what they sought and appealed to the other U.T.W. locals for support. When they refused, on grounds that the strike was an unauthorized one, the loomfixers appealed successfully to the U.T.W. Executive Council. Weeks of negotiation followed before a settlement was reached by arbitration; the U.T.W. signed a time contract with the Doherty firm which assured a union shop and the right to discuss grievances with management on a regular basis. There was some criticism of the slow pace of the U.T.W. negotiators, and some friction between the locals because of the loomfixers' unauthorized action, but the U.T.W. gained members as a result of the strike.

In an attempt to weld the three Paterson locals into a more cohesive force, the U.T.W. encouraged the formation of a Textile Council in the city. Similar in structure and function to the governing body of the old United Silk Workers of America, the Textile Council was composed of five delegates from each local. Meetings were held semi-monthly, with special sessions at the request of one of the associated locals, and the council worked closely with the national office. In order to call an "authorized strike," two-thirds of the council members had to vote approval before referring the matter to the U.T.W. for final authorization. If the U.T.W. Executive Council approved the strike action, the local involved would be entitled to financial assistance.[4]

Under this arrangement the U.T.W. could exert strict control over its Paterson affiliates, act to discourage the undisciplined strike actions of the past, and fashion a businesslike and financially sound organization on solid A.F.L. principles. The I.W.W., already active in Paterson, scornfully dismissed the Textile Council as "nothing but a dues collecting agency with the old craft scabbery."[5]

The I.W.W. began its organizing efforts among the country's silk workers almost as soon as the founding convention had adjourned. By September 1905, General Organizer Wade Shurtleff had already established two locals in the New York City area—Local 176 in Manhattan and Local 190 in Brooklyn—and was working toward the same end in College Point, Long Island, and in Paterson and Hoboken. In mid-1906, the Paterson local was formed and, on the petition of William Glanz, was issued a charter by the I.W.W. on December 8, 1906. Silk Workers Industrial Union Local 152 set forth immediately on an organizing drive led by Rudolph Katz, an S.L.P. member and broad-silk weaver. Although no branch of the silk industry was ignored, Katz had his greatest success among the dye-house workers. Virtually unorganized, the low-paid dyers' helpers worked under conditions which made them particularly susceptible to the appeals of the industrial unionists. As a result, Katz could claim in one of his early reports to the General Executive Board that "scores" of helpers and finishers had joined the I.W.W. local.[6]

Unlike the later-formed U.T.W. Textile Council, I.W.W. Local 152 encouraged militancy among its members. Before it was one-year-old, in fact, it had led two strikes against Paterson silk firms. It had also, through the threat of a strike, succeeded in helping the dyers in some of the larger shops gain a $1 per week raise. As a result of these actions, the New York organizer of the I.W.W. could report in April 1907 that there was "splendid progress at Paterson." According to his account, large numbers of weavers were joining Local 152, hopeful of obtaining a wage increase similar to the one granted the 6,000 dye-house workers. The dye firms had believed that the raise would thwart I.W.W. activities in their branch of the industry—and their strategy did sap some of the dyers' interest in the union—but it had made the I.W.W. more attractive to the weavers. In no other city, by the end of 1907, did the fortunes of the dual union look more promising. The *Industrial Union Bulletin* conveyed the enthusiasm and optimism of those on the scene: "The I.W.W. movement in Paterson, New Jersey, is flowering like a green bay tree; every day adds to its strength and all the workers in the city are interested."[7]

Paterson's prominence was accorded proper recognition by the national body: Katz was elected a member of the General Executive Board in 1907 and, the following year, the silk city was chosen as the site for a convention of all I.W.W. textile locals. Katz called the twenty-two delegates to order at the first session in Textile Workers' Hall and served as the temporary chairman. Local 152 was represented by ten delegates, a number which testified to its numerical strength, and played a major role in the formation of the N.I.U.T.W.[8]

The May 1908 Convention was the culmination of the first period of I.W.W. activity in Paterson. For the next two years, internal dissension among the early leaders of Local 152 robbed the organization of its earlier vitality. To make matters worse, the silk industry went into a slump, throwing thousands out of work and resulting in a sharp drop in the local's membership. When the N.I.U.T.W.'s national secretary prepared his report to the Fifth Convention of the I.W.W. in 1910, he was forced to admit that it was difficult to carry on any organizing work in Paterson. In August 1910, in its special coverage of the textile industry, *Solidarity* confirmed that the situation was bleak in the silk center. Yet, the tone of the weekly's piece was optimistic: the nature of the work force, the A.F.L. high dues and conservative strike policies, and the absence of dominant trusts in the silk industry indicated that "an industrial union using the right tactics and methods" could do well among the silk workers. All that was deemed necessary for an I.W.W. resurgence was an improvement in the economic condition of the industry.[9]

The depression in the textile industry unquestionably had a deleterious effect on union membership and activity, but equally threatening to Local 152 was the rift in the union between the faction of S.L.P. members and those who were either nonpolitical or associated with the S.P.A. Even before the convention which formed the N.I.U.T.W., there was tension between the two groups in Paterson: William Glanz, one of the most important early leaders of the I.W.W. in that city, protested in April 1908 the growing antipathy toward the S.L.P. expressed by national spokesmen of the industrial union. Once a member of the S.P.A., Glanz at the time was a member of neither socialist party but was in sympathy with "the aims and objects" of the DeLeon organization. He was concerned that the I.W.W. was about to undergo "another struggle similar to the Charles O. Sherman affair" and criticized the direction in which the union seemed to be moving.[10] Glanz's fears about the internal division within the I.W.W. were borne out during the May convention in Paterson, where a struggle broke out between the advocates and opponents of nonpolitical industrial unionism. The decision to launch the N.I.U.T.W. and to put it under the direction of James P. Thompson, it was later admitted, "was shaped by a desire to keep [textile] development out of DeLeon's hands."[11]

The actions taken at the Third Convention of the I.W.W. (1908) had a particularly adverse effect on the textile local in Paterson. The silk city had been one of the strongest centers of the S.L.P. and its S.T.&L.A., and Katz was a devoted disciple of DeLeon. Thus, almost immediately after the convention in Chicago, Paterson's S.L.P. faction called a meeting of its own to protest the action of St. John and the "Overalls Brigade." The district councils of New York and Paterson, along with representatives from a number of other locals, met in the New Jersey city on November 1, 1908. Laying claim to the I.W.W. name, the Paterson gathering elected new general officers, voted to establish a new official newspaper, and chose New York City as the union's headquarters. Shortly after the Paterson meeting, and after its actions had been affirmed by a referendum, the headquarters of the DeLeon organization was moved to Hamtramck, Michigan, and later to Detroit, where Herman Richter served as general secretary-treasurer. After first relying on DeLeon's *Daily People*, in January 1912 the Detroit-based I.W.W. established the *Industrial Union News* as its official organ.[12]

The Detroit organization began its existence as an industrial union scornful of the A.F.L., the S.P.A., and the Chicago-based I.W.W. of St. John. In the words of Katz, the first two of these were simply "the obverse and reverse of the same medal . . . trimmers and politicians." Detroit spokesmen attacked Debs's party and the Gompers union in venomous phrases typical of the intra-labor disputes of the day, but their best sallies were reserved for the antipolitical Chicago union. The Detroiters characterized the St. John organization as "a retrograde movement, trying to use the methods of barbarism in the era of civilization."[13]

Describing the Chicago leaders as men who "catered to a physical force, an anarchist element, possibly for the sake of revenue," the DeLeon organization contrasted its position: "We stand for constructive industrial unionism, no anarchy, no dynamitism, no gallery play, no sensational kindergarten 'stunts.' We are not boys playing at being soldiers. We leave the counterfeit I.W.W. and other erratic organizations to proceed along the blind alley of irrational, uncivilized methods."[14] From the moment of its formation, the DeLeonists stated and restated their hatred of the Chicago group. Katz, Richter, and the others never tired of retelling the treachery of the 1908 Convention and seldom lost an opportunity to attack their former associates. Often to the detriment of the mass of unskilled workers both I.W.W.s sought to organize, the two groups spent a good part of their energy fighting each other.

Nowhere was the struggle between the Chicago and Detroit adherents more heated than in Paterson. Badly split even before the "Overalls Brigade" succeeded in reshaping the industrial union in 1908, Local 152 was torn in two by the creation of the competing I.W.W.[15]

On October 23, 1908, DeLeon's *Daily People* printed a set of resolutions, signed by Glanz, which presumably detached the Paterson local from the St. John body and declared for the faction then headquartered in New York City. This first action in the struggle for control of Local 152 was immediately countered by St. John, who sent organizer Frank Bohn to the silk city to take possession of the furniture and other property in the I.W.W. rooms. Katz, who along with Glanz had declared his loyalty to the S.L.P. group, swore out warrants for the arrest of Bohn and local Chicago supporters Adolph Lessig, Ewald Koettgen, and Paul Colditz on charges of breaking, entering, and stealing property valued at $600. Released on bond furnished by the Chicago General Executive Board, Koettgen retaliated and had Katz arrested on the charges of perjury and false arrest. The Chicago supporters in Local 152 followed this with the passage of a set of resolutions disclaiming the Glanz report of affiliation with the DeLeon faction, endorsing the action of Bohn, and reaffirming association with the Chicago organization.[16]

On paper at least, Local 152 remained part of the St. John union which had disavowed political action. Katz continued to claim that he represented the true sentiments of the membership of the Paterson local, but he eventually organized his supporters into Local 25, affiliated with the Detroit I.W.W. By 1910, therefore, there were two I.W.W. locals in the silk city, both ready to claim the leadership of the still unorganized mass of workers and each eager to gain recognition as the local of the "true" I.W.W. Nationally, the weight of numbers was on the side of the Chicago faction, which had a total membership of 9,137 (4,300 in the textile industry) as compared to 3,475 members (a scant 300 in textiles) in the Detroit union.[17] In Paterson, however, the two I.W.W. locals were of more equal strength.

Improved conditions in the silk industry, after the decline of 1907–1908, permitted the mill hands to assert themselves in renewed union activity in Paterson the following year. Beginning in December 1909, the first of what would become an almost constant rash of strikes began under U.T.W. leadership. From that point through 1919, the city became a battlefield of contests between workers and their employers and among the labor organizations represented there.

The strike of some seventy broad-silk weavers at the Stehli Silk Company was the first of similar protests by Paterson weavers dissatisfied with their wages and conditions of employment. In the early months of 1910, employees of the Paragon Silk Works, the Victory Silk Company, and Doherty & Wadsworth also walked out of the mills. With the exception of the workers at the last of these establishments, each strike ended with some improvement in the prevailing piece rates, a result of the willingness of the employers to compromise with their workers rather than jeopardize their newly restored prosperity. All of the broad-silk weavers' strikes of 1909–1910 were spontaneous outbursts, with no coordination between shops and no prior approval by the Paterson Textile Council. Of the strikes in this period, the council approved only two, and none was formally authorized by the U.T.W.

Despite pleas for financial support, the broad-silk strikers were left to their own resources.[18]

The Doherty & Wadsworth strike was unique, involving the demand of Broad-Silk Weavers' Local 607 for a closed shop and the removal of four weavers who did not belong to the union. That strike of 170 weavers dragged on through the summer and resulted in considerable friction between the shop local and the U.T.W. At Doherty & Wadsworth, the strike was confined to only one department of the mill; other workers continued their work as usual, even crossing the picket lines established by Local 607. The fact that loomfixers, twisters, and warpers, all organized in U.T.W. locals, refused to support their fellow U.T.W. members, on grounds that the union had a contract with the employer, infuriated the less skilled weavers. In September 1910, in fact, they came close to withdrawing from the U.T.W. in order to establish an independent union. They did not disaffiliate at this time, probably because the U.T.W. Executive Council reversed its earlier refusal of aid and voted a small donation to each striker, but the relations between Local 607 and the parent body remained strained.[19]

A crisis between the Paterson broad-silk weavers' local and Golden's union eventually came over the question of increased loom assignments in the broad-silk shops. By the end of the first decade of the twentieth century, the Paterson producers of cheap silk goods (messalines) confronted serious competition from Pennsylvania establishments which they believed threatened their very existence. In the eastern Pennsylvania cities, where throwing mills and plain weave shops predominated, business improved by 97 percent between 1907 and 1913, with manufacturers there said to be "making fortunes." During the same period, the New Jersey silk city, where most of the best grades of broad silk (taffetas) were produced, business expanded only 22 percent and its manufacturers made only "moderate profits."[20]

Although the Paterson owners often overstated their penurious condition when confronted by demands from their employees, the New Jersey firms were hampered by a number of factors. One of these, concerning the special inducements of Pennsylvania cities, was a matter over which the Paterson establishments had no control. But the initial provision of free building sites and tax incentives to relocate in Pennsylvania represented only the first advantage to the firms moving into the eastern portion of that state. Of longer duration was the benefit which accrued to them from the abundant supply of unskilled women and children eager to find employment. This resulted in a wage scale in the Pennsylvania concerns which was substantially lower than in the New Jersey mills. According to the *Annual Report* of the New Jersey

Bureau of Statistics of Labor and Industries in 1913, female weavers in the broad-silk shops of Pennsylvania earned an average weekly wage of $7 and children received an average of $5 per week; in New Jersey, the averages for employees in broad silk and ribbon silk combined was $11.50 for women and $14 for adult males, who made up a much higher proportion of the industry's work force than in the competing state. A further handicap to the New Jersey silk firms was the legislation passed in 1892 which regulated the hours which could be worked in factories; the fifty-five-hour week maximum was between three to five hours less than in other silk-producing states.[21]

A fourth factor which hindered the Paterson firms relative to their Pennsylvania competitors concerned the organization of the industry in the two locations. In contrast to Pennsylvania, where three-fourths of the silk concerns were owned by large corporations, Paterson continued to be a silk-producing center characterized by many small shops. The resultant loss of efficiency, cut-throat competition, and lack of capital for modernization all had adverse effects on the New Jersey industry.[22]

The industries in the two major silk-manufacturing states differed in one last major area: the type and number of looms worked by the weavers in the broad-silk branch. Among the developments in the silk industry around the turn of the century was the invention of improved looms which enabled a single broad-silk weaver to tend more than a single machine at one time. In many silk mills in Massachusetts, Rhode Island, and Pennsylvania, weavers began running three and four looms (even six for the plainest of goods). Since the workers were paid by the piece, the mill could reduce the piece rate schedules while the weavers' earnings remained stable or even improved as a result of greater production. Firms which continued to run on a one- or two-loom system were disadvantaged by the higher piece rates they had to pay and by the smaller output of their weavers. In contrast with the Pennsylvania firms, where the three- and four-loom use was almost universal, as late as 1912 only 30 of the nearly 200 broad-silk weaving establishments in Paterson had weavers tending more than two looms. Many of the New Jersey firms, as a consequence, had reduced the piece rates of their employees in order to compete, and this reduction was the cause of the increased number of strikes among the weavers in that branch.[23] One obvious solution to this problem, although available only to the larger firms with sufficient capital to do so, was to introduce the multiple loom system in Paterson. Following the industry's recovery from the depression years, the Henry Doherty Silk Company decided to take that step.

In 1909, the Doherty Company operated four silk mills in Paterson, producing mainly taffetas and other high grade silks. Confronted with competition from Pennsylvania establishments, Henry Doherty, Jr., concluded that he could not continue the two-loom arrangement under which the firm then produced even the cheaper silks. Thus, this old and well-established broad-silk firm decided to build a large and modern new mill in Clifton, about three miles from Paterson. Doherty signed an agreement with the U.T.W. prior to the construction of the mill in which the union accepted the four-loom system in return for a union shop and the fixing of piece rates by arbitration. Under this arrangement, the mill was completed and the multiple loom system instituted in the largest broad-silk concern in New Jersey.[24]

When the new Lakeview mill opened, the Doherty Silk Company put most of its weavers on the four-loom production of messalines, which were then in great demand, and reduced its production of the two-loom silk taffetas. Operating at full production in a factory with the most modern machines, and with the Textile Council's approval of its agreement with the U.T.W., the company was confident that it held the key to the establishment of industrial harmony among the silk workers of the Paterson area.

Doherty miscalculated concerning the manner in which his broad-silk weavers would accept the new four-loom assignments. The U.T.W. had been amenable to the introduction of the more efficient machines in return for certain concessions from the company, but the silk workers themselves were quick to voice their dissatisfaction. In addition to the potential displacement of men by machines, one weaver possibly doing the work of four, the introduction of the multiple-loom system threatened to alter the nature of the entire Paterson silk industry. The substitution of plainer silks for the fancier weaves, as in the Doherty replacement of taffetas by the cheaper messalines, promised to transform the New Jersey industry to the image of Pennsylvania. As emphasis shifted to the cheaper goods, the skilled male workers could face displacement by the lesser skilled women and children who then dominated the industry elsewhere. Wages would then drop and the weavers would face worse conditions than before. For all these reasons, some silk workers protested the Doherty action.[25]

On February 9, 1911 a group of over sixty weavers at the Henry Doherty Silk Company struck for an increase in piece rates for silk woven under the multiple-loom system. Their total wages had increased, due to their greater productivity, but the rate per yard had been reduced, and they sought a return to the old schedule. Later that day the weavers' action was discussed at a Textile Council meeting, where the delegates decided that no support should be given the participants in the unauthorized strike: the business agents of the three U.T.W. locals agreed that the Doherty firm was justified in expecting the weavers to work four looms. Later, when the broad-silk weavers in Local 607 submitted a grievance against the company to the U.T.W. Grievance Committee, with the hope of some meaningful support, the union committee simply recommended that the matter be arbitrated, as provided in the earlier agreement with the firm. By the time this action was taken, however, the strikers had returned to work.[26]

The three-day strike in February thus did not flare into a wider confrontation over the loom issue, but it did bring to the fore an issue which would dominate the industrial struggle in Paterson for the next two years. The attitude of the Textile Council and the extreme caution of the U.T.W., moreover, served to erode the weavers' confidence in the A.F.L. textile union and make them susceptible to the inducements of other labor organizations in the city.

Katz, the leader of the Detroit I.W.W. in Paterson, was the first to take advantage of the weavers' dissatisfaction with the U.T.W. position on the loom issue. Following the conclusion of the three-day strike at the Doherty facility, and while U.T.W. organizer Miles worked without success to get the company to agree to arbitration under the 1909 agreement with the union, Katz began his effort to enroll the broad-silk weavers in his local. Attacking the U.T.W. for its reluctance to offer concrete support in the earlier walkout and appealing to those workers who had allowed their membership in Local 607 to lapse, he promised the Doherty weavers that his union would not shrink from taking decisive action in their behalf. At this point, business agents James Starr of the Horizontal Warpers' local and Thomas F. Morgan of the Loom-fixers' and Twisters' became alarmed at Katz's progress and obtained Henry Doherty's agreement to arbitrate the matter of piece rates. Discussions were in progress when Katz began to urge the weavers to strike at once. With Detroit I.W.W. encouragement, on November 10, 1911, five hundred weavers in the Doherty Lakeview mill walked out in protest over the four-loom system.[27]

On the day that this second Doherty strike began and while the business agents of the two U.T.W. skilled locals were still confident that the arbitrator would report in favor of the union, the Paterson Textile Council met in special session. In response to the question of whether the broad-silk weavers were defecting to the I.W.W., the Local 607 representatives gave assurances that they would stay with the U.T.W. The broad-silk delegates did state, however, that they expected the Loomfixers and Twisters and the Horizontal Warpers to stay off the job during the strike then in progress. Miles responded by promising only that the U.T.W. would insist that Doherty continue the arbitration and that he would call a strike of the other Textile Council member locals if the owner refused. This did not satisfy the broad-silk men. Protesting the council's delay in authorizing strike action, they declared that such extreme caution was "the crux of the trouble between their local and the parent body."[28]

The weavers' representatives on the Textile Council were not aware of it at the time of the special meeting, but the possibility of settlement through arbitration was almost nonexistent. While Miles was arguing for a "civilized" settlement of the issue dividing the owner and his employees, Doherty was drafting a letter to Judge Walter C. Cabell of the Passaic County District Court calling off the arbitration. The silk owner informed the judge, who was serving as the arbitrator, that the weavers' strike had negated the written agreement between his company and the U.T.W. and that he was no longer obligated to honor his promise to settle all grievances through arbitration.

Doherty, clearly exasperated over what had taken place as a result of Detroit I.W.W. intervention, issued a statement to the Paterson newspapers explaining his course: "We have had nothing but trouble since we became a union shop. There are two places in Paterson paying more for weaving on plain looms than any others, and, between us, we have had more bother, more strikes, committees, conferences, etc., than all the other firms put together. Most places have no unions at all, but there are two weavers' unions in our mill. They have no confidence in their own leaders, and have even suggested that their own representatives were fixed by some of the big concerns."[29] Caught in the rivalry of two antagonistic labor organizations, each one as interested in advancing its own fortunes as in the welfare of the workers, Doherty was determined to stand fast.

Although the strike initially caused the complete closing of the company's two mills—the new Lakeview in Clifton and the older facility in rented lofts in Paterson proper—the owner began to reopen his establishments with nonunion workers. He maintained that he was "not opposed to labor unions when properly managed," but refused to change his stance. The strike, Doherty told the press, was "one of the most senseless . . . we ever heard of, apparently without just cause or reason . . . by submitting to it, we would lose the respect of all decent people; consequently, no matter what may happen we would never give in to such a thing, and for those who desire to work, we say that we shall not, under any circumstances, discharge any of the weavers that we are now gradually taking on."[30] The stalemate, with neither side willing to concede an inch, continued on into December.

The strike remained confined to the two shops of the Doherty Company, but the field of contention was not limited to the clearly defined lines of management versus labor. Present from the beginning of the protest over the multiple loom system, the competition between the unions in the textile industry increased and became more complex as the strike wore on.

Paterson became a center of attention for all those who had a basic sympathy for the workers. In New York City, the socialist daily *Call* informed its readers that "it would be suicidal to let the company install the four-loom system and . . . throw out on the street half of their employees," and urged "all labor and other progressive organizations" to contribute to the strike fund.[31] The *Call* did not mention the I.W.W. involvement in the strike, but the S.P.A. paper worked to provide the financial support which the Detroit faction was unable to generate and which the U.T.W. was unwilling to grant. There was, to be sure, a political motive for the party's action—1912 was an election year and it sought to attract labor support—but its hope for benefit from the Paterson strike was pale compared to that of the Chicago I.W.W.

The New Jersey silk workers had long been considered prime organizing material by the N.I.U.T.W., and in 1908, St. John had gone to extraordinary lengths to keep Local 152 out of the grasp of DeLeon, but the Chicago organization in 1911 lacked a local organizer of Katz's ability. As a result, and because of the Chicago faction's involvements elsewhere, Detroit's Local 25 had been able to assume the leadership of the disaffected weavers. The N.I.U.T.W., however, was not willing to stand aside and permit the silk workers to join Local 25 by default. When it became evident that the Doherty strike would not be easily settled, Thompson canceled his scheduled speaking tour through New England and rushed to Paterson. His arrival in December began the Chicago organization's attempt to turn the Doherty confrontation into a general strike of all silk workers for the eight-hour day.[32]

The competition between the two I.W.W.s added spice and not a little confusion, but it was the conflict between the U.T.W. and the Detroit I.W.W. which was the center of attention during the 1911 Doherty Company contest. Despite U.T.W. organizer Miles's promise that the union would call an authorized strike in the event Doherty refused to continue arbitration, the A.F.L. union did not honor that commitment. Instead of joining the strike at the Doherty facilities, members of the two skilled U.T.W. locals remained at work, standing beside those weavers who had refused to walk out and those who had been hired to replace the strikers. Not surprisingly, this and the Textile Council's stance was galling to the representatives of Local 607. On January 23, 1912, after two months of disillusionment, that local's representatives attended their last meeting of the Paterson Textile Council; shortly thereafter, U.T.W. Local 607 disbanded. Golden was later to write of the collapse of the once promising broad-silk weavers' local: "All the weavers were asked to do was to take pattern from the splendid achievements attained by our other local unions."[33] He made no mention of the U.T.W.'s inadequacies or broken promises.

In the sixth week of the strike, when it was too late to revive the already comatose broad-silk weavers' local, the Doherty firm's loom-fixers, twisters, and warpers finally joined the walkout. As soon became evident, this action was not taken because of any genuine sympathy for the striking weavers. Rather, it occurred because as the strike wore on, weavers in other broad-silk mills had become extremely critical of the skilled operatives at Doherty's—to the point that they were threatening not to work with members of the two U.T.W. locals in their own shops. Starr and Morgan called their members out because, having witnessed the decline of Local 607, they had no wish to see their own organizations suffer a similar fate.

From the moment the skilled workers joined the strike, they attempted to get the weavers to compromise and return to work. Late in January 1912 the two business agents convinced the striking weavers to attend a special, non-I.W.W. meeting to discuss the possibility of ending their strike. Starr and Morgan sparred with the uninvited Katz concerning the relative merits of accepting a compromise or holding out for the total abolition of the multiple loom system, but nothing was resolved. Several similar meetings followed the first one of January 26, with the script and the actors much the same. Finally, the local U.T.W. leaders called a secret meeting of a select group of weavers (mainly the most skilled English-speaking segment), had a committee elected to meet with Doherty, and opened negotiations to affect a settlement. On February 12, after a number of these weavers returned to work under the pretext of an agreement, the skilled craftsmen declared the strike over and returned to their places in the mill. Despite denials by the Detroit faction's Anti-Four-Loom Strike Committee that the issues had been resolved, all but a few of the workers followed suit.[34]

The Detroit I.W.W. had to acknowledge that the three-month strike had ended in defeat, with little change in the loom assignments or pay schedules of the Doherty firm. The only immediate achievement of the lengthy struggle, some consolation to Katz and his organization, was the weakening of the U.T.W. in Paterson. As a result of the strike's disappointing outcome under U.T.W. orchestration, particularly as compared to a successful strike for higher wages under Detroit I.W.W. direction by silk workers in Long Island, the U.T.W. broad-silk local in

Paterson disbanded and its members joined the more militant industrial union. The Paterson Textile Council, reduced to delegates from only the two skilled craft locals, went out of existence in April 1912.[35]

The February 12 agreement with the Doherty firm, worked out by only a fraction of the weavers with the encouragement of the two skilled U.T.W. locals, clearly infuriated the broad-silk weavers in the city. Katz, along with Detroit organizers Boris Reinstein and Frank Young, sought to exploit the anger to build up Local 25 and to gain support for a general strike to improve the conditions of employment in the broad-silk branch. That the weavers were not in a docile mood was evidenced two days after the Doherty plant resumed full operations when a fight broke out between those still on strike and the "scabs" who had returned to the Lakeview mill. Quick action by the police ended that skirmish, but nothing could be done to control the general feeling of anger prevalent among the weavers. Confrontations at the plant gates continued.

While the Lakeview workers engaged in these altercations, Local 25 began to arrange for a meeting of representatives from every broad-silk mill in the city. At the first gathering, those present repudiated the Doherty settlement, endorsed the formulation of a uniform price list to be presented to all the shop owners, and went on record in favor of a general strike in the broad-silk shops to support the wage demands. Several meetings followed the first, with Katz urging the shop representatives to recommend to their fellow workers that they join Local 25 as a preliminary to possible strike action. On February 19, at a mass meeting held in the Paterson Auditorium, the assembled weavers were urged to approve the scale of wages drawn up by the I.W.W. committee, endorse the demand for recognition of the union, and demand the right to maintain shop committees in each shop.[36]

The Detroit I.W.W. men did not ask for the prohibition of the three- and four-loom system, an issue of crucial importance only to the weavers in the relatively few shops producing cheap silks and able to finance the new looms, nor did they include a demand for a shorter work week as the Chicago local had urged during its brief involvement in the earlier strike. This new struggle would be limited to the wage issue, with an accompanying request for union recognition.

The new schedule, which was approved at the Paterson Auditorium meeting, provided for an increase ranging from 22 percent for the higher priced silk goods to 28 percent for the lower, an average new wage of $12 for a fifty-five-hour week. Since the silk industry was then enjoying a period of peak prosperity, it was hoped that the manufacturers would agree to the new price lists without necessitating a general strike. Katz told the weavers at the February 19 meeting that a number of manufacturers supported the new scale and that others were expected to join them. In reporting the results of the meeting to the press, moreover, the I.W.W. leader emphasized that "no general strike is imminent in the broad-silk mills," and repeated that he expected most of the owners to agree to the wage demands. To allay fears or to spike rumors, he stated that hours was not an issue and that his organization would demand similar wage increases from the Pennsylvania mills in order not to place the New Jersey firms at a competitive disadvantage.[37]

Although the nature of the weavers' demands was known immediately after the meeting at the Paterson Auditorium, it was not until February 23 that the new price lists, on paper imprinted with the I.W.W. seal, were delivered individually to each employer by a shop committee. On that day, in anticipation of possible trouble, Police Chief John Bimson stationed men at all of the larger broad-silk mills. The weavers reported to work at the regular time and the various shop committees proceeded to deliver the price lists to management, giving the owners until eight o'clock to consider and accept the wage increases. Seventeen smaller shops accepted the terms, but the majority of the some 120 firms refused to grant the demands. The weavers in the latter shops thereupon abandoned their looms and marched off the job. Of the estimated 6,000 broad-silk weavers in Paterson, about one-fourth took part in the walkout on this first Friday morning. I.W.W. Local 25, with an estimated 1,000 members when the day began, claimed that 2,500 more joined in the first hours of the strike.[38]

The larger broad-silk establishments, most directly in competition with the Pennsylvania firms, took a determined stand against the proposed increase in piece rates. Through their organization, the Paterson Broad-Silk Manufacturers' Association, the employers labeled the demands "absolutely unworkable" and argued that they were already at a disadvantage compared to companies elsewhere. The more the manufacturers expressed their unwillingness even to discuss the proposed schedules, the more weavers walked off the job. By quitting time on the first Monday of the strike, the usually conservative estimates in the local newspapers put the number of strikers at 3,500. To make matters worse for the Paterson broad-silk employers, the dye-house workers began to talk of joining the weavers. On Monday several hundred dyers' helpers presented their own demand for a wage increase—$1 per week —and indicated that they would be willing to strike to obtain what they sought. The operations of virtually every broad-silk mill were already affected by the strike, although none had been forced to suspend work entirely. If a large number of dyers walked out, the broad-silk and ribbon mills would have to shut down for a lack of dyed goods.[39]

Local 25 tried to exploit the dyers' grievances while its leaders sought to meet the employers' major argument that they could not grant the weavers' pay schedule because of the lower piece rates in Pennsylvania shops. Almost as soon as the first weavers walked out of the Paterson mills, Katz announced that he had wired national headquarters to send textile organizers to Allentown and Mauch Chunk in preparation for strikes there. To further the possibility of acquiescence on the part of the Paterson firms, the strike leaders urged the weavers to keep the strike peaceful. They were successful in this: the strikers attempted to dissuade others from entering the mills each morning, but there were no disturbances around the broad-silk mills. The weavers, as a result, gained the sympathy of a number of groups in the city. Even the Executive Board of the Paterson S.P.A. endorsed the S.L.P.-led strike and called on all workers to lend the weavers their support. Meanwhile, the members of the Paterson Broad-Silk Manufacturers' Association vacillated between threatening to close all of the shops and offering to meet with their weavers on a shop-by-shop basis. On Tuesday, February 27, the latter tactic was approved: the employers' organization proposed settlement talks if the strike committee would not interfere or demand union recognition. Katz responded that union recognition was not necessary and that the strike would end if the price list was accepted.[40]

Just as the employers appeared willing to begin negotiations with the individual shop committees, the Chicago I.W.W. interjected itself into the situation. National organizer Thompson had deserted the silk city for Lawrence when the strike broke out in that New England textile center, and the St. John organization had been too fully occupied there to provide much early assistance to Lessig, Koettgen, and the other Paterson leaders. However, when it became apparent that the rival I.W.W. had taken advantage of the silk workers' dissatisfaction, had more than tripled the membership in Local 25, and might succeed in winning a wage increase for over 5,000 weavers, the Chicago I.W.W. determined to intervene. Local 152 began to circulate reports that Haywood would soon arrive in Paterson to take charge of the strike and to expose the Katz faction as imposters who were attempting to capitalize on the fame of Lawrence. For its part, Local 25 warned the silk workers about the Chicago organization: "The 'I'm a Bum' outfit are trying to engender confusion by bringing W. D. Haywood, that misfit in the Socialist movement, who with his wild talk about General Strike does more to hinder the revolutionary spirit of the working class than all the reactionary forces operated by the working class."[41] The Chicago I.W.W. did try to capture the Detroit group's support, but until the conclusion of the Lawrence strike and the Ettor-Giovannitti trial in fall of 1912, its presence in Paterson was sporadic.

The first week of the 1912 strike was a confusing round of walkouts in shops previously little affected, of settlements in shops that had early been hit, and of renewed strike activity in shops where the returned weavers had mistakenly thought a settlement had been made. The broad-silk manufacturers individually accepted and then reneged on the price lists, threatened total lockouts, and then offered wage increases if the workers would disavow the union leadership. Meanwhile, Katz maintained order, traveled to Pennsylvania's silk centers to agitate among the weavers there, and raised funds to keep the strike going. On the sixth day of the strike, twenty-two shops were reported to have settled, but between 4,500 and 5,000 weavers were still out. On Friday, March 1, rumors circulated that a general settlement was imminent. Both sides discounted this, but the rumor was given some credence by the settlement at the Empire Silk Company, a firm which employed over 250 weavers and was the first of the larger establishments to agree to the new price list.[42]

Important breaks followed during the next two days, beginning with the announcement by the Weidmann Silk Dyeing Company that it would grant its 1,425 employees the wage increase they demanded. This action effectively removed the threat of the dyers joining the strike and may have prompted the weavers to soften their position on union recognition. At a meeting on March 3, the Executive Committee of the strikers met to discuss whether the broad-silk owners should be compelled to sign the price lists which had been printed under the I.W.W. seal. It was decided that the manufacturers could signify their acceptance of the new schedules merely by posting the new piece rates in their shops; the price lists need not carry the union seal, and the acceptance of the weavers' demands would not mean that concessions had been made to the union. Following this decision, some 2,500 to 3,000 returned to work at the higher piece rates. Only some of the largest firms—among them Dexter & Lambert, Victory Silk Company, Pelgram & Meyer, and Paragon Silk Company—held out longer.[43]

The broad-silk strike ended without any recognition of I.W.W. Local 25, but its result could only be construed as a victory for the Detroit organization. The manufacturers had agreed to the price list which had been prepared by the union, albeit without accepting the affixed union seal, and over 5,000 weavers received wage increases; in addition, the threat of the I.W.W. enlisting members from among the low-paid dye-house workers had been more than a small factor in the $1 per week pay increase in that branch of the industry.

Local 25 enjoyed a marked increase in its membership following the settlement and used the Paterson struggle as a springboard for similar organizing gains among the silk workers in New York City, Long Island, various Pennsylvania cities, and other New Jersey silk centers. In mid-March, workers in Allentown and in Hudson County, New Jersey, struck for wage parity with the Paterson weavers and joined the Detroit I.W.W. The silk manufacturers, the *Industrial Union News* boasted in April, "were being shown . . . that the I.W.W. [Detroit] is no union to trifle with."[44] Even a more impartial observer would have to admit that the union's accomplishments in the early months of 1912 were impressive. Only the Chicago I.W.W. sneered at what Lessig called the "S.L.P. gang." Passing over the fact that the DeLeon followers had waged a successful fight for a minimum wage list, the Paterson leader of Local 152 labeled the strike a defeat because it had left the multiple loom system intact.[45]

The Lawrence strike tended to obscure the battle waged by the broad-silk weavers of Paterson, but the early settlement of the latter conflict attracted wide attention. Comparisons between the two textile strikes were inevitable, particularly in the interval between the settlement in Paterson and the capitulation of the American Woolen Company in the Massachusetts city. One article of this nature characterized the Lawrence struggle as a defensive one, initiated by unorganized workers lashing out to hold onto the weekly wage they had been receiving, marked by at least some early violence, and accompanied by a tension which threatened to flare into other outbursts given the spark. Paterson, on the other hand, was viewed as an aggressive action (waged to gain a general wage increase), which followed a long period of union preparation, and was conducted in a peaceful fashion under the tight discipline of its leadership. The Paterson strike had not generated any heroes of the magnitude of Ettor, Giovannitti, and later Haywood, but the writer credited the rather unknown Detroit leaders with a major victory.[46]

It was this sort of comparison and the promise that the Detroit faction would build on its Paterson success to undermine the N.I.U.T.W. among the eastern silk workers, which prompted the Chicago group's attack on the broad-silk strike's accomplishment. If Local 25 was determined to increase its leadership among the silk workers, Local 152 was equally committed to thwarting that effort. In the months following the March settlement, both organizations competed for the allegiance of the New Jersey textile workers—the result was "one of the rare strikes in American labor history in which both factions of the I.W.W. were simultaneously engaged."[47]

Immediately after the March 4, 1912 settlement, when all but between 700 and 800 broad-silk weavers had returned to work, the Detroit I.W.W. announced its intention to organize the workers in the other branches of the silk industry. Already counting some forty dyers' helpers among its members, the Katz group put particular emphasis on the dye houses. None of the workers was ignored, however. The skilled twisters were wooed, under the assumption that all of the silk employees were "tired of A.F.L. pro-capitalist tendencies," and in mid-March local newspapers reported that the ribbon weavers were being organized in preparation for a strike in that branch.[48]

Meanwhile, Local 25 remained active and visible in the support it provided to those broad-silk weavers who continued on strike against the shops which had not agreed to the new price list. When, as occurred on March 14, some firms reneged on their agreements to honor the minimum wage scale, the local encouraged the weavers in those shops to resume their walkout. At least in a desultory fashion, the Detroit leaders also launched periodic attacks on the multiple loom system in use at the Doherty Silk Company.[49] The Detroit organization's greatest activity, however, was among the silk and other textile employees of West Hoboken, Bayonne, Union Hill, Passaic, and other New Jersey cities. It was in these locations outside of Paterson that the two I.W.W.'s came into the most direct and heated conflict.

Consistent with its statements during the early days of the Paterson broad-silk strike, the Detroit faction had begun in late February 1912 to organize the silk workers of Hudson County, New Jersey. On March 11 it staged its first mass rally at Schuetzen Park in Union Hill. Addressing those assembled in Polish, Italian, and English, the speakers urged organization under Detroit I.W.W. auspices as a first step toward obtaining the Paterson price list for the 2,500 weavers in that area. Similar meetings followed and, as more and more workers joined the union, plans were made to call a general strike in the mills of West Hoboken, Union Hill, Bayonne, and Jersey City Heights. Finally, on March 22, an estimated 6,000 weavers in more than fifteen establishments in northern Hudson County quit work after presenting the individual employers with formal demands for the new piece rates. Katz led the movement, and the procedure he followed in preparing for and calling the strike was exactly the same as that pursued earlier in Paterson. As had been the case in that city, some of the mills in Hudson County settled within days after the strike began. Larger firms, such as Schwarzenbach-Huber, which employed over 3,000 workers in its various shops, resisted the wage demands and forced a more prolonged struggle. The strike without exception was orderly: the workers followed the cautionary warnings of the I.W.W. leaders not to provoke the mill owners or police.[50]

While Katz was busy with the silk workers of Hudson County, Boris Reinstein agitated among the worsted workers of Passaic County. A Russian immigrant, S.L.P. member, and rather provocative figure, Reinstein whipped up considerable enthusiasm from the low-paid immigrant workers who had long been virtually ignored by the U.T.W. On March 14 some 300 weavers at the Forstmann & Huffman Company mills in Passaic and nearby Garfield struck for higher wages. Their action precipitated similar strikes at most of the principal worsted mills in Passaic, Clifton, and Garfield. Nearly 1,600 of these textile workers were idle by March 19, and ten days later over 40 percent of the almost 10,000 worsted operatives in the Passaic area were out. In the third week of March, the Detroit I.W.W. was conducting strikes throughout northern New Jersey and had a membership estimated at 15,000.[51]

The Detroit I.W.W. controlled the strike activity in the various New Jersey cities without direct challenge from other unions until March 27, when the Chicago faction began to make its presence felt. Thompson had visited the Passaic area on two occasions the previous week, but it was not until then that St. John's organization made its move to divert worker support from its competitor. The first challenge from the N.I.U.T.W. came over strike tactics with Thompson and his associates urging greater militance in extending the strike to all workers employed in the Passaic shops. In place of the no-picketing policy of the Detroit leadership, the Chicago organizers counseled that the endless chain of pickets, which had been so effective at Lawrence, be employed to coerce those still working to join the strike. At a rally led by Reinstein in Passaic on March 27, moreover, a Chicago agitator's call for an end to the DeLeon policy of nonviolence received some vocal support, and some in the crowd, particularly many of the Italian strikers, walked out of the Detroit meeting in response to the urging of the Chicago interlopers. This action was followed by other defections from the Detroit I.W.W. by those inspired by the victory recently won by its Chicago competitor at Lawrence.

The fact that the Detroit leaders had promised a wage increase within a week, as had occurred for most in Paterson, and that none was forthcoming after two weeks off the job, made some of the strikers amenable to a change in tactics and leadership. Reinstein's demeanor did nothing to stem the disaffection. When he removed Frank Domo, a competitor for the leadership of the strike, from his position as treasurer of the Passaic local, the Detroit I.W.W. lost considerable support among the Italian workers. The day after Reinstein's ill-advised action, more than 500 Italian strikers met with Thompson to form a Passaic local of the N.I.U.T.W. Clearly, the Detroiters were losing control.[52]

April 1 brought the first potential break in the Passaic strike: the Gera Mills and Forstmann & Huffman Company announced a pay increase of between 5 and 10 percent if their employees immediately returned to work. Reinstein refused the offer, replying that he would accept no settlement which did not include recognition of union shop committees. Without such recognition, he warned the strikers, any increase would be only temporary; once the workers accepted an offer and returned to the mills, the owners would break their word and the men would be powerless against a subsequent reduction.[53]

Reinstein's position made sense—recent history in the textile industry had shown that employer acquiescence to wage demands in peak production periods had usually been followed by reductions during slow times—but narrowing the issue to union recognition made the Detroit I.W.W. increasingly vulnerable to attacks from the Chicago organizers. One could not blame the Passaic worsted workers, the majority of whom were foreign born and who had previously accepted their conditions of employment docilely, for being tempted by the offer of immediate gain. The strikers at Forstmann & Huffman and Gera Mills did not accept the carrot offered them to return, but every day that they remained out of work while some of their shopmates stayed on the job made them more willing to accept new strike tactics and to consider alternative leadership.

The Passaic strike both widened and became more violent during the first week of April. On the same day that the two companies made their offer, the strike was given a big boost when more than 1,500 employees of the Botany Worsted Mills struck the company's Passaic facility. Thompson's entreaties at a mass rally the day before, and word that Bill Haywood would soon arrive in New Jersey, prompted the action. Haywood arrived the night that the strike began, and the Chicago I.W.W. opened its campaign to organize the textile workers the following day. While the Botany strikers held meetings in Passaic, Haywood and Thompson addressed the Forstmann & Huffman strikers in Garfield. The N.I.U.T.W. message at all these gatherings was the same: the workers had to change their tactics, pull from work those who had not yet joined the strike, and unite in one large industrial organization.

Haywood, during his stay in New Jersey, spared nothing in his attack on the Detroit organization. At the meeting in Garfield, for example, he told silk workers there:

Reinstein and his associates are sailing under false colors. They are not a faction of the I.W.W. They got the confidence of the people here because they represented themselves as I.W.W. men. Some of them have told the workers that they had been in charge at Lawrence. That the men who have been conducting the Passaic strike for two weeks now, under the pretense of being I.W.W. men with headquarters in Detroit, are not I.W.W. men at all, can be seen from the fact that they still stand for the craft organization. They have only called out the weavers here. We propose to make the strike general and call out every worker in the mill.

Haywood urged his audience to appoint a strike committee of its own, made up of members from each nationality group, to frame new demands and to employ more militant tactics. Stirred by the appearance of the hero of Lawrence, the workers did what he urged.[54]

Within three days of Haywood's speech, the only time he spoke to a mass audience during the strike, skirmishes broke out between the strikers and the Garfield police guarding the Forstmann & Huffman mills. The first break in the previously peaceful conduct of the strike was not serious, but the authorities took firm action, refusing the Chicago I.W.W. permission to hold meetings in Garfield and ordering hall owners not to rent their facilities to the union. Orders also were issued prohibiting the strikers from picketing the struck mills. On April 4, denied speaking facilities in Garfield, Thompson led a group of his supporters to McKray's Hall in Passaic, where Reinstein was addressing a meeting of his followers. After warning that his organization would not tolerate any preaching of violence, Reinstein allowed his Chicago counterpart to address the assembly. Both leaders spoke at the meeting and each told the strikers to forget differences between the two I.W.W. factions and work together. This was a promising display of solidarity. It was followed, later in the afternoon, by a meeting of the Executive Committees of both I.W.W. groups at which it was decided that a joint price schedule would be drawn up to halt the confusion of each faction submitting separate wage demands to the employers. Some of the Detroit leaders, skeptical of the Chicago organization's intentions, tried to prevent this agreement, but the action made sense to strikers unschooled in the labyrinthian complexities of radical thought.[55]

It required only one day to terminate this uneasy alliance and to demonstrate that Reinstein had made a tactical error in opening his meeting to Thompson. The next morning, following a harangue by a Chicago I.W.W. speaker, pickets at Forstmann & Huffman again clashed with police. This time the altercation was serious, with injuries on both sides. When Thompson led some of the participants to the hall where

Reinstein was speaking, the Detroit leader told him he could not remain. Reinstein later defended his action on grounds that he feared the police would deny his local access to speakers forums, but Thompson used the incident as proof that the Detroit leader was in league with the police to restrict the direct actionists' right to speak. Overnight the issue of free speech had entered the struggle. With the Detroit faction cast in the villain's role, the local S.P.A. lined up behind the N.I.U.T.W. If this was not damaging enough to the Detroiters, the strikers appointed a committee of six to urge Reinstein to cooperate with the Chicago local.[56]

The strikers might not have been aware of it, but the destruction of the Detroit faction rather than cooperation with it was the real intent of the Thompson strategy. Any reader of the April 6 issue of *Solidarity* would have discerned this. Under the headline "Don't Be Flimflammed by the Katz-DeLeon Crowd Masquerading in the Name of the I.W.W.," the writer in the Chicago organ began: "'Cur DeLeon, the Lying Heart,' ... is just now working overtime in his futile effort to prevent the I.W.W. from becoming a power in the land." Then followed a rather lengthy rehash of the events of the 1908 Convention (with DeLeon and "his small following of fanatical parrots" blamed for the upheaval there), charges of financial mismanagement by Katz in Paterson, and this conclusion: "Apart from their [DeLeon and Katz] ignorance of the problem they are dealing with, their utterly vicious hatred of the I.W.W. will cause them to go to any length to set back the genuine industrial union movement set in such vigorous motion by the Lawrence strike."[57]

Such statements, more creative than accurate, would have provoked men considerably less volatile than DeLeon and Katz to explode in kind. The Detroiters did so in the following issue of the *Industrial Union News*: "In all those places where the I.W.W. is engaged in conducting *bona fide* strikes, that aggregation of slummists calling themselves I'm-a-Bummery and sailing under the colors of the I.W.W. have attempted to put in their dirty work and break up the strikes by engendering confusion, and trying to throw discredit upon the leaders of the strikes and the I.W.W."[58] With exchanges of this sort, in the press and in meetings before the textile workers, cooperation was impossible and direct confrontation almost inevitable.

The position of the then stronger Local 28, affiliated with the Detroit I.W.W., was not improved by the Passaic authorities, who might have been expected to use the antagonism between the two I.W.W. factions to undermine the strike. Soon after reports circulated in the press that Haywood would be arrested if he reappeared in the city, the commissioner of public safety in Garfield denied this intention and blamed Reinstein for the agitation against the Lawrence leader. According to the commissioner, it was Reinstein who told the local authorities that Haywood advocated violence and should be arrested. On the same day that this official denial was issued, the S.P.A. appointed a delegation to the Detroit strike committee to urge cooperation and an end to the battle with the Chicago group. Reinstein refused to entertain such a notion, but his hand was weakened when the committee members decided to consider the proposal for joint action. The next day, coinciding with a report that some of the strikers were returning to the mills as a result of the "impractical methods employed by the Detroit faction," the New York *Call* published the statement made by the S.P.A. representatives to the Detroit strike committee. The strike, the members charged, was "utterly devoid of system," the strikers were torn by dissension and had lost faith in their leaders. The committee of S.P.A. men concluded that the strike was "certain to be lost" unless the two warring locals united.[59]

This position of the party and the change of tone in the New York daily's coverage were undoubtedly influenced by the contention between the S.P.A. and S.L.P., but both the diagnosis of the strike situation and the prophesy of defeat were accurate. Beginning with the weavers at the Forstmann & Huffman mills in Garfield and Clifton, members of Local 28 drifted away from the union and returned to work. The last of the striking weavers, those employed at the Dundee Mills, returned to their looms on May 1. The strike, which lasted from twenty-four to thirty-six days, ended in failure; most returned to practically the same conditions which had existed before.[60]

When the return to the mills began at Forstmann & Huffman, Thompson did not attempt to keep the workers out, as might have been expected. Instead, probably content that their defection from the strike represented a repudiation of the Detroit leadership, he looked to the future. The N.I.U.T.W. leader announced that when all the weavers had returned to the mills, the Chicago organization would begin its work to organize along industrial rather than craft lines. New demands would be formulated and a strike called after sufficient progress was made in the membership drive. Reinstein worked for a time to keep the strike going in the six mills where weavers were still out and he continued to talk of the promise of victory. But on April 26, when only two companies were still affected, he advised the remaining strikers to return to work. On May 3, 1912, Reinstein left Passaic.[61]

All that remained to do was to assign blame for the strike's failure —with the Detroit's *Industrial Union News* and the Chicago's *Solidarity* offering the expected explanations. There was more than a grain of truth in the assessment of each I.W.W. organ: the former's charge against the intervention of the Chicago organizers and the latter's criticism of

Reinstein's leadership. The view of both that the strike would have been successful without the interunion rivalry is less certain. The chances of victory would have been better if each faction had not expended energy attacking the other—the examples of the earlier Paterson and Lawrence strikes suggest this—but lack of the financial resources to continue the struggle could well have forced capitulation of even a unified effort. This is the conclusion of the most recent study of the Passaic strike of 1912.[62]

The defeat might also have been influenced by the fact that the Detroit I.W.W. had overextended itself. Even at the height of the strike, the DeLeon faction did not concentrate all of its attention there. Katz, by most accounts a more skilled and effective organizer than Reinstein, left the Passaic struggle in the latter's hands while he continued his efforts elsewhere in New York, New Jersey, and Pennsylvania. While Local 28 fought to win its wage demands in Passaic, Garfield, and Clifton, Local 27 initiated a similar strike among the silk workers in Astoria, Long Island, and Paterson Local 25 was forced to resume its earlier struggle in the broad-silk mills of that city.[63] Nationally never as large as the Chicago organization and endowed with fewer capable leaders, the Detroit I.W.W. attempted too much and promised more than it could deliver. When the St. John organization was free of the Lawrence strike and its legal aftermath, it could both capitalize on its reputation won there and take advantage of the agitational activities of its rival in New Jersey. The Detroit faction had succeeded in organizing thousands of textile workers for at least a short time, although its membership dropped almost as rapidly as it had soared, and those who had followed under the Katz banner had seen what organization under strong leadership could mean to them. This was evident in Paterson and helps to explain the later attraction of the Chicago I.W.W. in that city.

The March 4 settlement in the silk center under which the majority of the striking broad-silk weavers returned to work with an increase in piece rates proved to be both an incomplete and short-lived victory for Detroit Local 25. The larger mills never acceded to the union's demands and their weavers either returned to work under the old schedule or remained on strike after that date. Those shops which had agreed to the new rates, moreover, did not long honor their settlements. As soon as business slackened, there was an almost general repudiation of the March agreement, with the owners arguing that they could not afford to maintain the higher rates and could not do business in the face of the alleged interference of shop committees. One month after most of the Paterson weavers had returned to their looms, another strike broke out among the broad-silk operatives. The largest number of workers involved in this contest never exceeded 1,500 at one time, but the strike was less peaceful than the earlier one.[64] It also featured a much greater involvement by Local 152, supported by the national leaders of the Chicago I.W.W.

Although much of the effort of Haywood, Flynn, Thompson, and others immediately after the Lawrence strike was directed toward raising money for the Ettor-Giovannitti defense fund, the conclusion of the New England strike did permit them more frequent visits to the New Jersey textile towns. Given greater support from the national office, Paterson leaders Lessig and Koettgen began to rebuild Local 152 and agitate among the disgruntled silk workers. At first, the attention of the Chicago organization focused on organizing the ribbon weavers and dye-house workers, where Detroit Local 25 had made few inroads, but Local 152 did not neglect the broad-silk weavers. Late in March, when the Chicago faction led a strike of the ribbon weavers in the Pelgram & Meyer mill, it also sought to convince those in the broad-silk department of the firm, most of whom belonged to Local 25, to join its members in the walkout. The Chicago I.W.W. held mass rallies and shop meetings in the city, during which Thompson, Trautmann, and Flynn would retell the story of Lawrence and hold forth the promise of a similar victory in the silk center. The speakers also preached industrial solidarity and the effectiveness of the Lawrence strike tactics.[65]

As the broad-silk strikes continued on into May 1912, the manufacturers began to press the city authorities for action, threatening to move their shops out of the state unless the claimed disturbances were halted. Perhaps as a consequence of such threats, the Paterson officials began to take stronger measures against picketing and union meetings. Both I.W.W. locals were affected by the firmer stance; by May 10 more than fifty members of Local 25 were languishing in the Passaic County Jail, and the Chicago leaders were forced to hold their mass rallies outside of the city limits. In the last week of the month, the Detroit organization, which controlled most of those weavers still out, attempted to break the stalemate. Appealing to the manufacturers to reopen negotiations, the two sides met at the Y.M.C.A. to discuss settlement. But the result of the meeting was not promising. The president of the Silk Manufacturers' Association told the strikers' representatives that the owners would not concede to the weavers' demands, reserved the right to install any number of looms that they wished, would not deviate from their position on the open shop, and would have no negotiations with the Detroit organization. If the weavers wished to return to work, the union men were told, they would have to do so at a wage of from two to three cents lower per hour than that established in March. These terms, submitted to a strikers' meeting the following day, were refused. Local 25 leaders thereupon promised to urge the two U.T.W. craft locals to join the strike and assured the members that an effort would be made to call out those still working in the struck mills.[66]

The Detroit organization also tried to step up its strike activities by calling out pickets to dissuade workers from entering the struck shops, but the intransigence of the owners and the unwillingness of the U.T.W. locals to take part in what now appeared to be a lost cause offered little hope. The strike gradually began to wind down. On May 31 its demise was accelerated when Katz was arrested for picketing outside of the Siff & Cohen mill and sentenced to six months in jail. The Detroit organization tried to use the arrest to marshal support—the Chicago I.W.W., in fact, charged that Katz had courted arrest for that purpose—but the removal of the S.L.P. leader marked the end of the Paterson broad-silk weavers' struggle to obtain the higher wage. The strike was over by the time Katz was released on August 12.[67]

The defeat was almost a death blow to Local 25 but had little adverse effect on the Chicago local. Organizer Koettgen reported that while the Paterson workers were "deserting Katz like rats from a sinking ship," the future never looked brighter for Local 152. Charges that members of the Chicago union had "scabbed" during the weavers' strike, made by Katz and denied by Koettgen, did little harm. More deleterious, but to the Detroit faction, was the fact that Katz had consistently refused the urgings of some of the strikers to join with Local 152 in a unified effort against the broad-silk employers. Although Thompson's claim that his organization favored such joint action was most certainly insincere and self-serving, Katz's open refusal made him appear to be the one more interested in his organization's preservation than in the weavers' victory. If any benefits accrued from the long 1912 contest waged against the broad-silk shops, it was to the Chicago I.W.W.[68]

In the fall of 1912, when the silk industry began to move into its prosperous season and out of the spring doldrums which had helped to defeat the Detroit-led strike, Local 152 became increasingly active. Both Flynn and Haywood spoke in the city in September. Although their purpose was to raise money for the Ettor-Giovannitti trial which was about to begin in Salem, Massachusetts, their appearance provided a boost to the organizing efforts of the N.I.U.T.W. local in Paterson.[69]

In mid-November, apparently pleased with the progress of his union, Koettgen announced the formation of an Eight-Hour League, composed of members from all branches of the silk industry, to begin work to obtain the shorter day. He promised that the league would work also to abolish the three- and four-loom system in the broad-silk shops and would soon set a date on which the workers in all of the silk mills would strike simultaneously to win these demands. A socialist leader of the industrywide strike in 1913 claimed afterward that the league predated I.W.W. involvement in championing the silk workers, but the reverse was true. The Eight-Hour League was organized by Local 152. It existed as a separate entity at the outset, seeking to enlist members from every mill and shop in the city, whether I.W.W. sympathizers or not. But after the league gained support and obtained the endorsement of the S.P.A., it was merged with the Chicago local. Throughout November and December of 1912, the movement for the eight-hour day and the abolition of the multiple-loom system gathered momentum. Local 152 prospered along with it.[70]

On January 23, 1913, before plans for a general strike were finalized, approximately 800 broad-silk weavers at the Doherty mill in Lakeview left work in protest against the continuance of the multiple-loom system in that plant. This action represented only the dissatisfaction of workers personally involved with the loom issue rather than a response to any specific call to action by a union, but the Chicago local was clearly in sympathy with the strikers. The Lakeview weavers only precipitated I.W.W. action somewhat earlier than planned.[71]

The Doherty strikers were an influence in altering the issue priorities of Local 152. Instead of the eight-hour day as the primary objective, with the loom question secondary, the new outbreak at Lakeview propelled the loom matter to first place. Lessig later testified to the 1914 Commission on Industrial Relations that the number of shops in Paterson which had adopted the multiple looms had increased significantly in 1912 and that "the workers were . . . generally panic-striken from that cause," but this is doubtful. There was, however, enough concern over the possibility of technological unemployment among the workers to permit the I.W.W. to use the Doherty loom issue to agitate for a general strike in Paterson.[72]

Within hours after its broad-silk weavers walked out of the Lakeview facility, the Doherty Company agreed to reduce the number of looms worked to two and granted an increase of one cent per yard on all goods manufactured in the plant. This concession was made with the provision that similar action would be taken by all other mills using multiple looms within thirty days; failure to bring about a general agreement would allow Doherty to reestablish the three- and four-loom assignments. It was on this understanding that the striking broad-silk weavers returned to work. The protest which they had begun, however, could not be ended so simply. Spurred on by the Doherty weavers' action, shop meetings had been held in many of the other broad-silk shops in Paterson. Actions differed and demands varied dependent upon the conditions in each shop, but the net result was a general expression of discontent and a willingness to take action. Nearly 125 weavers at Audiger & Meyer joined Local 152; some 300 weavers in the Aronson Mill began plans for an assault on the multiple-loom system in operation there, and other shops called meetings as a preliminary to a scheduled I.W.W. mass rally on January 30.[73]

Three days before the general meeting was to take place, 500 weavers at the Doherty plant struck again, protesting that the company had not lived up to its agreement to abolish the four-loom system. Explaining that he was caught between those of his workers who wanted the higher wages they could earn operating more than two looms and those who wanted the three- and four-loom assignments ended and higher piece rates paid on two machines—a situation not inaccurately described by the owner as "Heads you win, tails I lose"—Doherty gave up hope of any agreement which would satisfy all of his employees. The company position, that it would "agree to pay by any list that is generally adopted, and for any system that the majority wish to work under," was not shared by other broad-silk firms.[74]

The resumption of the Doherty strike provoked similar walkouts in shops where the multiple loom system was also in operation. Doherty strikers massed at the gates of other mills to persuade weavers to join in their protest and were able to convince a number of them. By the time Koettgen opened the mass meeting of broad-silk workers at Helvetia Hall on the night of January 30, workers from the Doherty Company, Abraham D. Cohen, and the Aronson plant were out in protest against the three- and four-loom system. It was evident that weavers were divided on the loom issue, but when Koettgen introduced a resolution which stated opposition to the multiple looms, the delegates voted their approval.[75]

By February 1 the strike at Doherty Company had become plant-wide and the I.W.W. had demonstrated its support, but there was little hope of victory on the loom issue unless the strike could be extended throughout the industry. In fact, when weavers at other plants showed a reluctance to strike their employers in any number, some of the Doherty weavers returned to work during the first week of February. Some of these protested that the I.W.W. had not lived up to its promise to extend the strike, thus in effect pressuring that organization to action. Seeing the possibility of the strike ending without any success and never reluctant to take militant action, Local 152 met in closed session on February 18 and voted approval for a general strike of all silk workers.[76]

Following the vote for the general strike, leaders of Local 152 worked to gain the support of as many shop committees and labor groups as they could. A meeting was arranged with the loomfixers and twisters to ask them to consider joining the fight, and meetings were arranged with the ribbon weavers and dye-house workers to explore the manner in which they would support the broad-silk weavers. Although the U.T.W. locals proved unwilling to accept the call for a general strike and the ribbon employees voiced their reluctance to participate, the movement did gain momentum. Flynn and Tresca, called from the New York hotel strike as events in Paterson moved toward a climax, joined Ettor, Giovannitti, and the local leaders in stirring up support. On February 24, 1913 the call went out for all silk workers in Paterson to leave the mills at eight o'clock the following morning.[77]

Chapter 4

Launching the General Strike

> In many respects this strike will be remembered as one of the most notable that has occurred in the history of the country, in that it illustrates the astonishing readiness with which a large army of wage earners whose living depended on their daily labor were moved to quit work . . . reduce themselves and their families to dependence upon charity for the commonest necessities of life, all at the insistance and demand of a few irresponsible, reckless agitators—perfect strangers to them all, who were utterly ignorant of everything relating to the affairs of the great industry, the control of which they were intent on securing through the instrumentality of its thousands of deluded or intimidated operatives.—N.J., *36th Annual Report of the Bureau of Statistics of Labor and Industries* (1913), p. 180.

On the eve of the announced general strike, a capacity crowd filled Turn Hall in Paterson to hear the rallying speeches of the national I.W.W. organizers and to be briefed on the procedures for the following day. Flynn and Tresca, who had addressed gatherings of silk workers frequently during the preceding weeks, were among those who spoke at the mass meeting. Well known by the workers of the city, and popular for their roles in Lawrence and the recent highly publicized hotel strike in New York City, they received a warm welcome. The loudest cheers, however, came when Koettgen read a telegram from St. John stating that Haywood was on his way to take charge of the battle. News that the hero of Lawrence would lead the assault on the silk manufacturers gave promise of victory.[1]

The optimism of the workers and their I.W.W. spokesmen was not wholly unrealistic. The Paterson textile employees had shown a greater willingness to protest their conditions than had their Lawrence counterparts prior to the 1912 Massachusetts strike, more workers were members of unions in the silk city, and the I.W.W. had carried on a campaign of agitation for months before its call to strike. Yet, a disinterested assessment of the situation in Paterson would have exposed problems.

On the Monday evening before the strike was to begin, even the usually inflated estimates of the I.W.W. faithful did not put the membership of Local 152 at more than 900 out of the some 25,000 workers

employed in all branches of the city's silk industry; of this number between 400 and 500 had been enrolled only since the beginning of the
month, most of these from the Doherty mill. Although Koettgen told the
Turn Hall crowd that he expected some 10,000 workers to strike the
next morning, agitational activities among the ribbon weavers, dye-
house workers, and skilled craft members of the two U.T.W. locals had
produced only minimal support for a general strike. This suggested a
repetition of past experiences in Paterson, when workers employed in
the various branches of the silk industry had rarely been able to present
a united front against the owners. The dye-house employees, for example, had received little support from the weavers during their 1902
strike and still resented that fact. Even in the broad-silk mills, where
the unskilled and semi-skilled workers had shown a marked inclination to strike in recent years, divisions existed between the two-loom
weavers and those who worked the more sophisticated multiple looms.
Only two of the broad-silk shops in the city were thoroughly organized
at the moment the strike was called; most had only a few I.W.W. members. As the crowd streamed out of the hall to prepare for the next
morning's events, therefore, the prospects for a successful general strike
were even at best.[2]

On Tuesday, February 25, the silk workers reported to work as
usual at 7 a.m. An hour later, according to the prearranged plan, between 4,000 and 5,000 of them responded to a signal from designated
shop chairmen and walked off the job. According to a press report that
afternoon, forty-five shops were at least partially affected by this initial
action; with the exception of the United Piece Dye Works and Fore-
mann, Stumpf & Sharp, where a few dyers joined the strike, all of these
were broad-silk weaving establishments. As the strikers left the shops,
some formed a parade of sorts to march toward Turn Hall where a
meeting had been planned. Others began to congregate around those
mills where the workers had remained working, hoping to convince
them to join the strike. The atmosphere at the hall and around the shop
gates was more festive than angry, but the forewarned city authorities
wasted no time in taking strong action. Chief of Police Bimson, while
acknowledging that there had been no violence or serious disorder,
called out the entire force of his department to handle the strike. Squads
of officers were sent to each of the larger Paterson mills and Bimson
himself led a contingent to Turn Hall, where Tresca, Flynn, and Patrick
Quinlan were to address the some 2,000 workers gathered there. The
first two strike leaders, and by some later accounts Quinlan as well,
had already spoken when Bimson appeared, ordered the meeting to disperse, and arrested the three agitators. Tresca, Flynn, and Quinlan all

refused the option of leaving the city and thus avoid prosecution, and were arraigned in police court on charges of inciting a riot and held in lieu of $1,000 bail. Following the policy which he termed "preventive medicine," Bimson also posted men at the railroad station to arrest Haywood, rumored to be on his way from Ohio, if the I.W.W. leader attempted to enter the city. As the Paterson *Guardian* stated approvingly in its afternoon edition, the police had the situation "well in hand."[3]

The Paterson newspapers almost without qualification applauded the swift action taken by the chief and reported with confidence that his removal of the "outside agitators" had demoralized the strikers. "Who said John Bimson was getting too old to be the chief of police of this city?" the *Morning Call* asked in its editorial. "He was right on the job yesterday and by his prompt and vigorous action proved to the world that Paterson is not another Lawrence. . . . The movement was squelched at the very start and squelched very effectively." Only the socialist newspapers in the area, among them the Passaic *Weekly Issue* and the New York *Call*, condemned the police action. The former, in words that would later result in the arrest of its editor, characterized the police as "a bunch of drunken Cossacks" and "professional strike-breakers," and labeled Paterson as "the City of the Blues, the hotbed of brass-buttoned anarchists." The New York *Call* was more measured in its attack but was equally clear in denouncing "the brutality and violence of old John Bimson." The *Call*, however, saw some benefit accruing from the police response. Rather than breaking the general strike movement, as the local *Guardian* stated, the socialist daily believed that the police action would provoke outside support and encouragement to the workers.[4]

If the Paterson officials hoped that the arrest of the strike leaders and the massive display of force would end the strike before it had really gotten underway, they misgauged the temper of the workers and the dedication of the I.W.W. organizers. When Flynn, Tresca, and Quinlan were released on bail, the latter two after spending the night in the county jail, the threat of a trial and conviction if their cases were pursued did not force them from the city or temper their ardor. Nor was it evident that the workers' enthusiasm for the strike was diminished by the measures taken by the police. Bimson's arrests—twenty-five strikers were taken into custody the second day of the strike and held overnight for arraignment—did not encourage an end to picketing or a return to work. Although the New York *Times* reported that the strike was on the verge of collapse (declaring that only 1,200 were still out on Wednesday) because of the police policy, there was more truth in *Soli-*

darity's contention that the treatment of Tresca, Flynn, and Quinlan had increased worker support. Quinlan, writing in the I.W.W. weekly, declared that the response of the authorities had transformed the strike.[5]

By the beginning of the second week, the Paterson *Evening News* was concerned that the city officials had fanned rather than quenched the workers' militance:

> There is a growing sentiment that the police made a mistake in arresting out of town agitators without their having committed any overt act. There is a principal of American citizenship as old as the Republic and as deep-rooted as the American love of liberty, that the right of free speech and the right of men to gather together peaceably . . . is an inalienable one.
>
> This is the day of the square deal and an action as serious as that making public arrests of speakers discussing labor problems in a city like Paterson, which is essentially a laboring town, is one that should not be taken in ill-advised haste.[6]

Chief of Police Bimson, whom Flynn described as "a stupid bemoustached walrus" contemptuous of the new immigrants in the city, had unwittingly provided an issue which the strike leaders could turn to their advantage.[7]

On the morning of February 27, Koettgen led a delegation of strikers to meet with Mayor Andrew F. McBride and protest the actions of his chief. Although professing his basic sympathy for the workingman and recalling that he had risen from a working-class background to become a physician and successful politician, McBride supported Bimson. The mayor maintained that the I.W.W. organizers had no interest in Paterson and that their actions would only work to damage the city's reputation. He further questioned the motives of Flynn and the other outsiders, whom he charged came only as "press agents of the radical Socialist movement." The loom issue, the Democratic son of Irish immigrants argued, was a sham which exposed the strike's leaders "to more than the suspicion that they are seeking to advance, not the interests of their followers as workers, but of themselves as agitators." If the I.W.W. organizers were sincere in their expressed concern for workers, he challenged, they should go to the Pennsylvania silk centers and work to make conditions there comparable to those existing in Paterson.

McBride ended his interview with Koettgen and the others by proposing that a committee of five — made up of two strikers, two manufacturers, and one impartial citizen — be established as an arbitration body to attempt a settlement. When this suggestion was put to the Central Strike Committee the following night, the proposal was refused. By that time and as a measure of how ineffective the city's early repressive actions had been, a reported 8,500 workers had left the mills. The strike still was mainly confined to the broad-silk weaving shops, but the dye-house workers were joining the initial protesters.[8]

The dye shops, as the strike leaders well knew, were the key to the success of the general strike movement. From almost the moment that the strike began, pickets were placed near those establishments in an effort to call out the predominantly Italian and Polish dyers' helpers. Despite the posting of police and private guards and the frequent arrests of the picketers, each day a few more of the dye-house employees responded to the call to strike. The first important break came at the giant Weidmann facilities on the twenty-seventh, when some thirty Italian helpers left their work. Since that firm alone employed almost one-third of the approximately 6,000 workers in that branch of the industry and since action by the Weidmann dyers would be followed by those employed in the smaller shops, their action was significant. The *Evening News* was correct when it commented that the growing discontent in the major dye houses meant that "the trouble would assume enormous proportions." The worst fears of those who had hoped for an early settlement were realized on March 1 when dyers at Weidmann's and the National Silk Dyeing Company, the two largest dyeing establishments in the city, walked out en masse. Speaking before a meeting in Turn Hall later that morning, Flynn could report that almost the entire work force employed in the dye houses was out. For the first time in recent memory, a weavers' strike had spread to include the dyers. The next step was to induce the skilled weavers in the city's ribbon shops to follow suit.[9]

The 6,000 ribbon workers were among the best-paid silk employees in Paterson. Predominately English-speaking, identifying little with the immigrant workers in the other two branches of the industry, they had no interest in the multiple-loom issue and were paid at a level higher than that which could drive them to engage in doubtful causes. Lacking the issue which could move the broad-silk weavers and the desperation which could compel the dyers to action, the ribbon-shop weavers were nevertheless susceptible to the call for a shorter day. It was that issue, coupled with the strong-arm tactics of the local authorities, which the strike leaders emphasized in their appeals to the ribbon-shop employees.

In their work among the third major group of silk workers, the organizers were helped considerably by the local and state S.P.A. The socialists, concerned about the abridgement of free speech and assembly, had early voiced their support of the strike. Following the arrest of Quinlan, Flynn, and Tresca on the first morning, the secretary of the

Socialist party of New Jersey, Wilson B. Killingbeck, rushed to Paterson to protest the police action and the Passaic County organization raised bail for party member Quinlan. As previously noted, the Passaic *Weekly Issue*, the official organ of the party in Passaic County, condemned Bimson's response from the start. Such socialist actions aided the strike and broadened its support among the workers. When Killingbeck was arrested and temporarily detained for his speech in Paterson on February 27, and when the police confiscated the offensive number of the *Weekly Issue* and arrested editor Alexander Scott the next day, the S.P.A. involvement increased. In the I.W.W. appeals to the ribbon-shop workers, leading members of the state party stood side by side with the union organizers.[10]

On March 2, with more than 12,000 silk workers out on strike, the socialist contribution was made even more evident when the first of what would become weekly Sunday mass rallies was held at Haledon. A small community on the outskirts of Paterson, within easy walking distance, Haledon was a socialist stronghold in New Jersey; in November 1912 it had given S.P.A. presidential candidate Debs a plurality and had elected a socialist mayor and two justices of the peace. Haledon would become an oasis to which the strikers could retreat when the Paterson authorities sought to prevent their gathering. On farmland donated for the purpose by a party member, the Paterson workers could have their resolve strengthened in a pastoral setting far removed from the surroundings of their daily lives. On the occasion of this first meeting at Haledon, held under the auspices of the S.P.A., a crowd estimated at between 12,000 and 15,000 listened to addresses by Flynn, Tresca, Scott, and Killingbeck. Almost a carnival atmosphere prevailed as the speakers reported the growth in the number of strikers, expressed confidence that the ribbon workers would hold a strike vote, and predicted that the employers would soon capitulate if all would stand together.[11]

The ribbon-silk weavers met the following evening at Helvetia Hall in Paterson to decide whether a strike vote should be taken in the ribbon shops. Those present decided to have shop committees gauge the sentiment and report their findings at a meeting the next evening. Rumors and conjecture concerning the outcome filled the city through the day. The conservative press was certain that there would be no strike, since the ribbon weavers had "no grievances" and were not interested in staging a sympathy strike, but the New York *Call* was confident of a different result. To give the narrow-silk weavers an extra incentive to make that decision, St. John again wired that Haywood would soon arrive in the city. The *Call* assessment proved correct. On March 4, 1913—the day that Woodrow Wilson was inaugurated as president—workers in about one-half of the ribbon shops voted to join the workers in the other two branches. By this action, the silk industry of Paterson was on the verge of complete paralysis.[12]

The strike of 400 ribbon-silk weavers at the Augusta Silk Company on March 4 marked the beginning of the tie-up in the ribbon shops. Gradually, in one establishment after another, workers in other shops followed suit. By March 6 some 2,500 ribbon weavers were on strike; two days later it was claimed that only 500 still remained at work. At this point the second stage of the silk strike began. Effective agitation and the miscalculations of the Paterson authorities had prompted an estimated 23,900 to desert their places of employment: 11,000 in the broad-silk branch, 6,000 in each of the other two, and 900 skilled craftsmen made idle by the suspension of operations in some shops. When Haywood finally arrived in the city on March 7, it was time to formulate demands and turn to the creation of an effective strike organization.[13]

Although they could not have known it at the time, the silk manufacturers and their sympathizers would have months to ponder the question of how a strike of such proportions could have been launched. Their conclusion, not altogether reassuring as the strike hardened into a test of endurance, was that there was no rational explanation for the workers' action. With the exception of the multiple-loom issue, which directly affected the weavers in only 20 of the more than 150 broad-silk shops in Paterson and its vicinity, the workers had expressed few grievances and had presented no demands to their employers. Mayor Mc-Bride later asserted that no more than one-quarter of those who went on strike were dissatisfied with their conditions; the remainder, in his opinion, had joined the strike "in the spirit of a lark" and with the expectation that they would return to work after two or three days. This was not simply the obtuse observation of a beholden public official. Individuals on all sides shared the mayor's view. A writer for the *National Civic Federation Review* maintained that not more than 5 percent of the silk workers in Paterson were dissatisfied when the general strike was called, and Thomas Morgan, the business agent of Loomfixers' and Twisters' Local 439, testified to the Committee on Industrial Relations that "the great majority of those . . . on strike had no definite understanding as to what they were on strike for." Even Louis Magnet, once prominent in the S.L.P. in Paterson and one of the ribbon-silk leaders during the strike, conceded that he knew of no clearly stated grievance save that of the three-and four-loom issue when the strike activity began.[14]

To the manufacturers, public officials, and middle-class citizens of the silk city, the fact that the strike began before any demands were presented to the employers was proof that there were no grievances other than those associated with the loom question. In their view, the general strike was simply the product of agitation by radical and irresponsible outsiders, who fabricated lies to initiate the strike and then used intimidation to prevent the workers from returning to the job. They argued that if the silk employees had expressed their dissatisfaction with conditions to their employers, there would have been no need to strike; they continued to maintain that if the strikers would deal directly with their own employers, there was no need for the strike to continue. In the words of the *Annual Report* of the New Jersey Bureau of Statistics of Labor and Industries, the strike was simply the work of "outside agitators" who sought to advance their "openly avowed propaganda of revolution."[15]

The I.W.W. leaders in Paterson would have quarreled with their depiction as self-seeking opportunists with no interest in bettering the conditions of the silk workers, but they did acknowledge that many went on strike without any well-formed grievance or aim. Local 152 secretary Lessig later testified that there had been no clearly expressed opposition to hours or general working conditions, and Flynn stated that many walked out "because of the brutal persecution of the strike leaders and not because they were so full of strike feeling."[16]

That is not to say that the strikers had no justification to leave their shops. There was a general feeling of dissatisfaction, with some specific grievances held by groups of workers or by isolated individuals, which could be exploited by skilled agitators. Paterson Rabbi Leo Mannheimer, who sympathized with the strikers and later tried to affect an equitable settlement, believed that the I.W.W. involvement was "merely incidental." In his opinion, the cause of the strike was the dreadful conditions in the silk industry—buildings which were firetraps, lack of sanitation, low wages and long hours, and housing conditions which were deplorable. It was the general quality of the workers' lives in Paterson, both on and off the job, which generated a sense of unrest.[17]

Low wages were perhaps the most widely voiced grievance. The ribbon weavers, who pointed out that piece rates had declined 40 percent in some shops since the 1894 price schedules, were particularly vocal on that issue. Increased production due to technological advances compensated for the reduction in piece rates, but weavers, accustomed to think in terms of pay per yard woven, saw this as a remunerative loss. The workers also complained of employers' unfair and discriminatory practices: the allocation of the best material and looms to favored weavers, the arbitrary and excessive system of fines "for every conceivable offense," and the use of particularly skilled workers as pacemakers to set production quotas in a shop. These practices were made more odious by the fact that those who objected to them faced blacklisting or early layoffs when production was reduced during slow periods. Mindful of all these concerns, Magnet attributed the general strike to "deepseated grievances in the minds and the hearts of the strikers, produced or caused by the manner in which the employers had been treating them for . . . four or five years."[18]

Even the Paterson *Evening News* discounted the notion that the strike was solely the product of outside agitation. "It is useless to try and ignore the dissatisfaction that exists among the working people in the silk industry," it editorialized on February 25. "It is silly for the manufacturers to try and prove that outside agitators are the entire cause of the trouble, for it is self-evident that if the workers were entirely satisfied with their condition the arguments of the professional agitators would not be of sufficient weight to induce them to quit their looms."[19]

The I.W.W. was successful in inducing over 23,000 silk workers to go on strike by appealing to the general sense of dissatisfaction and frustration, refusing to present specific demands which might hold appeal to only a segment of the workers, and capitalizing on the initial actions of the Paterson authorities. It was only after the strike had become general that the union turned to formulating specific demands which would appeal to workers in each of the three branches. While this was being done, the anticipated appearance of Haywood was sufficient to keep the strikers from returning to the mills.

Haywood arrived in the New Jersey silk center from Akron, where the I.W.W. was also engaged in a strike, and immediately involved himself in the textile battle. Met at the Erie Depot in the city by several hundred strikers and two city detectives assigned by Bimson, he received his first orientation at police headquarters, where he was escorted to meet with the chief for some cautionary advice. As he walked through the streets of the strike-bound city, the enthusiasm generated by his appearance was evident. On every side the word was passed: "Haywood is here, Haywood is here." Later that afternoon of March 7, the Lawrence hero gave his first address to a meeting of ribbon-silk workers at Helvetia Hall.[20]

Two days later, and after spending most of Saturday speaking before various groups of strikers, Haywood attended his first mass rally at Haledon. He avoided talk of specific bread and butter demands, and used the occasion for an exposition of the class struggle. Part of his speech was quoted as follows: "We will have a new flag, an international flag. We will take the flag of every nation, dip them in a common dye pot and then take all out together. Then you will get a flag of one color—the red flag, the color of the working man's blood, and under that we will march." The *Evening News*, which printed this excerpt and which throughout the strike expressed its sympathy for the workers, was angered by such revolutionary talk. "Haywood or no other leader has any right to utter anarchistic remarks such as those," it protested. "The cause of labor was never helped by any such utterance."[21]

What the paper did not understand was that such speeches were part of the broad strategy of the I.W.W. As Flynn later stated, "the first period of the strike meant for us persecution and propaganda, these two things. Our work was to educate and stimulate." She continued: "Stimulation in a strike means to make that strike, and through it the class struggle, their religion; to make them forget all about the fact that it is for a few cents or a few hours, but to make them feel it is a 'religious duty' for them to win that strike."[22] This was Haywood's first contribution: to give the strikers a sense of purpose larger than themselves.

Strike demands were not made until two weeks after the strike began. Meanwhile, city officials complained that the "outside agitators" cared only for inciting revolutionary zeal and the manufacturers professed bewilderment at their workers' action. On March 11 whatever confusion existed was ended by the publication of the demands:

Ribbon Shops:	1) The eight-hour day (forty-four hour week)
	2) Weavers limited to the operation of one loom
	3) A minimum wage of $3 per day
	4) A wage increase of 25 percent for fixers and twisters
	5) Institution of the 1894 piece-work schedule
Broad-Silk Shops:	1) The eight-hour day (forty-four-hour week)
	2) Abolition of the 3- and 4-loom system
	3) A minimum wage of $12 per week
	4) An increase in piece rates of 25 percent
Dye-Houses:	1) The eight-hour day (forty-four-hour week)
	2) Time and one-half for overtime
	3) Maximum overtime of one hour per day
	4) A minimum wage of $12 per week for dyers' helpers
	5) Minimum age for apprentices to be sixteen

6) Minimum wage for apprentices: $9 per
week for the first six months, $12 per
week thereafter

7) No discrimination against those on strike.

Nothing was said about recognition of the I.W.W. However, the presentation of the demands by the union was construed by the manufacturers to mean that their acceptance would result in all of the advantages of contractual recognition.[23]

On the day that the demands were made public, strike headquarters attempted to remove the I.W.W. as an issue in the strike, anticipating the employers' contention and already cognizant of the distinction being made between the local silk workers and the "outsiders." It was announced that the I.W.W. organizers would not serve in any formal capacity or on any committee established to talk settlement with the employers; the strike demands would be presented by delegations made up entirely of local workers.[24]

This pronouncement of abstention was not simply a ploy to defuse a potentially obstructive issue. One of the basic tenets of the I.W.W. was that leadership should come from the aggregate rather than be assumed by a small cadre at the top. Fred W. Thompson, an I.W.W. leader in the 1920s and the union's chronicler, stated flatly that I.W.W. strikes were always run by the strikers. This point was particularly emphasized in Paterson. *Solidarity*, for example, printed the following account of a meeting between Rabbi Mannheimer and Haywood at Turn Hall, when the rabbi asked to speak to the strike's leader:

"The strike has no leaders," answered Bill.
"It hasn't! Well, who is in charge of it?"
"The strikers."

Flynn, who later came to doubt the wisdom of rank-and-file leadership in the Paterson strike, described the role of the I.W.W. organizers and propagandists in that city: "We were in the position of generals on a battlefield who had to organize their forces, who had organized their commissary department while they were in battle, but who were being financed and directed by people in the capital."[25]

The organization of the strike in the silk city reflected the emphasis on local and mass leadership. The strike was entrusted to a Central Strike Committee which was made up of two delegates from each of the broad-silk, ribbon-silk, and dye shops in the city. If each shop had sent representatives that would have meant a body of some 500 members; in fact, although the number taking part fluctuated, only about one-half of that number participated. The committee, which according to Flynn had a majority of members who were not in the I.W.W., met each night and was responsible for the formulation of broad strike policies. Its nucleus was established even before the strike became general and expanded as new shops joined the movement. As the membership grew, subcommittees were formed to take charge of such things as propaganda, information, relief, and the like. In addition to the Central Strike Committee, which sought to involve large numbers of workers as active participants and to coordinate all shops and branches of the industry, there was also an Executive Committee. Made up of between fifteen and twenty members, this smaller body was composed entirely of local members of the I.W.W. It proposed matters to be taken to the Central Strike Committee, had the most direct connection with the national leaders, and played a role larger than Flynn and the others would have one believe.[26]

At the bottom level of organization were the shop committees, which met irregularly and usually at the behest of the Central Strike Committee, and the branch committees, which represented the special concerns of the strikers in each major division of the industry and usually held daily mass meetings. To a large degree the organization developed in Paterson mirrored that used the year before in Lawrence. In the silk strike, however, there was no formal organization along ethnic lines (although special meetings were held for the various nationality groups where they could be addressed by native speakers), and a greater reliance on shop and branch organization. These differences were less the result of conscious planning than they were of the peculiar characteristics of the Paterson industry and its less ethnically heterogeneous work force.

For a strike which had "no leaders," Paterson had a rather large number of prominent advocates. All decisions were submitted to the mass of strikers through the Central Strike Committee, the branch organizations, and the individual shop meetings, but the role of the national organizers was crucial. They functioned as spokesmen for the strikers, the source of virtually all information from the workers' side published by the press; were present at the Central Strike Committee's nightly meetings, as well as the daily branch meetings held at Turn Hall and Helvetia Hall; raised funds to sustain the relief effort, speaking in cities throughout the East for that purpose; and were the inventors of the tactics employed throughout the strike. They continued to maintain that they acted solely as advisers, a claim which the local union leaders took pains to confirm, but it is evident that their advice was followed without challenge almost to the end. Without their efforts, the broad-silk weavers' protest against the multiple loom system could never have been transformed into a general strike, nor could the contest have been continued for so long a period. Haywood, Flynn, Tresca, and Quinlan remained in Paterson throughout the strike and epitomized the battle.[27]

By far, Haywood was the most prominent member of the quartet of outsiders. Born in Salt Lake City in 1869, of stock which he described as "so American that if traced back it would probably run to the Puritan bigots or the cavalier pirates,"[28] he was raised in the rough and raw environment of the mining camps of the late nineteenth century West. The death of his father in a mining camp when he was three educated him early to the inherent dangers of the miner's life; when he entered the mines himself at fifteen—after he had already amassed a varied employment record as farm hand, fruit-stand operator, messenger boy, and hotel worker—he learned at first hand the life of a hard-rock miner. In 1896, after an unsuccessful stint as a farmer forced him back into the mines, Haywood joined the W.F.M. and began his steady climb in that organization; within four years Haywood was elected secretary-treasurer of the union and took up residence in Denver. It was from that Colorado city that he was taken to Boise to face charges in the murder of the former governor of Idaho in 1906. As previously discussed, that trial propelled the tall, one-eyed miner into national prominence and helped to change the direction of his life. Although Haywood had taken a leading role in the formation of the I.W.W. in 1905, it was not until after his acquittal in the Steunenberg trial, and his disagreement with his co-defendant and W.F.M. President Moyer, that he began to play a major part in the industrial union he had helped to found. When he took over for Ettor and Giovannitti in Lawrence and led the textile workers there to victory, he became a hero to workers in industrial centers throughout the country.[29]

Haywood was a complex man whose talents and convictions were variously described by his contemporaries and have been subsequently debated by scholars. Although newspaper accounts tended to depict him as "a rough-neck making melodramatic appeals to the mob," Andre Tridon, an I.W.W. member and American correspondent for the largest syndicalist paper in France, viewed him as a simple, direct man who spurned "soap-box platitudes" and appealed instead to the workers' desire to improve their condition.[30] Frank Walsh, chairman of the Commission on Industrial Relations before which Haywood testified for over three hours in 1914, described the I.W.W. leader as a "rugged intellectual," and was impressed by "his facility of phrasing, his marvelous memory and his singularly clear and apt method of illustration."[31] But most have agreed with Max Eastman, the socialist intellectual who knew Haywood during the Paterson period and later patterned the character Jo in his novel *Venture* after him, that the big westerner "sensed things better than he understood them, and was more at home in figurative than analytic language." [32]

None disputed the effectiveness of his speeches, nor the genuine compassion he had for the workers whom he addressed. Eastman remembered his "Gibraltar-like bearing" and "a voice like velvet," a combination of power and gentleness which was remarked upon by more than a few who knew him. Goldman wrote that his "most notable characteristic . . . was his extraordinary sensitiveness. This giant, outwardly so hard, would wince at a coarse word and tremble at the sight of pain." [33]

Despite Tridon's disclaimers, Haywood was most effective as a platform speaker who could move an audience by his often utopian pictures and anger conservatives by his bombastic attacks on the status quo. J. Ramsey MacDonald, who met him at the 1910 Copenhagen conference, termed him a "bundle of primitive instincts, a master of direct statement," but "useless on committee" and quiet and unnoticed among the world figures assembled there. Yet, when MacDonald saw Haywood address an audience of English workers, he became aware of his ability as a speaker. "He made them see things," the British socialist wrote, "and their hearts bounded to be up and doing." [34]

Haywood functioned in Paterson more as an inspirational agitator than an effective strike organizer; as was true in Lawrence, where he inherited the strike organization fashioned by Ettor, he arrived in the silk city after the essential structure of the strike force had been formed. His greatest contribution was in maintaining morale and keeping aflame the enthusiasm of the mass of strikers.

Flynn retained "unforgettable memories of Big Bill surrounded by stunted, undernourished little ones at the children's meetings; of his tender sympathetic appeals at the women's meetings; of his simple, plain language, and his gestures." [35] James P. Cannon described a typical Haywood speech:

> With his commanding presence and his great mellow voice, he held the vast crowd in his power from the moment that he rose to speak. He had that gift, all too rare, of using only the necessary words and of compressing his thoughts into short, epigrammatic sentences. He clarified his points with homely illustrations and pungent witticisms, which rocked the audience with understanding laughter. He poured out sarcasm, ridicule and denunciation upon the employers and their pretensions, and made the workers feel

with him that they, the workers, were the important and necessary people. He closed as he always did, on a note of hope and struggle, with a picture of the final victory of the workers.[36]

Although Haywood has been seen as a pragmatic unionist, "both cautious and expedient,"[37] the I.W.W. leader in Paterson emphasized less the strikers' bread-and-butter demands than his vision of their future. Certainly a portion of one Haywood speech to the silk workers suggests more than a touch of a visionary streak and illustrates what Cannon meant by his "picture of the final victory." In describing the new silk plant which would take the place of the numerous small "cockroach" shops after the workers assumed control of production, Haywood told his audience:

> It will be utopian. There will be a wonderful dining-room where you will enjoy the best food that can be purchased; your digestion will be aided by sweet music, which will be wafted to your ears by an unexcelled orchestra. There will be a gymnasium and a great swimming pool and private bathrooms of marble. One floor of this plant will be devoted to masterpieces of art, and you will have a collection even superior to that . . . in the Metropolitan Museum. . . . A first-class library will occupy another floor.
> The roof will be converted into a garden. . . . Your workrooms will be superior to any ever conceived. Your work chairs will be Morris chairs, so that when you become fatigued you may relax in comfort.[38]

How relevant this was to strikers who had by then existed for months without receiving a pay envelope is uncertain. But Haywood, an odd admixture of conflicting characteristics, managed to keep thousands of diverse silk workers out on strike week after week against seemingly insuperable odds. In the process, he lost over eighty pounds and almost ruined his health on their behalf.[39]

Usually appearing with Haywood at strike meetings and rallies, and presenting a fascinating study in physical contrast, was the twenty-three-year-old Flynn. Already termed by some the "Joan of Arc of labor wars," she seemed destined to succeed the legendary "Mother" Jones as the foremost female labor agitator in the country. "She's a little woman, is Gurley Flynn, and Irish all over," *Outlook* described her a few years later. "The Celt is in her gray-blue eyes and almost black hair, and in the way she clenches her small hands into fists when she's speaking."[40]

Born in Concord, New Hampshire, the oldest of three daughters of an Irish immigrant mother and first generation father, Flynn could scarcely remember when she was not involved in some radical cause.

Her mother, Annie Gurley, was a feminist and Irish nationalist who helped promote her radical attachments and provided "lifelong material and moral support." Her father, a religious skeptic who had left the Catholic Church in his youth, was a socialist who voted for Debs in 1900. "We were conditioned in our family to accept Socialist thinking long before we came in contact with Socialism as an organized movement," Tom Flynn's daughter recalled. Given direction by both of her parents—reading Edward Bellamy's *Looking Backward* at an early age on her mother's suggestion and trailing along with her father to socialist meetings before she was out of her childhood—Flynn at fifteen tried to start a socialist club among her classmates at Morris High School in New York City, where the family then lived. Goldman remembered hearing the fiesty youngster speak at the girl's first open-air meeting. "She could not have been more than fourteen . . . at the time," the anarchist leader wrote, "with a beautiful face and figure and voice vibrant with earnestness. Later I used to see her in company with her father at my lectures. She was a fascinating picture with her black hair, large blue eyes and lovely complexion. I often found it very hard to take my eyes off her, sitting in the front row at my meetings."[41]

Flynn was, in fact, fifteen when she delivered her first public speech, at the Harlem Socialist Club on the subject of the status of women. At sixteen she joined I.W.W. Local 179 and made her first appearance under its auspices at a meeting to protest the Haywood-Moyer-Pettibone arrests; later in 1906 she took part in an unsuccessful I.W.W.-led strike against the General Electric plant in Schenectady. The same year, while still in high school, she overcame her parents' hesitancy and attended the I.W.W. convention in Chicago as an elected delegate of her local. It was there that she met Jack Jones, a Minnesota miner and W.F.M. member in his thirties, whom she married in January 1908. Two years later, after many separations caused by Flynn's organizational work, the marriage foundered. Driven to distraction by her husband's fascination with the "system"—"his wheels and charts on the I.W.W. and a complicated plan he worked out to revise the calendar"— she went off alone to join in the Spokane free-speech fight then in progress. Although pregnant at the time, she courted and won arrest for her activities in that Washington city. Released by a jury which William Z. Foster described as "visibly affected by her charms," she returned to New York where she gave birth to a son. She was then twenty years old.[42]

The marriage was a casualty of her feminist inclinations and her growing commitment to the I.W.W. She wrote in her account of these years:

His [Jones] attitude was undoubtedly a normal one, but I would have none of it. I did not want to "settle down" at nineteen. A domestic life and possibly a large family had no attractions for me. My mother's aversion to both had undoubtedly affected me profoundly. She was strong for her girls "being somebody" and "having a life of their own." I wanted to speak and write, to travel, to meet people, to see places, to organize for the I.W.W. I saw no reason why I, as a woman, should give up my work for him. I knew . . . I could make more of a contribution to the labor movement than he could. I would not give up.[43]

Following her return to her family in the South Bronx, Flynn became a prodigious worker in the cause of industrial unionism. A frequent lecturer for the N.I.U.T.W. in New England, arrested for her activities in Philadelphia among the workers of the Baldwin Locomotive Works, she could be found wherever the I.W.W. was engaged. She gained national prominence as a result of her involvement in the Lawrence struggle and the colorful hotel workers' strike which followed and was one of the first on the scene when Paterson Local 152 issued its call for help. With a will of iron and courage to match, she devoted herself to the cause of the silk workers.

When Flynn arrived in Paterson, her romance with Tresca was at its height. Eleven years older than Flynn, Tresca was born in southern Italy, the son of a wealthy landowner in Pulmona. Almost as precocious as his later Irish lover, by the age of twenty-two he had organized a local branch of the Socialist party there, started his revolutionary newspaper, *Il Germe* (The Seed), and become secretary of the Italian Workers' Union. Indicted for libeling a local politician, found guilty and sentenced to eighteen months in prison, Tresca fled Italy and, after a stay in Geneva, immigrated to the United States in 1904. He spent three years as editor of the official organ of the Italian Socialist Federation in New York City, then resigned from the S.P.A. and moved to Pennsylvania, where he became editor of an Italian anarcho-syndicalist paper called *L'Avvenire* (Tomorrow) in New Kensington. It was in western Pennsylvania that Tresca met Giovannitti. When Ettor and Giovannitti were arrested in Lawrence, the latter recommended that his countryman be called to take up the work among the Italian workers of the textile city. Tresca responded and shortly thereafter met Flynn. "Carlo had a roving eye that . . . roved in my direction in Lawrence," Flynn later wrote. It was a "a very dramatic event for me then and one destined to have far-reaching consequences."[44]

Married and the father of a daughter, Tresca left his family and followed the yet undivorced Flynn to New York, where they provided the romantic interest in the hotel strike. Although not a member of the I.W.W., preferring his role as an army of one, he joined her in Paterson, where he was invaluable in appealing to the largely Italian dye-house workers of that city. On the first day of the general strike, he added to an already impressive American arrest record—police in Pittsburgh, Lawrence, and New York City had found his provocations intolerable— and was among the three arrested at Turn Hall.

A tall, slender man, it was said that "his Van Dyke beard and eye-glasses gave him the appearance of a poet." However, most who knew him during this period of his life would have agreed with Eastman, who described Tresca as "the most pugnaciously hell-raising male rebel . . . in the United States." This view was shared by Michael Dunn, the Prosecuting Attorney of Passaic County during the Paterson strike. In his testimony before the Commission on Industrial Relations, Dunn held Tresca responsible for inciting most of the hostility of the strikers. "I think he is one of the worst men in the United States today," the New Jersey official testified.[45] Eastman, who included Tresca in his book, *Heroes I Have Known*, wrote of him: "Tresca never makes trouble. He merely goes where trouble is, cultivates it, cherishes its fine points, props up the weak ends, nurtures and nurses it along, so that from being a little, mean, and measly trouble it becomes a fine, big tumultuous catastrophe approaching the proportions of a national crisis."[46] Flynn would not have disagreed with this characterization. "Tresca," she wrote, "was very resourceful—a good strategist in struggles."[47]

Quinlan, the last of the four most-prominent "outside agitators" in Paterson throughout the strike, was a socialist of more conventional bent than either Haywood or Flynn; he had little of the antipolitical or anarchistic sentiments of his three associates and worked closely with the S.P.A. in Passaic County. Born in 1883 in the village of Kilmallock, Limerick, he was the son of a farmer, dry-goods merchant, and horse trader who brought the family to the United States when Quinlan was four. Several years later, he was sent back to Ireland to be educated for the priesthood and remained in his native land until his early teens. He rejoined his family in 1900, learned about industrial conditions firsthand in a variety of manual jobs—coal miner, steel worker, longshoreman, machinist, and others—and became active in the labor movement.[48]

Quinlan joined the Longshoremen's Protective Association, a S.T.&L.A. local, and became a member of the S.L.P. in Newark, New Jersey. There he formed a close association with James Connolly, the Irish socialist agitator who would later die in the 1916 Easter Uprising, and worked with him in organizing efforts in that city. When the I.W.W.

was founded, the two men established locals of that union and joined in the effort to bring unity between the S.P.A. and S.L.P. in New Jersey. Connolly and Quinlan also worked together on the Haywood-Moyer-Pettibone Defense Committee and were among those who formed the Irish Socialist Federation at the New York City home of Flynn's father in March 1907. When DeLeon opposed the formation of the Irish Federation, both Connolly and Quinlan left the S.L.P., Quinlan to join the party of Debs.[49] In the years between 1907 and 1913, Quinlan worked as a S.P.A. organizer among the Irish in Massachusetts, enlisted members for the Amalgamated Association of Iron, Steel, and Tin Workers, served several months as a reporter for the New York *Call*, and lectured on Ireland for the Board of Education in New York City.[50]

Quinlan had known Flynn from his work with the Irish Socialist Federation and probably knew Tresca through the latter's early involvement with the Italian Socialist Federation in New York and New Jersey. Both men had worked for unity between the two socialist parties in New Jersey but had taken different paths when the rift could not be healed—Quinlan moved from the S.L.P. to the S.P.A., Tresca from the S.P.A. to an independent course. In Paterson, despite their differences, the three veterans of the labor and socialist struggles worked well together, and with Haywood. Quinlan's contacts with S.P.A. leaders in New Jersey and New York were invaluable in raising money and attracting socialist press support. Like his associates, he was an effective speaker, of whom the *Appeal to Reason* wrote: "His sarcastic tongue, his knack for picking up an armful of wrongs and hurling them at society in a single sentence, and the depth and intensity of his thin face . . . fairly compelled attention."[51]

Of the local silk workers, there were five men who played particularly important leadership roles in the prolonged strike. Two—Lessig and Koettgen—were most closely associated with the outside leaders. Koettgen, whose brother owned Helvetia Hall, was a Swiss-German who had lived in Paterson some fifteen years and had worked as a weaver. An early member of the I.W.W., he was elected to the Executive Board of the N.I.U.T.W. in 1910 and attended the I.W.W. convention the following year as its elected delegate. For several months before the Paterson general strike began, Koettgen worked full time as a paid organizer for Local 152. As a member of the General Executive Board of the I.W.W., he held the most prominent position among the union's members in the silk city. The forty-one-year-old Lessig, with whose family Flynn often stayed when she remained overnight in Paterson, was secretary of Local 152 and a broad-silk weaver at the Benjamin E. David shop when the strike began. A native of Philadelphia, he had worked as a weaver since his arrival in the New Jersey city in 1902. During the strike, he chaired the daily meetings of the Central Strike Committee and was a member of the Executive Committee. Like Koettgen, he was active in the N.I.U.T.W., becoming its secretary-treasurer in 1914.[52]

Edward Zuersher was a ribbon-weaver and a union loyalist who served on the Executive Committee. Less well-known than Lessig or Koettgen, he was a member of the S.P.A. and a later officer of Local 152. Zuersher had been a resident of Paterson for some twenty-five years and was the most active I.W.W. member among the ribbon-silk workers. When the strike began, he worked as a weaver in the small Fisher Company shop.[53]

Despite Zuersher's position in the I.W.W. strike organization, the most active and vocal ribbon-silk weaver during the strike was Louis Magnet, who was then employed at the Sweeney Silk-Ribbon Manufacturing Company. A resident of Paterson for over twenty years, he had a long history of involvement in labor organization: in 1902 he was the spokesman for the Paterson S.T.&L.A. local and a member of the S.L.P. Although not in any union in 1913, he was a member of the S.P.A. and an outspoken representative of his shop on the Central Strike Committee. Magnet was often quoted in the press, to the chagrin of the I.W.W. leaders, and was later blamed for encouraging the workers in the ribbon branch to seek an independent settlement.[54]

The leader of the dye-house workers, Thomas Lotta, played a role comparable to Magnet during the strike, although he was a loyal I.W.W. member who served on the Executive Committee of the strike organization. Little is known about his background beyond the fact that he was a dyers' helper of Italian origin. Along with Tresca, and later Ettor and Giovannitti, Lotta helped to keep the support of the Italian workers in the dye houses.[55]

The appearance of Haywood on March 7 completed the circle of strike leaders and the presentation of the workers' demands four days later gave the industrial conflict its focus. From March 11 onward, events in the silk city would center on the effort to maintain sufficient solidarity among the strikers to force an industrywide settlement.

The first reaction on the part of the manufacturers did not promise an early resolution of the contest. The day Haywood arrived in the city, and before the demands had been formally drawn up, thirty-six ribbon establishments joined in a statement concerning their position vis-à-vis the rumored eight-hour day issue. Such a shortened week, the signers declared, would add as much as 25 percent to their operating costs, which would force them out of the market and result in the closing of their Paterson mills.[56] When a delegation of three weavers presented the formal demands to each ribbon shop on March 12, they knew what to expect and were not disappointed. Each manufacturer turned down what was asked. But if the owners expected to frighten their workers by their threat of closing, they were not successful. At the Helvetia Hall meeting at which the rejection was reported, the hall rocked with applause and approval when one weaver declared his defiance: "I will stay out until next winter if necessary."[57]

The summary rejection by the ribbon manufacturers was soon matched by the owners in the other two branches. On the evening of March 13, over one hundred manufacturers, representing all three divisions of the industry, met to frame a united response to the strikers. The resultant statement, addressed "To The Silk Workers of Paterson," was published the next day. Containing seven parts, and labeled an "ultimatum" by the press, it read:

1) The present intolerable conditions are due to the domination of professional agitators and a small minority of silk workers; . . . 90 percent of our workers have been kept from their daily occupation through fear of this minority.

2) Our mills are open, and will be kept open, for employees who are desirous of returning to their work. We shall use all lawful means to protect them from injury. . . .

3) The employers find it impossible to grant any of the demands . . . and it must be thoroughly understood that work can be resumed only under the conditions that existed before the present disturbance.

4) The employers are anxious that their employees work under the most healthful conditions possible and that each employee shall receive fair and just treatment at all times. If any individual employee shall have a complaint to make of any kind, such complaint will receive proper consideration.

5) Nothing is to be gained by prolonging this strike. So far as the eight-hour day is concerned, its adoption by us would destroy Paterson industrially; such a movement must be nation-wide, and then Paterson would be found in line.

6) As regards the three and four loom system, it is applicable only in the case of the very simplest grade of broad silks, and . . . has for a long time been worked successfully and on a very large scale in other localities. Paterson can not be excluded from this same privilege. No fight against improved machinery has ever been successful.

7) We all desire permanent peace. This peace can only be obtained by living under, working under, and defending the American flag.

Signed by the Ribbon Manufacturers' Association, the Broad-Silk Manufacturers' Association, and the Master Dyers, the statement made it clear that the employers planned to stand together for patriotism and against the "unreasonable" demands of outside anti-American trouble-makers.[58]

With the lines clearly drawn between the strikers and their employers, other segments of the community established their positions. Of the four major newspapers in the city, only the *Evening News* evidenced any sympathy for the strikers. Politically independent, and designated early in the strike as the official organ for the English-speaking ribbon workers, it posited that the workers had genuine grievances and that the owners' refusal to meet with the strikers was a serious mistake. As for the I.W.W., which the other papers attacked viciously from the outset, the *News* preferred to reserve judgment until the union made known its aims and answered the charges that it was an anti-American organization bent only on revolution. If such allegations were true, the paper expressed confidence that the workers would disassociate themselves from such leadership. But, it pointed out, even if the I.W.W. was a destructive and anarchistic union, as the manufacturers alleged, the owners had only themselves to blame for its strength among the local silk workers—past refusals to deal with more conventional organizations and the blacklisting of workers who dared to protest shop conditions had left the employees with no choice but to accept whatever external aid was offered. The *News* did temper its support of the workers' justifiable bid for better treatment, however. Alluding to some of the strikers' demands, it cautioned that the employers could only be expected to agree to what was fair and reasonable. "It is," one editorial concluded, "only a waste of time to make a demand . . . which is out of all proportion."[59]

In contrast to the evening independent, the other Paterson newspapers were justifiably termed either antiworker or antistriker.[60] The *Morning Call*, a Republican daily, early took the position that the strike would be short-lived and continued throughout to report imagined breaks in the workers' ranks, accounts seen as a tactic designed to provoke a mass stampede back to the mills. The day after the demands were presented, for example, the paper stated: "The only new thing about the silk strike is that it seems to be going to pieces, disintegrating, by its own weight." Certain that "the whole trouble will soon be over," the paper opined that it was "not very likely that the silk operatives of Paterson [would] permit themselves again very soon to be forced from their work by a lot of professional agitators."[61]

The Paterson *Guardian*, the Democratic evening paper, followed a similar line, attributing the strike to outside agitators and reporting the imminent collapse of the movement. Seeking to exploit the long-standing division between the immigrant workers and the English-speaking ones, the latter termed the "best class of workers" by the paper, the *Guardian* predicted that the more desirable group would "have nothing to do with the I.W.W., its leaders, its methods, or its doctrines."[62]

The last of the papers, the Paterson *Press* and its *Sunday Chronicle*, were perhaps the most vehemently opposed to the strikers. Edited by John L. Matthews, who termed the I.W.W. "a menace to the community," the Republican *Press* came close to advocating vigilante action to drive the agitators from the city.[63] With the exception of the moderate and conciliatory *Evening News*, then, press sentiment was strongly on the side of management. Only the Passaic *Weekly Issue* and the New York *Call*, both socialist papers with a limited readership, supported the strikers in the greater New York City area.

Not all members of the community assumed the prevailing press position of support for management and little recognition of the legitimacy of the strikers' grievances. A number of prominent citizens at least reflected the more moderate stance of the evening independent, offering their good offices to attempt a settlement. One of these was Rabbi Mannheimer. Claiming that he acted on behalf of some prominent silk owners, the leader of the Congregation B'nai Jeshurun in Paterson called a meeting of nine strikers, three from each branch of the industry, the day the strike demands were submitted to the owners. It soon became apparent that the rabbi had had no offer of mediation from the manufacturers, that he had acted only because "someone had to do the work and everyone else seemed to be afraid." Lessig and Koettgen, who were among those present, took issue with Mannheimer's tirade against the I.W.W., and the session ended. The owners' reaction to the meeting was a curt disavowal of any association with the Mannheimer intervention.[64]

The rabbi continued to work for a settlement, even though he was aware that many in his congregation disapproved his actions, and remained vocal in support of the workers. In early April, over the objections of many in the synagogue, the trustees voted not to continue Mannheimer's services.[65] His dismissal served notice to others concerning what they might expect if they attempted to intervene without the sanction of the silk manufacturers.

The workers' most consistent friends in the early days of the strike came from the socialists, who were accustomed to the opprobrium of the city's business and political leaders. Killingbeck continued to appear at strike meetings and rallies, S.P.A. members offered bail to those jailed under Bimson's no picketing order, and party newspapers across the country carried sympathetic accounts of the silk workers' uprising. In an interpretation shared by many, Scott saw Paterson as proof of what could be gained if the I.W.W. and S.P.A. worked in harmony together.[66]

Although the *Industrial Union News*, organ of the Detroit I.W.W. and the S.L.P. faithful, questioned the motives of the S.P.A. in Paterson and continued its tirades against the "imposters" of the Chicago union, even that monthly offered its support to the strikers. Local 25 had shrunk to minuscule proportions after its efforts in 1912, but its members participated in the strike and were provided relief by the Detroit office. The Detroit I.W.W. declared at the outset that it would "not retaliate for the acts of ignorance and shortsightedness" that it had suffered in the previous strike and carried through on this promise. Thus, the strike leaders were not distracted by the sort of internecine conflicts which were often present within the radical-socialist camp.[67]

In the first weeks of the strike neither side seemed particularly interested in working toward a settlement, although each professed a desire for one. Offers to try to bring the strikers and their employers together—made with varying degrees of sincerity by Mayor McBride, a merchant-businessman-clergy group, and Mannheimer—received little affirmative response. Rather than agree to sit down with a delegation of strikers, the manufacturers directed their energy to transforming the conflict into one in which Americanism was the central issue. Taking Haywood's Haledon flag speech as a cue and an opportunity, the owners began plans for a massive display of their own national allegiance.

On March 17, the day designated as Flag Day in Paterson, the stars and stripes flew from every mill, with the expectation that the strikers would rush back to work under the national standard. This dubious manifestation of managerial patriotism added color to the drab mill district but otherwise had little impact. The strikers responded with a parade, with flags galore, led by a banner which proclaimed:

> We weave the flag.
> We live under the flag.
> We die under the flag.
> But dam'd if we'll starve under the flag.

On the following Monday, the appeal to patriotism having been unsuccessful, the American flags were removed from the mills.[68]

While the owners tried to exploit Haywood's promise of the international red flag, the strike leaders were busy trying to defuse the manufacturers' contention that the competition from outside silk concerns made it impossible to grant the demands. The general strike movement had barely gotten underway in Paterson when the I.W.W. leaders promised to carry the fight for improved conditions to the silk shops of Pennsylvania and New York City. After the great majority of Paterson workers had been induced to leave their shops, the union organizers increased their efforts to extend the strike to other silk centers.

The area around Allentown, which after Paterson contained the heaviest concentration of silk workers, was the first to feel the expanding impact of the New Jersey battle. On March 12 some 600 dyers' helpers at the National Silk Dyeing Company and the Lehigh Dyeing Company struck. The predominantly Italian workers had many of the same grievances as their Paterson counterparts —conditions, in fact, tended to be worse in the Pennsylvania shops—and had earlier expressed their willingness to strike in support of the New Jersey strikers. What precipitated their action, however, was the posting of police guards around the dye houses the previous day. The National Silk Dyeing Company, which was the second largest dyeing establishment in Paterson, hoped to prevent an extension of the strike to its East Allentown facility by this action; instead, its workers were infuriated by the appearance of armed guards. Local I.W.W. men helped to create sentiment for the strike, and were aided by the Paterson unionists. Koettgen, who had made previous trips to the city, rushed to Allentown the day the first dyers walked out. Three days later, Haywood and Tresca also appeared in the city. Although their efforts to get all of the silk workers in the vicinity to join the dyers were not successful, the dyers' strike continued and the Paterson men made frequent visits there.[69]

Meanwhile, Quinlan was active among the silk workers of Hazleton and Williamsport, Pennsylvania. By March 20 some 1,200 workers at the Duplan Silk Company in Hazleton were out on strike and an I.W.W. local had been established. Early in April four dye houses in Philadelphia were hit by a strike of some 400 helpers. The I.W.W. never managed to tie up the Pennsylvania silk industry to the extent that it did in Paterson, mainly because of the special characteristics of the textile industry in that state, but the successes it did register made it evident that the dissatisfaction of the silk workers in the country was widespread.[70]

Closer to Paterson, the I.W.W. organizers made better progress in their appeal to disaffected employees in the silk industry. On Saturday, March 15, the workers at the Smith & Kauffman ribbon shop in Harlem voted to strike and the following Monday, Flag Day in Paterson, some

700 of the company's operatives failed to report to work. Union leaders predicted that by the week's end some 4,000 silk workers in the New York City area would be out and, to give credence to this boast, sent organizers to College Point, Astoria, and the other silk communities.

The strike at the large Smith & Kauffman ribbon shop, which came after the New York ribbon weavers had sent a delegation to Paterson and was voted at a meeting addressed by a visiting group from New Jersey, was an important breakthrough for the I.W.W. organizers. Not only did it extend the strike in the ribbon branch of the industry, where the better-paid weavers had shown some reluctance to strike in Paterson, but it actively involved the New York socialists in the silk struggle. Many of the shop's workers were party members and their participation helped generate financial and press support which was crucial to the continuation of the contest. Once the Harlem firm's weavers joined the strike, moreover, they became active in convincing other shops outside of Paterson to follow suit.

Workers in the Smith & Kauffman annex in South Norwalk, Connecticut, struck the day after the main shop was hit. Shortly thereafter, in Astoria and College Point, Long Island, weavers at the Star Ribbon Company and Meineppo Silk Company appealed for organizers and began to talk strike. On March 20 some 300 ribbon weavers at the latter shop in College Point, under the leadership of Local 527, walked off the job. Shops throughout metropolitan New York swelled the growing number of strikers until, by March 26, an estimated 6,000 silk workers in that area were out. According to John Steiger, the socialist leader of the Smith & Kauffman weavers, only the Astoria workers resisted the call to join the mass action.[71]

In addition to the work of extending the Paterson strike to encompass the entire silk industry, the I.W.W. leaders spent the first weeks of the strike in perfecting tactics and establishing an effective system of relief. This, in the categorization of sociologist Ernest T. Hiller's study of strike behavior, was the crucial third phase of what he identified as a "typical strike cycle": the maintainence of group morale, which followed organization and the initiation of concerted action.[72] Flynn well recognized the importance of morale and the need to keep strikers occupied during the period they remained out of work. "Continual activity" was part of the agitators' most important job, she recalled, "and we lay awake many nights trying to think of something more that we could give them to do."[73]

The job of maintaining morale among the silk workers was made somewhat easier by the example which the earlier strikes in Lawrence and Little Falls provided. During the twelve-week Little Falls textile strike, the I.W.W. leaders used mass picketing, mass parades, and demonstrations "to make each individual feel that it [was] upon his participation that the success of the strike depended." When the authorities of that New York city barred such activity, the nightly hall meetings remained the only vehicle for preventing the corrosive boredom and depression of the idle workers. The continuous oratory soon proved tiresome, however, at which point the meetings changed their nature. As one observer wrote of the strike, "every night . . . there was practically a continuous vaudeville."[74]

The activities planned in Paterson followed closely those employed in Little Falls. The emphasis, as Quinlan later explained, was on mass action: "Big strike meetings were held. Picketing was carried on en masse. Funerals, parades, and everything connected with the strike were done on a large scale. The only time group action was resorted to was when the workers discussed their affairs in shop meetings and here group action ended."[75] Morale, as much as the local proscription on Sunday meetings in Paterson, was the reason for the weekly outdoor rallies in Haledon.

Because Monday is most often the critical day in a strike, when the employers make their greatest effort to get the workers back and when the strikers are most apt to be discouraged, Sunday activities were crucial "in order to keep spirit from going down to zero." For this reason, Flynn recounted, the decision was made to go to Haledon—"to give them novelty, to give them variety, to take them en masse out of the city . . . to a sort of picnic over Sunday that would stimulate them for the rest of the week."[76]

To overcome divisions and counteract any sense of isolation, which could destroy morale, another tactic employed in Paterson was to involve various distinct groups of individuals. Thus, there were special meetings for female workers; planned gatherings for the wives and children of strikers, designed to keep up enthusiasm on the homefront; and special ethnic events at which immigrant workers could be addressed in their native languages. All of these cut across branch and shop lines. Frequent exhortations to victory, song fests, performances by outside artists, dances, a circus, and every other form of diversion imaginable were employed during the strike. When Hiller wrote of the various ways in which morale could be upheld in a strike, he could and in fact did use Paterson as a textbook example.[77]

None of these tactics, of course, could convince strikers to remain off the job in the face of abject want and unbearable hardship for their families. Provision had to be made to provide for those in need through the establishment and operation of a relief agency. Here again the system employed at Lawrence and Little Falls provided the model. Since the I.W.W. had from its inception followed a low initiation and dues policy, in reaction to the alleged "fat cat" mentalities of the A.F.L. "bureaucrats" and in recognition that the low-paid industrial worker could not afford a heavy assessment, a first priority was to solicit funds to augment the thin union treasury.

Shortly after the manufacturers' "ultimatum" precluded the probability of an early resolution of the issues, the Central Strike Committee sent a circular of appeal to labor organizations throughout the country. Addressed "To All Wage Earners and Friends of Labor," it made its appeal under the declaration: "An Injury To One Is An Injury To All." Similar requests for aid were sent to socialist organizations and fraternal groups which were thought to sympathize with the workers. A final source of aid came from collections taken up at the "free" lectures given by I.W.W., socialist, and anarchist speakers.[78] The initial response in Paterson to the plea for financial assistance was gratifying. The *Evening News* announced that it would contribute $5 per week to the strike fund, to demonstrate its sympathy for the workers; the Purity Co-operative, a socialist bakery in the city, notified the Central Strike Committee that it would donate $1,000 worth of bread; and the Passaic S.P.A. signified its intention to offer all aid within its power. Finally, at a meeting on March 17, the Sons of Italy, a fraternal organization which claimed 1,000 members in its nine local lodges, voted to levy a weekly assessment on its membership, estimated to bring in $384 each week.[79]

There was a constant need for financial aid, especially as the strike wore on, but the Paterson strike leaders received enough in contributions to provide help for the most distressed. A committee of fifteen strikers, composed of representatives from each of the three branches of the industry, established the policies governing strike relief and oversaw its disbursement. This body met each day at which sessions the members would hear appeals for aid and issue relief orders to those whose requests were granted. At the outset, money was provided the applicants; later, orders on local merchants were given, two per week, in amounts varying with the size of the family. Toward the end of the strike, the committee established a commissary to dispense food and other necessities. Relief was provided all those on strike, whether or not the worker was a union member: the applicant simply had to provide certification from his shop committee that he was indeed not working. According to the New Jersey Bureau of Labor Statistics, over 800 families were receiving some kind of aid from the Relief Committee by the end of the second month of the strike.[80] The rest lived on savings, the income of family members employed outside of the industry, or relief provided by external agencies. Many spent money only on food, allowing their rent and utility bills to accumulate.

By March 20 the New York *Times*, by no means a newspaper friendly to the workers' cause and clearly hostile to the I.W.W., was reporting that the silk industry was showing the effects of the three-week strike. The supply of dyed goods was reputedly being diminished, a condition which would soon affect the few weaving shops which had continued to operate, and the ribbon firms had exhausted their stock of fancy silks. The implication was that the manufacturers in these branches would soon make some small concessions and that the strike would then end.[81]

This appraisal had some substance, for the previous day the Broad-Silk Manufacturers' Association, Ribbon Manufacturers' Association, and Master Dyers had issued their first statement since their declaration of March 13. "We have always been willing, and are ready at any time, to hear any grievances that our employees may have," the joint statement began, but the owners maintained that they would meet only with their own employees. If this attempt to separate the strikers from the union and the Central Strike Committee was thought to hold any hope for a break, management was soon disappointed. The Press Committee of the strike organization responded that the workers had the same right to chose an organization to represent their interests as the silk owners had to select one to represent those of management. The Central Strike Committee, it stated, was "prepared to meet with the managers on a common ground based on fairness and justice." Both the *Evening News* and the *Morning Call* ran editorials urging the two sides to get together—the former "regardless of the I.W.W." and the latter on a shop-by-shop basis without union interference—but neither side was ready for much give and take. In fact, if the strikers interpreted the statement of the owners' associations as did the New York *Call*, the employers' "change of front" gave the workers reason to hold firm. It was, the socialist paper declared, "an indication that the bosses are feeling the effects of the strike and are ready to make concessions."[82]

With the appearance of deadlock underscored by the statements of the two sides, third parties again tried to act as intermediaries. On the day of the exchange of official statements by owners and the strikers' Press Committee, an unnamed "local man of prominence" traveled to Trenton to explore the possibility of state intervention. Governor James F. Fielder's reaction did not offer much hope, however: he deplored the effects of the strike on the city's economy but disavowed any intention to intervene. "A safe and just settlement of such an industrial difficulty could readily be made by voluntary arbitration," Fielder wrote the Paterson man. "The intelligent men on both sides ought to be able to find a method of meeting and discussing the questions at issue as public-spirited and unselfish citizens in a great industrial community."[83]

The afternoon that the governor's letter was published, at the Board of Trade rooms in City Hall, a group of professional men met to see what a public-spirited third party might do. Members of the five-man Committee on Industrial Conditions and Trade Disputes of the Paterson Board of Trade, they surveyed the situation which was bringing the city's business to a halt. Finding that the Board of Trade by-laws prohibited interference in labor disputes as arbitrators without the request of one of the affected parties, the committee invited each side to take that step. It also appealed to State Senator Peter J. McGinnis to introduce a resolution calling for the appointment of a joint legislative committee to investigate the strike. When McGinnis assured the Board of Trade that he would do what was requested, a sense of hope permeated the city.[84]

On March 25 the assemblyman from Passaic introduced a resolution in the lower house, calling on the governor to appoint a committee to investigate conditions of work, wages, and the like in the silk industry. It passed the House that day. However, Senator McGinnis delayed the introduction of a similar resolution in the upper chamber. Declaring that a committee could only bring out the facts, that it had no power to make a settlement, the senator expressed his concern that a legislative committee would only cause delay in resolving the strike. When McGinnis finally introduced the resolution which he had promised, it was defeated. Quinlan blamed the defeat on the manufacturers' reluctance to have their business affairs aired in a public forum, but it is doubtful whether either side welcomed interference from Trenton at that juncture.[85]

As the fifth week of the strike began, no progress had been made toward a settlement. The three manufacturers' associations remained firm in refusing to deal with the workers on anything but a shop basis and, convinced that economic want would soon put an end to the conflict, were willing to bide their time. The I.W.W. leaders, who had control of the Central Strike Committee, refused to consider anything but an industrywide settlement and were certain that the employers would have to capitulate. Each side watched the other carefully for any sign of weakness.

Figure 1. Textile Workers of Lawrence, Massachusetts, Celebrating Their Victory over the American Woolen Company, 1912. Courtesy of the Archives of Labor and Urban Affairs, Wayne State University.

Figure 2. William D. Haywood. Courtesy of the Archives of Labor and Urban Affairs, Wayne State University.

Figure 3. Elizabeth Gurley Flynn. Courtesy of the Labadie Collection, the Department of Rare Books and Special Collections, the University of Michigan Library.

Figure 4. Carlo Tresca. Courtesy of the Labadie Collection, the Department of Rare Books and Special Collections, the University of Michigan Library.

Figure 5. Arturo Giovannitti and Joseph Ettor. Courtesy of the Archives of Labor and Urban Affairs, Wayne State University.

Figure 6. Patrick Quinlan, Carlo Tresca, Elizabeth Gurley Flynn, Adolph Lessig, and William D. Haywood (left to right). Courtesy of the Labadie Collection, the Department of Rare Books and Special Collections, the University of Michigan Library.

Figure 7. E. Strokins, Frederick Sumner Boyd, Pat Lumbar, Thomas Lotta, Adolph Lessig, William D. Haywood, Ewald Koettgen, and Arturo Giovannitti (left to right). Courtesy of the Archives of Labor and Urban Affairs, Wayne State University.

Figure 8. Elizabeth Gurley Flynn and William D. Haywood with Strikers' Children in Paterson. Courtesy of the Archives of Labor and Urban Affairs, Wayne State University.

Figure 9. Sunday Rally of Paterson Strikers in Haledon, May 1913. Courtesy of the Archives of Labor and Urban Affairs, Wayne State University.

Figure 10. Elizabeth Gurley Flynn Addressing Paterson Strikers, June 1913. Courtesy of the Archives of Labor and Urban Affairs, Wayne State University.

Chapter 5

"Until Hell Freezes Over"

The chances of settlement seem no nearer than it did the first week the trouble began.—*Evening News*, April 7, 1913.

"Stay with this strike even though you starve to death, for it is better to die than have the children go back in the mills in perpetual slavery."—William D. Haywood's speech at Turn Hall, April 15, 1913. Quoted in the Paterson *Evening News*, April 15, 1913.

The Paterson strike bids fair to last ten months. . . . The Paterson workers have had to live mostly on hope, which now has become simply grim determination.—Phillips Russell, "Living on Determination in Paterson," *International Socialist Review*, 14 (August 1913), 100.

From the beginning of the strike, the manufacturers and the business-oriented newspapers in Paterson had expressed dismay that the English-speaking workers had joined the less-skilled immigrants. In their view, this unnatural alliance of previously antagonistic elements could not withstand the hardships of a prolonged battle. Thus, as the strike settled down to a contest of endurance, the owners sought to exploit the ethnic divisions among the workers. Almost daily, the press carried stories of breaks in the strikers' ranks, of shops which had reopened as strikers returned to the mills, and of the desire of the English-speaking element to sever connections with the Central Strike Committee. Every display of tension between the English-speaking strikers and the "foreigners" was given wide coverage; if there was no incident to report, potentially divisive issues were introduced to provoke one. The newspapers, for example, reported at length an alleged altercation at a Turn Hall strikers' meeting between Italian workers and their English-speaking shopmates, supposedly sparked by the latter's habit of leaving the hall whenever speeches were delivered in Italian, and, when the press reminded the strikers of the hardships their families were enduring, the point often was made that the English speakers suffered most because they had nothing like the Sons of Italy to provide relief.[1]

Reports of expected mass returns to the shops and of acrimony between various groups of strikers were largely fabrication, but there was enough truth to them to concern the leadership. Workers in some shops did begin to return to work after a few weeks and others were clearly anxious to bring the strike to an end. Ribbon leader Magnet, for example, urged the intervention of third parties—elected officials, clergymen, merchants, or whatever—and sentiment for this grew among the nonunion strikers. To counter possible defections, and also to keep the workers actively involved in the strike, the I.W.W. began to increase its picketing. In response, city authorities augmented the police guard around the larger mills and began to use firemen to reinforce them. Large plants like Weidmann's, which began to transport strike-breakers by boat to its plant along the Passaic River, hired private guards to assure even greater protection. The strikers were cautioned against the use of violence by Haywood and the others, but the increasingly volatile situation made an outburst almost inevitable. On March 25, before the gates of the Doherty mill, the first skirmish took place between pickets and some English-speaking weavers who had returned to work. Although the police quickly dispersed the crowd before the confrontation had advanced much beyond the pushing and shoving stage, the incident demonstrated the increasingly angry mood of the strikers as the stalemate continued.[2]

The altercation at Doherty's, which resulted in the arrest of seven pickets, was the signal for a change in tactics by the Paterson authorities. During the first two weeks of the strike, the city officials had followed a get-tough policy which they thought would bring it to an early end. The arrest of Flynn, Tresca, and Quinlan on the first day of the general strike was designed to warn "outside agitators" to keep out of the matter or face the consequence of long prison terms; the mass arrests of the first pickets were to serve notice on the strikers that the city meant to uphold the right of others to remain at work; the treatment of Scott for his editorial in the *Weekly Issue* was meant to caution sympathizers to watch their language. This strategy, however, had not produced the desired end. The strike had spread, in part *because* of the police action, and more rather than fewer outside sympathizers appeared in the city.

On March 11, the last instance of the initial big-stick policy occurred: Tresca was arrested for disorderly conduct in picketing the Weidmann plant. After spending the night in the county jail, his second stay in that facility, he was found guilty of the charge in Recorder's Court and sentenced to six days. The colorful strike leader was soon released under heavy bail, but the Italian community was incensed over his treatment. Whether because of the Sons of Italy's strong protest or the fact that arrests seemed to be little deterrent, the release of Tresca was followed by the abandonment of the early police tactics. For two weeks there was no occasion for talk of "brass-buttoned anarchists."[3] The Doherty incident, coupled with indications that at least some strikers were ready to return to work if they could be protected against feared I.W.W. reprisals, led to the return of the earlier policy of arrests and intimidation.

When the Doherty mill was again the scene of mass picketing on March 28, forty strikers were arrested for refusing the police order to leave the area. Charged with disorderly behavior and held in jail overnight, they formed the vanguard of hundreds who would be similarly treated. In its edition that day, the Evening News was concerned what might follow. "If the present police tactics continue," it warned, "there will be a great deal of trouble in the city." It went on: "There is a growing feeling . . . of restlessness and brewing trouble. The strikers and police have already clashed in one or two instances and there is a general feeling that a storm is brewing and is about to break. At their meeting today, the strikers were very much incensed over the story of a beating of a woman by a police officer." Whether the rumor of police brutality alluded to had a scintilla of substance, such stories were believed and did not bode well for the peace of the city. The Police and Fire Commission read the mood of the strikers and authorized the appointment of twenty-five temporary policemen. In turn, the I.W.W., while advising the strikers to remain orderly, declared that if the city police did not treat the workers fairly, the union would organize its own police force. In this atmosphere, word began to circulate that preparations were being made to send the state militia to the city.[4]

On Sunday, March 30, the renewed strict policy of the Paterson authorities was directed against Haywood. The strikers had planned a meeting for that day at Lafayette Oval in East Paterson and had circulated word of it throughout the city. When the local officials refused to grant permission for the open-air rally, the location was moved to Haledon, where socialist Mayor William Brueckman had extended an invitation. Shortly before the meeting was to begin, Haywood and a few others went to the Oval to inform those gathered there that the site had been changed and to lead them to Haledon. A crowd estimated at near 2,000 began forming behind I.W.W. leaders for the walk to the socialist borough when the Paterson police arrived, broke up the "parade," and arrested Haywood and Lessig on charges of unlawful assemblage and disorderly conduct. The following afternoon, after the two men had spent the night in the county jail, Recorder James F. Carroll found Haywood guilty of disorderly conduct and sentenced him to six months imprisonment.[5]

During the morning of Haywood's hearing in police court, over fifty pickets were arrested, most for refusing to suspend their activities in front of the Weidmann plant. They were taken to the jail to await their turn before Carroll, a willing partner in the city's attempt to break the strike, who acted as the city police magistrate. A political appointee, named to his two-year term by the Board of Fire and Police Commissioners, Carroll was a key figure in the judicial intimidation of the strikers.

In all criminal proceedings, the Recorder's Court held the preliminary hearing, determining guilt or innocence in nonfelony cases and setting sentence. With the exception of domestic relations cases and a few other specified matters, there was no provision for a jury trial in that court. Felonies, which included the crime of unlawful assembly, were not tried in Recorder's Court, but the recorder conducted the preliminary hearing, determined whether the individual charged would be bound over for trial in the Court of Quarter Sessions, and set bail. Thus, whether a striker was charged with a felony or a misdemeanor, his first contact with the "law" was before Recorder Carroll. Under the charge of unlawful assembly, strike leaders and pickets would be held in lieu of bail set at between $500 and $2,000, impossible amounts for most of those arrested; when bail was reduced after a few days, as it usually was, those released had to function under the threat of future trial and punishment. The preliminary hearing, termed by two later investigators as a "travesty on justice," was in most cases not followed by further action—the serious charge of unlawful assembly was primarily a tactic of the police authorities "to put a damper on the activities of the strike leaders."[6]

The most conservative elements in Paterson approved the swift action of the police and the recorder in their handling of Haywood, but others in the city were troubled. The *Evening News* was one of the latter. In an editorial entitled "Making a Farce of the Law," that paper commented: "Haywood has done many things, no doubt, which entitled him to arrest and imprisonment, but if the evidence presented in the Recorder's Court was all that the city has to base its case on, the *News* predicts that Haywood will be at liberty again in short order. Nothing is to be gained in this strike trouble by violation of the law, either on the side of the authorities or of the strikers."[7]

The newspaper's prediction of Haywood's speedy release proved accurate: on April 5, after he had spent six days in the crowded jail, the I.W.W. leader was released by order of New Jersey Supreme Court Justice James F. Minturn. The *News* applauded the action, pointing out that the treatment of Haywood had been a tactical error as well as a legal mockery. "Nothing," it stated, "binds men more firmly together and makes them more determined in any position . . . than the oppressive or unlawful acts of the officers of the law." The New York *Call* shared this sentiment, commenting that the action against Haywood was a blessing to the I.W.W. and would prove an asset to those on strike.[8] Bimson and Carroll had almost succeeded in creating a martyr in the Ettor and Giovannitti mold—Justice Minturn, in a sense, had saved the local authorities from themselves.

Minturn's action was not, however, the only thing which prevented the I.W.W. leaders from exploiting Haywood's arrest and turning it into a propagandist's dream. Even while Haywood was awaiting his preliminary hearing before Recorder Carroll, strike leaders and their socialist allies began to organize protest meetings to use the arrest to the advantage of the workers, and the initial reaction to the police work at Lafayette Oval seemed all that they could hope. But the mood of the public was changed by two speeches delivered by Frederick Sumner Boyd, one of the outside speakers. On March 31 and again on the following day, Boyd addressed protest gatherings in words so intemperate that much of the sympathy for Haywood was transformed into anger against the union. Flynn later suggested that Boyd might have been a provocateur, hired by the manufacturers to discredit the strike leaders, and Conlin has concluded that it was "likely" that Boyd's speeches were aimed at provoking antiunionist sentiment. Although no such charge was made at the time, the *News* stated later in 1913 that the outsider's appearance "did as much as any other one thing to hurt the cause of the strikers."[9]

Outside speakers were often used in I.W.W. strikes, but Paterson attracted more than the normal complement. Not only did the appearance of new speakers vary the oratorical diet of the strikers, but they were immune from blacklisting and could, in Flynn's words, "speak fearlessly about the conditions" under which the workers toiled.[10] In the days immediately following Haywood's arrest, when word went out for speakers to fill his place, such prominent socialists as Emil Seidel, the former mayor of Milwaukee and the 1912 vice-presidential candidate of the S.P.A., and Hubert H. Harrison, a black party member from New York City, were among those who appeared at Turn and Helvetia Hall meetings. Less well-known among the outside speakers was Boyd, a twenty-eight-year-old Englishman.

Born in London of parents whose radical sentiments made their home a refuge for foreign and domestic dissidents, Boyd became a socialist, street speaker, and labor organizer at an early age. Acquiring some reputation as a union activist in England, he was one of those who attended the 1910 International Socialist Congress. It was there that he first met Haywood, who seemed to Boyd a refreshing exception to the rather tepid professional and opportunistic socialists who dominated the meeting. Later that year he left England for the United States, where he continued his socialist activities, by some accounts joined the I.W.W., and tried to make a living as a journalist. An observer at Lawrence, where again he admired the work of Haywood, Boyd joined Leslie H. Marcy, associate editor of the *International Socialist Review*, in authoring a panegyric to the I.W.W. victory there. In December 1912 he became a contributing editor of *The Masses*, for which he had written a 1911 piece on the phosphate poisoning of workers. A resident of New York at the time that the Paterson strike began, he willingly responded to the call for speakers following Haywood's arrest.[11]

On the morning of March 31, at the regular meeting of the dyers' helpers and broad-silk workers at Turn Hall, Koettgen introduced Boyd as a New York socialist who had come to help the strikers win their battle. Mounting the platform, the young Englishman delivered a speech which would become infamous in the annals of the New Jersey strike. According to members of the press who were in attendance, the Boyd harangue had two notable parts, both equally offensive to citizens of the city. The first of these, quoted in the *Evening News*, was an ill-advised if not totally stupid reference to the symbolism of the American flag: "Those stars represent the badges of the cop . . . the badge of men who club women and . . . beat up defenseless men in your jail and they represent all the brutality and all the law's despicable cunning and all of the brutality of the police in this and every other city of America today. . . . The stripes represent the prison bars. . . . This flag is no symbol of justice. It is rather a symbol that the workers are in the subjection of the police and the prison bars." Boyd, in that short flight of oratory, managed to reintroduce the issue of patriotism and give credence to the manufacturers' claim that the I.W.W. leaders and their adherents were un-American revolutionaries who deserved any treatment measured out to them by the constituted authorities.

Such talk would have been folly regardless of who uttered the words; the fact that they were delivered by an Englishman in the accent of a recent arrival simply made matters worse. "In his reference to the American flag the memories of 1776 are brought to mind," the *News* protested. "He is an example of the typical character of Englishman who every chance they get assail the Stars and Stripes."[12]

As if the flag portion of the speech was not enough to undo the propaganda value accruing from the treatment of Haywood by the city officials, Boyd followed it with an advocacy of sabotage. The persistent admonishment of the I.W.W. leaders to avoid violence and all provocation was erased in the public mind by Boyd's suggestion that the strikers use the ill-defined but alarming French tactic. Flynn later wrote a pamphlet in which she attempted to explain sabotage and rid it of its connotation of undisciplined violence. "Sabotage," she wrote in defense of Boyd, "means primarily the withdrawal of efficiency. Sabotage means either to slacken up and interfere with the quantity, or to botch in your skill and interfere with the quality, of capitalist production or to give poor service. Sabotage is not physical violence; sabotage is an internal, industrial process."[13] Unfortunately for the I.W.W. and ultimately for Boyd, who was eventually sent to the state prison for his words, few at the time wished to grasp such an explanation or condone the tactic which was relatively unknown in the country. They preferred to believe that "destruction of property was the keynote of the red-fire speech."[14]

By the time that Boyd delivered a second address in the same vein the following day, many of the strikers and virtually all of the socialist supporters of the strike were rushing to disassociate themselves with the intemperate young Englishman. Convinced that "such speeches . . . do not help the cause of the strikers at all," Glanz, head of the Passaic County S.P.A., and State Secretary Killingbeck tried to undo the damage of their New York colleague. The two socialists were present at the Turn Hall meeting and agreed with those who shouted on every side: "Get that man down, he will surely break the strike." They immediately protested Boyd's speech to the meeting's chairman Lotta and to I.W.W. organizer Koettgen, both of whom, according to Killingbeck's later recollection, shared their concern. But this was only the beginning of the protest of Glanz and Killingbeck, whose alarm over the impact of Boyd's speech on the strike was at least matched by their fear of what his comments could do to the S.P.A. Killingbeck later explained in defense of his actions: "If Mr. Boyd had simply represented the I.W.W., we would have had no right to protest." The fact that the speaker was known as a member of the S.P.A. prompted Glanz and the secretary to disavow any connection with Boyd's remarks, visiting the various newspaper offices in Paterson to issue a public statement to that effect.[15]

The reaction of the strike leaders was somewhat more ambivalent than that of the two New Jersey socialists. Quinlan was the only outside strike leader publicly to disassociate Boyd from any involvement with the strike organization. According to Quinlan, the Englishman had "simply come to Paterson as a volunteer speaker," was "not connected with the I.W.W. in any way," and had in fact recently been expelled from the Socialist party for advocating violence. Flynn and Tresca avoided public comment on the content of Boyd's speech, but they did defend him before the Central Strike Committee, which had notified the I.W.W.

leaders that the Englishman should not be permitted to speak before the workers again. Flynn objected to the committee's decision, on the grounds that the issue of free speech was involved, and argued that "a socialist, a minister or a priest, a union organizer, an A.F. of L. man, a politician, and I.W.W. man, an anarchist, anybody should have the platform."[16]

Despite the protest of the strike committee, Boyd continued to appear in the silk city and speak at strike meetings. On April 3, he shared the platform at Turn Hall with Tresca and Quinlan, and on the following Sunday he addressed the rally at Haledon along with Haywood, Lessig, Quinlan, Koettgen, and Giovannitti.[17] That Haledon celebration of Haywood's release the previous day ended for a time the appearance of Boyd as a speaker. Once his right of free speech had been defended and upheld, he quietly disappeared from the strike platforms. However, he continued to support the strikers in a concrete but less visible fashion until the workers returned to the mills.

April 1 marked the beginning of the sixth week of the strike, and tempers in the silk city were clearly wearing thin. "How Much Longer?" the Paterson *Guardian* asked in its editorial the following day. There had still been no discussions between the two sides on a settlement; all that the workers had heard was, in the paper's words, "the blatherings of Boyd, the race appeals of Tresca, and the casuistry of the Flynn woman, cleverist of all the bunch of outside agitators."[18]

The *News* clearly shared the exasperation of its evening competitor, but was less willing to limit its comments to broadside attacks on the I.W.W. Instead, the independent paper presented "A Business-Like Suggestion for the Settlement of the Strike" in its April 1 edition. It was the *News*'s contention that a number of the smaller silk manufacturers, those without annexes outside of the city, were willing to grant the weavers' demands for increased pay and reduced hours and that their workers were anxious to come to terms. All that prevented them from returning to work was the I.W.W. insistence that the strikers remain out in a body until every shop agreed to the workers' demands. There was, the paper suggested, a better way to demonstrate solidarity than to all starve together: the strikers should return to work in those shops willing to grant wage and hour demands, and in those broad-silk mills where use of the three- and four-loom system was impossible; they should then be assessed between 10 and 20 percent of their weekly earnings to support those still on strike against other establishments. If this were done, "the strikers would be beating the manufacturers with their own money," and the strike would come to an end. Since only the I.W.W. seemed committed to an industrywide settlement, the paper further urged that the workers form their own independent union, led by local men who understood the situation in the silk industry.[19] From the appearance of this editorial onward, the question of shop-by-shop versus industrywide settlement became a dominant one.

Several days after the appearance of the paper's recommendation, the matter of independent settlements was raised by Magnet at the morning meeting of the ribbon workers in Helvetia Hall. Over the objection of Koettgen, whose former employment as a ribbon weaver qualified him to sit on the strike committee in that branch, the members voted to take a position midway between the industrywide stand of the I.W.W. and the shop-by-shop plan of their official newspaper organ. The Press Committee of the ribbon weavers was authorized to issue the following statement:

> The ribbon weavers wish it to be understood that if the manufacturers want to settle with them, it is not necessary for them to have any dealing with the I.W.W. leaders at all or with anyone else outside the ranks of the ribbon weavers' delegates.
>
> There are 168 accredited delegates representing the ribbon weavers of Paterson. These delegates are ready at any time to name a committee to meet with the manufacturers and discuss terms of settlement, the final result of the meeting to be referred back to the entire body of ribbon weavers' delegates, who will then vote on it.

The press release concluded with the challenge that "if the manufacturers really want to settle the question they have raised as to the I.W.W., it is eliminated in this way."[20]

Overlooked by those who had long predicted defection by the English-speaking workers, who formed the majority in the ribbon branch, the conclusion was more important than it seemed. Rather than expressing a willingness to break with the Central Strike Committee, the release was a tactical device to force the employers to admit that the union was not the only matter delaying settlement. Moreover, the fact that I.W.W. organizer Koettgen would be a party to the negotiations, as an accredited delegate, would make it impossible for the ribbon manufacturers to deal with representatives of their workers without consulting one of the acknowledged leaders of the union. The News, although applauding the ribbon workers for their "fair and equitable" proposal, recognized that it offered little hope. When the manufacturers responded with a reiteration of their position that only settlement on a shop basis was acceptable, the paper concluded that there was "no other course than a fight to the bitter finish."[21]

Others were somewhat more optimistic. At almost the same time that the ribbon weavers were framing their statement to the manufacturers, a group of local clergymen met to see whether they could bring an end to the strike. At the instigation of Reverend Anthony H. Stein, the rector of Our Lady of Lourdes Roman Catholic Church, some fifty clergymen gathered at the Y.M.C.A. to discuss what the religious leaders of the community could do to break the impasse between the workers and their employers. At this first meeting on April 3, a committee of five was formed to speak with both sides in the conflict. Under the chairmanship of Father Stein, the committee met twice with representatives of the manufacturers' associations to urge the owners to negotiate with a committee of the workers. The silk men steadfastly refused to do so, arguing that the strikers were dominated by the I.W.W. The only way the strike could end, they told the clergymen, was for the strikers to return to work and then deal directly with their own employers. Stein and his associates had no better luck in their session with a committee of the strikers. The clergymen were told that even if a meeting with the owners could be arranged, any decision to confer would have to be submitted to the various shop committees and then to the Central Strike Committee. A number of the church leaders involved in this effort continued to be active in the efforts to end the strike, but this early attempt to use "moral influence" foundered because of the intransigence of both protagonists.[22]

With the collapse of the clergymen's effort, there seemed more than a little truth to Haywood's cry of April 7: "The strikers in this city will stay out until hell freezes over and then fight on the ice to the finish."[23]

On the evening of the day that Haywood made this promise, the elected officers of the city took over from Stein and the other churchmen in mounting a drive to bring a settlement. The strike was then in its seventh week. Thomas Quigley, president of the Board of Aldermen, acting on a resolution passed by the board, extended an invitation to the citizens of Paterson to attend an open forum to discuss the strike. Those specifically invited to the meeting in the council chamber at City Hall included the mayor, the five state assemblymen and one senator from the county, a committee from both the Board of Trade and the Paterson Trades and Labor Council, and representatives from each branch of the silk industry's workers and owners. This action by the Board of Aldermen was the first taken by any municipal body to affect a settlement.[24]

The I.W.W. leaders urged the strikers not to attend the public meeting, which had been moved to the high school auditorium because of the interest expressed by the public. However, the ribbon weavers were quick to accept the invitation and, at their regular morning meeting at

Helvetia Hall, elected three delegates to represent the workers in that branch. The dyers' helpers and broad-silk weavers, meeting later in the day at Turn Hall, followed suit. With the acceptance and selection of representatives of the businessmen's Board of Trade and the A.F.L.-dominated Paterson Trades and Labor Council, only the silk manufacturers neglected to appoint official spokesmen.

The meeting, called to order by Alderman Quigley, drew a crowd of 2,000. The large attendance was indicative of the community's concern over the long strike, but it soon became evident that the town-meeting approach to the problem was not particularly well suited to bring results. Everyone, it seemed, wanted to have the floor, and solemn deliberation was virtually impossible in such a setting. Over the din created by Quigley's refusal to allow Killingbeck to present his views, the crowd heard Magnet, Lessig, and George Alyea of the ribbon, broad-silk, and dye-house workers respectively; Samuel McCollom, head of the Silk Manufacturers' Association; representatives of the Board of Trade; and a number of clergymen, including those who had served on the earlier committee of churchmen. Since few of the speakers addressed themselves to the comments of their predecessors on the platform, simply reading prepared statements they had drafted, there was little debate and no give and take.[25]

Mayor McBride, the first speaker in the long line of orators, ended his remarks with a plea that the participants forget their differences for the evening and strive to come closer to an agreement which would terminate the strike. After the warm applause which followed this request had subsided, speaker after speaker proceeded to ignore McBride's words.

Magnet and Lessig reiterated the weavers' grievances and repeated that the strike committee stood ready to meet with the manufacturers at any time. In addition to offering nothing that had not been heard before, Magnet's comments were particularly disheartening. Speaking for the ribbon workers, whose defection from the strike ranks had been prophesized since virtually the first day of their participation in the strike, Magnet declared that unit's whole-hearted support of the strike committee and charged the employers with trying to "arouse race and religious divisions" among the workers. He also challenged the much-reported contention that his group was afraid to return to the shops. "It is a base reflection on the courage and manhood of the English-speaking workers," he declared, "to say that they have been intimidated by the foreigners and would be back at work now if it was not for that fear. We English-speaking workers are not shaped by any such metal. We are not cowards and we cannot be coerced or intimidated."

Following the comments of the strikers' representatives, McCollom rose and read a resolution passed by his organization. Briefly, it declared that the owners refused to meet with any committee of employees representing the strikers as a body but were ready to meet with their own workers, if they were independent of the I.W.W., to discuss any grievances they might have. William R. Little, who spoke for the Board of Trade, substantially repeated McCollom.

Much of the rest of the evening was taken up by the clergymen, some of whom urged the workers to return to work and seek settlement through their shop committees while others advised the strikers to break with the I.W.W. and organize behind the A.F.L. Father Stein attempted to read a set of recommendations which had been prepared by the committee of clergymen, but few could hear him because of the shouts and catcalls from the audience. According to Stein's later summary, given before the Commission on Industrial Relations, the substance of his remarks was: "That the strike was led by men who advocated lawlessness and anarchy and was foredoomed to failure; that we placed ourselves on record for justice between all men at any cost. We called upon the manufacturers to meet their employees in a spirit of fairness, and we suggested . . . a Federal or State probe." When Magnet was allowed to respond to the priest's statements, he denied that the I.W.W. controlled the situation and stated that the workers wanted only "to secure fair treatment and livable conditions." On this note, the speeches came to an end. The last act of the evening was the aldermen's passage of a resolution calling for the establishment of a fifteen-man committee—composed of five representatives each from management, the workers, and the Board of Aldermen—to continue the night's work.[26]

The reaction to the meeting at the high school was, as could be expected, mixed. Both the strikers and the manufacturers saw little benefit arising from it. The former maintained that the aldermen's intervention had come too late to be productive; the latter complained that their position was clear and nothing could be gained by having to repeat it. What was most evident at the open meeting was the anti-I.W.W. sentiment of outside parties, particularly of the Board of Trade and the clergymen, and the general support of the manufacturers' position vis-à-vis shop-by-shop settlement.

Father Stein's comments were particularly resented by the workers. The New York *Call* spoke for many of them in the audience when it stated that "the average clergyman who butts into labor troubles in this manner is too obtuse to know that he is offensive." It continued: "Clergymen should be kept out of these affairs until they develop sense enough to understand that workingmen are possessed of some human intelligence . . . and to regulate their remarks accordingly. These men have had such long experience of talking without fear of contradiction from their pulpits and altars, that they finally come to think that their babble will go anywhere."[27]

If the nonunion strikers had hoped that third parties might bring about a settlement, the meeting tended to make them wary. The workers did not subsequently refuse offers of outside groups to attempt to bring the two sides together, but they heard enough at the high school not to accept the arbitration of supposedly disinterested third parties from such community leaders.

Even the single tangible outcome of the public meeting, the call to establish the committee, brought no progress. Two days before the first scheduled meeting at City Hall, the manufacturers notified the Board of Aldermen that no representatives from the owners' side would appear. The strikers agreed to send five spokesmen, and the aldermen tried to get the manufacturers to reconsider, but McCollom simply reaffirmed the earlier decision. The meeting planned for April 14 did take place— attended by Magnet and William Westerfield for the ribbon weavers; Joseph Matthews and Lessig representing the broad-silk workers; and Lotta speaking for the dye-house men—but no owner was present. With the exception of Alderman Rogers's suggestion that a resolution be drawn up asking for a federal investigation, the meeting was simply a repetition of the earlier discussion.[28]

City Hall had tried to put the strikers in a mood more receptive to negotiation by halting the arrests of pickets and releasing a number of those who had been arrested earlier. But with the disappointing result of the high school meeting and the collapse of the aldermen's efforts to bring discussion between the two sides, the arrest policy was resumed. The special policemen hired by the city to augment the regular force and the private guards employed by the larger mills kept pickets away from plant gates as some workers entered and left work.

On April 17, the night that the aldermen's committee met for the last time, the long-threatened bloodshed became a reality. A group of private detectives in the employ of the Weidmann Company, the scene of earlier confrontations, opened fire to protect themselves against a group of stone-throwing strikers. Valentino Modestino, a nonunion machinist employed by the Nicholson File Works, was wounded by a stray bullet as he sat on his porch nearby. When Modestino died shortly thereafter, the strike had its first victim.[29]

The I.W.W. leaders immediately reacted to the incident, appealing to Mayor McBride to end the use of O'Brien agency men in the city. (They received only a vague promise to punish those responsible for the death if they had broken the law.) More typical of the union was the attempt to exploit the killing for propaganda purposes: as soon as Modestino died, plans got underway to stage a mass funeral for the fallen worker.[30]

According to Steiger, the New York socialist and ribbon weaver who penned his account of the Paterson strike after he had become one of the I.W.W.'s most vocal opponents, Mrs. Modestino was visited shortly after her husband's death by Haywood, Tresca, and Flynn. The three strike leaders urged the woman, about to give birth to her fourth child, to allow them to hold a large public funeral for Modestino. They promised to pay all the bills, provide $30 a month to support her family, and see to the education of her children. The woman agreed and on April 22 the martyred machinist was buried in ceremonies orchestrated to have the greatest publicity effect. A crowd of 5,000 mourners, each wearing a red carnation or ribbon, followed the hearse in a procession through the streets of Paterson; Flynn rode in the first carriage with the grieving widow, and Haywood, Tresca, and Lessig marched at the head of the column of solemn strikers. At the graveside in Laurel Grove Cemetary, Tresca delivered a speech in Italian which ended with chilling advice to the mourners: "Blood for blood should be your motto."[31]

On the day before the burial, Golden arrived in Paterson to see what the U.T.W. could accomplish. Late in March the local Trades and Labor Council had asked the A.F.L. to intervene in the strike, but this was the first appearance of a national figure from that labor organization. With Golden's arrival, the Paterson citizens were treated to "the singular spectacle of two great labor organizations warring one against the other."[32]

The belated intervention of the A.F.L. mirrored the interference of the Chicago I.W.W. in the Detroit-led textile strikes in New Jersey the year before. In both instances, a concern for the plight of the workers seems to have been secondary to organizational self-interest on the part of the intruding union. In the earlier contest, the interunion rivalry had contributed to the loss of the strike and the virtual demise of the De-Leon local in Paterson; in 1913 the immediate consequence was to divert attention from the central conflict between the strikers and their employers. By mid-April, many in the city had accepted the owners' contention that they would negotiate with a reputable labor organization and believed the press reports that a large number of the strikers were disenchanted with the I.W.W. and ready to accept alternative leadership. The appearance of U.T.W. officials offered an opportunity to test both beliefs.[33]

When the general strike was declared late in February, the U.T.W.

membership in Paterson was confined to a small number of skilled workers in two craft locals. The once-promising Local 607 Broad-Silk Weavers no longer existed, and the A.F.L. textile union was clearly in decline in the silk city. Starr and Morgan, the leaders of the horizontal warpers and the loomfixers and twisters respectively, attributed the U.T.W.'s loss of members to the inability of the mass of workers, particularly the recent immigrants, to understand the need for organization. Starr later stated to the Commission on Industrial Relations: "The biggest majority . . . of the foreigners can't see a form of organization whereby they won't be allowed to strike just as soon as they are organized. They have got some radical ideas in their heads, and until those radicals have been supplanted with others by some kind of organization that don't stand for such things as what they would like to have and like to have carried out, we are going to have trouble going right on with those people."

There was some truth to what Starr said—many of the workers were impatient with the cautious policy of the U.T.W. and its unwillingness to finance unauthorized strikes. Certainly, they could not understand the refusal of the A.F.L. locals to strike in sympathy with the broad-silk weavers the year before. But the disenchantment with the federation was also due to the attitude of the skilled craft members toward the relatively unskilled foreign born. As Starr's testimony in 1914 made evident, the immigrant workers were viewed in a condescending if not overtly hostile manner. For reasons of union policy and attitude, therefore, the U.T.W. was seen by many of the silk workers as unsympathetic to their needs.[34]

The skilled workers affiliated with the U.T.W. locals in Paterson did not join the weavers who walked out of their shops in the early days of the general strike. Morgan's attitude was that the strike action represented simply a body of disorganized people who had no idea what they were seeking. Only after loomfixers, twisters, and warpers were thrown out of work by the closing of their shops did the local U.T.W. business agents become involved in the strike. It was not until March 27, at a meeting of the Trades and Labor Council in the Paterson Labor Lyceum, that the leaders of the city's A.F.L. locals decided to go on record in support of the silk workers: the delegates present passed a resolution which promised aid and offered the participation of the council on any arbitration committee which might be formed. "We were anxious at that time to help these people out of the trouble they got into," Starr later explained. "We were not looking for any glory out of the matter; did not care whether they organized in the A.F.L. or not, but wanted to help them out." For this reason, or probably a less disinterested one, the Trades and Labor Council appointed a committee to meet with a delegation of the strikers. The Evening News, for one, was optimistic that this action by the A.F.L. locals in the city would result in movement toward a settlement. "Out of the darkness of the present deadlocked strike situation . . . a bright ray of light came today," that paper enthused.[35]

It is doubtful whether more than a few of the strikers were willing to act in concert with the A.F.L., as Starr contended, but any possibility of such cooperation was ended by the reaction of the I.W.W. leaders. Following Haywood's arrest at the Lafayette Oval, which occurred three days after the resolution was voted by the Trades and Labor Council and might not have been unrelated to it, Flynn invaded a meeting of the council committee and some of the strikers to advise what the A.F.L. locals could do if they were sincere in their offer to help.

To demonstrate their support for free speech and assembly, and to protest the actions of the police, Flynn called for a twenty-four-hour sympathy strike by all union members in the city. Then, to expose the A.F.L.'s true sentiments to the mass of strikers, the Central Strike Committee issued a proclamation addressed to "Fellow Workers of Paterson" in which the sympathy strike was urged: "Fellow workers, if these vile deeds can be committed against silk mill workers fighting today for just demands, they can be inflicted upon electrical workers, street car workers, railroad workers, teamsters . . . and any and all others.

"This is the time to fight! Fight now! Strike in sympathy with your fellow silk workers." The proclamation concluded with an invitation to all workers to attend the Haledon rally that Sunday and there declare a citywide strike for the following day.[36]

The Trades and Labor Council, meeting jointly with the Building Trades Council, categorically refused to call the strike. The I.W.W., a spokesman for these bodies declared, knew very well that the A.F.L. locals could not break their existing agreements with employers and take such action. This refusal, he insisted, did not mean that the A.F.L. offer of aid was insincere — the federation would do all that it could and was "open to any overtures which may be made by businessmen, clergy, etc.," to participate in bringing about a settlement.[37] To underscore that point, the Trades and Labor Council elected delegates to attend the aldermen's high school meeting—among these Morgan and Starr—and announced its planned participation in the press. Whether the other A.F.L. representatives attended the April 9 meeting, however, is unclear; when Quigley invited a statement from the council, there was no response. This silence, whether from nonattendance or a reluctance to speak before the large number of hostile strikers in the audience, was indicative of that body's stance in the days following its refusal to authorize the sympathy strike. Not until Golden's arrival in Paterson over a week later did the federation reemerge as a factor in the silk strike.

The occasion for Golden's appearance was an announced mass meeting to be held on April 19 under A.F.L. auspices. Declaring that the federation's position had been deliberately misrepresented by the I.W.W. agitators, the Trades and Labor Council planned the gathering to refute the "libels levelled against it." The I.W.W., in return, charged that the U.T.W. leaders saw that the strike was almost won and wanted to "inject their influences at the eleventh hour and claim the glory of the victory." It urged the strikers not to attend. Magnet, however, argued that the U.T.W. appearance would afford the workers an opportunity to hear both sides of the interunion contest; but instead of simply an A.F.L. gathering, he suggested that the two labor organizations agree to a formal debate of the strike issues. Specifically, Magnet proposed that Golden debate Haywood at the armory, where the meeting had been scheduled, and that Flynn and Tresca engage in similar exchanges with U.T.W. organizer Sara Conboy and an Italian representative of the A.F.L. This plan received the support of the I.W.W. leaders, but was not accepted by the Trades and Labor Council. When the A.F.L. proved unreceptive to Magnet's proposal, Quinlan and other I.W.W. people urged their followers to attend the federation's meeting and attempt to capture it.[38]

In the interval of two days between the time the meeting was announced and its convening, the prospect of a major confrontation between the two rival unions became increasingly probable. Quinlan and Haywood used every strike gathering to urge the I.W.W. supporters to attend and to demand a hearing. The former suggested what the public could expect: "We will get to the armory and see what these fellows have to say. If they attack the I.W.W., we will demand the floor and an opportunity to defend ourselves. If the A.F.L. puts its nose into the dispute between the strikers and the manufacturers—a dispute that is strictly between the two—we will punch it for them." Some kind of altercation appeared likely when, the morning of the meeting, the Trades and Labor Council issued a statement about the I.W.W. intention. Pointing out that the industrial unionists had been holding meetings for eight weeks without the interference of the A.F.L., the council declared that it would not tolerate disruption by the I.W.W.[39]

By 6 p.m. on the evening of April 21, two hours before the meeting was to begin, crowds began to form around the Fifth Regiment Armory. No sooner were the doors opened than a rush of strikers poured into the hall, calling out slogans and shouts for the I.W.W. Even discounting the obvious prejudice of its account, there was considerable truth in the statement in *Solidarity* that it "was an I.W.W. and not an A.F. of L. meeting."[40]

When Golden and Conboy entered the building, they were immediately approached by Koettgen, who asked that I.W.W. organizers be allowed to speak. The expected refusal was given. Koettgen then jumped to the stage and announced that the I.W.W. had been barred from participation and a prearranged demonstration erupted in the audience. One newspaper account reported that "if it had not been for the prompt action of Bimson, the armory floor would have been the scene of a riot." With police prodding, Haywood, Tresca, and Flynn were escorted to the door, followed by a contingent of strikers. The meeting then began. Golden and Conboy had to struggle to be heard over the boos and catcalls of the I.W.W. supporters who had remained in the armory before Chief Bimson ordered all disturbers evicted from the building. When this was done, the U.T.W. leaders were free to berate the rival organization before those who remained. Conboy, described by the press as "physically robust, possessed of enormous energy, and an habitually vehement speaker who brooked no opposition," showed her toughness that evening. Shouting over the noise of the hecklers, she delivered a memorable one-liner: "If that Bill Haywood gives me any back talk, I'll scratch his other eye out."[41]

The accounts of the armory meeting suggest that truth as well as beauty is in the eye of the beholder. Those who wished to believe that the silk workers were anxious to have a "reputable" union represent them reported that a large crowd listened attentively to the U.T.W. speakers once the "anarchists" had been cleared from the hall. The New York *Times*, for example, headlined its story of the event "Strikers Denounce I.W.W. Leadership" and informed its readers that the U.T.W. speakers were given quiet attention by the thousands who remained at the meeting. The I.W.W. and socialist accounts, on the other hand, proclaimed that Conboy and Golden had spoken to empty seats after most of the audience had left to hear Haywood, Tresca, and Flynn address a rival gathering at Turn Hall. The only agreement was that the confrontation between the two labor organizations lived up to expectations, and in fact was more unruly than had been anticipated.[42]

Scott believed that the intervention of the A.F.L. was counterproductive—that the federation's action only "resulted in welding the forces of the strikers and increasing their loyalty to the I.W.W." Haywood maintained that the armory meeting was "the funeral of the A.F.L. so far as Paterson was concerned."[43] The I.W.W. leader was correct, although this was not immediately evident. That the workers were drawn more closely to the I.W.W., as the socialist editor contended, is more doubtful.

In the days immediately following the meeting, at least, a number of the strikers were critical of the I.W.W. actions at the armory. Magnet argued that the workers should not have been led out of the hall before they had had an opportunity to hear what the U.T.W. had to offer and how the union could help the strikers; he and others pointed out that an organization that professed to stand for free speech had shown little inclination to assure that right to outsiders. The ribbon weavers' spokesman was sufficiently disillusioned with the I.W.W. to call a group of fellow nonunion weavers together to discuss the possibility of forming a local union, independent of both the A.F.L. and the I.W.W. Although nothing came of his meeting at Probst's Hall, the fact that it was held and had the support of some of the leading S.P.A. men in the county—those whose tie with the I.W.W. had loosened following Boyd's speeches—was an indication that there was a growing dissatisfaction with the progress of the strike. On the same morning as Magnet's meeting, either coincidentally or to encourage his independent movement, a number of ribbon firms hinted that they were ready to talk settlement. Frank & Dugan, Kramer Hat Band Company, Taylor & Friedman, and Graef Hat Band Company were among those at least rumored to be willing to offer a 15 percent wage increase and the nine-hour day.[44]

The boost in morale provided by the Modestino funeral, worker acceptance of the I.W.W. contention that the A.F.L. appearance was proof that the strike was almost won, enthusiasm generated by a planned May Day parade, and the soon evident insincerity of the ribbon manufacturers' proposal prevented the break in ranks. When the narrow-silk shop committees met with their individual owners, at the request of management and over the objection of the I.W.W. advisers, they were offered no concessions; instead, they were asked how many would return to work if assured police protection. If Magnet was willing to divorce himself from the I.W.W. and support a separate settlement in the ribbon shops, the manufacturers' unwillingness to grant even a small concession made his position impossible. The optimism engendered by the signs of weakening in the ribbon branch was totally destroyed when McCollom declared that there would be no compromise.[45] Scott's contention that the loyalty to the I.W.W. increased following the appearance of the U.T.W. in Paterson was true only in the sense that it became clear that there was no place else to turn.

In the days following the armory meeting, it was apparent that the A.F.L. textile union held little appeal. On April 23, the federation opened its organizational drive to recruit silk workers. That same day Assemblyman James Matthews, secretary of the Trades and Labor Council, announced his plan to bring about a settlement under the leadership of the A.F.L. Matthews, a member of the local Brewery Workers' Union, urged the strikers to desert the I.W.W.—a union which the employers would "never recognize"—and affiliate with the more respected U.T.W. To encourage them to do so, Golden announced that the customary initiation fee would be suspended and that new members, regardless of earlier union affiliation, would be eligible for immediate relief assistance. The A.F.L. rented space for headquarters, sent in special textile organizers from other parts of the country, and began to issue confident progress reports concerning the number of silk workers enrolled. Three days after the membership drive was begun, for example, it claimed enrollment of 1,200 new members, 700 of these during the previous day. Meanwhile, the I.W.W. stationed pickets in front of the federation's office and increased its oratorical attack on the rival union. For a period of three weeks, the leaders of the two organizations fought for the loyalty of the silk workers of Paterson and the New York area.[46]

The A.F.L. continued to issue optimistic reports of its success, but Koettgen's contention that the federation was losing rather than attracting members proved the more accurate. On May 17 the A.F.L. spokesman announced that the union was abandoning its fight with the I.W.W. until the workers understood that "what they really need is craft unionism." "They wanted the I.W.W., let them have it," Morgan stated to the press. "Let them have so much of it that it will make them sick."[47]

Morgan later maintained that the U.T.W. suspended its organizational efforts when it became clear that it would not reach its goal of enrolling the majority of the silk workers. The truth is that the A.F.L. drive was almost a complete failure and the U.T.W. organizers admitted as much in their reports to the union's 1913 convention. Golden attributed this to the "nefarious work" of the I.W.W., but Thomas Reagan, the New England organizer who had been dispatched to Paterson to take charge of the campaign, reported that "nothing could be accomplished because [the workers] were not in sympathy" with the local union people. U.T.W. Secretary-Treasurer Albert Hibbert urged that new emphasis be put on appealing to the foreign-speaking workers. "In the coming year," he advised, "we shall have to double our efforts to get the foreign element to come into our organization, and in order to do that successfully it will be necessary that we secure competent men of their own nationality, men in whom they have confidence." Hibbert thus put his finger on a major cause of the A.F.L.'s rout in Paterson. For years the U.T.W. had spoken almost exclusively to and for the skilled English-speaking elite in the silk industry; it could not expect the Polish and Italian workers, in the midst of a general strike, to desert an organization which promised them so much for one which had given them so little.[48]

In the period from the armory meeting to the abandonment of the craft unionists' organizing campaign, the A.F.L. advocates were not the only individuals active in Paterson. The city officials, who throughout the strike pursued alternately the carrot or stick approach, resumed the attack on the strike leaders.

On April 25, as the A.F.L. began its drive for members, a grand jury returned indictments against Haywood, Tresca, Flynn, Quinlan, and Lessig. On the same day, forty-eight pickets were taken into custody at the Harding Mill and Frederick Koettgen, the proprietor of Helvetia Hall, was arrested on charges of keeping a disorderly house. Koettgen's problems ended in Recorder's Court when the complaint on which he was arrested could not be found, but the strike leaders to whom the hotel keeper often rented rooms were less gently treated. Lessig, charged in the grand jury indictment with unlawful assembly stemming from the LaFayette Oval incident four weeks before, was arrested at his home that evening. Tresca, Flynn, and Quinlan, indicted for their speeches at Turn Hall on the first day of the strike, were taken into custody the following morning when they arrived in Paterson from New York City. Flynn was charged with inciting to personal injury; Tresca with inciting to personal injury, inciting to assault, and unlawful assembly; and Quinlan with inciting to personal injury, inciting to assault, and advocating burning and destruction. Bail for the four was set at between $1,000 for Lessig and $7,000 for Quinlan. Haywood who was in Schenectady appealing for strike funds in that strongly socialist New York city did not return to Paterson until two days after the arrest of his associates. The city authorities, concerned that there might be violence if they attempted to arrest him at the Paterson railroad station, where a large crowd of strikers awaited his arrival, arrested the I.W.W. leader as his train stopped in Passaic. On Wednesday, April 30, the five strike leaders were arraigned before Judge Abram Klenert, who set May 7 as the date on which their trials would begin in the Court of Quarter Sessions.[49]

While the I.W.W. leaders awaited trial, final preparations were made to use the tactic which had been so successful in generating sympathy for the Lawrence workers the year before—the evacuation of strikers' children. The day after the armory meeting, Boyd and Sanger were in Paterson to begin arrangements for taking care of children in the homes of New York socialists. Sanger had played an active role in the Lawrence evacuations and was a frequent companion of Haywood's in New York City; Boyd, who had substituted other activities for that of orator after the criticism he had received the month before, served as the secretary of the Children's Committee.

The Paterson authorities reacted strongly to the suggestion that local children needed to be cared for elsewhere, but they showed better judgment than their Lawrence counterparts. Mayor McBride responded to the first hint that such a move was contemplated with a statement that the city could provide for its citizens without outside assistance. When plans for the evacuation proceeded, the former president of the Charity Organization of Paterson visited McBride to assure him that the I.W.W. plan was both unnecessary and potentially harmful to the children involved. He told the mayor that his organization was prepared to help all those who were in need. McBride's office then issued a public statement to that effect.[50]

The night before the mayor's announcement, Flynn held a special meeting for children and their parents at Turn Hall. The large attendance, estimated at over 600, prompted Flynn to propose a variation in the tactic used in Lawrence. She declared that she had decided to test the administration's sincerity and would lead a delegation to "swamp the Mayor's office with kids." Unfortunately for Flynn, the city had the better of this round. When the superintendent of outdoor relief countered that all children deposited at City Hall would be sent to the Almshouse and then turned over the State Board of Guardians, which would find them foster homes, the I.W.W. plan was abandoned. Instead, it was decided to use the upcoming May Day celebration as the occasion for sending the first contingent of children from the city. On that day, about fifty children, ranging in age from five to fifteen, assembled at Helvetia Hall, where their parents committed them to the care of a committee from New York led by Sanger, Boyd, and Jessie Ashley.[51] Several other groups of children were sent to homes in the New York area in the next two weeks.

The evacuations were clearly designed to gain publicity and sympathy for the Paterson workers, as they had been in Lawrence, but the I.W.W. generated neither the coverage nor the indignant reaction that it had obtained in the New England strike. The Paterson authorities avoided the mistake of trying to prevent the exodus, and there was no repetition of the scene at the Lawrence railroad station. The children simply left the city amidst whatever fanfare the I.W.W. strategists could muster, remained out of the city for varying periods of time, and then quietly were returned to their families.[52]

On May 1, while the I.W.W. staged its May Day celebration and the first children were being escorted to homes outside the city, a group of some forty Paterson businessmen met at the Eye and Ear Infirmary Building to try their hand at ending the strike. Claiming to represent the "third party" involved in the contest, those whose livelihoods were being threatened by the prolonged strike, they passed a resolution calling upon U.S. Senator William Hughes and Congressman Robert S. Bremmer to initiate a federal investigation of industrial conditions in the city. This call, which if answered could have resulted in hearings similar to those Berger had instigated the year before, received a moderately friendly response from Hughes. But Bremmer and Mayor McBride opposed such intervention. The Paterson strike was later one of the industrial conflicts investigated by the Commission on Industrial Relations, but there was little support for such action while it was being waged.

The businessmen's action did, however, help to prompt McBride to take a more active role. On May 4, three days before the trials of the I.W.W. leaders were to begin in the Court of Quarter Sessions, the mayor issued the following statement: "I have waited patiently for a moment to intervene. Until the present hour mediation would have been without fruit and its purpose misinterpreted as the temper of both parties was high and unbending. I believe at last that the time is now ripe to act. I do not believe that we should seek for aid outside." The *Evening News*, no friend of the Paterson administration, commented: "After eleven weeks of sidestepping, Mayor McBride has at last been smoked out by the force of public opinion, and has done what he should have done over two months ago."[53]

The forty-four-year-old McBride, mayor of Paterson since 1908, had indeed kept a low profile to this time. He had supported if not orchestrated the carrot and stick policy of Chief Bimson, however, and was not looked upon as a friend or an impartial party by the strike leaders. His fellow Irishman, Quinlan, described the physician and former president of the Paterson Board of Health as "the leader of the Catholic and Irish-American elements" and as the type "who would start a fly-killing crusade, but would leave the manure heaps and swamps severely alone."[54]

Late in March the ribbon-shop strikers, encouraged by the *News*, had begun to put pressure on McBride to declare his position vis-à-vis the strike. Soon after the paper's campaign had begun, a delegation of ten ribbon weavers, led by Magnet, handed the mayor a list of twenty-four questions for which they demanded answers; the first, "are you in sympathy with the strikers?" was followed by equally pointed queries on his views concerning conditions in the mills, police conduct, and the like. The mayor took some days to draft a point-by-point response in which he skillfully avoided committing himself to either side. His answer to the question of why he believed that the workers had gone on strike exemplifies the position he assumed: "Many persons left their work because they had just grievances, others out of fear, many in sympathy with the former, others through the influence of agitators." Until weeks later, when the city's businessmen prompted him to take action, he kept out of the crossfire of the conflict as best he could, urging only that two sides should meet and resolve their differences.[55]

Whether because he wished to forestall a federal investigation or, as he claimed, because the time was opportune, Mayor McBride announced on May 4 the creation of a committee of twenty-five citizens to attempt a settlement. Chaired by John W. Griggs, a former governor of New Jersey, the committee was composed of businessmen, clergy, public officials, and professional men. There were no silk manufacturers or strikers included among the members.[56]

The initial response from both sides to McBride's committee was less than enthusiastic. Haywood, who observed dryly that the mayor was rather late in taking action, maintained that it would be best to have the workers and their employers settle the matter themselves and made it clear that the committee had no recognized authority. McCollom reserved comment on the position of his association until it could meet, but individual manufacturers let it be known that they were dubious about the committee's worth. When the list of the committee members was given further scrutiny, protests were lodged concerning some. The strikers in particular questioned the impartiality of Griggs, on grounds that he had formerly been the counsel for the Weidmann Silk Company.[57]

Despite the criticisms and reservations, the committee held its first meeting on May 6 in the Council Chambers at City Hall with all but two of the mayor's appointees present. Following introductory remarks by McBride and the formal election of Griggs as chairman, the basic question of what the body could and should do was raised. Former Judge Francis Scott began the discussion with a resolution that five-man committees of investigation, conciliation, and finance be established as a first step. At this point, division over the role of the committee became evident. Reverend David S. Hamilton of St. Paul's Episcopal Church, who had been a member of the earlier clergymen's committee, observed that the judge's proposal would accomplish nothing but consume valuable time and urged the membership to take immediate steps to bring the two sides together. When Scott reminded Reverend Hamilton that the committee had no authority to compel either party to meet, as the clergyman wanted, the latter responded that "if that is the case, we may as well go home." After considerable debate on what could be done, which featured a ringing attack on the I.W.W. by Dr. Walter Johnson, Scott's resolution was passed and the meeting was adjourned. The next evening the committees of investigation and conciliation met and drafted a letter to the manufacturers and the strike committee asking each side to state its case.[58]

The I.W.W. was swift and uncompromising in its response. Flynn thought it ridiculous that men like Griggs should assume they could settle the strike. In reference to Dr. Johnson's much-quoted remark that the good citizens of Paterson should run the I.W.W. out of the city, she declared defiantly: "If we are to be removed by a vigilance committee, it will be in pine boxes." Notwithstanding the objections of Haywood and Flynn, however, a delegation of strikers—including Magnet, Lessig, Koettgen, and Lotta—did make at least one appearance before the mayor's committee. (Subsequent meetings were thwarted by the presence of pickets in front of City Hall to prevent any appearance by self-appointed striker representatives.) Individual owners also appeared at a separate session with the committee, although they were as unresponsive as their union adversaries. On May 23, when it was obvious that neither side was prepared to budge from its long-established position, the spokesman for the Committee on Investigation acknowledged that it had "not been able to accomplish anything." The mayor thanked the members and disbanded the committee. "There did not appear to be a possibility . . . of getting either side to yield," McBride later testified to the Commission on Industrial Relations. "Both sides were unruly, unyielding, and there was a lot of feeling existing on both sides, so that it was impossible to have any amicable arrangement settled upon."[59]

McBride may have launched the committee to coincide with the trial of the five strike leaders, under the assumption that settlement was more possible when the "outside agitators" were otherwise engaged. But if that was his thinking, he miscalculated. The scheduled trials were just the sort of thing which the I.W.W. relied upon to maintain strike morale and elicit sympathy.

The proceedings began first against Quinlan; following the anticipated conviction of the colorful Irishman, Tresca, Haywood, Flynn, and Lessig were to be tried in order. As a large crowd gathered outside of the court house on May 7, booing the police and cheering the appearance of the defendants in a manner not unlike a sports event, Haywood led the way into the building. The youthful Flynn followed, dressed in "a Panama hat trimmed with a flowing blue dotted ribbon and a claret colored tailor-made gown." Tresca, Quinlan, and Lessig, meriting no such society-page description, trailed along behind.[60] Despite the fanfare which attended the creation of the citizens' committee, the center of public attention was the drama unfolding in the courtroom.

During the morning session, the jury was selected and Assistant Prosecutor Munson Force presented the charges against Quinlan. Testimony began that afternoon. The first witness for the prosecution, Detective Sargeant Adolph Keppler, told the court of hearing Quinlan's speech at Turn Hall on the morning the strike began. According to Keppler, and six other witnesses who followed him and parrotted his account, Quinlan had urged his listeners to force the nonstrikers to leave their shops by any means necessary. Despite the efforts of defense attorneys, Henry Marelli and Gustave Hunzinger, the testimony of the prosecution witnesses, all policemen, could not be shaken.

The second day of the trial was taken up by the defense. Quinlan swore that he had not spoken at Turn Hall and that he had arrived at the meeting just as Bimson's men were breaking it up. Lessig and Flynn confirmed that Quinlan had not spoken to the strikers that morning. When striker Luigi Paduchi took the stand to support the leaders' testimony, Force broadened his line of questioning in an attempt to influence the jury:

Q: Are you an anarchist?   A: Yes.
Q: Do you believe in God?   A: No.
Q: Do you believe in Law?   A: No.

Although each question was met by the objection of the defense, Judge Klenert ordered Paduchi to answer.

The summations were presented on May 9: Marelli dismissed the charges against Quinlan as "a police frame-up, pure and simple," and charged that the prosecutor sought only to break the strike; County Prosecutor Michael Dunn completed his remarks by comparing Quinlan to the infamous McNamara brothers. At 1 p.m. the case went to the jury. The following morning, after being sequestered for the night, the foreman informed the judge that the jury was hopelessly deadlocked and could not reach a decision. When Klenert had dismissed the jury, Dunn announced that he would ask for a new trial for Quinlan and that the cases of the other strike leaders would follow as planned.[61]

The determination to pursue the case against Quinlan had the full support of the Paterson press. The *Sunday Chronicle*, for example, had none of the doubts that had divided the jurors. It commented:

The mistrial of Patrick Quinlan, the I.W.W. agitator, is a severe disappointment to all right-minded citizens, and unless retrieved will be a grave misfortune to our country. It will be looked upon outside as a travesty on our boasted system of New Jersey justice.

In the next trial, it is not too much to expect that witnesses whose avowal of anarchistic sentiments and disbelief in God make their oaths worthless, should be excluded. It is an insult to the majesty of the law, and even of common sense, to admit testimony of this kind.[62]

This was an interesting but not unique conception of judicial "travesty."

The county prosecutor did not waste time in pursuing Quinlan's conviction. Just forty-eight hours after the first jury declared its deadlock at seven for acquittal and five for conviction, the Irish socialist leader was back in the Court of Quarter Sessions for the start of his second trial. The script was expected to be the same, with the jurors asked to choose between conflicting accounts of an event over two months before, but early Sunday morning an incident occurred which set a different mood in the community. A few blocks from the Erie Station in Paterson, a Chicago express train was halted by the quick action of its engineer just short of rocks piled on the track. The local police immediately blamed the I.W.W. and claimed that the sabotage attempt was meant to dissuade the Erie from transporting strikebreakers into the city. Both Flynn and Haywood denied that the strikers were involved, charging instead that the manufacturers had staged the incident to discredit the union on the eve of the Quinlan retrial.[63]

Several hours before the second trial began, the Paterson police were out in full force in front of the larger silk mills to protect those who wished to return to work. At the Weidmann facility, considered a key to the strike by both sides, forty-five pickets were arrested and taken before Recorder Carroll. Justice was swift: all were found guilty and given ten days or a $5 fine.[64]

On this background of increased tension in the city, the second Quinlan trial opened. The jury, selected in less than an hour, heard much the same testimony that had been presented to the earlier panel, although the defense introduced three new witnesses. Two of these were Reverend Percy Stickney Grant, pastor of the Episcopal Church of the Ascension in Manhattan, and George Gordon Battle, a prominent New York lawyer, who testified to Quinlan's good character and reputation. The last and most important new witness was Emmett Drew, a reporter for the Paterson *Morning Call*. Drew told the court that he had been present at the Turn Hall meeting of February 25 and was certain that the defendant had not spoken. Although his testimony seems supported by the absence of Quinlan's name in the newspaper accounts of that day, it was to no avail. Two hours after the case was handed to the jury, a verdict was reached: Quinlan was guilty as charged.[65]

With the exception of I.W.W. and socialist papers, press comment on the conviction was generally favorable. The *Nation* declared that it was "necessary for the law-abiding citizenship of the country to assert itself" against the I.W.W. "The issue really before the people of New Jersey," it asserted, "is not whether Quinlan is guilty, but whether the law is supreme"; in the Quinlan case, the "fundamental question was . . . the law and the safety of the nation." The New York *Times*, in its approving editorial, similarly skirted the issue of Quinlan's guilt or innocence and used the occasion to issue a sharp attack on socialists and members of the I.W.W. "It is time that the public should understand the real aim of the strikes taken in charge by the leaders of the I.W.W.," it declared. "They seek to destroy." Then, in response to those who would declare their concern over a larger issue in the case, the *Times* continued: "The cry is at once raised that they are exercising only their constitutional right of free speech, and that police interference is unlawful and oppressive. It is difficult to understand how sane persons, not themselves of the I.W.W. . . . can with the slightest pretense of sincerity express such views.

"Never has free speech ever meant the license to exhort mobs to burn and destroy." None of the Paterson newspapers criticized the verdict. In their view, Quinlan was at least guilty of being a member of dangerous organizations, a crime serious enough to warrant punishment. Most saw the conviction as an important turning point in the strike as well. With the removal of the I.W.W. agitators, the *Evening News* argued, "the strike would disintegrate."[66]

Quinlan's conviction brought the threat of similar verdicts when other strike-related cases were brought to trial, but the I.W.W. leaders showed little sign of being intimidated. Flynn rushed from the courtroom after the verdict to preside over a strike meeting at Helvetia Hall, where she delivered a particularly angry speech; Ettor announced that he would appear at a protest rally the next day at the Lafayette Oval and promised to take charge of the strike in the event Haywood was imprisoned; and other I.W.W. organizers pledged to continue the fight despite the consequences. Even Quinlan, whose sentencing was to await the conclusion of the other trials, was not cowed into silence. Rather than serving to silence the strike leaders or to encourage the workers to return to work, as some had predicted, the trial had the opposite effect. Quinlan's conviction, as the more objective *Survey* commented, "stirred up bitterness among the strikers."[67]

The Thursday rally at the Oval was indicative of the workers' reaction. Between 10,000 and 15,000 attended the protest gathering, a fulldress affair at which all the prominent I.W.W. leaders were present. In addition to Flynn, Haywood, Tresca, and Ettor, the state S.P.A. men also spoke in condemnation of Quinlan's treatment. The dramatic impact of the verdict could be seen by the appearance of Killingbeck, Glanz, and Magnet sharing the platform with Boyd, whose earlier speeches they had so vehemently criticized. The text of most of the speeches was similar, although there were promises of new tactics. Lessig, for example, asked every workingman in Paterson to strike on a specified day the following week, promising thus to tie up the entire city and "throw it into darkness." Haywood used the occasion to announce plans for the enactment of the Paterson struggle in a pageant to be held in a New York City theater to raise sufficient funds to assure victory. Quinlan showed his disregard for possible reprisal by the sentencing judge by calling Paterson "a thoroughly rotten town" and advising a boycott of every merchant who advertized in newspapers hostile to the I.W.W.[68]

During the weekend of May 17–18, the strike leaders kept up their attack on the city authorities, perhaps spurred to greater heights of indignation by the arrest on Saturday of socialist editor Scott for his editorial in the Passaic *Weekly Issue*. While Scott spent the evening in jail, Quinlan spewed out his sentiments in a vitriolic speech at Union Square in New York City. Sharing the platform with Flynn, the hot-tempered Quinlan declared that the strike would be won even if the I.W.W. had "to wipe the city off the map," and turned his venom on the city officials. Paterson, he charged, was run "by a lot of ex-prize fighters and ex-saloon keepers," and the recorder was the worst among them; Carroll, who had presided over Quinlan's initial hearing, "had about as much knowledge of law as an ordinary pig in Barnum and Bailey's circus had about electricity."[69] The next afternoon, one of the largest gatherings to that time assembled in Haledon to hear Tresca, Haywood, Flynn, and Koettgen join Quinlan in his attack on the alliance between the silk owners and the city authorities. The extent to which the struggle had attracted outside attention was demonstrated by the appearance of Upton Sinclair, who urged the workers to keep up their struggle.[70]

The conviction of Quinlan on May 14 began a week of increased tension in the silk city. The police, under orders to crack down hard in an attempt to bring an end to the conflict, confronted strikers whose long weeks of inactivity had made them quick to anger. Although the I.W.W. still cautioned its followers against violence, the speeches which the leaders delivered to protest Quinlan's treatment were provocative. The daily branch meetings featured such angry addresses that a delegation of citizens demanded that the mayor and councilmen take action to prevent such sessions. On May 19, the presence of detectives and a stenographer from the prosecutor's office at Turn Hall provoked a near riot, as the attending strikers hurled ugly threats at the intruders. The wholesale arrests of pickets, seeking to prevent the trickle of returning workers from turning into a broadening stream, added to the explosive atmosphere. When the city officials closed the meeting halls on May 19, strikers trudged daily to Haledon, forming lines of marchers who seemed to need only a spark to set them off. Boyd, who now appeared with greater frequency as a speaker, contributed to the oratorical bombardment of the Paterson authorities. "There is no country except bloody Russia where conditions exist as they do in Paterson," he declared at one Haledon rally. "America is nothing but a land of cruelty and tyranny."[71]

On May 20 the strike entered its thirteenth week with settlement no closer, but with each side carefully watching the other for any sign of weakening. The strike had long since reached the stage where any professed or hinted inclination to settle was looked upon as an indication of weakening resolve and as a signal for the adversary to stand fast. Strike sympathizers began to report a division within the manufacturers' ranks between the large and small concerns, with the former most adamant in refusing all demands, and used this to urge the strikers to await the expected capitulation. The New York *Call* reported that the manufacturers were becoming desperate and "on the verge of ruin" and promised the strikers that victory was near if they would hold together a while longer.[72] Meanwhile, the manufacturers reported an increased number of strikers returning to work and forecast an imminent break in the workers' ranks. When some members of the Central Strike Committee protested the inflammatory speeches of the I.W.W. supporters, again specifically taking offense at Boyd's remarks, this was construed by the employers as an indication that the "responsible" strikers were willing to break with the union and seek a settlement.[73]

With reports that some of the manufacturers and a portion of the strikers were anxious to settle, there was some optimism that the strike was nearing an end. Once again the *News* began to urge a shop-by-shop settlement, encouraged by the fact that the workers in the A. W. Price broad-silk shop had accepted the company's offer of an eight-hour day and a 10 percent wage increase. But the agreement between this small weaving establishment and its some forty workers did not prove to be the beginning of a general return to work by employees in other shops. The Price Company became the scene of frequent skirmishes between pickets and police rather than the model for settlement throughout the industry. The Central Strike Committee interpreted the company's offer as a sign that all the manufacturers would be forced by economic necessity to seek an industrywide agreement; manufacturers saw the weavers' return there as an indication that workers in other shops would be forced by their condition to settle on a similar shop basis. But the Price agreement, hailed as "the first important move between employer and employee," was an anomaly rather than a sign of weakening by either protagonist. On May 24, both the manufacturers' associations and the Central Strike Committee denied that a general settlement was imminent; spokesmen on both sides indicated that there was little likelihood of an early resumption of work.[74]

The month ended with no greater cause for optimism. Despite frequent newspaper accounts that more and more strikers were anxious to settle, that the I.W.W. was losing the support of increasing numbers, and that a general return to work was near, the true situation was one of continuing stalemate. The steady diet of meetings and rallies proceeded as before, pickets continued to patrol in front of the mill gates, and the police and recorder were kept busy arresting and sentencing dozens of strikers daily.

Early in June, the monotony of the situation was broken by the trial of Scott. Why Prosecutor Dunn determined to begin the proceedings against the editor at that moment, while at the same time postponing the trials of the I.W.W. leaders and Quinlan's sentencing, is unclear. However, either for tactical or political reasons, the Paterson authorities throughout the strike seemed to pursue socialist spokesmen more vigorously than the better-known I.W.W. organizers. Quinlan, more clearly a socialist than I.W.W. advocate, was by no means the most prominent of the strike generals; yet he was the one who received the harshest treatment. Perhaps the precipitating factor in bringing Scott to trial was the increased activity of the Passaic County S.P.A. toward the end of May, when it attacked the closing of the halls and began to urge a federal investigation of the strike. The Passaic editor could have been seen as a convenient target against whom the local politicians might strike back at the third party critics.[75]

Scott's "crime" was his authorship of the blistering editorial against Bimson and the Paterson police in the February 28 issue of his Passaic weekly. He was tried under a New Jersey antianarchist statute, passed after the assassination of President McKinley, which made it a criminal offense to attack any part of the state or federal government. The prosecution charged that Scott's description of the Paterson police was a violation of that 1902 law.[76]

The trial before Judge Klenert in the Court of Quarter Sessions began at 10 a.m. on Monday, June 2, and was "one of the quickest in the history of Passaic County." Assistant Prosecutor Force opened his remarks with reference to the McKinley assassination and the subsequent passage of the New Jersey statute, and then read the Scott attack on the Paterson police. He was followed by Captain John Tracy, who testified that he had been present at a strike meeting at which Scott read the offending editorial. Defense attorney Henry Carliss acknowledged Scott's authorship, but argued that criticism of the police did not constitute hostility to government. If the editor was convicted, Carliss asserted, free speech would be a "dead letter" in New Jersey. The case was in the hands of the jury by noon and two hours later the verdict was in: Scott was guilty. Klenert set sentencing for June 6 and turned to hear the cases of forty-four strikers charged with unlawful assembly for their picketing activity in mid-April.[77]

Although the jury recommended mercy, and few expected that the maximum sentence of fifteen years and/or $2,000 fine would be levied, Scott's sentence was a harsh one. Klenert gave the socialist editor an indeterminate term of from one to fifteen years and levied a fine of $250. Bail was set at $3,000 pending appeal.[78] The conviction and penalty unleashed an avalanche of criticism from journalists and libertarians across the country. There was considerable truth in the statement that the treatment of Scott promised to make "the question of free speech a national topic" as well as "change the popular temper toward the strike."[79]

The Paterson authorities gained nothing from the editor's conviction; if anything, the city had staged the sort of spectacle which the I.W.W. liked to provoke on its behalf. Upton Sinclair, one of the many prominent Americans to help publicize the quality of justice in New Jersey, termed the Scott conviction "the most outrageous legal persecution that had ever been recorded." Closer to home, the pastor of the Unitarian Church of Hackensack preached a sermon on "Why the Unitarian Church Is Interested in Free Speech" and the trustees of his church voted to allow Flynn and Tresca to speak before them.[80]

Shortly after the trial in the Court of Quarter Sessions, a group of prominent citizens sent a petition to President Wilson urging a federal investigation of the strike and Paterson's violation of constitutional rights. Following a brief outline of the issues, the strike's progress, and the actions of the city officials, the petition urged intervention to "protect the . . . fundamental rights essential to the life of a free government."[81] At no other time during the strike was the sentiment higher in favor of the textile workers of New Jersey. The I.W.W. was at last receiving the sort of national attention which had been of such importance in winning the Lawrence struggle.

The peak of the drive for publicity—the long-planned pageant of the Paterson strike—was yet to come. The evening after Scott was sentenced, the drama was enacted at Madison Square Garden. As Ralph Chaplin, I.W.W. editor of the *Industrial Worker* and *Solidarity*, later wrote: "This strike produced some of the most spectacular defense features in labor history. Bob Fitzsimmons, the fighter, and Bertha Kalich, the actress, contributed their talent at benefit performances. But the famous Paterson Pageant was by far the greatest strike-benefit and publicity stunt on record."[82] Flynn, albeit not enthusiastic at all about the impact of the pageant, termed the June 7 performance the "great dividing point" in the strike.[83]

Chapter 6

The Pageant

Within the last ten years, the intellectual proletarians of advanced tendencies have entered every radical movement. They could, if they would, be of tremendous importance to the workers. But so far they have remained without clarity of vision, without depth of conviction, and without real daring to face the world. . . .

The intellectual proletarians who are radical and liberal are still so much of the bourgeois regime that their sympathy with the workers is dilletante and does not go farther than the parlor, the so-called salon, or Greenwich Village.—Emma Goldman, "Intellectual Proletarians," *Mother Earth*, 8 (February 1914), 366, 369.

The men and women who affixed their names to the petition to the president following Scott's conviction represented one segment of the heterogeneous group of middle- and upper-class easterners who sympathized with the struggle of the New Jersey silk workers. Of the journalists, clergymen, and social workers who comprised the majority of the signers, most knew from first-hand observation the conditions of work and life in the country's industrial centers. With a few notable exceptions, they were among the moderate reformers who were both concerned by the existence of poverty amidst affluence and alarmed by indications that workers might accept radical solutions to their problems. The bombing of the Los Angeles *Times* building in 1910, followed by the trial and eventual guilty plea of the McNamara brothers over a year later, had convinced them that a virtual state of war existed in the country. Led by Paul U. Kellogg of *Survey*, a committee of "militant economists, social workers, churchmen, and civic leaders" began to urge a federal investigation of industrial conditions as a first step in remedying labor problems through orthodox means.[1]

John Bates Clark, one of the so-called militant economists, stated the position of this group when he wrote in support of an investigation:

No one can guarantee that a commission will be able to answer... the questions that chiefly perplex us; but it should be able to do much in that direction, and at least put us in the way of getting answers we seek.

The supreme question is a moral one. Is labor generally getting its due?

A belief that the laborer is wronged and that he will never get justice without a revolution accounts for the growth of dangerous parties which constitute the extreme left of the labor movement.

Maintaining that most citizens believed that advances could be made "without revolution," Clark and his associates argued the need for reform legislation.[2]

Although the sincerity of the *Survey* group cannot be doubted, their advocacy of a Commission on Industrial Relations was, as Clark revealed, prompted by the fear of radical appeals as well as by a commitment to the workers' welfare. There were, however, others of like background and profession who were not similarly motivated. In the early years of the century, many so-called intellectuals—lawyers, journalists, educators, and the like—actually sought the type of radical solutions which their reformist counterparts wished to contain. In the important socialist center of New York City, for example, much of the leadership of the S.P.A. came to be provided by those outside of the working class. The party's mainstay there during its formative years had been the immigrants, predominantly Jews from Eastern Europe, who worked in the needle trades. But around 1905 socialism's attraction broadened. As Morris Hillquit later wrote in his autobiography, the party "began to attract ever-growing numbers of men and women in literary and academic circles. Socialism became popular, almost a fad."[3]

The "fad," as Hillquit rather scornfully referred to the attachment of nonproletarian types, was not restricted only to middle-class intellectuals. There were also at least a smattering of millionaire socialists in the period before the Great War. "Perhaps it was the 'cult of Something Else,'" David Shannon has written, "perhaps it was a feeling of guilt brought by having plenty in the midst of poverty, perhaps it was a sincere desire to right the world's wrongs, but whatever the motivation, there were comrades who were . . . actually men of wealth."[4]

The intellectual and millionaire socialists and their more conservative progressive brethren had a positive influence on the labor movement. Using their pens and pocketbooks, they both publicized and financed many of the struggles of the period. The so-called Uprising of the Twenty Thousand, the 1909 strike of shirtwaist workers in New York City, is an example. The largest strike of women workers in the United States to that time, it was supported by the broadest spectrum of individuals and organizations. The S.P.A., the Women's Trade Union League, and the suffrage movement's Political Equality Association provided valuable assistance. Clearly the contributions of writers, clergymen, and the comfortable were a factor in that successful strike.[5]

Most of the intellectuals found their place as members of the right wing of the S.P.A., but some proceeded further and became great admirers of the antipolitical I.W.W. Although the leaders of that radical industrial union saw society as clearly divided between capitalists and wage earners and engaged in incessant attacks on intellectuals who "sought to lead those of whose lives they know nothing," the intellectuals were not put off. Many commented upon their fascination with the radical union, often in dismay or with ridicule. "Just at present Syndicalism is the pastime of a great many Americans, so-called intellectuals," Goldman wrote disdainfully in January 1913. "Not that they know anything about it."[6] Similarly, in a piece concerning direct action, the *Independent* commented:

> What is surprising is not so much that untrained foreign workmen should be taken captive by leaders who tell them that the world belongs to them; but that well-educated literary writers, men who never did a stroke of industrial work, should in their emotionalism and their utter absense of any basis of fine ethics, be carried away by the rough, lawless force of a policy which reeks not of God or man. It seems beautiful to them. They follow Haywood much as a bunch of giggling girls go wild over the physical prowess of a quarterback. Their naive, childlike faith in the new policy is queer to see.[7]

However bizarre the attraction might have seemed to anarchist Goldman, the reformist *Independent*, or even the I.W.W. organs, the industrial union was extremely appealing to a number of younger writers and artists. Whether this was due to the I.W.W. origins and association with the romantic West, its irreverence, the heroic figure of the cyclopean Haywood, or whatever, many "of artistic and literary temperament" were happy to help the union fight its battles.[8]

The Lawrence strike in 1912 first attracted the attention of the younger intellectuals to the I.W.W., and many traveled to that New England city to witness or partake of the exhilaration of the underdog's battle against the textile barons. When the scene of the union's activities shifted the next year to Paterson, less than twenty miles from New York City, these and other enamored intellectuals were ready and able to participate more fully in the I.W.W. struggle. Some took part in fundraising activities, others wrote sympathetic accounts of the heroic struggle being fought at their doorstep, and more than a few took Sunday excursions to form part of the audience at Haledon. Their most significant contribution was the pageant which they conceived and staged at Madison Square Garden in June. This artistic tour de force was the creation of a fascinating group of individuals within the orbit of two New York phenomena: the Greenwich Village salon of Mabel Dodge and the group of artists associated with the flamboyant monthly, *The Masses.*

The Masses, accurately described as "a meeting-ground for revolutionary labour and the radical intelligentsia,"[9] first appeared in January 1911. Founded by Piet Vlag, a Dutch organizer of cooperatives and the manager of a cooperative restaurant in the basement of the Rand School of Social Sciences, it was first subsidized by wealthy insurance executive Rufus Weeks. Thomas Seltzer served as its first editor; John Spargo, Gustavus Myers, W. J. Ghent, and Eugene Wood were among the contributors; and Art Young, Charles Winter, and Maurice Becker did cartoons. Despite the talent which Vlag was able to attract, *The Masses* had a small circulation and perpetual money problems. When its second editor, Horatio Winslow, proved no more successful than Seltzer in overcoming the magazine's chronic problems, Vlag urged, in the summer of 1912, that it merge with a feminist publication in Chicago. The original founders were reluctant to concede defeat, however, and decided to call in yet another editor; Young recommended the twenty-nine-year-old Eastman as a candidate for the thankless job.[10]

Eastman later recalled: "One day . . . in late August I received a letter scrawled with a brush on a torn-off scrap of drawing paper. . . . It said: 'You are elected editor of *The Masses*. No Pay.'" Eastman knew little about the condition of the magazine and was not interested in becoming an editor—especially one without salary. But he agreed to put out a December edition, try to raise some money, and write a few editorials; if the necessary funds were obtained, he agreed to join the cooperative and write a monthly column. "Before we had the experimental number out," he wrote, "I was to all intents and purposes president and general manager of *The Masses* Publishing Company as well as editor of the magazine."[11]

Under its new editor, *The Masses* became both a livelier and more left-wing publication. Vlag and the earlier contributors stood in the center or to the right of the S.P.A., held no sympathy for anarchists, and paid little attention to the I.W.W. Eastman refashioned the magazine. It became a more radical publication, its pages open to both anarchism and syndicalism. Following the Lawrence success, the affection for the I.W.W. increased. The Paterson strike, one student of literary radicalism has observed, was in some ways "the central event in the life of the magazine."[12]

The Masses had a truly distinguished group of writers and artists on its staff.[13] One of the best known, and the one to play the most active role in the Paterson strike, was twenty-six-year-old John Reed. Those who knew Reed in this period all have described him in markedly similar fashion. Julian Street remembered him as "reckless to the point of foolhardiness," a young man who sought adventure and liked to regale his friends with stories of his exploits. "His heart," wrote Street, "was that of a mischievous boy throwing snowballs at the world's silk hat. Presently he began to conceive this snowballing as a serious duty to be performed for the welfare of humanity." Harvard classmate Robert Hallowell described him as "a born non-conformer" with "the body and mind of a man who could fight, and the temperament of a Knight of romance." He was "a creative force rather than a great intelligence," Orrick Johns remembered Reed. "He loved to be where things were going on. . . . The things that stood out about him were his big lunging youth, his audacity, speed, and his wide and sensitive human sympathies."[14]

Walter Lippmann knew Reed at Harvard as "the most inspired song and cheer leader that the football crowd had had for many days" and concluded in 1914 that he had not changed. In a *New Republic* article, Lippmann described his college classmate:

> Reed has no detachment, and is proud of it, I think. By temperament he is not a professional writer or reporter. He is a person who enjoys himself. Revolution, literature, poetry, they are only things which hold him at times, incidents of his living. Now and then he finds adventure by imagining it, often he transforms his own experience. He is one of those people who treat as serious possibilities such stock fantasies as shipping before the mast, rescuing women, hunting lions, or trying to fly around the world in an aeroplane.[15]

Reed was too much the juvenile dilettante for the more serious and profound Lippmann, but most found him captivating. Sanger, who worked with him during the Paterson strike, commented that both right-wingers and those far to the left "loved Jack Reed." She saw, as did Street and *Masses* associate Floyd Dell, that Reed differed from many of the young intellectuals who loved to proclaim their radicalness. "Most of these men were merely vocal," Street wrote. "Jack longed to translate his new-found beliefs into action."[16]

When Reed established himself in Greenwich Village in 1911, that area of New York City had become something of a mecca for such young dissident spirits. Hutchins Hapgood, who lived elsewhere but was spiritually drawn to it, described the Village as "not so much a physical locality as a symbol of a new American Bohemia that appeared all over the country."[17] Prior to World War I, before the Village was discovered as quaint and transformed into a high-rent area too expensive for the genuine artists and writers, the atmosphere there was exhilarating. Rebels of all persuasions felt free to fashion their own variety of escape. The spirit of Bohemian rebellion took many forms, but one unifying feature was "an aesthetic love of poverty." Those who were not genuinely penurious, affected it.[18]

For many, it was only a short step from sympathy or emulation of the poor to attachment to those individuals or movements which presumed to speak for the downtrodden. By no means were all of the Village's young dissidents enamored with socialism, anarchism, or the syndicalism of the I.W.W., but all three found their supporters there. At gatherings of *The Masses*' staff, at the Liberal Club located over Polly's Restaurant on Macdougal Street, or in the confines of the varied dwellings of the habitués, such radical proponents as Goldman and Haywood were given an honored place. In 1913, when the intellectuals talked about "social revolution and the worker, the Wobbly or the Paterson striker was the prototype of the proletariat, and the I.W.W. the organization of the revolution."[19]

Late in 1912 the area around Washington Square became home to the woman who would draw the diverse elements of Greenwich Village together: Mabel Dodge and her husband Edwin, a "Boston architect of independent means," moved into a second-floor residence in a brownstone at the corner of Fifth Avenue and Ninth Street. Born in 1879, the daughter of a wealthy Buffalo banker, Mabel and her second husband (the first, Karl Evans, had been killed in a hunting accident in 1902) had recently returned to the United States after a decade's residence in a villa outside Florence.[20]

Accustomed to the stimulating artistic life which she had lived in Italy, Mabel now found herself in a strange city where she knew no one. She was busy enough at first, decorating her apartment in her own inimitable fashion: white woodwork, white walls, white bearskin rug before the white fireplace ("a repudiation of grimy New York"); delicate French furniture, all in pale tones, which she had shipped from Florence; and a white porcelain chandelier from Venice, "covered with birds and flowers in canary yellow, turquoise blue, green, all the lovely gay colors—life-sized canaries perched among the gentians, blue birds among the roses." She created the rooms to be her "refuge from the world."[21]

But the refuge soon seemed more like a prison. "There was," Dodge later remembered her first weeks in New York, "no life in anything about me. A rumble-rumble on the streets outside, and inside a deathly stillness wherein one could hear oneself draw every breath." She felt ill, bored, depressed, purposeless. "Much of the time I lay listless on the pale French gray couch, dangling a languid arm, eyes closed before the recurrent death of the sweet antiquities about me that lapsed lifeless between whites."[22]

Her husband, anxious to find diversions for her, tried to introduce interesting people into this eclectic but empty environment. Carl Van Vechten was the first notable to "animate" the lifeless rooms, but a more important early acquaintance was the sculptor Jo Davidson, whom Edwin Dodge met one day in the Village and brought home with him for a drink. Davidson, an old associate from Paris days, became her link to the fascinating assortment of writers and artists who lived in or were a part of Greenwich Village. Edwin Dodge's chance encounter with the sculptor and the invitation to the Fifth Avenue apartment was the beginning of her total immersion in the world of art and rebellion. "It was ironic," she later wrote, "that Edwin, in his effort to help me, launched the boat that sailed away and left him behind."[23]

Lincoln Steffens and Lippmann were among the early visitors to the Dodge residence, but the most important literary figure whom Davidson brought to Mabel Dodge's door was Hutchins Hapgood, brother of the editor of Collier's. Hapgood, then writing for the New York Globe and living with his wife and four children in Dobbs Ferry, became her closest confidant and her entree into the world of radical labor.[24] Hapgood wrote of their early association:

> When I first met her, she was completely innocent of the world of labor and of revolution in politics, art and industry. She lived in the purely conservative world, although her restless energy and her enormous temperamental instinct created frequent ructions in that world. But to these ebullient and transforming emotions she gave no thought. There was no mental form to her surging and changing inner existence. When Jo took me to her place, I existed in the midst of a changing New York and a changing America. I was connected with all the isms and all the radical hopes and enthusiasms. . . . My world excited Mabel; and she wanted to get into it.[25]

Hapgood loved to talk, and Dodge proved to be the perfect audience; they were, in a sense, two lost souls who had remarkably much in common. Eastman said of Hapgood, in words equally applicable to Dodge: "He seems to have puttered endlessly, like a grandmother over some tangled knitting, with a thing called 'life,' and had never taken enough actual stitches to give it shape."[26]

Hapgood's work on the Globe, where he wrote tri-weekly signed articles on subjects of interest to him—including sympathetic pieces on the I.W.W., Haywood, Flynn, and Tresca—did not consume much of his time. He could, therefore, spend a good part of his day enjoying the rather eccentric ambience of Dodge's parlor; the two exchanged confidences concerning the disappointments of their lives and discussed their mutual search for "It" (Dodge's term) and "the Infinite" (Hapgood's).[27]

Through Hapgood, Dodge met the anarchist group centered around Goldman and *Mother Earth*, the I.W.W. leaders who were directing the fight in Paterson, the circle of young writers and artists around Steffens, Sanger and her S.P.A. associates, the Eastmans and *The Masses* contributors, and the whole galaxy of labor leaders, poets, and theater people of the day. All who came to visit were dissidents of one sort or another, sharing a sense of rebelliousness, but the various groups were more like "different constellations" than a united whole. In fact, each "fragment in the same large puzzle" seemed to think little of the others.[28] Steffens had no admiration for "the creed-bound radicals, whether socialists, anarchists or single-taxers"; Eastman ridiculed Steffens's "obscurantism" and his "kittenish delight in paradox" and dismissed Hapgood as a "sentimental rebel"; Hapgood thought Eastman "lacked social impulse" and that Goldman had "no intellectual message to give"; and Goldman lumped all the "intellectual proletarians" into the category of "dilletantes."[29] Dodge, however, loved them all. To her, Goldman was "a homely, motherly sort . . . rather like a severe but warm-hearted school teacher"; Steffens possessed a "rapier-keen mind"; and Sanger was a "Madonna type of woman," the first Dodge knew who was "openly an ardent propagandist for the joys of the flesh."[30] All of them were welcome in her home. Dodge "collected people and arranged them like flowers," Christopher Lasch has written of her, "She loved to combine people in startling new juxtapositions."[31]

Dodge, who confessed that she had "never read the news" except when it was about herself "or some friend or enemy," now found herself "caught in the whirlpool of contemporary agitation." At Steffens's suggestion, she transformed the accidental and unplanned gatherings of her radical and literary friends into Wednesday night Evenings. "Socialists, Trade-Unionists, Anarchists, Suffragists, Poets, Relations, Lawyers, Murderers, 'Old Friends,' Psychoanalysts, I.W.W.'s, Single-Taxers, Birth Controlists, Newspapermen, Artists, Clubwomen, Woman's-place-is-in-the-home Women, Clergymen, and just plain men all met there and . . . exchanged a variousness in vocabulary called, in euphemistic optimism, Opinions!"[32]

Few who attended an Evening, or knew someone who had, could refrain from writing about the experience. Dodge made such an impression that she was used as a character in novels written by two of the circle: she appeared as "Edith Dale" in Van Vechten's *Peter Whiffle*, and as "Mary Kittridge" in Eastman's *Venture*. The latter includes a description of an Evening during which Haywood took part in the discussion of art and revolution. A philosophical anarchist introduced the subject at a sign from the hostess:

> He says, in effect, that as regards proletarian art he believes in art and he believes in the proletariat. He makes it plain that he is very earnest in both these beliefs, but leaves the impression that his belief in art is a little the more firm. . . . He introduces Bill Haywood as a master of the art of agitation.
> Bill sits there on a very small chair during this speech. Perhaps the chair is not so small, but it looks so with Bill sitting on it. . . .
> He has only one eye, and he peers about with it like a tame eagle. He examines his audience very thoroughly. . . . Then he says—very gently: "Fellow workers and folks!"[33]

It is obvious that Eastman was not impressed with the depth of understanding displayed at this gathering. Such occasions were memorable, however, as his account in *Venture* and the following from Sanger's *Autobiography* make evident: "The topic of conversation turned out to be direct action. Big Bill was the figure of the evening, but everybody was looking for an opportunity to talk. Each believed he had a key to the gates of Heaven; each was trying to convert the others. It could not exactly have been called a debate, because a single person held the floor as long as he could. . . . In the end, conversations were nil; all were convinced beforehand either for or against, and I never knew them to shift ground."[34] Sanger later admitted that it was "hard not to laugh about it" in retrospect, but at the time the participants took the Evenings very seriously. The mingling of I.W.W. direct actionists, moderate socialists, romantic artists, anarchists, and millionaires was significant. It was from this combination that the idea for a pageant of the Paterson strike was hatched.

Dodge, if one accepts her own recollection, first met Haywood and Reed through the good offices of Hapgood. One evening in late April of 1913 the Hapgoods were invited to a gathering at the apartment of Haywood's current mistress, a high school teacher in New York, and Hapgood, aware that Dodge was anxious to meet the I.W.W. leader, asked her to join them. After dinner at the Dodge residence, the three went to "B's" rather Bohemian place. In a large room, sparsely furnished and lit by candles, they found groups of men and women standing in clusters or sprawled on the floor talking quietly. Haywood, whom Dodge recognized at once, filled one of the few chairs. Soon the peripheral conversations died away and attention focused on the I.W.W. leader, who began to talk about the Paterson strike. He was concerned that people were not aware of the silk workers' struggle and complained that it had be-

come virtually impossible to get the New York newspapers to print the true story of the strike.[35]

What followed can best be told in Dodge's own words, an account undoubtedly embellished but one usually given credence:

"Why don't you bring the strike to New York and show it to the workers?" I asked in a small, shy voice.

Haywood, who hadn't noticed me before, turned his eye on me with an arrested look. I went on, feeling engulfed in blushes and embarrassment, but unable to be still, for this idea was speaking through me. I hadn't thought it consciously. It was another case of It!

"Why don't you hire a great hall and re-enact the strike over here? Show the whole thing. . . .

"Well, by God! Why Not?" I was excited now by my own inspiration that, coming to me without any volition or expectation of mine, appeared simply wonderful to me. . . .

"I'll do it!" cried a voice—and a young man detached himself from the group and assumed a personality before my eyes.[36]

The volunteer, of course, was Reed, whose meeting with Dodge had been delayed by his heavy writing schedule during the early months of 1913.[37]

A dramatization of the silk strike before a New York audience was not as eccentric an idea as one might think. As a recent student of the Paterson production has written, "the whole country was in the throes of a vigorous pageant renaissance" at the time.[38] Shortly before the meeting between Dodge and Reed, the American Pageantry Board was organized in Boston at which time "the value of the pageant as a short cut to reach people was emphasized."[39] Given the existence of the new enthusiasm for pageantry by civic-minded groups interested in raising funds or conveying a particular message, and given the twin commitments to art and revolution of the Greenwich Village intellectuals, a pageant to publicize and help finance the silk strike made enormous sense. When the evening broke up, Haywood had become interested enough in the idea to promise to broach it to the Central Strike Committee.[40]

During their first meeting, Dodge was more than a little enchanted by the brash and youthful Masses writer—she found Reed "lovable"—but the two did not meet again for some time. Reed, his enthusiasm fired by what he had heard that night, left early the next morning for Paterson. On a dark and rainy Monday morning, he walked the streets of the city, mingling with the strikers gathered in clusters outside the mill gates. At about 7 a.m. on April 28, as Reed and a few others sought shelter on a porch, a Paterson policeman—"doubtless a good, stupid

Irishman in time of peace," Reed wrote—attempted to break up the group. Reed refused the order to leave, was arrested on a charge of disorderly conduct, and hauled before Recorder Carroll. He soon received the treatment which had been meted out to many strikers before him: twenty days in the Passaic County Jail or, as he termed it, "Sheriff Radcliff's Hotel." When Reed was ushered into the jail, an old facility which he described as "full of vermin and disease," he found himself in the company of perhaps a hundred prisoners, "half of them strikers with foreign faces, quick gestures, an air of subdued excitement." Each new recipient of Carroll's justice, when brought in to swell the number, was greeted with cheers of welcome. Tresca, arrested two days before and held awaiting bail on the charges stemming from the February 25 Turn Hall meeting, was there, explaining the class struggle in broken English to a black prisoner. Reed approached him and tried to ask questions about the strike, but the Italian leader was suspicious of the well-dressed young man. It was not until later in the day, when Haywood joined the group following his arrest at the Passaic Railroad Station, that Tresca learned that Reed was a friend rather than a spy.[41]

Reed remained in the Passaic County Jail for four days before he was released on bail. During that time, Haywood introduced him to Tresca and Quinlan, had the strikers tell him their stories, and instructed him in the ways of labor agitation. Released on bail provided by Harvard classmate Edward E. Hunt, Reed returned to New York to find that he was something of a celebrity as a result of his experience. He probably regaled his friends with stories of his four-day confinement in the overly dramatic fashion he later employed in an autobiographical account: "In the jail I talked with exultant men who had blithely defied the lawless brutality of the city government and gone to prison laughing and singing. There were horrors in that jail too; men and boys shut up for months without trial, men going mad and dying, bestial cruelty and disease and filth—and all for the poor."[42]

Reed was somewhat more temperate in the piece he wrote for The Masses in the days following his release. It was evident, however, that he had been an apt student during the instruction he had received from Haywood and Tresca. The article, which began "There is war in Paterson," told of the valiant struggle of the silk workers against the combined forces of mill owners, local press, police, and courts. Although the circulation of The Masses was not large, his account did reach the intellectuals of New York and helped publicize the strike within that community. A Paterson police officer later stated that "jailing one lousy poet . . . attracted more journalistic attention than the hundreds of strikers" arrested by the department.[43]

By the time Reed was back among his friends in the Village, Haywood had gotten the strikers' assent for the pageant and enthusiasm was high for the project. Reed, who might have gone to Paterson initially on somewhat of a lark, had been deeply moved by his experience and became almost obsessed with helping the embattled workers. He appeared frequently at strike meetings, even to the point of overcoming his initial reluctance and addressing the gatherings, and insisted that his Greenwich Village friends see the situation at firsthand. Among those who visited Paterson with him were Dodge, Hunt, theater designer Robert Edmond Jones, Lippmann, the Hapgoods, and Eastman. Dodge, who was by that time infatuated with Reed, motored out to Haledon with the Hapgoods one Sunday, where they found Reed leading a crowd of workers in strike songs; Eastman attended a similar gathering and found a meeting which had "somewhat the aspect of a Sunday school picnic."[44]

Few within the Dodge circle were unaffected by the strike. The Hapgoods were among the New Yorkers who opened their homes to Paterson children, plucking a brother and sister from the grimy industrial city and depositing them in their suburban home under the care of their Italian nurse.[45] Reed and Dodge plunged into the preparations for the pageant. "I was engrossed by it," the Fifth Avenue hostess recalled. "I gave up everything to work on it. Reed was the executive. I kept having ideas about what to do and he carried them out."[46] Actually, it was Reed who was the moving spirit; he wrote the script, chose the scenes, and got his friends to help in staging the production. Some of his acquaintances disapproved of his jail experience and his association with the I.W.W. and hoped that he would "grow up and get over it," but a number contributed to his artistic effort. Jones, a Harvard classmate, staged the production and designed the striking cover for the program. The stage backdrop depicting the silk mills was painted by artist John Sloan, a contributing editor of The Masses.[47]

On May 19, at the two meeting halls in Paterson, Haywood introduced Reed as the director of the production which would be given on June 7 at Madison Square Garden. Reed then took off his coat and proceeded to lead the attending strikers in a song which he called "The Haywood Thrill." (He promised the singers that "the strains of the music, when it reached the ears of the manufacturers, would make them feel that the 'terror of death' was on them.") Following this "first rehearsal," Reed outlined the projected ten scenes in the pageant: I. Calling the Strike; II. Mills Closed, Picketing, Police Arrests; III. The Carroll Courtroom and the County Jail; IV. Armory Meeting; V. Mass Meeting at Haledon; VI. Funeral of Modestino; VII. May Day Parade;

VIII. Festival at Slate Mountain; IX. Evacuation of the Children; X. Turn Hall Meeting.[48]

From that day on, Reed was in Paterson almost daily, rehearsing the cast of strikers, returning to New York to work on other aspects of the production. Dodge, meanwhile, worked on publicity, fund-raising, and other attendant matters; she saw less and less of Hapgood and Van Vechten, who remained somewhat apart from the enterprise, and more and more of the group of New York socialists who played an active role. Occasionally she would watch Reed's rehearsals. "One of the gayest touches," she wrote appreciatively, was seeing him teach the strikers "to sing one of their lawless songs to the tune of 'Harvard, old Harvard.'" Many of Reed's college friends surely could not appreciate that touch! But there were many more radical outsiders who delighted in the work of the young writer. Sinclair, for example, wrote that he would remember always the sight of Reed, "his shirt sleeves rolled up, shouting through a megaphone, drilling those who were to serve as captains of the mass."[49]

The participating strikers reportedly were enchanted with the idea of re-creating their struggle on the stage and welcomed the diversion that the preparations provided. There was some difficulty in convincing any of them to play the parts of policemen and strikebreakers—the *Call* commented that it might be necessary to enlist Sinclair, Steffens, Hapgood, and their friends for those roles—but the promise of appearing at the Garden eventually overcame their reluctance. Although Flynn and Tresca were somewhat skeptical of the whole idea, Haywood became more and more enthusiastic as the days wore on.[50]

In New York City, among the noncreative types who were entrusted with the thankless chore of raising funds to mount the production, there was considerably less optimism that the idea could be carried through. Sanger's apartment became the command center for those who had to wrestle with the finances, and there came a time when the Pageant Committee was on the verge of cancelling the spectacle. As the production became more and more an artistically grandiose affair, costs mounted alarmingly: $1,000 to rent the Garden; $750 for the scenery; and some $1,000 more for publicity, programs, tickets, and the like. Shortly after the first meeting of the Pageant Committee, Sanger's home was the scene of a late night gathering to decide whether to continue. Haywood, Ashley, Giovannitti, and Boyd were among those who participated. If it had not been for the fact that a check for the Garden's rental had already been sent, the production might well have been dropped then.[51]

About a week after this meeting, the financial problems again

loomed so large as to threaten the event. At the instigation of Haywood, Sanger, Boyd, Dodge, and Reed, a meeting was called at the Liberal Club to which all members of the various working committees were invited. The enormous expenses of putting on the production and the fear that the floor seats could not all be sold at the planned $1.50 ticket price forced the leaders to raise again the question of cancellation. Among those who had been asked to attend was John Steiger, the socialist leader of the striking ribbon weavers at the Smith & Kauffman mill and the most prominent figure among the New York workers. There were about seventy people present when one of the members of the Pageant Committee announced that the Garden production could not be staged unless more money could be found at once. "I pleaded as hard as I could," Steiger later recounted, "because I felt that if we ran the show we would be in a position to hold out several months longer." He finally agreed to try to raise the money if one of the strikers was appointed assistant treasurer and if the Pageant Committee would promise to repay the loan before any other bills were settled. This offer and its conditions was accepted and the meeting ended. Shortly thereafter the New York silk worker provided the amount promised, and Rudolf Wyssman was named assistant treasurer. Dodge collected an additional $600 and, with some $1,000 more raised from other sources, the pageant was assured.[52]

By the end of May the only concession to the financial difficulties was that Reed's original plan for ten scenes had been reduced to a more manageable and less expensive six.[53] The strikers' attention was now firmly fixed on the upcoming event, which they expected would raise enough money to allow them to hold out until the owners had to capitulate. This possibility, and the publicity which would result from the production, prompted reaction in Paterson. The *Guardian*, representing the views of the city's conservatives in an editorial two days before the event, tried to impugn the union's motives:

> The men and women workers are now to be used as puppets in a "pageant" for the purpose of putting a few more dollars into the pockets of the I.W.W. agitators.
> The I.W.W. agitators hope to reap a rich harvest of dollars from the show. . . . If the strikers can only be induced to exploit their own misery and make a public spectacle of themselves to satisfy the idle curiosity of a New York audience, the I.W.W. agitators will succeed in their last effort to make money out of the Paterson strikers.
> That's why the agitators are too busy these days to do anything at the daily meetings but boom the New York show.[54]

The charge that I.W.W. leaders were labor charlatans bent only on profiting from workers' misery was one often leveled at the union to discredit it. The striking silk workers thus viewed the *Guardian* piece simply as another of the worn tactics employed by the opposition. Nothing could dim their enthusiasm. I.W.W. publicist Ebert accurately described their feelings: "The strikers hope to derive the largest sum of all from the Pageant. . . . One thousand of them are going to take part; and all look forward to a big success."[55]

While the striker-actors were busy polishing their roles, the Publicity Committee was hard at work trying to excite the hoped-for theater-goers. Rose Pastor Stokes, who served in this capacity along with Steffens, Walling, Sinclair, and Hapgood, worked to assure socialist support.[56] On the day of the event, she used the New York *Call* for that purpose: "Here, then, is a pageant, oh Daughters of the Revolution, that will set forth in thrilling episodes, not the glory and courage, the aspirations and struggles of a dead past . . . but a pageant that gives us history fresh from the hands of its makers and—more thrilling marvel still—with the makers themselves as the actors in the play. Hail the new pageantry! Hail the red pageant—the pageant with red blood in its veins."[57] Although Stokes did not mention the competing event by name, she wished to make it clear that the pageant scheduled that same evening at the Henry Street Settlement would be a lifeless presentation by comparison.

On Saturday, June 7, the Paterson performers began assembling at Turn Hall shortly after 8 a.m. Reed appeared an hour later, ran his cast through their last home rehearsal, and then led a procession of almost 1,500 strikers to the Delaware, Lackawanna, and Western Railroad Station. Marching in two divisions through the streets of the city, headed by a band playing lively marches, the troupe made quite a sight; "girls and men alike were bedecked with red ribbons, and in some instances wore a red rose or carnation, pinned to their garments." At 10:45 a.m. most of the contingent boarded the thirteen-car special train which would carry them to New York. "No one could doubt for a moment that the strikers were enjoying themselves to the utmost," the *Guardian* reported, "from the Italian musicians who found seats in the forward cars, to the members of the German Singing Society who stood in the baggage compartment . . . at the end of the train." While the happy riders sang and laughed their way by rail, about 800 others marched behind Tresca to join them for a rally scheduled for Union Square. The spectacle continued in New York City when both groups arrived there. A parade was formed and strikers marched up Broadway to the Garden, where they were to eat and then rehearse on the stage. The New

York supporters had prepared a lunch for them, and Sinclair, one of those on hand to greet the actors, was moved by "that mass, two-thousand half-starved strikers . . . rushing for the sandwiches and coffee!" Following the food and Reed's final instructions, those at Madison Square Garden joined the Tresca contingent at the rally.[58]

At 7:30 that evening, a full hour before the performance was to begin, the streets surrounding the arena were full of spectators hoping to enter. High above, on the tower of the building, the initials "I.W.W." were displayed in red electric lights. "It was," Phillips Russell wrote approvingly, "the first time that the significant letters had ever been given so conspicuous a place." But the crowds and the lights could not relieve the growing concern of the pageant promoters. Shortly before the scheduled curtain, their fears were confirmed: the house would not be sold out. The expensive boxes and the few cheap seats were filled, but the sections priced from $1 to $3 were largely empty and the hundreds who crowded the entrances for admission could not afford such amounts. Finally, after a hurried conference, the decision was made to admit workers at a quarter apiece and, at the last, some entered at no cost.

An audience estimated at close to 15,000 filled the Garden as the final preparations for the performance were ended, and hundreds more were prevented from entering by police fearful of crowding the aisles. The Garden interior was bright with the red colors of the I.W.W.—red banners on the walls, red sashes, ribbons, and flowers worn by many in the crowd. The only discordant feature in the sea of red was a single sign near the stage beside the third gallery. There, a huge banner proclaimed in green letters: "No God, No Master." The crowd muttered uneasily about it before Quinlan tore it down. While those seated waited for the pageant to begin, volunteers paraded the aisles, selling copies of the program, the Passaic *Weekly Issue*, *The Masses*, and books and pamphlets on syndicalism, socialism, and anarchism.[59]

As the house lights dimmed, Reed appeared in front of the stage and, megaphone at the ready, signaled for the curtain to be raised. The pageant began, and the audience watched as its six scenes unfolded:

Scene 1: Men going to the mills, pantomime of whether or not to strike. Suddenly all rushed from the mill yelling "Strike." Then the singing of the Marseillaise.

Scene 2: Pickets. Mills dark. Non-striker appeared, "booed" as he walked across the stage, but police get him into the plant; then police "booed." Police charge the pickets and arrest forty and march them to police headquarters.

Scene 3: Band played the "Dead March in Saul" and scene pictured funeral of Valentino Modestino, the Paterson laborer. . . . Coffin carried by four men and covered with Red emblem of I.W.W.; coffin opened and strikers filed by, each dropping in a red carnation. Then Tresca gave oration and Haywood spoke, pledging I.W.W. support for widow and child.

Scene 4: Green in center of Haledon—2,000 attending weekly Sunday meeting there. Singing by German quartette. Then speakers Quinlan, Haywood, Tresca, Lessig, Flynn—Haywood called for disapproval of Quinlan and Scott convictions. Strikers voted this and also voted to stay out on strike.

Scene 5: Departure of children from Paterson—with Flynn giving kids to "strike mothers" in New York City.

Scene 6: Helvetia Hall—Haywood, Flynn, Tresca, Quinlan spoke; strikers swore to stay out; band played Marseillaise and Pageant ended.[60]

Throughout the performance, the actors were joined by the sympathetic audience, which booed, cheered, and sang along with the cast of strikers. It was a memorable event for all, and there were few who were not moved by what had been depicted. Very late that Saturday night, as the strikers began the train trip back to Paterson, there was talk that the pageant would be returned to the Garden for a week-long run.[61]

Press reaction to the pageant was almost uniformly positive to it as an artistic production. *Current Opinion*, which printed excerpts from a number of the New York reviews (many papers sent their theater critics), summed up the sentiment: "Judged from . . . artistic standards and ideals . . . it seemed to be truly an artistic achievement." *Independent* commented that "no stage in the country had ever seen a more real dramatic expression of American life—only a part of it, to be sure, but a genuine and significant part."[62] *Survey*, which hailed the production as "without staginess or an apparent striving for theatrical effect," was perhaps most enthusiastic:

> The average man who went to look on and the social observer familiar with labor struggles left Madison Square Garden with a vivid new sense of the reality of the silk strike and of industrial conflict in general. . . .
>
> It conveyed what speech and pamphlet, picture and cartoon, fiction and drama fall short of telling. The simple movements of this mass of silk workers was inarticulate eloquence.
>
> Perhaps the thing that struck the observer most forcibly was the sort of people the strikers seemed to be and the absence of race prejudice. A large proportion were substantial, wholesome appear-

ing German-Americans who seemed utterly to lack the hotheaded emotionalism which most people think characterizes I.W.W. adherents.[63]

Haywood, who had complained that the Paterson struggle had been hampered by a lack of publicity, must have been enormously pleased by the amount of national attention which Reed's production received.

As an art form, even the conservative Paterson *Morning Call* had something complimentary to say. However, that paper and others like it were highly critical of the content. The *Call* termed the depiction of the strike a "laughable farce" and "an exaggerated and overdrawn travesty," while the *Guardian* saw it as "a public warning of possibilities which may result when elemental passions are exploited for political purpose and private gain." The latter also commented on the fact that the appearance everywhere of the "red flag of socialism and anarchy" and the absence of the American flag were silent proof of the I.W.W.'s "sinister menace to American institutions." The New York *Times* made the same point when it compared the Reed pageant with the one staged the same evening at the Henry Street settlement to celebrate that organization's twentieth anniversary. The Henry Street production, a pictorial representation of New York history from earliest times, was a pageant "with a vastly different purpose." In its editorial, "Two Pageants: A Contrast," the *Times* commented: "In the Henry Street celebration the motive was to exhalt progress, intellectual development, and the triumph of civilization. In the other the motive was to inspire hatred, to induce violence which may lead to the tearing down of the civil state and the institution of anarchy." The *Times* and the Paterson papers were alarmed by the implications of this new use of drama for the purpose of "stimulating mad passion against law and order."[64]

The media reaction to the pageant, whether enthusiastically positive or unreservedly negative, demonstrated that the production had achieved one of its goals—that of propaganda and publicity. The second aim, to raise money for the relief fund, at first also seemed to have been realized. The audience of 15,000, all presumed to have been paying spectators, made it appear that the pageant had been a great financial success, and initial estimates of the profits ranged from $6,500 to $10,000. In addition to the gate receipts, it was expected that the sale of programs and I.W.W. literature "by the ton" would provide a considerable amount of money for relief purposes.[65]

Unfortunately for the strike and the strikers, these figures were wholly inaccurate: the Paterson Pageant turned out to be a financial catastrophe. The Monday after the performance this was made painfully clear at a meeting of the Finance Committee held in Ashley's law office in New York City. Florence Wise, a member of the Women's Trade Union League and the designated treasurer of the Pageant Committee, informed the gathering—which included Haywood, Boyd, Wyssman, and Steiger—that instead of a profit, there was a large deficit. Steiger and Wyssman, representing the New York silk strikers who had loaned money for the production, could not believe what they heard. Steiger began specifying the amounts of money which he alleged had been given to the committee by three of his associates the evening of the performance; by his account, the total from these sources alone came to more than $2,500. In his later published memoir of the strike Steiger wrote: "While I was speaking, one of them asked me if I meant to accuse them of being dishonest. I replied that I simply meant to ask what they had done with the money. The answer was that they had put all the money uncounted into a satchel and had not counted it until Sunday, when they found it to be $1,560. They claimed that neither Siegrist or Malady had turned over such a sum as I had reported." When Steiger later contacted the two men named and they assured him that his understanding of their receipts was correct, the Smith & Kauffman weaver was convinced that someone had taken the money.[66]

In light of later disclosures, including a detailed financial account, it is doubtful that theft had anything to do with the lack of profit. Yet Steiger's conclusion appears to have been shared by many. Among the New York silk workers, the questioning of the pageant finances was the beginning of a hostility to the I.W.W. leaders which would play a part in the ending of the strike.

The Paterson strikers were not immediately informed that there would be little money for the relief fund, and they waited patiently for the thousands of dollars which they expected. Only when days passed and nothing materialized, did rumors begin to circulate that something was wrong. On June 12, six days after the show, Haywood finally told a Paterson meeting that his early estimate of a large profit had been in error; the Paterson relief fund would receive only $348, with an equal amount going to the strikers of New York. The I.W.W. leader, who had not been in the New Jersey strike city since the day after the Reed extravaganza, was understandably given a cool reception by his audience. The local press, which had been charging union exploitation for weeks, lost no time in spreading the word that the pageant, as they had warned, was simply another "of the many lemons the I.W.W. [had] handed the strikers." The New York Times, although it knew better, stated that it was "difficult to understand so low a profit for a jammed Madison Square Garden where seats sold for from $20 a box."[67]

If the accounts in the *Evening News* can be credited, the I.W.W. leaders only gradually acquainted the strikers with the financial details of the pageant. Haywood's initial statement in Paterson hinted that the $348 was simply a first payment to the relief fund and that the total proceeds were expected to be $5,000. Although he must have known this was not true, Haywood waited almost a week longer before he admitted that nothing more would be forthcoming. Reed accompanied the I.W.W. leader to this second meeting and tried to explain why the expenses had exceeded the receipts, but the workers were skeptical and sullen. When he tried to lead them in the songs they had once enjoyed, there was reportedly little response. Not only were the strikers disappointed with the material result of their theatrical efforts, they were suspicious when Reed told them that he planned to sail for Europe the next day to regain his health.[68]

The press continued to spread rumors concerning the pageant proceeds and the strikers, led by the New Yorkers, demanded a detailed accounting. Finally, the Finance Committee prepared a full report of the receipts and expenditures of the Garden production. With Reed in Europe with Mabel Dodge, and with many of the Greenwich Village enthusiasts and I.W.W. people apparently reluctant to get involved in the matter, the task of preparing the statement fell to Ashley, Wise, and Boyd. On June 24 their report was released to newspapers:

Receipts:	Tickets	$3,550.61
	Programs	264.01
	Parade Collection	70.56
	Petty Cash	47.00
	Pageant Collection	697.20
	Loans	3,016.02
	Total	$7,645.40
Expenses:	Production Costs	$5,506.85
	Paid to Strikers	697.20
	Loans Repaid	1,428.35
	Total	$7,632.30
Liabilities:	Bills	$327.63
	Loans	1,682.02
	Total	$2,009.65
On Hand:		$13.10
Total Deficit:		$1,996.55

The committee accompanied this disclosure with an account of the early difficulties, the discussions over whether the show should be cancelled because of financial exigencies, and the loans which had been made to allow the pageant to be staged.

The signed statement closed with a firm denial of the rumors, "inspired by malice," that funds had been misappropriated by the I.W.W. or that the show's artistic sponsors had profitted. All those associated with the production, the report declared, had donated their services. In fact, while the New York workers' loan had been repaid, over $1,500 of the deficit was owed to members of the group under attack; Reed, Dodge, the Sangers, Sinclair, and Ashley were among those whose loans would not be repaid.[69]

The Evening News, which had been particularly vocal in urging full disclosure, was satisfied with the report, and most of the rumors concerning misappropriation were put to rest. For this, Ashley must be given much of the credit. Member of a prominent New York family, S.P.A. activist since 1908, officer of the National American Woman's Suffrage Association, and supporter of many radical and labor causes, she was above suspicion. A generous contributor of both time and financial resources in I.W.W. causes in the East, she had given $1,000 to the Lawrence relief fund, had served as legal counsel for the Little Falls strikers, and had been active along with Sanger in attempting to convince the Hazleton, Pennsylvania, silk workers to join the strike in the early days of the contest.[70]

Ashley's appearance in Paterson to deliver and explain the financial report to the strikers was indicative of her courage as well as her commitment. Boyd, who accompanied her on this unpleasant mission, also showed that his sympathy for the workers was not limited to fair weather days. In Boyd's case, a heavy penalty was exacted for his appearance. When he arrived in Paterson to present the report on June 24, he was arrested on indictments charging him with inciting to riot, unlawful assembly, and advocating the destruction of private property. The English radical was sent to the Passaic County Jail in lieu of $4,000 bail and remained in "Sheriff Radcliff's Hotel" until July 11.[71]

Steiger, if his statements in 1914 can be believed, was not one of those satisfied with the financial report. In his privately published Memoirs of a Silk Striker: An Exposure of the Principles and Tactics of the I.W.W., a bitter attack on the union's role during the strike, he disputed the statement's account of private contributions and charged that the I.W.W. had stolen the profits. He wrote: "Shortly after I was expelled from the [I.W.W.], a man whom I know very well told me that, on arriving at Helvetia Hall, one day early in May 1913, he found Haywood, Miss Flynn, Lessig, and Koettgen seated around a table counting a large pile of money. He watched them count it twice, after which, he says, they divided it into four parts and pocketed it."[72] There is nothing to support this story and every reason to believe that the alleged witness either misinterpreted what he saw or that Steiger was simply leveling every charge imaginable to discredit an organization which, he had come to believe, had betrayed the silk workers' trust. However, Steiger's account of the strike and the pageant cannot be simply dismissed as a "mysterious 'private printed' attack on the I.W.W. by 'a silk striker' who wasn't in Paterson" or as "a deliberate garbling" of events based on the "biased state report of the strike."[73] Steiger was a genuine New York silk worker who had a close association with the strike and the Reed pageant. His later disillusionment led to many spurious charges, but not all of his comments should be dismissed out of hand.

When Steiger turned from charges of misappropriation to statements about mismanagement, there is the essence if not the kernel of truth. For example, he wrote: "The carelessness displayed in the management of the pageant is indicated by the fact that while 15,000 programs were printed and delivered no one thought of arranging for their sale. I discovered the enormous pile of booklets about 10 o'clock and immediately tried to sell them, but it was too late to dispose of them and three or four days later more than 10,000 were taken to Manhattan Hall; but they were never sold, except as waste paper."[74] The program was an impressive one, with the cover design by Jones and reprinted articles on the strike by Flynn, Koettgen, Boyd, and Haywood. Whether someone forgot to distribute them, as Steiger charged, or whether few could afford to purchase one, the fact is that the programs lost money. Printed at an expense of $282, the combined receipts from advertising and sales totalled only $264.50.

Anyone who bothered to look further than the bottom line of the financial report need not have attributed the $1,996.55 deficit to theft. At some point between the suggestion of the pageant and its performance, the event had turned from a fund-raiser to an artistic spectacular. Even after the emergency meeting at the Liberal Club, there seemed to be little attempt to cut costs. The transportation of the actors by special train required an expenditure of $681.28 and the New York City parade to the Garden consumed an additional $100.65.[75]

The pageant was a theatrical tour de force, but it had become essentially art for art's sake. "Haywood," the New York *Times* commented when the financial statement was released, "went blithely into the show business with the idea that anybody can give a theatrical performance and make money."[76] If this charge is true, he can be excused his naiveté. The New Yorkers should have known better! Steiger, discounting his extravagant charge that the I.W.W. leaders had pocketed part of the receipts, was not far off the mark when he wrote that "it was the reckless, almost criminal negligence of the Intellectuals that made the pageant a failure."[77]

In 1939, when Hapgood penned his autobiography, A Victorian in the Modern World, he included an observation of the young radicals of that day which might have stemmed from his own earlier experiences before World War I: "Fortunately for the cause of revolution, most of these egoistic followers of the cause are likely to fall away before very long. It becomes too arduous for them in the long run; or if not too arduous, they become bored with the dawning success of the movement. It is no longer a spectacular thing for them to play for. There are a few that remain . . . those who see how this social change may be shaped into forms which more perfectly satisfy the needs of men. These are indeed few."[78] Whether Hapgood had Dodge and her circle specifically in mind, the sentiments he expressed applied to at least some of those who had been involved in the Paterson Pageant. Many did not give up their interest in social causes, but almost all turned to other things shortly after the Madison Square Garden performance. The silk strikers, who had expected so much from that event, struggled on without them for over a month longer.

Those whose flight from their Paterson involvement was most abrupt were Reed and Dodge. On June 19 the two sailed aboard the Hamburg-American liner Amerika to spend the summer in Florence. Granville Hicks believed that Reed felt guilty about abandoning the strikers while the battle was still on and the controversy raged over the pageant receipts, but explained that he was exhausted by his efforts to put on the production.[79] Others have not been as sympathetic. John Stuart wrote of Reed after Paterson:

> If Paterson shook Reed, it did not shake him into making a lasting commitment to the labor movement beyond the episode of the strike itself. When his mother was appalled by what he was doing, he told her, "I am not a Socialist temperamentally any more than I'm an Episcopalian. I know that my business is to interpret and live Life, wherever it may be found—whether in the labor movement or out of it." In Paterson he had plunged joyously into his new role and the novelty of the experience gave him profound satisfaction. It was an exciting incident to be cherished in the course of living an exciting Life. But his active responsibility finished when he decided it was finished.[80]

Reed had been genuinely moved by the valiant struggle of the Paterson silk workers and drawn by the larger-than-life figure of Haywood, but the New Jersey strike was only an incident in his quest for "beauty and chance and change." When he returned from Europe, there were other struggles to attract him.[81]

Reed went off to Mexico to cover the revolution there for *Metropolitan Magazine* and Dodge returned to her white walls at 23 Fifth Avenue and "began to make a life" for herself without Reed. He wrote her "vivid, loving letters," but their affair and her involvement with the radical movement did not last more than a year. It was clear that she had become bored with the collection of labor radicals, anarchists, and assorted social activists she had once found so enchanting.[82] She wrote in her memoirs: "Well, I thought, as I faced forward into the year 1915, that is the end of that. I had said good-by forever to Reed in my heart. To the gay, bombastic, and lovable boy with his shining brow; to the Labor Movement, to Revolution, and to anarchy. To the hope of subtly undermining the community with Hutch; and to all the illusions of being a power in the environment. . . . Instinctively I turned more to Nature and Art and tried to live in them."[83]

Dodge gave up her Evenings, ignored "the continuous flood" of letters about "Birth Control, Industrial Relations, Free Speech, and all other forms of social maladjustment," and turned her attention to the Elizabeth Duncan School of Dance. She rented a house near the school in Croton and began to associate with "the affluent German-American owners of the silk mills in Paterson, whom Reed and I had tried to defeat with our pageant! Now we joined in sympathy, working together to help Beauty into the world." At her cottage in suburbia, "while in New York the women hurried to check the population, or to raise wages, or to 'swing' some urgent affair," Dodge and her new friends "sipped . . . wine and watched the beautiful plumes of the asparagus bed move as though a hand had passed over them."[84]

It is not surprising that Flynn, writing to a friend more than thirty years after the Paterson strike, did not recall Dodge with fondness. "Yes," the then-sixtyish Flynn responded to a query, "I remember that horrible rich woman, Mrs. Dodge. She patronized all the poor folks in Paterson insufferably. Was crazy about Jack Reed and other celebrities. Jessie Ashley helped a lot in the pageant. I don't recall Mrs. Dodge doing anything." Flynn would have agreed with the assessment of Dodge by one writer who attended an Evening: "She played with life as if it were a game in which the stakes were not very high."[85]

Others in the Dodge circle who had helped with the pageant were not as abrupt in severing their ties with political or social dissidence. Sanger, "thoroughly despondent after the Paterson debacle," concentrated her attention on birth control, concluding that "the whole question of strikes for higher wages was based on man's economic need of supporting his family, and that this was a shallow principle upon which to found a new civilization." She continued to see many of the old group, spending the summer of 1913 in Provincetown with Mary Heaton Vorse, Hapgood, and Ashley. The latter brought Haywood, in poor health after the Paterson strike, to enjoy the restful atmosphere of Greenwich Village's summer annex. Sanger and Haywood "rambled up and down the beach" together, giving each other the encouragement both needed.[86]

Ashley, now Haywood's mistress, continued her commitment to the silk strikers' cause, serving later as the head of the Paterson Defense League, which raised money for the legal defense of the strike leaders. At the time of her death in 1919, she was hailed as a true friend of labor. Goldman called her a "valiant rebel," and stated that "no other woman of her position had allied herself so completely with the revolutionary movement . . . giving personal service and much of her means."[87] In the winter of 1913–1914, in contrast to the negative response of Dodge, Haywood was able to enlist Steffens, Vorse, Amos Pinchot, and others in establishing the Labor Defense League; in their cases the pageant was not the end to their interest in or association with the I.W.W.[88]

Hapgood seemed to withdraw from any active involvements—he later termed the years between 1914 and 1922 ones of "the deepest discouragement and unhappiness"—but did keep up his contacts with Goldman, whom he visited in Berlin in 1922. By the time he wrote his autobiography, however, he had turned from revolution and revolutionaries. Of the radicals he wrote: "They are with the revolution either because it is an easy substitute for unexciting, painstaking, unheralded, and unnoticed sobriety in life and work, or because it is the only way they see to feed their own ego."[89]

The Paterson Pageant of 1913 set the strike of the New Jersey silk workers apart from similar labor confrontations of the period, but it also demonstrated that the romantic affection of many intellectual rebels of the Village could be both short-lived and irresponsible. The Madison Square Garden performance was, as Flynn observed, the great turning point in the strike. Heralded as the event which would turn the tide to victory, it was instead the beginning of factionalism and defeat.

Chapter 7

Demobilization

> Our folded hands again are at the loom
>   The air
> Is ominous with peace.
> But what we weave you see not through the gloom.
> 'Tis terrible with doom.
>   Beware!
> You dream that we are weaving what you will?
>   Take care!
> Our fingers do not cease:
> We've starved—and lost; but we are weavers still;
> And Hunger's in the mill!
> And Hunger moved the Shuttle forth and back.
>   Take care!
> The product grows and grows.
> A shroud it is; a shroud of ghastly black.
> We've never let you lack!
>   Beware!
> The warp and woof of Misery and Defeat. . . .
>   Take care!
> See how the Shuttle goes!
> Our bruised hearts with bitter hopes now beat:
> The Shuttle's sure—and fleet!—Rose Pastor Stokes,
>   "Paterson," *The Masses*, 5 (November 1913), 11.

The Haledon meeting on the afternoon following the pageant was some-what smaller than usual, but those in attendance were reported as particularly enthusiastic. Flynn, one of the principal speakers, used the occasion to attack Scott's conviction and aroused the crowd with her condemnation of the authorities' violation of free speech and assembly. Then, following remarks in Italian by Giovannitti, Haywood spoke to the gathering about the performance at Madison Square Garden. It was, he said, a success both as a fund-raiser and as a counter to previously biased press accounts of the struggle. "I would be willing to beg, bor-row, or steal to win this strike," he concluded. "This is the life of the I.W.W. and if it takes years, we plan to win this strike." The crowd, according to the account in *Solidarity*, was "elated" by the reports of the pageant's success and by Haywood's promise of victory. Even the New York *Times*, which would have preferred to report otherwise, had to concede from its observation of the Sunday rally that "the success of the Madison Square Garden venture [had] given new hope to the agitator and fresh courage to the strikers."[1]

Just the reverse proved true. Disclosure of the financial details of the pageant certainly was a factor in undermining the strikers' morale. After weeks of being assured that the performance would provide badly needed relief funds, nothing could assuage the disappointment felt by the thousands who had been out of work for over three months. Whether any believed that money had actually been siphoned into the pockets of the show's sponsors, as the hostile press contended, one can understand the resentment felt at Reed's hasty departure for Europe. The fact that Haywood appeared less and less frequently in the strike city following the pageant was also seen as a discouraging sign, as were the rumors that Quinlan had broken with the I.W.W. leader over matters relating to the event.[2]

According to Flynn, however, the seeds of discord associated with the pageant were sown well before the deficit became public knowledge, Reed went off with Dodge, or Haywood and Quinlan absented themselves for days at a time. Flynn, who was dubious about the event from the beginning and took little part in its preparation, was convinced that the publicity gained from the pageant was purchased at the cost of the workers' unity. From the beginning of the Paterson general strike, the I.W.W. had emphasized group leadership, group action, and solidarity; its aim had been to involve every worker in the struggle through mass meetings, mass picketing, and the like. Although divisions between the various branches of the industry and between the immigrants and the English-speaking workers did exist, the union leaders were remarkably successful in developing dedication to the whole. The pageant, in Flynn's view, undermined this. Reed's cast of striker-actors was enormous by most theatrical standards, but the thousand or so who were selected to perform in New York were only a small portion of the total number of strikers. When the special train pulled out of Paterson on the morning of the performance, Flynn later stated, it "left 24,000 disappointed people behind. . . . Between jealousy, unnecessary but very human, and their desire to do something, much discord was created in the ranks." Flynn also maintained that the pageant had the effect of diverting the strikers from more important work. "Turning to the stage of the hall, away from the field of life," the actors played the role of pickets at Reed's daily rehearsals rather than performed this duty in front of the silk mills. As a consequence, "the first scabs got into the Paterson mills while the workers were training for the pageant."[3]

Most recent students of the struggle in Paterson have agreed with

Flynn's view. In Conlin's words, "both the struggle at Paterson and the I.W.W.'s high hopes of a golden future in eastern industry dimmed with the Klieg lights."[4]

The week after the pageant, the press reported less picket activity than before and predicted that the contest would soon come to an end. In a long strike, a crisis is often caused by indications of discouragement or by employers' attempts to detach a portion of the strikers from the main body.[5] This was the situation in Paterson during the second week in June. Few strikers returned to work on Monday, June 9, but as the week wore on the shop owners began reporting more and more of their workers back on the job. The *Guardian* stated that as many as 6,000 former strikers were at work, that almost all of the dyers at the small Dundee mill had returned, and that the Weidmann Company was operating with a large number of its employees. The *Evening News*, less the employers' organ than its Democratic evening competitor, put the number of returning workers at no more than 500, but agreed that "many of the mills" were daily adding to their working force.[6]

The often inflated figures on returnees was one tactic employed by management's supporters in June; another was the circulation of rumors concerning the growing disaffection of the English-speaking ribbon workers. Here again the *Guardian* led the way. Issuing reports that the ribbon weavers in the smaller shops had returned to their looms, it prophesied daily that those in the larger establishments were about to follow suit. On June 11 the paper ran a full story of a purported break in the ribbon branch under the headline "English-Speaking Workers Aroused." It read in part:

> The principal feature in the strike situation today was the division between the English-speaking and foreign workers. No matter how this may be disguised, the fact remains that a serious division has occurred. . . .
>
> A number of elements enter into the situation now . . . which emphasize how the English-speaking workers have been exploited for the benefit of the agitators. To begin, not a thing that has been promised has been done. The strike has dragged along fourteen weeks, the little savings of the workers . . . exhausted, and still these agitators have the effrontery to stand up and declare that they are on the point of winning.

The piece ended with the falacious statement that the pageant had raised "at least $10,000" but that "not a penny" had come to Paterson. "The English-speaking workers," the paper stated, were convinced they would "never see their share."[7]

Amidst signs—both real and imagined—that the strike was cracking, the I.W.W. sought to increase its picketing and the city officials augmented the protection afforded workers who wished to enter the mills. With this situation, it is not surprising that clashes between the two forces increased. On Friday, June 13, several hours after some pickets were handed heavy jail sentences as a result of a skirmish with the police, a potentially serious incident took place. A large contingent of police was escorting a group of strikebreakers from the mills after work when they were met by an angry crowd of pickets. The two groups clashed and the officers, in an attempt to disperse the strikers, fired shots into the air. Most of the strikers ran, but sixty-eight of them stood their ground and were arrested. Flynn, later that evening, urged the strikers to respond to this action by increased picketing the next day and specifically encouraged mothers to take their children on the picket line. She explained that this "would train the children how to act as pickets so they could do the work when grown."[8] A more plausible explanation for her urging was that she hoped for an incident similar to that at the Lawrence station the year before.

Although Flynn encouraged the strikers to greater militance, Haywood promised to fight on "for years" if necessary, and Koettgen reported that the silk owners faced financial ruin if they did not soon capitulate, the resolve of some strikers had clearly weakened even before the night of the Reed production. The subsequent reports of an imminent defection by the ribbon workers did have some basis in fact.

A first sign of independence from the Executive Committee and I.W.W. leadership had come on June 5, when a group of ribbon weavers held a special meeting at Helvetia Hall. The reports of what occurred were imprecise, but those present did discuss the possibility of permitting workers to return to those shops willing to grant wage and hour demands and also weighed a suggestion that an amended list of demands be prepared and submitted to the owners. Later the same day, the Central Strike Committee met, and the question of moving toward a settlement along those lines was hotly debated with the result that a committee of fifteen was appointed to open discussions with the employers.[9] The Paterson press gave this action wide coverage. The *Morning Call* hailed it as "the first definite step" on the part of the shop delegates to meet with the manufacturers, and the *Evening News* interpreted it as proving its own long-held contention that the strikers were "not dominated by the I.W.W. . . . and were willing to talk [settlement] entirely independent" of the union.[10]

Flynn viewed this action by the Central Strike Committee as an attempt by a group of "conservative" English-speaking workers "to wipe the strike off the slate in order to leave the stage free for a political campaign." According to her, Magnet, who was named chairman of the committee and was the man most responsible for its creation, was motivated by his desire for the Socialist party's mayoral nomination.[11] Whether the narrow-silk weaver had ambitions in politics is unclear. But, even if he did seek political office, that aspiration was not at the root of Flynn's suspicions of him. Magnet, as both the I.W.W. leaders and the conservative press understood, was an individual whose unionism ran along rather conventional lines. Ideologically closer to the A.F.L. than most of the other local strike leaders, he increasingly believed that the I.W.W. demands were unattainable and its tactics often counterproductive. His conservatism was not so much a threat to the workers as it was to the revolutionary union which directed the fight.

On this occasion, the position of Flynn and the other I.W.W. leaders was strengthened by the action of the manufacturers. Instead of agreeing to meet with Magnet and his committeemen, thereby perhaps driving a wedge between the union and at least a portion of the striking workers, the Silk Manufacturers' Association refused to modify its stand vis-à-vis a general settlement. On June 10 the owners' organization sent a letter to the Central Strike Committee in response to the request for a meeting. "We affirm the position we took at the beginning of the strike," it informed the members, "and will only treat with our own employees at our own shops after they have returned to work on the same terms that existed when they left." In the cat-and-mouse game that was now being played in Paterson, the manufacturers had apparently interpreted the suggestion of the Central Strike Committee as a sign that the workers were weakening. With the evident decline in picketing in the days prior to the pageant and the return of some of the strikers, the owners did not believe that they had to compromise. They expected a massive return to the mills within days and, when that did not occur, privately admitted their surprise.[12]

Magnet and those who shared his position were caught between the intransigence of the owners on the one hand and the opposition of the I.W.W. leaders on the other. Nothing came of the creation of the fifteen-man committee except the indication that the union's hold on the Central Strike Committee was not absolute. This indication of independence, however, was significant. The Evening News, although clearly disappointed that the ribbon weavers' efforts were fruitless, began to push harder for the shop-by-shop settlement which had been debated at the Helvetia Hall meeting. By mid-June word circulated that sentiment for shop agreements was increasing and that the Executive Committee was about to sanction this approach. Lessig denied this, although he acknowledged that the matter had been discussed, but nothing could stem the stories that shop settlements were imminent. The fact that the *News* was the official organ of the ribbon workers, moreover, tended to give the reports substance.[13]

On June 17 the paper, in a story headlined "Strike Settlement on *News'* Plan Now Seems Likely," stated that the Central Strike Committee had decided on a new approach:

> During the next day or two a committee will be sent to every ribbon and broad-silk manufacturer; and to all the dye shops, to formally present demands . . . and to ask for the consideration of same.
>
> In the event of the manufacturers refusing to grant the demands as presented, they will be asked for a counter proposition by their own employees, and this counter proposition will be considered by the strikers as a body, and if a reasonable basis of settlement can be arrived at, the workers will go back.

If this account was true, it would mean that the strikers in each shop would deal with their own employer, as management had insisted, but that the settlement would be as uniform as possible throughout each branch.[14] The day after this story was published, the *Morning Call* proclaimed: "The strike is practically over."[15]

The *News* was accurate on this occasion, but the optimism of the *Call* proved premature. The first shop committees began meeting with their individual employers on June 18 to reiterate their demands and listen to the owners' counterproposals, but the results were not encouraging. Most of the shop committees reported a reception similar to the one accorded the Frank & Dugan ribbon weavers. Mill manager Moses Straus told those who met with him that the company had concessions to offer but asked whether the shop delegates were empowered to settle. When he was informed that the shop representatives were obliged to report back to the Central Strike Committee, Straus announced that, if that were the case, Frank & Dugan had no concessions to make. For the next two days, the employers made it clear that they would not accept any role for the coordinating body.[16] The silk manufacturers, sensing that total capitulation was at hand, refused to accept anything but a shop-by-shop settlement. The I.W.W., which had to accept the decisions of the Central Strike Committee but had opposed its endorsement of individual delegations, could thank its adversaries for the failure of the plan.

The manufacturers' refusal to accept even a minimal ratifying role for the Central Strike Committee was not, however, the end of the struggle between the I.W.W. loyalists and the nonaffiliated members of the strike's representative body. On the afternoon of June 19, over the heated opposition of Lessig and other union members of the Central Strike Committee, the majority of the delegates from the various mills voted to call shop meetings to poll their fellow workers on the question of a shop-by-shop settlement. At this meeting it was again clear that the greatest support for such a referendum came from the ribbon delegates; the dye-house representatives, with some support from a number of broad-silk committeemen, voted the I.W.W. position that there should be no retreat from the demand for a general settlement. The division in sentiment between the three branches of the industry became even more evident the morning after the meeting of the Central Strike Committee when 5,000 striking dyers assembled at the Riverside Casino and voted their disapproval of agreements by individual shops.[17]

During the interval between the vote of the Central Strike Committee and the scheduled completion of the referendum process on June 26, the I.W.W. leaders were tireless in their efforts to defeat the shop-by-shop settlement proposal. Their response to the rebuff they had suffered within the general representative body was immediate and somewhat unsettling to the Paterson citizenry. At an open-air meeting held at the Doremus Estate the night of June 19, Flynn joined Haywood and Quinlan in urging the industrywide settlement or nothing. In the course of Haywood's speech, termed his "hottest address . . . since his invasion of the city," the big westerner again vowed not to accept defeat. "If this strike is not won on the outside," he declared, "we are going on the inside, and there win it."[18] Three nights later in Boston, Quinlan repeated this implied threat of sabotage before an audience of I.W.W. sympathizers in that city: "God help the machines in the Paterson mills if the strikers go back to work defeated."[19]

All of the I.W.W. strike leaders equated the shop plan with defeat and the Sunday rally at Haledon prior to the referendum was used almost exclusively to attack the Central Strike Committee's action on those grounds. There, and at a strike meeting the following evening in Paterson, Flynn warned against accepting shop settlement: "Our ranks would be broken, and those that were on strike would be compelled to go back under the same conditions. That has been the trouble with the strikes in Paterson for the last forty years, the workers never won a strike because they were settled shop by shop." She concluded her speech on the eve of the voting: "We don't want any concessions. We want our demands."[20]

The morning of Flynn's rally, the I.W.W. had been heartened by the action of the workers in the single most important shop in the city. The

Weidmann dyers, almost 1,500 strong, voted early and announced that shop's overwhelming opposition to the shop-by-shop settlement. The dye-house workers had been expected to stand most solidly behind the I.W.W., but their confirmation of the union position by such a wide margin was important. Since the workers in the other two branches of the industry were dependent upon the dye houses for loom silk and since the Weidmann firm dominated that segment of the industry, even if the weavers were to defy their I.W.W. advisors, they could not long be kept at work. Although the *News* contended that 75 percent of the city's weavers supported the shop-by-shop settlement, even it now doubted that the plan would be approved. The paper's fears were confirmed on the afternoon of June 27 when the Central Strike Committee met at Helvetia Hall to receive the results of the referendum. The tally showed a clear victory for an industrywide settlement. The vote was extremely small—a mere 4,796 workers of the more than 20,000 on strike had participated—but the margin was wide: 3,700 opposed shop settlement and only 1,007 supported it. The dye-house workers voted in the largest numbers and were mainly responsible for the outcome. However, in the weaving establishments, even among the English-speaking element, the vote for the proposal was disappointing.[21]

The defeat of the shop-by-shop settlement plan was a significant victory for the I.W.W. Almost from the beginning of the strike, the silk manufacturers, the local press, and the city authorities had contended that the conflict was the work of a few outside agitators, that the workers had no real grievances, and that the English-speaking operatives would repudiate the radical union. The vote suggested otherwise. Even with the disappointing reports about the pageant and amidst accounts that the Paterson workers were on the verge of starvation, only some 1,000 men and women voted in support of the shop agreements. The Paterson *Guardian* alone attempted an explanation for the result, attributing it to the workers' general impression that the manufacturers would have to settle in a few weeks or risk losing the entire fall trade. The *News*, which took credit for the plan and had been most active in promoting it, simply reported the result of the referendum with no comment.[22] To that paper, the vote was apparently inexplicable.

Edward Zuersher, the ribbon-silk weaver and I.W.W. Local 152 officer at the time of the strike, later tried to explain the workers' vote to the members of the Commission on Industrial Relations. "They thought they could hold their ranks better by staying solid," he testified. "One of the reasons was that if one shop was to settle individually, even though they got their demands, that other workers would be jealous . . . and there would be a break in the ranks." Zuersher, in retrospect, regretted the referendum's result and believed that most shared his feeling. "A big majority of the workers realize that they made a mistake in not settling shop by shop when they first came out," he told the commission in 1914. "That is, there were some shops that, when they were called out on strike, especially in the ribbons, who would grant an eight-hour day and an increase in wages."[23]

Flynn did not agree with Zuersher, however. According to her, the crucial mistake of the postpageant movement for independent shop settlements was the Central Strike Committee's decision to hold the referendum rather than the workers' defeat of the proposal. When the committee "swallowed the bait" offered by the employers and decided to poll worker opinion on shop agreements, this, she emphasized, was construed by management as an indication of weakening. If the owners' tentative proposal for shop agreements had been understood as a sign of their weakening, if the Central Strike Committee had taken the position of "absolute surrender, all of nothing," Flynn contended that the strike would have been won. During the third week in June, she stated after the strike had become history, there had occurred "the most peculiar phenomena" she had ever witnessed in a strike—"the bosses weakened simultaneously with the workers." Even though the strikers defeated the shop proposal, the Central Strike Committee's willingness to hold the referendum had indicated a softening position and had encouraged the manufacturers to assume a more aggressive stance.[24]

Reports from Paterson at the time tend to support the I.W.W. leader's contention concerning the owners. Following the defeat of the referendum, the manufacturers seemed resolved to launch an even more concerted campaign to force their workers back into the mills. On June 28, for example, they announced that pickets' names would be recorded and those identified would be blacklisted from the industry. (The I.W.W. countered defiantly that it would increase the number of pickets.) "There is," the News reported, "every indication that from this point on the strike . . . is going to resolve itself into a bitter war."[25]

The day after the paper voiced its concern, the strike had its second fatality. On Sunday, June 29, a silk striker by the name of Vincenzo Madonna was mortally wounded as he visited with friends on a Paterson street. According to reports in both the New York Times and the New York Call, he was shot as a result of an altercation between his group and a former Paterson silk worker who had left the city to accept a job in the mills of Astoria, Long Island. The local police identified Madonna as part of a band which had attacked the Astoria "scab," a charge the wounded man denied before he died. Whichever version of the actual shooting incident was accurate, there was no disagreement that the death resulted from a clash between strikers and a strike-breaker. The I.W.W. considered Madonna a martyr to the cause and stage-managed a funeral similar to the one held earlier for Modestino.[26]

The day after the Madonna shooting, Flynn went on trial on the charges stemming from her Turn Hall address on the day the general strike was called. It had been the announced intent of the county prose-cutor to try all the strike leaders in consecutive jury proceedings in May, but Quinlan's conviction was not immediately followed by the trials of Flynn, Haywood, Tresca, and Lessig. One reason for the delay, although certainly not the only one, was the application by their attor-neys for a trial before a "foreign" jury. Contending that the accused could not get a fair hearing by a panel made up of Passaic County citizens—an argument which was ridiculed in the press—they sought jurors selected from outside the immediate area. Late in May, Supreme Court Justice Minturn granted their application, the first time such a request had been honored in decades in Passaic, and ordered that the jurors be drawn from Hudson County rolls. With that matter settled, Prosecutor Dunn told the press that the Flynn trial would begin on June 23.[27]

Koettgen welcomed Dunn's announcement. "The trial," he wrote in *Solidarity,* "is likely, in one way, to prove beneficial to the strikers. It will give their cause great and renewed publicity. Elizabeth Gurley Flynn is, thanks to her youth and ability, a public character, whose every utterance, opinion and activity is seized upon by the press. . . . In other words, she makes good copy."[28] Concern that the trial would in-deed prove advantageous to the strikers and might influence the refer-endum scheduled the day after the trial was to begin probably was responsible for the additional delay. In any event, it was not until June 30 that the second I.W.W. trial began.

The night before the Flynn case was to be heard, Chief Bimson disclosed that his department had uncovered a plot to blow up the Strange Silk Mill, a large building which covered a city block and housed over twenty small silk concerns. Bimson's allegation of a resort to sabotage—reminiscent of the one made the morning of the Quinlan trial almost two months before—was denounced by the union as an attempt to influence the Flynn jurors.[29] The coincidence of the two "plots" and the Quinlan and Flynn trials would seem to suggest that the I.W.W. contention had substance. Certainly nothing more was heard of the plot or any subsequent investigation. The authorities, tenacious if not imaginative, showed only their desire to discredit the strike leaders by any means possible.

On Monday, June 30, the twenty-three-year-old Flynn, smartly dressed and with her young son beside her, watched intently as Judge Klenert called the courtroom to order. Haywood was not present, but Quinlan, Tresca, and Lessig were among the spectators. Following the impaneling of the Hudson County jurors, the state called its witnesses —policemen and several mill foremen—who testified to the content of the defendant's speech and the scene around the mills on the morning of February 25. The prosecution sought to create a picture of an angry crowd of several hundred strikers roused to the point of explosion by the fiery words of an impassioned revolutionary. Defense attorneys Marelli and Hunziger, when they had their turn, called a number of workers to the stand to give their quite different account of the strike's beginning hours. On the afternoon of the second day of the trial, Flynn testified in her own behalf, refuting the police testimony and giving her version of what she had said at Turn Hall. After summations by both sides, the jurors retired to decide which of the conflicting sets of witnesses was most credible. The jury was charged before noon on Wednesday and continued its deliberation into the evening. At 9:30 p.m., amidst word that it was "hopelessly deadlocked," it was sequestered for the night. Late in the afternoon of the following day, after another long attempt to reach a verdict, the foreman informed Klenert that the twelve could not agree. The judge, who had earlier urged the jury to break its deadlock, accepted the impasse and dismissed the panel. The prosecution immediately promised a speedy retrial, but four days later Assistant Prosecutor Force announced that the four indicted I.W.W. leaders would not be tried until early September.[30]

The strikers and their sympathizers were understandably pleased at the outcome of the Flynn proceedings. But their celebration was sobered by an unexpected turn in the courtroom while the jury was out. On Thursday morning, when it appeared that there would be no decision in the Flynn case, the authorities apparently determined to snatch their victories where they could. As courtroom principals and spectators milled around waiting for some word from the juryroom, Quinlan was suddenly brought before Judge Klenert for sentencing on his earlier conviction. The Irish socialist stood in disbelief as he heard himself receive a fine of $500 and a term of from two to seven years in Trenton State Prison. He was locked away in the Passaic County Jail by the time the Flynn jury declared its deadlock. On Monday, following the long holiday weekend during which it was impossible to obtain his release on bail pending appeal, Quinlan was deposited at Trenton.[31]

The same morning that he sentenced Quinlan, Judge Klenert arraigned editor Scott on a grand jury indictment of criminal libel. This charge stemmed from an editorial Scott had written in the March 29 number of the *Weekly Issue* and was quite separate from his earlier conviction under the 1902 anarchist statute, which he was then appealing. Judge Klenert, who had sentenced Scott to from one to fifteen years for his attack on the Paterson police, set bail on the criminal libel charge at $1,000, which ordinarily would have sent the editor to join Quinlan in "Radcliff's Hotel." Scott, however, appeared in the Court of Quarter Sessions with Dr. Morris Korshet, a well-known Passaic socialist, who furnished bond and thus procured the journalist's release. Although obviously disappointed at the failure to win a conviction against Flynn, the forces of law and order had some reason to celebrate on the occasion of the nation's birthday: Quinlan was in jail facing a long term in prison; Scott had been convicted on one charge and was under indictment for a second; and Flynn, Tresca, Haywood, and Lessig were threatened with conviction on assorted charges. Meanwhile, almost forgotten in the other legal battles associated with the strike, Boyd was beginning his second week in the County Jail, still unable to raise $4,000 bond.[32]

Every kind of pressure was applied to strikers and their supporters in the weeks following the defeat of the referendum. Koettgen, who to that point had managed to escape the legal difficulties of his I.W.W. associates, was arrested on July 16 on the charge of assault and battery, stemming from his physical response to a striking dyer's statement that he was a "grafter." His confinement in the County Jail was brief, thanks to the $500 bail provided by his brother Frederick, but he too was now threatened by further legal action. On the day that Koettgen's temper precipitated his arrest, the mayor of Haledon began to see the implications of his support of the Paterson strikers; Passaic County Sheriff Radcliff notified Brueckman that some silk manufacturers had complained of the lack of protection afforded them in the socialist borough. Mayor Brueckman and two of his deputies were arraigned before the Justice of the Peace on charges that they had been in a crowd which had threatened a group of men working at one of the silk mills. On July 21, the same day that it dismissed charges against the man accused of the Madonna shooting, the Passaic Grand Jury indicted Brueckman for malfeasance in office. The detailed charge specified that he had appointed deputies and town marshals who were I.W.W. supporters and had no qualifications to serve as law officers, had not maintained law and order in Haledon, and had taken part personally in picketing the silk mills. The day of Brueckman's arraignment and release on $2,000 bail, the Haledon Council refused a permit application for an I.W.W. meeting.[33] By the end of the third week in July, the authorities had done almost everything possible to intimidate the strike's leadership and its most prominent supporters.

During this period, reports of a break in the strike ranks increased. There was no rush back to the mills, and the I.W.W. was able to stem and even reverse the tide for a time, but slowly the stalemated situation began to shift in favor of the employers. July began on an encouraging note for the union: workers at the Weidmann Silk Dyeing Company, an estimated 1,000 strong, met at the Riverside Casino to discuss the rumor that the company was willing to offer a minimum wage of $12 per week and a nine-hour day and reaffirmed their position not to accept any compromise. But the situation in the other two branches of the industry was not as bright. With the marked decline in picketing activity, despite the constant urging of the strike leaders, scattered numbers of strikers in the weaving shops returned to work. At the ribbon delegates' meeting on July 2, representatives from two establishments told of tempting concessions offered by their employers: two-thirds of the over ninety weavers at John Hand and Sons were already at work under a 10 percent pay increase and twenty highly skilled workers at the Miller Hat Band Company were reported anxious to accept a promised 15 percent increase and a nine-hour day. Receipt of these reports prompted the delegates to call a general branch meeting for July 7 to hear shop committees from every ribbon shop in order to determine whether there should be a change in strategy. The situation among the broad-silk weavers was similar to that in the ribbon branch of the industry. Although most were holding firm for a general settlement, shop meetings were held daily, and some of the weavers in the smaller shops had gone back to work.[34] With the exception of the dye-house workers, therefore, sentiment for separate settlement appeared to be increasing among the strikers.

An estimated 2,000 ribbon weavers attended the July 7 general meeting at Helvetia Hall. The subsequent account of what transpired indicated the situation in that branch as the strike entered its twentieth week. Of the forty-one establishments for which shop reports were made, twenty-three reported that one or more workers were back at work. The total number still on strike in these shops exceeded the returnees by a margin of 2,171 to 380. Only five shops had a majority back on the looms, and these were among the smaller ribbon concerns. At the five New York shops represented at the mass meeting, the picture was somewhat different: a greater percentage had returned than in New Jersey, although those on strike also were in the majority by a margin of two to one. Even taking into account the possibility of some deliberate distortion on the part of the ribbon branch's shop committees, the most skilled workers in the industry were not willing to capitulate.[35]

On the day of the Helvetia Hall mass meeting, eighty-six firms in the Silk Manufacturers' Association issued a statement declaring that they would not deviate from their position on the ten-hour day, fifty-five-hour week. Recognizing that some of the smaller firms had granted a shorter day, conditional on its eventual acceptance by the majority of the silk firms, the signers declared that there would be "no use in parleying about the matter" and that there would be no acceptance of the eight- or nine-hour day unless this were accepted in every silk-producing state. This "ultimatum" of July 7 was accompanied by the announcement that every silk mill in the city of Paterson would be open the next day to receive workers willing to accept the fifty-five-hour week; those who refused to return at a date to be specified, would not be rehired.[36]

The announcement by the association, an organization dominated by the larger firms in the industry, made compromise on the increasingly prominent issue of the shorter day unlikely. It also made it evident that the nine-hour concession made by some of the smaller firms, contingent on its later acceptance by all, represented only a short-term gain by a few workers. Although the acquiescing employers may have been acting in good faith and under economic pressures which the larger concerns did not feel to such an extent, the workers were suspicious of their motives and concerned that they were being used to break the strike and pressure their comrades back under the old conditions. Thus, the day following the issuance of the "ultimatum" by the eighty-six larger companies, a number of those who had returned on the conditional nine-hour basis rejoined the strike.[37]

Increasingly, the situation fluctuated: workers would return to a shop one day and walk out the next. The number at work seemed to increase at least slightly each day, but as long as the larger establishments—such as Weidmann, Henry Doherty, Frank & Dugan, and Pelgram & Meyer—remained obdurate and their workers did not weaken, there appeared to be no end to the strike. The smaller firms and their employees operated on the periphery of the action; their maneuvers, straws in the wind which were variously interpreted by the generals on each side, were only skirmishes in the real battle.

The first significant break in the strikers' ranks came from among the ribbon workers employed by the Smith & Kauffman Company in New York City on July 18. As mentioned earlier, there had been a number of prior indications that the ribbon workers' allegiance to the I.W.W.'s "all or nothing" stance was softening. Following the referendum on the shop-by-shop settlement, a plan which owed much to the non-union leaders in that branch of the industry, some ribbon shop committees had continued to hold discussions with their employers. At the increasingly frequent sessions of the narrow-silk weavers at Helvetia Hall, shop delegates reported a few employers' apparent willingness to grant concessions on hours (however tentative) and affirmed that some had returned to work to test their firms' sincerity. Many of these workers did not remain on the job for long—the phenomenon of work and strike was most pronounced in the ribbon shops—but the fact that numbers did return, even briefly, was indicative of their willingness to settle by shop or branch if possible. At a mass meeting of the ribbon workers on July 16, in the course of reports from shop representatives present, the delegation from Smith & Kauffman announced that a meeting with management had been arranged for the following day and that this conference, the first direct communication since the strike began, might result in "some good." Since this statement was given in the context of similar reports from other shops and followed comparable discussions with management by a number of Paterson shop committees, the Smith & Kauffman report did not elicit much comment.[38]

The situation at Smith & Kauffman was not wholly similar to that existing in the New Jersey ribbon shops, however. The weavers in that New York establishment had gone on strike in sympathy with the Paterson workers with the expectation that their walkout would be of short duration. Although they had agreed to remain out until all units had settled, a number had objected to making this commitment from the outset and some had even voted against the strike for this reason. Nevertheless, the Smith & Kauffman employees joined the strike and even played a part in convincing other silk workers in the New York City area to join them. However, the enthusiasm of the New York ribbon weavers began to wane after the first month of the strike. Unlike their Paterson counterparts, whose resolve was continually being strengthened by the morale-boosting rallies, parades, and daily meetings, the out-of-state strikers were isolated and more easily discouraged. Steiger later alleged that his fellow workers became so disheartened that the shop committee sent representatives to Paterson "with the express instructions to bring back good reports, whether they were true or not."[39]

The Paterson Pageant, which the New York workers had helped to finance with a loan when it appeared that it would have to be canceled, proved a particularly bitter disappointment. Yet, that financial failure did not cause the Smith & Kauffman strikers to desert. Reluctant to return to work with nothing gained after months without pay, they still preferred to believe the I.W.W. rhetoric that the strike was about to be won. Even the later embittered Steiger continued his involvement in the strike, spending considerable time in Paterson and taking a leading part in attempts to raise relief funds; as late as mid-July, he and Ashley were in charge of the campaign to solicit money from socialist sources in New York. By this time, however, the situation of the workers was becoming desperate and relief agencies could not handle strikers' requests for aid. As contributions dwindled, the idea of a compromise settlement gathered support. Increasingly, I.W.W. insistence on industrywide acceptance of the original demands was seen by the New Yorkers as unrealistic.[40]

Steiger's account of the events leading up to the Smith & Kauffman settlement cannot be substantiated from other sources, and in a number of instances, his book's evident hostility to the I.W.W. clearly influenced his comments, but there is no obvious fabrication in his recounting of the details behind the agreement. Early in July, he wrote, he was informed by a friend that the Smith & Kauffman firm was quietly offering to train weavers to replace those on strike and that the company was taking this course because it believed that the strikers did not wish to settle. Convinced that this was a good time to attempt to assure the owners that the workers did want a settlement and were willing to discuss terms, Steiger asked his informant to pass that message along. Several days later, he was told that the company would be interested in meeting with a shop representative. Steiger claimed he was encouraged by some of his confidants to pursue the matter and thus he arranged an informal meeting with a company spokesman. As a result of their conversation, the owner's man proposed that additional workers be included in later talks with him. He further suggested that these be "accidental" meetings, since he was as "unwilling to ask for a committee as [the strikers] were to offer to send one." Following a number of discussions held at scattered places around Harlem, Steiger reported what had been done at a full shop meeting. The Smith & Kauffman workers endorsed his actions and authorized a formal meeting at which the two sides might reach an agreement. It was this action which the shop delegate reported at the branch meeting in Paterson on July 16.[41]

On July 18 a settlement at Smith & Kauffman was signed and announced to the press. It provided for a nine-hour day and a tentative price list which represented 20 percent less than the requested 1894 schedule but some 10 percent over what had been paid before the strike. The price list was made contingent upon its acceptance by 60 percent of the Paterson and New York ribbon firms and their weavers, but the shorter work week carried no such provision. Since the head of Smith & Kauffman was the vice-president of the Silk Association of America and his foreman was chairman of the wage committee of that organization, the agreement suggested association acceptance and seemed the break which had been so long awaited.[42]

The day after the agreement in New York City, Steiger and some of his New York associates attended a branch delegates' meeting at Helvetia Hall in Paterson. According to him, they were cheered when they completed their report of the agreement with the company. The shop delegates who were present, estimated as representing some 80 percent of the Paterson ribbon shops, discussed the New York wage terms at some length and then voted to accept local settlements along the same lines. The proposal of the nine-hour day, put to a separate vote, was endorsed with little opposition. The situation in the ribbon branch of the industry had thus become dependent upon whether the local companies would agree to the shortened workday and the tentative price schedule of the New York firm. Shop delegates were authorized to visit all of the employers to discuss such a compromise.[43]

The ribbon weavers were the first to act independently of the Central Strike Committee and to agree to accept less than the original demands. However, both the Paterson press accounts at the time and Steiger in his later *Memoirs* preferred to attribute the break in the strikers' ranks to others. Steiger, in that portion of his account of the New York settlement which most clearly showed his antiunion bias, claimed that I.W.W. machinations were responsible for his action in opening negotiations. According to him, several weeks before conversations were begun with the representative of the Smith & Kauffman firm, Koettgen, Lessig, and a third Paterson union leader had requested a meeting with some of the New York silk strikers. In the course of their discussion, the Paterson men supposedly admitted that the strike situation was bleak, and Lessig was reported to have suggested that the New Yorkers "try to get a chance to go back to work." Steiger interpreted this as evidence of "the hypocrisy and double dealing of the celebrated I.W.W. leaders" and as evidence that they were willing to accept the New Yorkers' defeat and then blame them for the loss of the general strike. By this interpretation, the I.W.W. cast the Smith & Kauffman workers aside weeks before Steiger decided to act independent of the Central Strike Committee.[44]

A Paterson *Guardian* story on the day of the Smith & Kauffman settlement lacked the detail (or the imagination) evident in the later *Memoirs of a Silk Striker*, but it too saw the ribbon workers' action as a "defensive" one. The narrow-ribbon weavers, whom the paper termed "the most intelligent group of the workers who went on strike," were pictured as forced to seek a compromise settlement because of the evident weakening of the dyers and the broad-silk weavers, who were "straggling into the mills in ever-increasing numbers." The *Guardian* explained that the ribbon workers, "wholly unsustained by any united support from the other workers," and suffering "undue hardship . . . because of the lack of stability displayed by the other workers," had taken the only sensible course.[45]

Whether one accepts or rejects such face-saving interpretations— and earlier indications of the ribbon weavers' interest in accepting some compromise settlement argues for the latter—by noon on July 18 the I.W.W. leaders could no longer boast of the silk workers' solidarity. Following the ribbon-shop delegates' votes at the morning meeting at Helvetia Hall, it remained only to see what the workers in the other two branches of the industry would do. The first signs did not promise a continuation of the strike. Without waiting for the delegates' meetings in the dye and broad-silk branches, the Central Strike Committee assembled shortly after the ribbon workers had ended their meeting. Once again Helvetia Hall was the scene of discussion on shop-by-shop settlement and, for the second time in one day, the I.W.W. position to hold out for a general agreement was rejected. After the receipt of reports concerning the number of silk concerns willing to grant concessions and a heated debate on the merits of individual agreements, the Central Strike Committee voted its endorsement of shop settlements on the basis of the nine-hour day and pay increases between 10 and 20 percent.[46]

At an outdoor meeting held at the Doremus Estate on Water Street that evening, the I.W.W. organizers pleaded for the continuation of the strike and attacked the Central Strike Committee's capitulation. Ettor, Tresca, Lessig, and Haywood shared the platform, but the latter was the center of attention. The Paterson *Morning Call*, displaying a sympathy which had never been apparent when the strike was at its peak, described the I.W.W. leader as he appeared that evening. "There are few things in the strike that were so painful to witness as were the feeble efforts of Haywood," it began: "This big, strong, robust type of manhood who came here in the perfection of physical health five months ago . . . was but the shadow of himself. His sunken cheeks and flabby white skin, his painful effort to stand with a small table for support, and the flopping of his clothing, many sizes too large for him with his fifty pounds lost weight, told all too plainly of a wrecked physical strength." The paper saw the Water Street meeting as the I.W.W.'s pathetic last hurrah in Paterson; while the leaders spoke of the victory that was about to be won, their faces told of "the total collapse of the strike."[47]

The following day, however, the "collapse" did not look quite as certain. At the Sunday meeting at Haledon, an estimated crowd of 5,000 responded with surprising enthusiasm to the urgings of Haywood, Tresca, Flynn, Lessig, Koettgen, and Scott. The New York *Call*, which had been predicting a general return to work on the following Monday, was impressed enough by the warm response to write that it was "not improbable that a large percentage, if not practically all, of the strikers" would refuse to go back.[48]

There were few pickets around the silk mills on Monday, July 21, despite the I.W.W. speakers' call for a massive picketing effort, but the number of workers who returned to their jobs was nevertheless small. The workers in the few shops which had already reached at least tentative agreement with the employers began work at 7 a.m.; the majority of the strikers in all branches of the industry awaited the result of meetings between their shop committees and management. This was true of the ribbon weavers as well as the workers in the dye houses and broad-silk shops.

By quitting time on the first full workday following the Central Strike Committee's endorsement of shop settlements, it was clear that the employers were pursuing as independent a course as the strikers. In the ribbon branch, where the situation was reported most fully, the early company responses varied widely. J. Rosen & Sons offered its weavers a 10 percent wage increase on one class of goods and no reduction in hours; Deise Hat Band Company followed the Smith & Kauffman proposal; Augusta Ribbon Company agreed to a modest pay increase but refused to offer the nine-hour day; Dexter & Lambert and the large Brandes Company refused any concessions; and Corbett Brothers insisted its weavers had to return to work before discussing terms. By Monday night the possibility of settlement in the ribbon segment of the silk industry, which had seemed so bright after the Smith & Kauffman agreement, did not look promising. The workers in shops where meetings had already been held and terms discussed had voted not to return without the nine-hour day. The ribbon manufacturers, on their part, were adhering to the decision of the larger firms not to grant a reduction in hours unless this became the rule in every silk-producing state. Only 7 small New Jersey firms of the 139 reporting had conceded the shorter day.[49]

On Tuesday, as shop meetings were held in every branch of the industry and more firms reported the return of some of their workers, the Central Strike Committee announced the suspension of its relief agencies. The contributions needed to run its food store, it told the press, had fallen so precipitously that it could no longer operate. That evening, obviously influenced by the critical relief problem as well as the workers' gradual return to the mills, Flynn came as near as she ever would to concede defeat. She told an audience of strikers:

> You realize what this strike is as well as I do. If the silk workers of Paterson had stood together longer they would have won. We have a serious situation . . . that none of us are responsible for. If there is any blame for this strike being lost it is up to those who threw up the sponge at the last minute, when victory was at their door, and went back to work.
>
> The result of their going back has had its effect already. It was shown in the stopping of relief funds. All over the country they have stopped sending funds in because the workers have gone back, and the word has spread that the strike in Paterson is over. There is no one to blame but your fellow workers who deserted you.

Flynn told the Water Street gathering that she would stand behind them if they thought they could "stick it out for a few weeks longer." Those who had reached the end of their endurance, however, were counseled to make the best settlements possible and then work to strengthen their organization "so that when the occasion to strike comes again," they would be "better organized and stronger." Ettor, who was in Paterson almost daily during the last month of the strike, followed Flynn and seconded her advice. Haywood, reportedly in New York too ill to attend, was spared the pain of acknowledging failure.[50]

The ribbon weavers took the first step toward ending the general strike of the Paterson silk workers, but it was the capitulation of the group which had stood most loyally behind the I.W.W. that forced Flynn and the other I.W.W. organizers to concede that the strike was over. On Tuesday, July 22, the dyers' helpers and finishers at the Weidmann, National, and Geering plants returned to work in such numbers that all three were operating at near capacity; only the smaller dye shops remained idle. That evening, the scheduled meeting of the dye-house workers was so poorly attended that Lotta was forced to postpone discussion for a day. At his request, the papers ran a front-page announcement calling on the workers in that branch to attend the Wednesday night meeting at Turn Hall to discuss whether to continue the strike, but the response was not much better than on the evening before. Only an estimated 150 dyers took part in the discussion—the great majority had made their decision at the plant gates and apparently saw no need to ponder what was already fact—and no formal action was taken. Instead, under Lotta's urging, the Turn Hall loyalists postponed a vote once again and called for a mass meeting the next day at the Doremus Estate.[51]

For the dyers and the broad-silk workers, the strike was in fact over. All that remained to be done was to call it off officially. No one, however, seemed willing to take that step. At the mass rally on Thursday, it was decided to place that responsibility with the Central Strike Committee, after it had received reports from each of the shop delegates, at its meeting the following Monday. But when that committee met at Helvetia Hall on July 28, it refused to make a recommendation to the mass rally scheduled to receive it the following night. After four hours of reports, which indicated that only twenty-one silk firms had made any concession concerning hours, and debate on whether to declare the strike over, a decision was put off. The nearest thing to one was the general agreement that there would be no official statement until the shorter work day was granted. This position was endorsed by those who attended the Water Street mass meeting the following evening.[52]

The strike was never declared over by the Central Strike Committee, the mass of workers, or the I.W.W. The New York *Call* declared the strike lost on July 29, but there was no similar statement at any time in the union newspapers. *Solidarity*, which had carried lengthy accounts of the struggle from the time of its inception, simply ceased mentioning it. In the July 26 issue, there was no word about Paterson![53]

The first to break and the last to give in were the Paterson ribbon weavers. On Tuesday, July 22, the day the largest number of broad-silk workers and dye-house helpers returned to their jobs, the press committee of the narrow-silk branch issued a statement declaring that the fight for the nine-hour day and a wage increase was still on. The next day, at a mass meeting at Helvetia Hall, these most skilled of the silk workers voted not to accept anything less than the Smith & Kauffman settlement, declared an assessment on those workers who returned to shops which had agreed to terms, and stated their intention of opening a relief station to help those in need. Regardless of what action the broad-silk weavers and the dye-house employees took, the ribbon men announced their commitment to continue the strike. When thirty-nine ribbon shops in the city issued a statement that there would be no compromise on the shorter work week, the situation in that branch seemed to stand as it had for weeks.[54]

Despite the resolution to stand firm on a settlement along the lines of the Smith & Kauffman agreement, the ribbon workers in Paterson began to return to work in growing numbers during the last week in July. By the end of the month only twelve shops reported their weavers still on strike: Sherr Silk Company, Johnson & Cowdin, Universal

Weaving Company, Dexter & Lambert, Harris Silk Company, Ashley & Bailey, Passaic Silk Company, Augusta Silk Company, Helvetia Silk Company, Corbett Brothers, Pelgram & Meyer, and Frank & Dugan. The number of silk workers in Paterson on strike, almost all in the ribbon branch, stood at approximately 2,000.[55]

At the close of work on Monday, August 4, only 600 workers at Johnson & Cowdin were still holding out for the nine-hour day and the New York price list. With the exception of the workers in some mills who walked out for a day or two at a time, the strike which had once paralyzed virtually the entire Paterson industry had dwindled down to a contest between one ribbon-silk company and its employees. The rest of the narrow-silk workers, almost all of whom had been forced to accept something less than the Smith & Kauffman terms, continued to express their dissatisfaction and issued regular threats to resume the strike. At the scheduled meetings of the ribbon weavers at Helvetia Hall, talk continued of assessments to aid the Johnson & Cowdin strikers, but there is little evidence that this was done; the support of the Johnson & Cowdin weavers was more rhetorical than real. Still, the tone of the gatherings made it evident that the ribbon workers were not happy with the treatment they were receiving at work. Those firms which had promised to discuss wages and hours once their people returned, showed little inclination to honor their words. As a result, at a meeting on August 13, the ribbon workers announced the plan to strike one manufacturer at a time, forcing a settlement in one shop and then striking another shop to force it into an agreement. The Paterson Ribbon Manufacturers' Association met the following day and responded to this threat. The Johnson & Cowdin strike, a spokesman for that organization announced after the meeting, was directed "against all Paterson ribbon makers" and would therefore be dealt with in that light. In response to the one-shop-at-a-time strategy announced by the workers, the members of the association agreed to offer every assistance to the struck company, even to the point of providing workers to operate its looms.[56]

This exchange of threats was the last on both sides. On August 20, Pelgram & Meyer, one of the largest ribbon companies in Paterson, reached an agreement with its workers. The settlement, which included a wage increase of between 5 and 15 percent but no reduction in hours, could not be construed as much of a victory for the weavers. But it was concession enough to reduce the discontent which had threatened to provoke a walkout in that shop. More importantly, the settlement prompted the Johnson & Cowdin firm to make a new offer to its weavers. Two days after the Pelgram & Meyer settlement was announced, the last large group of striking ribbon weavers accepted the company offer of a 5 percent wage increase. On Monday, August 25, the Johnson & Cowdin weavers returned to work.[57]

The continuation of the ribbon strike at the large Johnson & Cowdin facility, after almost all of the weavers and dyers had returned to their own shops, captured much of the attention of the community during August. The I.W.W., which was not involved in the attempt of the ribbon workers to salvage something from their long months on strike, no longer was the center of concern. However, this did not mean that the union leaders had ceased their activities in the New Jersey silk center. Nor did the virtual end of the strike mean that the Paterson authorities were willing to ignore the "outside agitators" whom they blamed for their difficulties. Toward the end of July the City Council agreed to dispense with the services of the special police, which by then had cost the citizens an estimated $10,000, but the regular law officers continued to keep a watchful eye on the strike leaders.[58]

Quinlan was the first to discover that the authorities were unwilling to forgive and forget. After three weeks of incarceration at Trenton, Quinlan had been released on $5,000 bail provided by *The Appeal to Reason* and had arrived back in Paterson on July 24. He took little part in strike activities upon his return—which lent support to the rumors that he had broken with the I.W.W. leadership—but instead became increasingly active in local socialist politics. His first stop in Paterson after his release on bail was at S.P.A. headquarters, where he was welcomed as a socialist hero by Glanz and other local party activists. While his former I.W.W. associates held rallies to urge the strikers to hold out, even while the strike was clearly crumbling around them, Quinlan spoke at political gatherings and argued for the election of socialist candidates as the best method to help the workers improve their condition. It was not long before his hot tongue got him into trouble again. On July 30, he was arrested for comments made at an S.P.A. meeting two days before and taken before Recorder Carroll on the charge of disorderly conduct. The recorder's initial sentence of one year in the county jail was reduced to ten days after Quinlan had spent one night in custody, but the message was clear—the city was in no mood to endure further agitation from the convicted Irishman. The *Evening News* attacked the treatment of the feisty agitator, but even it wondered at his provocative actions. "Quinlan," it wrote, "is a very foolish individual and used very poor judgement. He is of that rather odd type of irresponsibles who twist the lion's tail while his head is in the lion's mouth."[59] Quinlan, alone among the leaders of the general strike, would learn the full cost of challenging the political and economic establishment in Paterson.

While Quinlan was waging his own private war, the I.W.W. leaders were winding down the strike and at the same time denying it had ended. On August 1, the Children's Committee announced that the strikers' children would be brought back to Paterson for reunion with their families within the week. Two days later, under the care of Ashley, they quietly returned to the silk city. The tactic which had worked so well in Lawrence and which was designed to elicit sympathy and financial support for the strike, had not accomplished the desired end. The failure of the Paterson authorities to overreact minimized the outpouring of sympathy and the evacuation probably cost the relief fund more than it gained in donations.[60]

The I.W.W. continued to hold meetings in Paterson well into August —regularly scheduled gatherings at the Water Street headquarters on Tuesday and Friday evenings and an occasional rally at a new site in Haledon—but the crowds of thousands who had once listened to the union organizers dwindled to a few hundred at best. Flynn, Tresca, and Ettor appeared at most of the meetings, but Haywood and Quinlan rarely were in attendance. Most of the day-to-day work fell to Koettgen and Lessig, who tried to maintain the strike organization and worked to enlist members in Local 152. Both men refused to acknowledge defeat. In his reports in Solidarity, Koettgen promised that the silk workers of Paterson would be "heard from again in the near future," and Lessig, almost a year after the general return to the mills, told the Commission on Industrial Relations that the silk conflict had been "deferred" but not ended.[61]

Chapter 8

The Bitter Aftermath

... the flood of criticism about the strike is unabated, becoming more vicious all the time, drifting continually from the actual facts and involving as a matter of course the policies and strike tactics of the I.W.W. It is rather difficult for me to separate myself from my feelings about the Paterson strike, to speak dispassionately. I feel that many of our critics are people who stayed at home in bed while we were doing the hard work of the strike.—Elizabeth Gurley Flynn, "The Truth About the Paterson Strike," speech delivered at the New York Civic Club on January 31, 1914.

The New York *Call*, which had given valuable support to the New Jersey strikers, was alone among the once sympathetic journals in admitting that the strike had been something less than a success. On July 29, the day that socialist paper announced that the Paterson conflict was over, it attempted to assess what the twenty-two week struggle had cost those concerned. It concluded that everyone had lost something. The workers, it estimated, had denied themselves over $5,000,000 in wages, the manufacturers had lost as much in orders, the small landlords in the city had been deprived of a good portion of their rental income for periods ranging from two to five months, and "a score of small shop keepers, butchers, grocers, and clothiers were forced to close." Beyond the financial implications of the strike, which left few of the Paterson inhabitants wholly untouched, the paper counted five lives lost: Modestino and Madonna, two strikers who had committed suicide, and a landlord who took his own life because of financial difficulties caused by lost rents. Finally, it estimated that some 2,500 workers had left the city during the strike and that perhaps another 2,000 would be forced to seek employment elsewhere because of blacklisting or the closing of some small silk companies.[1]

Nowhere in this early assessment was there an indication that the strikers had gained any meaningful concessions as a result of their protracted fight. The multiple-loom system was not withdrawn from the broad-silk shops where it had been introduced, the fifty-five-hour week remained in effect in almost every establishment in the city, and only a few weavers had received any increase in wages. The Paterson strike, as later students of it have agreed, was deemed a defeat for both the New Jersey silk workers and the I.W.W.[2]

But this was not the impression conveyed by strike leaders, union spokesmen, some upper-class sympathizers, and most radical publications in the months following the operatives' return to the mills. The I.W.W. loyalists not only continued to maintain that the strike was still on, but refused to acknowledge that the silk workers had returned to the mills even temporarily defeated. The *International Socialist Review*, the left-wing socialist monthly which stood closest to the industrial union, shared this position. Although associate editor Mary E. Marcy did concede in the September 1913 number that "many of the demands were not granted," the tone of her editorial was decidedly positive. The Paterson strikers, she informed her readers, had "gained a shorter workday and a militant organization that [would] put them in a far better position in the next battle."[3]

The following month, in a tribute to Haywood, still in poor health as a result of his exertions in behalf of the New Jersey workers, a *Review* piece repeated this optimistic assessment:

> Haywood simply would not consider defeat and Comrade Koettgen . . . reports that unguessed benefits have been gained for the strikers through their long and gallant stand. Mill conditions have been much improved in many ways and the fighting spirit of the strikers is still holding the banner aloft. When conditions are ripe, they are ready to go out on strike again, down to the last man, woman and child. Koettgen also reported that the I.W.W. has a strong local in Paterson composed of several thousand dues-paying members and several thousand more who will throw their hearts into the movement as soon as they begin to recover from the last long fight.
>
> Haywood fought with the courage, the wisdom and the strength of ten men in Paterson, and the great work he accomplished there will live as long as the conflict between Capital and Labor endures.[4]

Solidarity published an even more exultant account of the material benefits derived from the strike, reprinting the assessment made by Giovanni DiGregorio in Tresca's former paper, *Il Proletario*. DiGregorio, who had been in Paterson during the struggle, thought "it necessary to disprove the idea that the strike ended in a fiasco." If one believed his account, the workers had achieved a great victory. "Is it not true that the mills now work only nine hours a day instead of ten as they did before the strike?" he asked. "Is it not true that there were gains in wages ranging from 15 to 25 percent? Is it not true that the four-loom system exists only in name and not in fact?"[5] Disinterested observers would have had to reply in the negative to DiGregorio's string of rhetorical questions, but denials, whether published or uttered, did not silence those who wished to see a victory in the outcome.

Even those I.W.W. supporters who admitted that the workers' condition in the silk industry had not been much improved as a result of the lengthy strike, still managed to be optimistic about the outcome. Victory and defeat could be judged by more than a single standard. In the months following the strike, a favored measure among the devout came to be the psychological rather than the material benefits of the struggle.

Goldman and Alexander Berkman were frank in admitting that the strike had been lost by the usual dollars and cents definition, but both viewed the Paterson battle as a valuable educational experience for the workers. Although they acknowledged that the strikers returned to their shops with the same hours and wages as before, the two anarchists emphasized that they had resumed work with a "stronger and more conscious revolutionary spirit."[6] Killingbeck and Quinlan agreed, differing only on what this educational experience meant for the future. In their view, socialism rather than anarchism would be the chief beneficiary of the aroused class consciousness of the silk workers: the strike had been a six-month-long school from which those involved had emerged with a feeling of solidarity and working-class commitment.[7]

There were, of course, those who saw the result as a total defeat for the Paterson strikers and the revolutionary union which had assumed leadership. The early editorials of the New York *Times* can be considered typical of the conservative press's reaction to the resumption of work. In its view the silk workers had gained nothing and had lost $5,250,000 in wages "for no other purpose . . . than to gratify the vanity of Haywood, Quinlan, and Elizabeth Gurley Flynn." The paper professed sympathy for the employees' losses and their prolonged suffering, but applauded the sound defeat of the I.W.W. "The firm stand of the Paterson officials and the businessmen of the city has tended to defeat an organization which is the avowed enemy of Government," it declared on July 25, "and the whole nation should be grateful to Paterson."[8]

The A.F.L. was also quick to comment on the strikers' return to the mills, using the occasion to boost its own brand of unionism and to attack the motives and tactics of its revolutionary competitor. Silent after its withdrawal from Paterson following the unsuccessful organizing drive in April, the federation was outspoken in its condemnation of the I.W.W. role in the silk strike. In the August number of the *American Federationist*, Gompers used Paterson to point out the general fallacies of the I.W.W.-led strikes:

We are not averse to inaugurating a fight, even a struggle of the unorganized, if there is some assurance that better things will come of it or that constructive results can be evolved. Leadership aiming at constructive policies and purposes is in strong contrast to leadership which lures the workers into unwise undertakings by holding out the belief that their past sufferings can be abolished forever, and that workers can immediately become the dominators of the situation. . . .

Neither wisdom nor sobriety has characterized those who dashed into the problems of Paterson and promised to work immediate transformation. Men and women have gone among perturbed suffering workers and inflamed their sense of injustice, found the feeling for revolt and incited the expectation of impossible results from mere agitation without practical organization. The workers have nobly done their part, have stood their ground with pathetic confidence in the hopes aroused by the frothy word-mongers—their misleaders. And what has been accomplished? Employers refuse to meet with men who loudly proclaim that one strike is but a prelude to another and another.[9]

Attacks by the conservative press and the A.F.L. were nothing new to the I.W.W. and, given the role that the media and craft unionists had played during the strike, their criticisms might even have redounded to the union's advantage among the Paterson workers. The same, however, could not be said of the socialist critique. Soon after the broad-silk weavers and dye-house employees returned to the shops, the New York socialists launched their assault on the industrial unionists' conduct of the silk strike. For months, charges and countercharges cluttered the pages of socialist and union organs until, as *Solidarity* editor Ralph Chaplin later wrote, a state of "ideological warfare" existed between the S.P.A. and the I.W.W.[10] The tenuous nexus between the two was broken in the bitter aftermath of the Paterson strike.

The S.P.A. in the first decade of its existence was a party whose membership was divided on a number of significant issues. One of these, as previously discussed, concerned the relationship between the party and the labor movement, with the lines drawn between those who sought to influence or "capture" the A.F.L. and those who despaired of achieving that end and instead supported the creation of dual unions. A second area of discord concerned tactical emphasis and divided S.P.A. members into so-called evolutionists and revolutionists. The former, who tended also to oppose dualism, held that socialism would be achieved gradually via political means; the latter were impatient with the evolutionist-reformist approach.[11] The split within the party was evident in the individual socialist leaders' reaction to the formation of the I.W.W. in 1905 and even after the deletion of the political clause at the 1908 Convention, S.P.A. members remained divided in regard to the union. The right wing denounced the nonpolitical stance of St. John's organization and the concept of class warfare which the I.W.W. increasingly seemed to encourage, but many on the party's left continued their association with the industrial union. Haywood, who was elected to the Executive Committee of the party in 1910, epitomized the connection which continued to exist between the two.

During the Lawrence strike of early 1912, socialists of all persuasions offered their assistance to the industrial unionists. The Massachusetts strike was an example of what might be achieved if the S.P.A. and the I.W.W. put aside their differences and worked together on behalf of the industrial workers of the country.[12] After Lawrence, some members of the S.P.A. urged a closer association between the party and the dual union, but the year between the New England textile victory and the outbreak of the Paterson strike saw greater acrimony and less harmony between the two organizations. Trade unionists like Max Hayes, who remained optimistic that the socialists could capture the A.F.L. and replace Gompers, were concerned that the party's association with the I.W.W. would be politically damaging. Those who placed their faith in the political process were naturally fearful that the union's talk of sabotage and revolution would have an adverse effect on the S.P.A. vote in the upcoming national election. Quite aside from the ambitions concerning the A.F.L. nexus and the 1912 political ramifications, it was, as William M. Dick has written, "a little too much to expect the leaders who spent their lives trying to increase votes to accept an organization that denied the efficacy of political action."[13] Shortly after the conclusion of the Lawrence strike, therefore, the S.P.A.'s right wing moved to disassociate the party with the industrial union and to expel those who advocated direct action.

Haywood became the obvious first target of those within the S.P.A.'s right wing. He, more than any other individual, symbolized the conflict between evolutionary and revolutionary socialism and between dual unionists and A.F.L. adherents. Moreover, his role in Lawrence and his position on the National Executive Committee gave him a prominence which was particularly threatening to the party's reformists.

The direct confrontation between the two distinct wings of the S.P.A. finally came at the party's May 1912 Convention in Indianapolis. At first it appeared that the delegates had taken to heart Debs's plea for less intraparty rancor and more toleration of differences.[14] On the potentially volatile issue of industrial unionism, the convention voted a tepid resolution which stopped short of endorsement but accepted its existence. Haywood and his supporters within the party agreed to this compromise, as they did to the plank proposed by the Committee on the Platform which stated the importance of the class struggle as the ultimate goal of the party while affirming its commitment to immediate reforms. At this point, however, the spirit of conciliation ended. Hillquit, speaking for the Committee on the Constitution, rose and recommended an amendment to the party's constitution which was clearly directed at the I.W.W. members and supporters. It read: "Any member of the party who opposes political action or advocates crime, sabotage or other methods of violence as a weapon of the working class to aid in its emancipation shall be expelled from membership in the party." This so-called antisabotage clause—Article II, Section 6, of the constitution—was approved by a vote of 191 to 90.[15]

When Article II, Section 6 was subsequently submitted to the party membership, it carried easily (13,215 to 4,196) despite Debs's opposition. The total vote was too small to call the referendum's outcome an enthusiastic endorsement of the convention action, but Berger—whom Haywood believed was most responsible for the measure—hailed the result as a mandate and called for the amendment's prompt use against the "anarchists and syndicalists" in the party.[16]

Early in December 1912, Haywood provided the excuse the right wing sought to remove him from his position in the party. Speaking at the Harlem Casino in New York City, the I.W.W. hero and S.P.A. official advocated direct action and attacked the socialist politicians. The New York *Call*, which reported his remarks fully the next day, began the movement to recall him under Article II, Section 6. "William D. Haywood," the paper declared flatly in its December 4 issue, "does no longer belong in the socialist party, and certainly not in the Executive Committee."[17]

Shortly thereafter, the New York State Committee, supported by its counterpart in New Jersey, formally initiated Haywood's recall. On December 28 the national party headquarters charged Haywood with advocating sabotage and direct action in violation of the S.P.A. Constitution, and party members were asked to vote on whether he should be removed from the National Executive Committee. The results of this referendum were announced in March 1913, shortly before Haywood arrived in Paterson to assume leadership of the silk strike. With perhaps a quarter of the dues-paying party members voting, the I.W.W. leader was expelled by a margin of 22,495 to 10,944.[18]

William Z. Foster, who in the course of a long career held membership in an impressive number of political parties and labor organizations and had by 1913 already joined and left both the S.P.A. and the I.W.W., was among those who saw Haywood's recall as "almost catastrophic" for the party. In his view, the victory of the right wing resulted in a sharp decline in party membership, the precipitous drop in socialist votes after the 1912 national election, and an almost immediate financial crisis for the S.P.A. Foster believed that Haywood's recall provoked "many thousands of Socialist workers" to leave the S.P.A. and dealt the party a blow from which it was "never able to recover fully."[19] Although there is by no means unanimity on this point, many scholars agree that the split within the party over the implementation of the antisabotage clause resulted in a serious decline in S.P.A. membership and potential.[20]

The party, however, was not alone in feeling the impact of Article II, Section 6. As Conlin has written, the antisabotage clause "marked a significant milestone in the decline of the I.W.W." as well.[21] The I.W.W. had in a sense chosen an independent path when it expunged the political clause from its constitution in 1908 and it rarely shrank from attacking the socialist "opportunists" when an occasion arose, but the industrial union was not as self-reliant as it liked to believe. The socialist support it received in Lawrence, particularly the financial assistance, was important to the success of that strike. Whether the I.W.W. leaders or the reformist socialists were in the end most responsible for the break, it can not be denied that neither the party nor the union profited as a result.[22]

According to Kipnis, the Lawrence strike marked "the end of the united Socialist participation in the economic battles of the working class"; the antagonisms between the right-wing party members and the I.W.W. supporters were thereafter so intense that the former refused to participate in the contests led by the industrial union.[23] This judgment must be qualified, however. Despite the fact that the Paterson strike was launched in the midst of Haywood's recall—a move which both the New York and New Jersey party organizations endorsed—the S.P.A. did not stand aloof from the silk workers' struggle.

During the early days of the strike, the New Jersey state party provided immediate and important aid to the union agitators and organizers. The day after the conflict began, State Secretary Killingbeck was in Paterson assuring the workers that the party would "do everything possible to help." Not only did he and other state party members appear frequently at strike meetings, but they shared the platform with Flynn and other I.W.W. speakers at Haledon and at the daily branch meetings. On February 27, as a result of his speech protesting the city's violation of the right of free speech in the arrests of the I.W.W. organizers, Killingbeck himself was taken into custody and detained at police headquarters. In addition to their services as speakers and Scott's editorial support in the *Weekly Issue*, the New Jersey socialists provided bail when Quinlan was arrested, made Haledon available as a meeting place, and took part in the early establishment of relief facilities.[24]

When Haywood was arrested at the Lafayette Oval on March 30, Killingbeck was among those who protested the police action and on two occasions spoke alongside Boyd. However, the provocative words of Boyd and other intemperate orators marked the beginning of tension between the New Jersey socialists and the union organizers in the city. Although I.W.W. leaders, particularly Flynn, defended the Englishman at the time and appeared with him at subsequent rallies in the city, by the end of the strike the political party and the industrial union were each scrambling to associate Boyd with the other. This was particularly unfortunate for Boyd—and in part explains his long stay in the county jail awaiting bail—but it was equally unlucky for the Paterson strikers.

The harmony which had existed between the S.P.A. and the I.W.W. was clearly strained by the incident. It was only shortly after Boyd's speeches that socialist Magnet raised the possibility of a settlement without I.W.W. approval and expressed his interest in opening a dialogue over issues with the manufacturers.[25] After the Boyd uproar, the collapse of the alderman's efforts, and the abortive attempt by the A.F.L. to organize the nonaffiliated silk workers, the S.P.A. activities in Paterson noticeably lessened. Haledon's Mayor Brueckman continued to offer the borough as an I.W.W. Sunday sanctuary, and socialists from outside the state appeared from time to time at strike rallies, but for weeks the Passaic and New Jersey socialist organizations played little role in the strike.

It was not until late in May that party leaders reappeared as newsworthy forces in the strike city. At that time the S.P.A. of New Jersey declared its intention to enter the fight against the Paterson officials' action in closing the halls to strike gatherings, and Killingbeck appeared in the city to hold a meeting as a test of the order and to affirm the party's commitment to free speech and assembly. With Magnet and Glanz most often officiating, the S.P.A. speakers began to urge a federal investigation of the local silk industry and the city authorities' abrogation of the constitutional rights of the strikers. The conviction of Scott on June 3, an action which both the S.P.A. and the I.W.W. hoped to exploit, prompted the party and the union to resume joint meetings.

The *New Review*, which had earlier deplored the party's treatment of Haywood as an action which had played into the hands of the Paterson silk magnates, applauded this and other new evidence of cooperation. If the S.P.A. rescinded its recall of Haywood and worked hand-in-hand with the I.W.W. leaders, the journal saw only benefits for the workers.[26]

The *New Review*'s editorial writer would not have been as optimistic about the fruits of socialist and I.W.W. cooperation if he had written a month later. In the weeks following the pageant, whatever unity that had existed between the two organizations in Paterson began to wane. When Reed's artistic triumph turned out to be a financial failure, as the workers' hardships increased and relief support ebbed, as there seemed no sign that the employers could agree to an industrywide settlement, the New Jersey socialists came out in strong support of shop agreements. Eventually the ribbon weavers in New York City and Paterson, many of them members of the S.P.A., broke with the Executive Committee and began to negotiate by shop. It was this move by the most skilled silk workers that began the rush back to the mills and brought the strike to an effective if not officially announced end. Shortly after the Smith & Kauffman agreement was announced, the I.W.W. leaders and the S.P.A. spokesmen were at each other's throats. For months thereafter, each side chewed over the question of blame for the Paterson defeat.

The first major volley in what would become incessant sniping from both sides was fired by Jacob Panken in the New York *Call* issue of July 26, the same day that Flynn told a gathering of strikers that the battle seemed lost for the moment.

Panken was a Ukranian-born Jew who had immigrated to the United States as a boy of eleven in 1890, worked at a variety of jobs, and graduated from New York University Law School in 1905. An active socialist and labor organizer, Panken prior to obtaining his law degree had served as an organizer for the International Ladies' Garment Workers' Union and the Purse and Bag Makers' Union.[27] He was no stranger to the I.W.W. leaders when the Paterson strike began, nor was he only a remote observer of events in the silk city during the contest. In 1912 Panken had been legal advisor to the Hotel and Restaurant Workers' Union, which had obtained an agreement with a number of New York City's establishments and was then seeking to improve the wages and conditions of other workers in the industry. In that capacity he had come into contact with Tresca, Flynn, and Quinlan, at whose instigation the general strike of hotel and restaurant employees was called on New Year's Eve. In retrospect at least, Panken questioned the I.W.W. tactics in the hotel strike and blamed the industrial union's leaders for its defeat as well as the decline of the once promising hotel workers' organization.[28]

Although he did not play a large role in the Paterson strike, Panken made at least one appearance at a strike meeting in Turn Hall: on March 20, introduced by Lessig and sharing the platform with Killingbeck, he addressed a group of Jewish strikers as the principal Yiddish speaker. There is no direct evidence that he performed a similar function on other occasions, but he at least claimed that he often met informally with the Jewish workers in the city and was kept informed of events in Paterson. Several weeks before the strike ended, according to subsequent accounts by Haywood, Koettgen, and Ettor, Panken was among a group of New York socialists who offered to act as intermediaries between the strikers and silk financiers to affect a settlement.[29]

Panken's letter, entitled "The I.W.W. and Paterson," was a lengthy review of the tribulations of the silk workers, beginning with the Detroit faction's strike in 1912. It was also a scathing attack on the motives and tactics of the I.W.W. as evidenced in Paterson and in earlier strikes in New York City. The kernel of his argument was that the I.W.W. was an organization bent on social revolution and insincere in its professed aim to improve the workers' immediate condition. The union's motive, he claimed, was apparent in the earlier hotel strike, when workers who had already obtained a satisfactory agreement with their employers were directed to walk out for no other reason than to show the impact of "direct action" and to "bring disruption." The fact that the hotel workers had lost more than they gained in the I.W.W. "fiasco" did not deter the union agitators from playing the same "irresponsible game" among the silk workers.

In Panken's estimation, the broad-silk weavers had a legitimate grievance on the matter of the multiple-loom system and could have won a victory on that issue under responsible leadership. But the I.W.W. was not interested in such a mundane victory. Under the fiction that all of the silk workers should strike for a few days to demonstrate their sympathy for the broad-silk weavers, and then return to their shops while the fight against the three- and four-loom system was pursued, the I.W.W. had gotten all three of the branches' workers to strike. At that point, the plan "changed" and the aim of a general strike for revolutionary purposes became paramount and other demands were put forward. Instead of the mass of workers returning to their shops to put pressure on the few companies which employed the multiple-loom system, and thus win a battle that could be won, the I.W.W. had preferred to lead 25,000 workers in a hopeless struggle over unobtainable demands.

The irresponsibility of fomenting a general strike was, in Panken's view, only exceeded by the insistence that all shops had to settle before any of the workers returned to their places. If the I.W.W. had not demanded the capitulation of all the employers and instead had allowed the workers to return to those smaller shops which were willing to make some concessions, at least some would have benefited. If those who did go back could have been convinced to sustain those who remained on strike, even more of the operatives might have won higher wages or some reduction in hours. The I.W.W., by its tactics, simply helped to accomplish for the silk manufacturers what they had been unwilling or unable to do for themselves—organize and work together. "In all industrial disputes it has been the policy to try to break the ranks of the employers when they were organized, especially when they fought as an organization," Panken wrote. "The policy, apparently, of the I.W.W. is not only to organize the workers, but also to organize the foes of the workers." Instead of using the tactic of divide and conquer at the outset, when some of the smaller firms were willing to come to terms, the outside organizers had encouraged employer unity.

According to his account of July 26, Panken had realized at the time of his visit to Paterson in March that the strike could not be won under the strictures imposed by the I.W.W. "After I had been in Paterson a half hour," he wrote, "I knew that the strike was in the hands of men who were not competent to cope with the situation." He had, he said, discussed with some friends whether he should make his views on the strike public at that time. All had cautioned him against doing so, on the grounds that the I.W.W. "would immediately accuse the Socialists of trying to break the Paterson strike." What prompted him to end his silence was the I.W.W.'s agitation among the tailors and barbers of New York City even as the New Jersey strike was faltering. This convinced him that it was "time to call a halt" to those who argued that "the social revolution [could] be brought on by a strike of barbers or hotel workers or silk workers."[30]

Panken's broad attack on the I.W.W. and his critique of its handling of the Paterson strike was followed by similar postmortems by his fellow socialists. Killingbeck was the first New Jersey party leader to air his views in the *Call*, the paper in which almost all the S.P.A. charges against the union were printed. Less critical than the New York lawyer and labor activist, Killingbeck acknowledged the educational value of the strike and expressed optimism about the silk workers' future gains. His major criticism was that the I.W.W. had ignored its own previous counsel to avoid long strikes. If the Paterson struggle had shown anything, he wrote, it was that "the short, sharp strike at frequent intervals, until demands are granted, should . . . be the future method of economic warfare."[31]

Korshet, a prominent figure in the Passaic County party organization, was the next to write on matters connected with the strike. His comments avoided any consideration of I.W.W. strategy or revolutionary intent, and concentrated instead on the S.P.A. contributions during the strike and the union's failure to credit the party for its work. Provoked by an article in the August issue of the *International Socialist Review*, which charged that the party had allowed Quinlan to be "railroaded to the penitentiary with hardly a murmur of protest," Korshet defended the S.P.A. role in Quinlan's behalf and contrasted that with the I.W.W.'s refusal to support Socialist party activities in local politics. The doctor reviewed the party's work in raising money for relief and bail, providing publicity in the *Weekly Issue*, and staging rallies in support of the strikers. This practical aid, he asserted, was of far greater value than "the wind-jamming, hell-raising and hallelujah-shouting . . . done by the I.W.W. star performers."

Korshet concluded his letter on "The I.W.W. and the Socialist Party" with the following words:

No well-grounded Socialist disputes the wisdom and necessity of industrial unionism. An industrial union in active cooperation with the Socialist party could be made a powerful weapon in an industrial or political conflict. But at present there is absolutely no common meeting ground, controlled as the I.W.W. is by men and women who, in private, call themselves Socialists, even joining the party, and in public not only dread announcing themselves as such, but seek to slight or slur the Socialist party at every opportunity.

The Socialist party has always fought for the working class, whether organized or unorganized, whether they were Socialist or not. But it is high time that Socialist party members understand thoroughly the attitude of the I.W.W. towards them. The I.W.W. regards the Socialist party as a sort of bourgeoise reform party, whose assistance it will grudgingly accept in time of need. . . . If the Socialist party does not profer enough help the I.W.W. stirs up an awful howl. If the party does too much, then it is accused of seeking political notoriety. In either case the help of the Socialist party is not appreciated or acknowledged and as soon as the I.W.W. wiggles out of trouble it turns upon its Socialist friends with the viciousness of a snake. The Socialists of Passaic County have learned their lesson.[32]

The doctor's statement concerning the S.P.A. contributions and the I.W.W. leaders' disdain for the party's efforts was subsequently affirmed by Haledon Mayor Brueckman and Passaic County Organizer Glanz. Brueckman, whose aid during the strike jeopardized his own political office, wrote to the *Call*: "I have read the article of Comrade Korshet and

I agree with him . . . in all details. It is a true and correct statement of facts and conditions."[33]

Korshet's piece and its confirmation by other New Jersey socialists prompted party members to reflect on the association between their organization and the I.W.W. From Brooklyn, New York, W. W. Passage directed a letter to the editor of the *Call* concerning the lack of "the most ordinary sense of courtesy and fairness on the part of I.W.W. leaders" in not crediting the S.P.A. role in Paterson. In his view it seemed "common sense for the Socialist Party at large to profit by the experiences of . . . Passaic County Comrades and make some provision to prevent the repetition of that experience in other places." Passage had a suggestion: "Suppose the individual members of the party who on many notable occasions have rescued labor leaders from tight places into which their foolishness had gotten them should serve notice upon the official committee of all future strikes that no funds or other support will be forthcoming from them if Ettor, Giovannitti, Haywood or any other speakers of this class who have derided political action, are employed as speakers or in any other important capacity in connection with the strike." He announced that it was his intention to follow that course in the future.[34]

The last shot in what Foner has termed the socialists' "vitriolic campaign of denunciation" against the I.W.W. in Paterson was fired by Steiger in 1914.[35] The Smith & Kauffman ribbon weaver, who had become an I.W.W. member after his shop had voted to join the general strike, repeated the charges made by other socialists but gave particular emphasis to the alleged corruption of the union leaders. Paterson, Lawrence, and Akron had proven to be "rich pickings" for I.W.W. agitators whose "chief interest" in the workers of those cities, he claimed, was how much money they could gull from them.[36] After detailing charges of how Flynn, Haywood, Tresca, and the others lined their pockets at the silk workers' expense—dipping into relief and defense funds, siphoning profits from the pageant, and exacting per diem pay for their work and "expenses"—Steiger gave his explanation for the industrial union's inability to win strikes or hold members: "Because they build their propaganda on lies—because they incite to crime—because they teach a doctrine of hate and envy. They promise an earthly paradise that can never be realized; they inflame the minds of their dupes to acts of violence by teaching that every deed is justified whether it is right or wrong." When the "artifically-aroused discontent" of the workers subsides and they "recover their common sense," they conclude that "better no organization at all than one like this." According to Steiger, members predictably left the union when they saw the false promises for what they were.

That was why the I.W.W. had no durability and was "merely a trouble-making organization" which actually impeded working class progress.[37]

To Goldman, the socialists' critique of I.W.W. leadership in Paterson stemmed from the party's "too-obvious view of making political capital out of the situation." She saw no point in responding to the S.P.A. attacks on the use of revolutionary ideas in labor confrontations and declined to do so.[38] But others, more intimately involved with the strike and the union, could not show such forbearance! The socialists' articles and letters elicited a response in kind, with *Solidarity* serving as the New York *Call*'s counterpart. For months and months, the long-standing contention between the right-wing socialists and the I.W.W. centered on the activities of each in Paterson.

Panken was the first and favorite target, with Ettor leading the assault on the New York lawyer for joining "the pack of wolves" who sought to bring "discredit upon the I.W.W." Hunger and nothing else lost the silk strike, Ettor emphasized in his August letter. The shop settlement plan, which Panken had contended would have brought victory, was clearly not a viable tactic; Paterson workers had fallen for that argument in the past and had reaped nothing but defeat. In fact, Ettor argued, the strike had been lost *because* of the "shop settlement discussion that was foisted upon the workers by a Socialist politician." As for the alleged crimes of the I.W.W. in the hotel, barber, and silk strikes, Panken's statements were nothing but malicious and purposeful lies against "the revolutionary honor of men and women whose boots [he] could not blacken." If there was any crime committed in Paterson, it came from the socialist labor leaders and lawyers on New York's East Side.

"For nearly four months," Ettor wrote, "no official effort was made by 'leaders' or 'legal advisors' of East Side unions to support in any way the Paterson workers." Instead of striking in sympathy with the silk weavers and dyers, or refusing to handle silk cloth produced by scabs or Pennsylvania workers, the organized clothing workers of New York remained on the job and fashioned clothes from silk. Men like Panken had "made no effort . . . to help the Paterson workers financially" or through any sympathetic action by their working-class followers. Ettor's "Open Letter To Jacob Panken" concluded:

> You exclaim that there must be a halt! Well, there will be no halt. As long as the workers are divided into multitudinous small unions, tied up by protocols, and betrayed to the bosses by as unscrupulous a gang of labor mercenaries as was ever gathered together. As long as men and women are used as cats' paws by a lot of "union lawyers" and red politicians. As long as a reign of bull-

dozing, hiring gangs, as long as the reign of lawyers and labor fakirs lasts, we will not halt in our efforts. You helped to start this seemingly fratricidal war. Now we will continue on our side, and "damned be he who first cries 'Hold! enough!'"[39]

Koettgen, some two weeks after this I.W.W. response to Panken, framed and published a similar reply. Charging that the New Yorker's article was "a poor attempt to discredit the I.W.W. in favor of the A.F. of L.," Koettgen picked Panken's statements apart on bits of detail—for example on the size of meeting halls, the number of workers on multiple looms, when the eight-hour day became an issue—and dismissed the more substantive charges as simply "misstatements of facts." The Paterson union organizer repeated Ettor's contention that the New York socialists had done nothing themselves to help the silk workers.[40]

Other similar articles followed in the I.W.W. weekly, differing in emphasis and in the particular epithets only.[41] Neither the socialist critics nor the union defenders seemed to tire of the question of blame. In this the union faithful put themselves in the odd position of denying the strike had been lost while at the same time attributing the defeat to the machinations of others.

The fullest response to Panken and the other detractors came finally from Flynn. On January 31, 1914, she used an invitation from the New York Civic Club to deliver a speech entitled "The Truth About The Paterson Strike." This, the most complete account and justification of the I.W.W. role in Paterson, was prepared because, fully six months after the strike had ended, the criticism had not abated. Since many of the critics had done nothing themselves to help the strike and some had never visited the New Jersey city while the fight was in progress or had gone there only once or twice as one "went on a holiday," she thought it time that someone who had been in Paterson throughout the struggle clear away the misconceptions and blatant falsehoods.

The task Flynn set for herself was a difficult one. By the time she gave her speech, the I.W.W. tactics in the silk strike had come under attack from virtually every direction: Berkman had criticized the leaders for not advocating and employing violence; Sanger had asked why the organizers had done nothing to bring the state militia onto the scene as in Lawrence; some had wondered why the I.W.W. had fled to Haledon rather than exploit the free speech issue in Paterson; and others had questioned the insistence on a general settlement, the unwillingness to compromise, and the use of relief funds.[42]

Point by point, Flynn responded to the second-guessers and armchair strategists and defended the strike leadership. To those who had advocated violence, either for its own sake as a revolutionary device or to elicit sympathy from a confrontation with police or militiamen, she countered that there had been no need for it and no certainty such direct action would generate the sort of response that Sanger envisioned. Her objection to this tactic in Paterson, Flynn made clear, was "not a moral or legal one, but a utilitarian one." During the first four months of the strike, the "mills were shut down as tight as a vacuum" and stood "like empty junk boats along the banks of the river"; how violence could be used "against non-existent scabs" was beyond comprehension. Violence for its own sake, moreover, could have been construed as weakness, an indication of desperation generated by knowledge that the strike was failing. "There is," she concluded on this point, "a certain responsibility about advocating violence. . . . Men and women who get out as strike agitators should only advocate [it] when they are absolutely certain that it is going to do some good other than to spill the blood of the innocent workers on the streets."[43]

To the extent that Flynn agreed that the Paterson strike had been lost—a word acceptable to her only if defined in narrow economic terms—the cause was threefold: the peculiar characteristics of the silk industry, the intolerable deprivation suffered by the workers due to in-sufficient relief funds, and the machinations of the unaffiliated, largely socialist, delegates on the Central Strike Committee. In Paterson, unlike Lawrence, the I.W.W. faced an adversary composed of over three hun-dred separate employers, ranging greatly in size, with some having out-side mills which continued in operation; there was "no company that had the balance of power upon whom [the union] could concentrate [its] attack." An additional difficulty was the fact that silk goods are not a necessity like coal or food. Since people could do without silk, the union could not get the "public by the throat" to have pressure exerted on the manufacturers.[44]

The nature of the silk industry thus provided an advantage to the owners. Meanwhile, the financial difficulties encountered wore away the strikers' strength. Setting the amount of relief money raised at $60,000 to maintain 25,000 strikers over a five-month period, Flynn pointed out that this meant an average of less than $.50 per month each. Hunger, she echoed Ettor, had prompted the workers back to the mills. "If all those critics all over the United States had only put their interest in the form of finances," she told her audience, "the Paterson strike might have been another story."[45]

Even against great odds, Flynn contended, the strike could have been won if it had not been for the English-speaking ribbon weavers, led by socialist Magnet, and the I.W.W. insistence that the strikers should control their own struggle. The I.W.W. organizers, acting only as advisors, were too dependent upon the dictates of the Central Strike Committee and were too much at the mercy of the mass of workers. The strike eventually wore down because Magnet and others like him in New York City were allowed to promote and sell the idea of the shop-by-shop settlement, despite the opposition of the union leaders. This was the crucial I.W.W. mistake and "one of the lessons" Flynn declared that she had learned at Paterson: "When the I.W.W. assumes the responsibility of a strike, the I.W.W. should control the strike absolutely through a union strike committee; there should be no outside interference, no outside union domination accepted or permitted, no Magnet permitted to pose as 'representing the non-union element.'"[46] Panken's charge of I.W.W. domination was, to Flynn, both false and ironic; it was the *lack* of union dictation rather than its existence that resulted in the strike's loss.

If Flynn challenged the New York socialist's allegations on the matter of control, thus transferring blame for the failure from the leaders to the led, she did give substance to his arguments concerning the revolutionary aim of the I.W.W. One of Panken's major criticisms of the union's role in Paterson had been that social revolution had been its principal interest. The young I.W.W. agitator did not challenge this. No clearer evidence of the two differing conceptions of labor organization can be asked than in the exchange between these two antagonists.

Flynn explained to the Civic Club:

What is a labor victory? I maintain that it is a twofold thing. Workers must gain economic advantage, but they must also gain revolutionary spirit, in order to achieve a complete victory. For workers to gain a few more cents a day, a few minutes less a day, and go back to work with the same psychology, the same attitude toward society, is to have achieved a temporary gain and not a lasting victory. For workers to go back with a class-conscious spirit, with an organized and a determined attitude toward society, means that even if they have made no economic gain they have the possibility of gaining in the future.

By Flynn's definition, a genuine labor victory had to be both economic and "revolutionizing." If one had to choose between the two, she stated, it was "better to gain in spirit than to gain economic advantage."[47]

Whatever cooperation that had existed between the S.P.A. and the I.W.W. while the Paterson strike was in progress came to be regretted by both during the bitter months that followed its conclusion. None of the New Jersey socialists stated it explicitly, but the message of all appeared to be that future I.W.W. excursions in the state would be viewed with considerably less favor than before.

The *Call*, whose contributions during the Paterson strike earned only I.W.W. abuse for not doing more, continued to attack the union at every opportunity. Thus, when a crowd of I.W.W. adherents tried to disrupt a socialist gathering in New York in March 1914, the paper devoted its editorial to ridicule those who had taken part: "The I.W.W. is not an organization, but a state of mind, and one that calls for the services of an alienist. In the crowd were many with strong voices and weak minds, the type that yawp and bluster, alternately crawl and threaten. . . . They have no intention of improving the condition of the working class. They are having excitement, and the more silly the excitement is, the more do they become drunk with it and desirous of further excitement."[48]

Paterson continued to embitter the I.W.W. toward the S.P.A. as well as the reverse. Thus, at the union's Eighth Convention in September 1913, the General Executive Board argued that the union had been betrayed:

> The professed neutrality of the Socialist politician and the socialist press towards labor organizations and their internal affairs have been proven false by the studied attacks made on the I.W.W. at times when the issue of the battle for better conditions hung in the balance. Professing friendship for the workers and rendering sufficient assistance in the fight to gain some measure of trust and confidence, they have stabbed the workers in the back by the publication of false reports, reflecting on the integrity of the organization and its officials, calculated to shut off support in the fight.[49]

I.W.W. General Organizer George Speed also used the occasion of the fall convention to attack the S.P.A. In regard to those who controlled the New York *Call*, Speed told the delegates: "They evidently have no more use for an economic organization of workers than they have for a bad cold. They use it only for the purpose of a vote-getter and the funds they worm out of its treasury. Their pretensions of impartiality are pure bunk. They fear the growth of the I.W.W. just as the capitalists fear it." The general organizer summed up his sentiments on the Paterson strike "in one word": "My word is, I regret there was a Haledon."[50]

The I.W.W.'s battle with the S.P.A. was not the only bitter contest following the strike in New Jersey, and at the Eighth Convention vituperation was not reserved only for the Hillquits, Bergers, and Pankens. The strike defeats suffered by the industrial union in Akron, Paterson, and Detroit (among the workers at the Studebaker plant) had eroded badly the optimism which had followed the successful Lawrence battle the year before. In fact, the prospects for the union by fall of 1913 seemed so dim to some within the I.W.W. that a number sought to re-examine and possibly redirect the organization's activities. It would not be correct to attribute the internecine battle fought at the convention solely to the defeat suffered at Paterson—seeds of discord existed well before the union agitators set foot in that city—but the disappointing results of the year's most prolonged strike surely contributed to the tensions within the I.W.W.

During the summer of 1913, signs of the union's possible disintegration were everywhere. First, it was undeniable that membership had declined precipitously. On the West Coast, I.W.W. leaders were engaged in a bitter struggle over the direction of the *Industrial Worker* which culminated in the suspension of its editor in July and the publication itself two months later.[51] If the union's difficulties were not already sufficient to assure a heated September convention, late in August *Solidarity* published a piece by "L.C.R." entitled "Sensationalism vs. Organizing Ability," which was a harsh critique of union past practices and raised the question of the I.W.W.'s future as a labor union.

"L.C.R." was Ben H. Williams, the editor of *Solidarity* from its inception in 1909 and a man described by Dubofsky as "perhaps the most astute I.W.W. theoretician." As a founding member of the industrial union, a former member of its governing board, and a close observer of its agitational activities in the East, his views carried weight.[52]

Williams began his piece with a sharp attack on existing union methods: "If the I.W.W. is going to organize the working class then we will have to make a great change in our attitude towards the labor movement and in the methods that we are using now. At present we are to the labor movement what the high diver is to the circus. A sensation, marvelous and nerve thrilling. We attract the crowds. We give them thrills, we do hair-raising stunts and send the crowd home to wait impatiently for the next sensationalist to come along." In words closely paralleling those of Steiger, Williams accused the I.W.W. organizers of stirring the workers "into a religious frenzy," appealing to their emotions "with cheap phrases and flowery language." Once the workers were aroused to strike, and while they were still mesmerized by the "spectacular stunts" and oratory of the agitators, the union would enlist scores of members. "Many of them," Williams wrote, "would just as soon join the salvation army as the I.W.W." When the dynamic speaker removed himself from the scene or when the strike he provoked was ended—whether in victory of defeat—all the advances in membership "would go up in smoke."

The I.W.W., he wrote, would have to have "less of the sensational and more quiet organization" in order to survive as a union. It had to work to maintain and build on the membership acquired during a strike and not, as happened in Lawrence and Akron, neglect those who had rallied to the union's standard in response to the "high diver's" act. Williams believed that the appeal of industrial unionism was strong but that the past "brass band" approach, the reliance on peripatetic crowd-arousing agitators, would continue to retard I.W.W. growth. "Unless we can organize the workers without doing the spectacular," he warned, "we are doomed."[53] On this less than cheerful note, the I.W.W. faithful began assembling in Chicago for the September 15–29 meeting.

The divisive issue at the Eighth Convention concerned "centralization" versus "decentralization," a matter which Brissenden likened to the controversy over states rights on the political scene. Although the sides did not divide cleanly along sectional lines, the revolt against centralization of power in the General Executive Board centered in the West. The year before there had been some discussion of the matter of centralization and local control at the union gathering, but there was no real confrontation and nothing was resolved. During the intervening twelve months, the differences in opinion had become more acrimonious and the line between the two camps more sharply drawn. Clearly, the defeats suffered in the strikes during the preceding year did nothing to mitigate the matter.[54]

In 1913 those who wished to minimize the power of St. John and the General Executive Board lost little time in introducing a set of resolutions which would accomplish this end and, following reports from the officers and general organizers on the progress and prospects of the union, most of the rest of the convention was spent in their debate. Among the resolutions designed to curb the authority of the central organization, which was already a weaker body than that created at the founding convention, were the following:

1. that locals have the right to select an Auditing Committee to go over defense funds, accounts of papers, free speech fights, etc.;
2. that the editors of the I.W.W. papers be elected by and be directly responsible to the rank and file;
3. that no officer hold office for more than two years;
4. that no G.E.B. member hold any other salaried position in the organization;
5. that the office of General Organizer be dispensed with;

6. that the G.E.B. be abolished;
7. that a full itemized account of funds in I.W.W. strikes and defenses be given to any local on demand;
8. that the Convention be abolished.[55]

If the more extreme of these resolutions were passed—the abolition of the General Executive Board, the position of general organizer, the annual convention—the I.W.W. would be left with an impotent secretary-treasurer standing as a figurehead over a collection of almost autonomous locals. Ben Williams, who saw the issue as one "between INDUSTRIAL ORGANIZATION, according to the present requirements of capitalist development, and a REACTIONARY LOCALISM, which ignores capitalist development," warned that if the anarcho-localists carried the convention, the result would be "the complete disintegration of the I.W.W."[56]

The motions which reflected a dislike for central authority and a suspicion of financial irregularity in high places were evidence of only part of the divisions among the delegates. The dissidents also questioned the organizational methods of the union. In words which indicate clearly the differences in philosophy within the I.W.W. in 1913, Delegate Sautter told his fellow representatives: "We hold this in the West . . . we want to educate the working class—in the East they want to organize. . . . We want to organize on class lines, on educational lines. We don't want men coming into the organization by the thousands and going out by the thousands. I would sooner have ten men class conscious, educated, than a thousand that know nothing about Industrial Unionism." Sautter specifically mentioned the membership drives and advances in Paterson, Lawrence, and Akron during the strikes in those cities as something which should be avoided in the future.[57]

It is interesting that such opposites as Williams, in his preconvention attack on the "high-divers," and Sautter, during the heated debates in Chicago, were alike in their criticism of the union's recruiting efforts. Where they differed—and it was a significant difference—was in the alternative which each man put forward. *Solidarity*'s editor, more a unionist than a revolutionary, sought to increase and hold membership through greater attention to sound organizational techniques and greater emphasis on gaining improved conditions for the workers. The westerner, who cared little for numbers or modest job-related advances, was interested most in fashioning an organization of class-conscious revolutionaries, a cadre of the pure of heart.

When Sautter introduced a motion to issue temporary strike books rather than membership cards to those who applied for admission to the I.W.W. during a strike, a significant and lengthy debate on the proposal got underway. At issue was the very nature of the organization: unionist or revolutionary. Among the most vocal opponents of the motion were Koettgen and Speed, who maintained that education without organization was meaningless. Speed, as much under fire by the decentralizers as St. John, argued that "in a strike such as the Paterson strike there is more real educational work done . . . than . . . by street corner meetings any time or any place." Sautter was eventually voted down by a vote of 21 to 7, but the result was anticlimactic. The fact that such a matter could be debated at length was an indication of the deep divisions within the organization which Paterson had helped to expose.[58]

The supporters of St. John and centralization were able to defeat their opposition on all of the resolutions proposed by the predominantly western localists. After almost two weeks of interminable debate, the motion to abolish the General Executive Board was defeated 76 to 43 1/2, the office of general organizer was narrowly retained by a vote of 18 to 11, and the annual convention was upheld by a vote of 22 to 10.[59] By the time that the last of these three key resolutions was moved, it would not have been surprising if the delegates had voted to abolish the annual meeting in disgust over what they had been forced to endure.

The parliamentary haggling at the 1913 Convention reached the point of absurdity on more than one occasion and the petty attacks were almost beyond belief. For example, when one delegate moved to send a get-well card to Haywood, whose illness prevented his attendance in Chicago, this innocuous gesture provoked opposition. Some of the decentralizers objected because there were other I.W.W. members who were sick and it was not right to single out one man for such special consideration. This pettiness prompted Delegate Kelly to voice his impatience: "Fellow Workers, when Local 84 sent me up here I understood I was a delegate to a convention of the I.W.W., but it seems to me that I fell into a personal mutual condemnation society. It reminds me of an Irish Wake about three o'clock in the morning after everybody has forgotten all about the deceased."[60] Kelly was not alone in expressing his disgust. "We cannot do away with the Convention by legislating it," Delegate O'Brien stated from the floor. "I think you will see the Convention done away with next year by none of us coming; but it will never be done away with so long as the workers are suckers enough to send suckers here."[61]

While the aroused delegates hurled epithets, argued about greeting cards, booed, and hissed, and generally carried on like an undisciplined bunch of rowdies, those in the gallery watched the proceedings and tried to fashion some coherent meaning from the spectacle. Ben Reitman, one of the observers, gave his reaction in *Mother Earth*:

> As I sat in the hot, stuffy, smoky room of the Convention hall day after day, and heard the discussions, and saw how little regard the delegates had for grammar and the truth, and realized that most of the delegates knew as much about the real labor movement as they did about psychology, and that they cared little about the broad principles of freedom and did not have a vision of a new society . . . I marveled at the big things the I.W.W. have done during their short career. . . . And I said to myself, "God, is it possible that this bunch of pork-chop philosophers, agitators who have no real, great organizing ability or creative brain power, are able to frighten the capitalistic class more than any other labor movement ever organized in America?"

"And then," Reitman recalled his reaction, "I wondered how they did it."[62]

Berkman, Reitman's fellow anarchist, was equally unimpressed with what he had witnessed. Disappointed with the outcome of the convention, Berkman termed the gathering "a sad failure." The defeat of the decentralizers and "the apparent willful ignoring of the supremely important questions of aims and methods" confirmed his belief that the I.W.W. was caught in a "tide of conservatism and faint-heartedness." Suggesting that the lack of militancy and the unwillingness to use revolutionary methods had been the cause of the Paterson defeat, Berkman hoped that "the real militants and revolutionists of the I.W.W." would take the silk defeat as a lesson.[63]

Koettgen viewed the gathering from the vantage point of one whose side had triumphed and interpreted the results in a very different fashion. The member of the General Executive Board termed the Eighth Convention "epoch-making" and saw the defeat of the decentralizers as a vindication of the work the leaders had done among the industrial workers of the East. "There is," he reported in his masterpiece of optimistic overstatement, "no doubt that in the coming year the organization will make great strides."[64]

A more objective observer at the convention, or at least one not identified with either faction within the I.W.W., was labor economist Robert F. Hoxie, who offered his interpretation of the head-spinning spectacle he had witnessed in a series of articles in the *Journal of Political Economy*.[65] As a result of his study of the I.W.W. and particularly his observations during the 1913 Convention, Hoxie concluded that the American public had nothing to fear from the revolutionary union. The public, he wrote, had been "unduly frightened by the impressionistic school of reporters and magazine writers into total misconception and tremendous overestimate of the power and significance of the I.W.W." What the Eighth Convention revealed to him was an organization of modest membership which had "failed utterly in its efforts to attach to itself permanently a considerable body of men representative of any section of the American workers." According to his estimates, dues-paying members numbered around 14,000, a sharp decline from the periods of strike activity. Convention representation from Akron indicated a membership of less than 200, as compared to the estimated 6,000 claimed during the rubber strike earlier in the year; Lawrence, which may have had as many as 14,000 union men at the time of the 1912 victory, could count fewer than 700 eighteen months later. In the entire textile industry, using the constitutional provision of 1 convention vote for every 50 members as a yardstick, Hoxie set the number of union members in good standing at no more than 1,600.[66]

The numerical weakness of the I.W.W. was not the union's only deficiency. Hoxie emphasized also the financial and philosophical problems which the organization confronted in the late months of 1913. The financial report of St. John gave more than enough supportive evidence of the first of these difficulties. According to it, the union had less than $370 on hand as of the first of September; the Akron strike fund, the Little Falls strike fund, the Lawrence strike fund, and the Paterson strike fund showed deficits of $135.50, $865, $716, and $122 respectively.[67]

The dismal financial picture, the result of the low-dues policy coupled with almost incessant strike activity, was in Hoxie's view a serious impediment to the I.W.W.'s becoming an effective foe of the industrial establishment.[68] But, this observer concluded, the I.W.W. posed no genuine threat primarily because it had an unsolvable and "perpetual dilemma" concerning its identity: "The bulk of the American workmen want more here and now for themselves . . . and care little for the remote future of the revolutionary ideal. These will have none of the I.W.W. The others have not, and under the existing conditions cannot develop, the capacity for sustained organic effort. Whichever way the organization turns, then, it seems doomed to failure."[69] Some I.W.W. members insisted that the organization could be both a labor union *and* a revolutionary body, but the contentions of the 1913 Convention suggested that a significant number believed that one of these roles must be given clear priority. The decentralizers opted for the latter; Williams urged the pursuance of more straightforward industrial organization to build up a stable membership. The "fundamental conflict of ideals," present from the founding of the organization and painfully apparent at the

Eighth Convention, predestined the demise of the industrial union. "The truth is," the labor economist wrote in November 1913, "the I.W.W. is not an organization but a loosely bound group of uncontrolled fighters."[70]

The internecine battling over tactics and goals which Hoxie witnessed continued long after the 1913 Convention was history. However, the most serious implication for the future of the I.W.W. was the questions raised about its very existence. Debates over particular strike tactics, ultimate aims, and concentration of power were nothing compared to the doubts expressed concerning dual unionism itself.

Foster, who joined the I.W.W. in 1909, had early become convinced that the slow growth of the industrial union was the result of its isolation from the mainstream of the labor movement in the United States. When he could not persuade his fellow delegates at the 1911 Convention of the wisdom of attempting to capture and radicalize the A.F.L.—the tactic of "boring from within"—he left the I.W.W. and formed the Syndicalist League of North America to pursue this strategy.[71] The victory at Lawrence and the impressive membership gains registered among the textile workers shortly thereafter tended to mute for a time Foster's criticism of dual unionism, but Akron and Paterson spurred him to a more vigorous attack.

In mid-April of 1913, Foster had used the occasion of the defeat of the rubber workers in Akron to question again the tactics and assumptions of the I.W.W. He argued that the union had to come face to face with the fact that a "conservative working class" would not accept revolutionary unionism without education and that the I.W.W. had to accept the difference between theory and practice.[72] Three months later, as the Paterson strike was entering its last month, Foster expanded on this theme of "theory and practice." According to his analysis, the I.W.W. had been formed "on the theory that labor unions were never known to change, but were governed by fixed principles." Its founders had believed that nothing could alter the craft unions and that the only hope for the mass of workers was the creation of a new labor organization which stood for permanent and "fundamental principles" of its own. Foster argued that the concept of immutability was clearly no longer valid, that both the craft unions and the I.W.W. had changed. Under the pressure of new industrial realities, the former were "repudiating the 'harmony of interest' slogan," were federating or amalgamating, and were even loosening their attachment to the "sacredness of the contract." At the same time, Akron and Paterson made evident that the I.W.W. was modifying its own founding principles and was evolving into an organization quite different from that proclaimed in 1905. It now engaged in long strikes (for which it had formerly attacked the

A.F.L.), it had in the barbers' strike in New York reversed its stand on no contractual agreements with the employers, and it was in Paterson engaged in the "typical 'dime against dollars' strike" which had long been the hallmark of its union adversaries. The increased cry for decentralization among some I.W.W. members and the questioning of the old boast of "no leaders," also indicated that the I.W.W. was moving toward a new structure and leadership. Since, in Foster's estimation, the I.W.W. and the craft unions were approaching each other, it was time to put an end to dual unionism.[73]

In early 1914 Foster's position received the support of Tom Mann, a founder of the Workers' Union of Great Britain and Ireland and a leading British syndicalist. Mann had spent some twenty weeks in the United States in the latter part of 1913, lecturing and observing the labor situation. In August he had shared a platform with Haywood at a New York City lecture and had also spoken before a gathering of Paterson silk workers at I.W.W. headquarters on Water Street. Mann appeared under the auspices of the industrial union and was considered a friend and supporter of the dual organization.[74] But in the January 1914 number of the *International Socialist Review*, in an article entitled "A Plea For Solidarity," the Englishman criticized dualism and endorsed Foster's tactic of "boring from within."

Mann praised the good work of the I.W.W. in the free speech fights and among the migratory workers in the western part of the country, but he could see few permanent or tangible results from the union's efforts. "It seems to me," he wrote, "any fair minded person, unwilling to be unwarrantly optimistic, must frankly admit the results are utterly unsatisfactory." Noting that the industrial union had no more than 14,000 members at the time of the Eighth Convention, he asked whether such a small return from so much effort did not "call for inquiry as to whether the present lines are the right ones?"

Mann argued that the I.W.W. had overemphasized economic revolution to the detriment of union organization and was thus a devisive agency in a situation which called for industrial solidarity. "If the fine energy exhibited by the I.W.W. were put into the A.F. of L. or into the existing trade union movement," he maintained, "the results would be fifty-fold greater." It was, he wrote, "the duty of the revolutionaries to become members of existing unions, when dual unions exist, merge them at once, unite all on the basis of industry, and tactfully and persistently spread a knowledge of industrial solidarity." This done, he expressed certainty that "three-fifths of the rank and file of the existing unions" would be ready to take whatever "sensible action" was required. It was "pitiable to find A.F. of L. men berating the I.W.W. and vice versa"; such existing warfare between the two could only hinder real working-class progress in the United States.[75]

Mann's comments provoked an extended and often-heated debate among American radicals who always enjoyed such exchanges and rarely left an attack unanswered. Two months after the English labor leader's article appeared, the *International Socialist Review* published the reactions of Debs and Haywood to Mann's plea. Debs's piece, which carried the same title as the syndicalist's, agreed with the need for greater solidarity but urged unification of a different sort. Essentially what the S.P.A. leader advocated was a return to the principles and coalition of the I.W.W. at its inception. His primary call was not for coalescence with the A.F.L.—the "boring from within" tactic—but rather for the reunification of the two branches of the I.W.W. (Chicago and Detroit), the merger of the S.L.P. and the S.P.A., and the Chicago organization's reestablishment of ties with political actionists. The founding principle of revolutionary unionism, utilizing political action as well as industrial, promised the sort of future success which to that point had eluded the I.W.W. The victory at Lawrence, which Debs maintained would have been impossible "without the cooperation and support of the Socialist party," demonstrated what could be accomplished on behalf of the industrial workers of the country. Instead of learning the lesson of Lawrence, however, the union had become more anti-political and anarchical. What followed were the failures of Akron and Paterson, strikes which Debs argued could have been won.[76]

After calling upon the S.P.A. to delete Article II, Section 6, from its constitution and advising the I.W.W. to foreswear sabotage, Debs concluded on a note of hope: "The conditions of today, the tendency and the outlook, are all that the most ardent socialists and industrialists could desire, and if all who believe in a united party backed by a united union and a united union backed by a united party will put aside the differences, strike hands in comradely concord, and get to work in real earnest, we shall soon have the foremost proletarian revolutionary movement in the world." He urged all socialists and all industrial unionists to join together in this spirit of true solidarity.[77]

Since Haywood's article appeared concurrently with the Debs piece, the I.W.W. leader could not respond to the socialist's blueprint for future success. He did, however, indicate what he thought of Mann's advice. Haywood made it clear that those who advocated working with the established trade unions did not understand the I.W.W. aims. Industrial unionism was not, he emphasized, simply an amalgamation or federation of federations. Such a suggestion as Mann had put forward would find "no audience among industrial unionists who [had] for years been preparing the ground for a new structure of society." The I.W.W. stood for the class struggle and would not compromise its ideals by joining with those who advocated "contractual relations with the exploiters." Far from being a failure, as Mann had maintained, the I.W.W. in its short existence had far exceeded the growth of other labor organizations in their formative years. In Haywood's view, moreover, membership figures were not meaningful measures of success or failure. The I.W.W. had engendered "a feeling of fellowship among the down-trodden and oppressed, unskilled and unorganized" and had spurred "among the lowest strata of wage slaves in America a sense of their importance and capabilities such as never before existed." This was its greatest accomplishment.[78]

Haywood's line of argument and justification of the I.W.W. course was later repeated by Ettor. Like Haywood, he could not entertain the notion of union with the A.F.L. or a compromise of I.W.W. principle:

> Can there be any dispute that if the I.W.W. struck bargains with employers, compromised its principles . . . had the employers collect dues, and acted as "good boys" generally, we should have a half-million members? There is no such doubt. . . . But rather than sacrifice our principles, kow-tow to all sorts of freak notions, declare a practical truce with the enemy, and have a large number of dues-payers, we have preferred to be true to our purposes in spite of all opposition. Our men have sweated blood in carrying on the propaganda for a real revolutionary labor body—revolutionary in methods as well as final purpose.

Nothing, Ettor indicated, would convince the I.W.W. to compromise its convictions. The I.W.W. was committed to "the solidarity of labor for the revolution, and not solidarity with politicians, labor betrayers, craft unionists, priests and preachers, Militia of Christ and Civic Federation."[79]

Defeat, particularly a series of defeats, often calls forth criticism and sometimes encourages a modification of position which victory does not evoke. The Paterson failure, following closely the loss in Akron, elicited a plethora of criticisms and suggestions from every quarter, internal and external, for months afterwards. But it did not immediately cause a fundamental change in I.W.W. philosophy or practice. The organization beat down the challenge of its individualistic decentralizers; it did not merge with the Detroit faction, reinstitute the political clause or mute its attack on the socialist evolutionists, seek to capture or cooperate with the A.F.L., or turn itself into a propaganda league. Whether any of these changes would have altered the union's prospects is not certain, but the organization's adherence to its beliefs and aims clearly did not bring growth or reap benefits. In 1914–1915, the I.W.W. suffered a substantial loss of strength and membership. Less than 2,000 votes were cast in 1914 in the election for general secretary of the union, one indication of the decline in membership, and at the Ninth Convention only twenty-five delegates attended.[80]

The 1914 Convention, even with the paucity of delegates, nevertheless proved to be a significant one for the I.W.W. In the course of a discussion on organizing strategy, Frank Little, a member of the General Executive Board, proposed that the union embark on a concerted effort to organize the migrant workers in the midwestern grain belt and urged that the existing locals in that area, each separately tied directly to the central office, be merged into an industrial branch with its own secretary and organizing committee. Little's proposal was adopted by the convention and in spring of 1915, nine locals joined together to establish the Agricultural Workers' Organization (A.W.O.). The A.W.O. proved almost an immediate success—even reporting surplus in its treasury of over $14,000 by the end of its first year—and as a result, the structure of the I.W.W. was altered at the 1916 Convention to provide for industrial unions of a similar type. In addition, the convention delegates voted to launch campaigns to organize the lumber, mining, and shipping industries. With these actions, the I.W.W. entered what Philip Taft has called its third stage: "For the first time the I.W.W. was functioning regularly as a labor organization, using its monies to organize slowly and systematically some of the industrial areas it had staked out for itself. The I.W.W. publications began to stress the virtue of employment, improving conditions on the job, and the organization of the unorganized. The soap boxer lost his dominant position." According to Taft, these new developments might have led to I.W.W. permanency as a force in industries where large numbers of unskilled workers were employed had not World War I intervened.[81]

The organizational changes, following the lines urged by Williams after the Paterson debacle, were accompanied by changes in the leadership of the industrial union. St. John, who had served as secretary-treasurer of the I.W.W. since 1908, chose not to stand for reelection in 1914 and left Chicago headquarters for the life of a prospector in New Mexico. (Haywood replaced him as the highest officer in the organization.) In 1916 Ettor submitted his letter of resignation as general organizer. Although he claimed exhaustion from his long work as the union's most prodigious organizer, it is clear that the new emphasis of the union and A.W.O. activities in the grain belt were factors in his decision. "During the past eighteen months," he wrote the General Executive Board prior to the 1916 Convention, "I have suffered many disappointments, and they have further served to disillusion me as to the possibility of the General Organizer being of any practical value in the present state of the organization."[82]

Under new leadership, with a revised organizational structure, operating more as a union and less as a revolutionary body, and with evidence of success among the agricultural and lumber workers, the future seemed brighter for the I.W.W. in 1916. There was, however, some less favorable news which had to be reported to the delegates at the Tenth Convention in fall of that year. It concerned the N.I.U.T.W., formed in 1908 as the first industrial organization within the I.W.W. In March 1916 the General Executive Board suspended the once promising N.I.U.T.W. because of its small membership and its deficits of over $6,000.[83]

Fred W. Thompson attributed the demise of the textile industrial in part to the depression of 1914, when "the socialist activities appeared to offer a better outlet for whatever aspirations for a new social order these workers had retained from their strikes and past experiences," but he also acknowledged another factor, using words strikingly similar to those of Hoxie in describing the I.W.W.'s "perpetual dilemma": "To some extent this decline of the National Industrial Union of Textile Workers came from the difficulty in hitting the right balance between an industrial union program so different from prevailing thought that it struck most workers as alien, and a program so confined to job unionism that it lacked the spirit and vision necessary to hold workers together."[84]

The victory at Lawrence in 1912 had propelled the I.W.W. to national prominence, but its promise for the future had been dashed by the near-total defeat in Paterson the following year. If Lawrence demonstrated the potential of the I.W.W. among the country's textile workers, the struggle in the nation's silk capital raised questions concerning the very nature and direction of the industrial union.

Chapter 9

The Crucial Test

The real force in the labor history of 1913 . . . will undoubtedly be the I.W.W. . . . . If they continue to increase in membership during the coming year they will become an organization which will have to be reckoned with when it comes to the settlement of labor disputes.— Hezekiah N. Duff, "What of the Year 1913?" *Square Deal*, 11 (January 1913), 487.

Paterson has had its notoriety in the past, and we who think a great deal of our city and are interested in its prosperity and welfare did not want to have a repetition of . . . Lawrence.—Testimony of John W. Ferguson, United States Commission on Industrial Relations, *Final Report and Testimony on Industrial Relations*, 64th Congress, 1st Session, Senate Document #451, (Washington, 1916), vol. 3, p. 2580.

This is the life of the I.W.W. and if it takes years, we plan to win this strike.—William D. Haywood, quoted in Paterson *Evening News*, June 9, 1913.

In the months after the silk workers' return to the mills, second-guessers and those with twenty/twenty hindsight dissected the I.W.W. role in Paterson from every conceivable vantage point. From outside the industrial union, in particular, pundits offered their gratuitous opinions on why the strike had failed. The I.W.W. could expect the withering critiques which emanated from its proven adversaries: the business establishment, devotees of craft unionism and the A.F.L., the law and order crowd, and conservatives in general. But, as previously discussed, the criticisms hurled at the leadership of the strike came also from those who had previously worked closely with the syndicalist organization and from those who had provided it some measure of support during earlier labor contests.

Students of the I.W.W., most writing in the 1960's, have in their treatment of the Paterson strike included some of the same charges which were leveled by either friends or foes shortly after the silk strike petered out.[1] A number emphasize the "perpetual dilemma" inherent in the dual nature of the organization from its founding: a class-conscious revolutionary body and an industrial union concerned with the plight of unorganized and ignored workers.[2] Others discuss the shortcomings of specific parts of the I.W.W.'s policies: on dues, membership, contracts, and the like.[3]

There is substance to many of these criticisms. The constitutional provision of minimal initiation fees and low monthly dues, fashioned as a policy in contrast to that of the A.F.L., was particularly unsuited to an organization which so frequently advocated the weapon of the strike.[4] Expecting workers on the picket line to carry on without much semblance of a union relief fund is an example of a less than practical approach to the conduct of a long strike. The bare-treasury policy, more suitable to the hit and run actions of migrant workers in the West than to the industrial struggles in the East, made the I.W.W. particularly dependent upon the financial support of others,[5] and yet the union rarely missed an opportunity to ridicule or even attack those whose contributions were important. The I.W.W.'s often-stated disdain for the S.P.A. politicians, not infrequently voiced concurrent with its appeals for funds, might well have been even more counterproductive than it actually was. During both the Lawrence and Paterson strikes, the union was fortunate that party members did not allow the volleys fired at them to prompt withdrawal of their relief contributions.

The union's insistence on no contractual agreements with employers, coupled with fairly consistent statements that one strike was merely a prelude to the next, can also be questioned.[6] If, in the words of the I.W.W. faithful, settlement meant nothing more than a temporary truce, a breathing space before an opportune time to disrupt a company's production once again, one can understand the employers' disinclination to come to terms. The strategy of striking when the moment is right can be successful in gaining at least temporary gains, but it can also tend to make owners more intransigent than they might otherwise have been. Clearly, in Paterson, the mill owners showed scant willingness to discuss the matters at issue and even seemed resigned to risk financial disaster rather than settle a strike which the I.W.W. promised would be followed by another.[7]

The manner in which the I.W.W. conducted its organizing drives and the role which the national leaders played in strikes, attacked by Williams and others at the time, also warrants criticism. As one observer wrote on the first point in 1913, "no one use[d] the word 'organization' oftener or practice[d] it less" than the I.W.W.[8] The union was able to attract large numbers of workers to its ranks during the strikes in the East, but in every instance there was little attention paid to holding them when the contests ended. In McKees Rocks and Lawrence, for example, membership in the I.W.W. local dwindled to practically nothing within a few months of victory as Williams's "high divers" went off elsewhere to practice their art. Once a strike was over, even a successful strike, the battlefield was soon deserted for another.[9] This haphazard attention to organizational longevity had two important effects: it prevented the union from acquiring any permanent membership growth and it assured that union campaigns could not be built upon previous organizing efforts but always had to be constructed anew.

Flynn discussed the second organizational deficiency in the I.W.W. —its emphasis on group leadership—in her 1914 response to critics of the Paterson strike. The national leaders' role as advisers to the mass of strikers was not, she stated in retrospect, a particularly appropriate way to wage a battle which affected thousands. Flynn, in fact, listed this as one of the reasons why the silk strike was lost and argued that victory could have been obtained if the union had assumed genuine control. Her argument as it pertained to Paterson, which appeared to absolve the I.W.W. leaders of blame for the defeat, seems faulty as well as self-serving. But there is truth in the contention that strikes, in general, have a better chance for success if there is firm direction from the top.[10]

If the I.W.W. suffered from its own lack of organization and coordination, it displayed a particular genius for inspiring these qualities in its adversaries. In Paterson, the strike prompted a commonality of purpose among owners and the general public which had been rare in the past. Although the employers by no means spoke with a single voice during the conflict, the three silk associations did join together against their I.W.W. adversaries. In the community at large, moreover, the union leaders seemed to go out of their way to promote the overreaction of groups which might have been supportive or at least neutral in the strike.

Shichiro Matsui, in his history of the silk industry, makes this point as well as any other student of the contest: "While many representatives of the various interests in Paterson, not directly involved in the struggle, regarded the strikers' demands as not wholly unreasonable, they were deterred from openly urging the manufacturers to come to an agreement with the strikers by the fear that such action might be regarded as in some way constituting an approval of the anarchistic and revolutionary aims set forth in the constitution of the I.W.W." He argues that it was "this dread of anything that might suggest approval of the revolutionists that prevented the rallying of public opinion in support of the strikers."[11]

Even accepting as valid much of the criticisms of contemporaries and later students of the I.W.W., however, one can not blame entirely the initiation-dues policy, the emphasis on no contracts, group leadership, or the leaders' intemperate words for the defeat in the New Jersey silk center. Nor should one be too harsh in emphasizing internal weaknesses for the union's ultimate decline in the industrial East or be too confident that if the I.W.W. had followed "proper" tactics it would have been successful.[12] In any assessment of the I.W.W. before 1915, particularly of its role in Paterson, two points must be considered: the fate of earlier and later attempts at industrial organization in the country, and the fact that the union's efforts in the silk city followed successful strikes in the textile centers of Lawrence and Little Falls the previous year.

To blame internal failure and misguided principles alone for the decline of the I.W.W. in the East after 1913 ignores the fact that other challengers to the A.F.L.'s brand of organization had been even less successful in their efforts to establish viable alternative unions. Debs's American Railway Union, formed in 1893 and successful in its strike against James J. Hill's Great Northern line soon after, was the victim of its failed contest with the Pullman Palace Car Company the following year and joined the list of union dead. DeLeon's S.T.&L.A., created by the S.L.P. leader in 1895 as a direct challenge to Gomperism and the "labor fakirs," similarly demonstrated its inability to make substantial gains and to endure as a viable labor body. The ineffective W.L.U. and A.L.U., founded largely out of frustration with the dominant strategy of the A.F.L., also bear testimony to the poor track records of alternative unions in the period before 1905. And it should be noted that none of the dual unions mentioned shared the "misguided" or "self-defeating" policies of the I.W.W. In fact, Haywood was essentially correct when, in response to Mann's critique following the Paterson debacle, he pointed out that the I.W.W. had demonstrated a growth and durability far beyond these predecessors.[13]

The record of the U.T.W., like that of the fleeting textile organizations formed earlier, affords ample proof that it was no easy task to make lasting inroads in that important industry. Up to 1913 the U.T.W. had not shown itself to be a potent force in confrontations with the textile firms of the country. Again, the slow growth and modest success cannot be attributed to the same "impractical" strategy and tactics which brought the demise of the N.I.U.T.W.[14] The A.F.L. textile union emphasized the building up of a large war chest before a strike, demonstrated no reluctance to enter into contractual agreements with employers, was structured into a hierarchical chain of command in which leadership was tightly held at the top, and showed little inclination to alienate the establishment by provocative rhetoric. It clearly had liabilities in making itself a force in the textile industry, as evident in its role in both Lawrence and Paterson, but they were not the same as those attributed to the I.W.W. If one blames the Paterson defeat primarily on I.W.W. policies and revolutionary aims, how can one explain the dismal record of a union which followed along the opposite road?[15]

Those who emphasize the I.W.W.'s shortcomings in terms of broad approach and specific tactics to explain the defeat at Paterson and the demise of the N.I.U.T.W. seem to minimize another important fact: the victories which the union won the preceeding year in both Lawrence and Little Falls. In Paterson the I.W.W. organizers adhered to the same basic policies and followed the same strike tactics as in the two earlier textile confrontations.[16] The question to ask, therefore, is why the New Jersey silk strike failed while the contests in Lawrence and Little Falls succeeded. The reasons for the Paterson defeat must be sought beyond whatever deficiencies the I.W.W. possessed at its founding.

There is a tendency to emphasize the similarities in the textile strikes of 1912–1913, particularly the contests in Lawrence and Paterson, for the industry had certain common characteristics irrespective of the particular product or geographic location. Whether in wool, as in Lawrence, or in silk fabrics, as in Paterson, the industry was inordinately susceptible to seasonal and cyclical economic fluctuations. Workers in textiles, no matter the product, were almost routinely faced with layoffs or forced reductions in hours or wages due to the country's general economic climate, the demands of the marketplace, or the changing tastes of the consuming public.

In all the branches of the textile industry, technological advances had diminished the reliance on highly skilled operatives, and relatively unskilled workers of foreign birth comprised a large and growing portion of the labor force. Due to technological changes as well, the number of female workers and youngsters of both sexes was increasing. Women and children, viewed as supplementary family providers rather than principal breadwinners, received wages lower than what were paid to mature male workers, and employers saw them as attractive cost-saving replacements. In all textile cities, therefore, job displacement and wage reductions were genuine threats and cause for concern.

Like their counterparts in Lawrence and Little Falls, most Paterson textile workers were poorly paid, worked at piece-rate wages, and toiled long hours under work and safety conditions which were of low standard. Although specific points of grievance differed from city to city, the broad outline of the workers' dissatisfaction was the same: six days' work per week at low pay, poor shop conditions, speedups on the line, a system of fines for every conceivable infraction of the rules or faults in the woven fabric, preferred treatment of favored workers to the detriment of others, and the threat of blacklisting for those who spoke up against conditions or tried to organize their co-workers.[17]

Following the successful strike at Lawrence among workers in the same industry and laboring under similar conditions, it is not surprising that I.W.W. organizers would view Paterson as an inviting prospect for another victorious contest. In fact, on the surface at least, Paterson seemed to offer even better chances of success. With its long history of labor unrest, the marked proclivity of the silk workers to transform grievances into militant action, and the apparent radical inclination of Paterson's working class population, the New Jersey silk center appeared to be a particularly promising site for an I.W.W. strike.[18]

Lawrence and Paterson were fairly large cities, with populations of approximately 86,000 and 123,000 respectively, and each had a substantial proportion of its workforce employed in the textile industry. In Lawrence, some 30,000 were employed in the mills along the Merrimack, with an estimated 60,000 of its citizens dependent on the textile industry.[19] Paterson and the surrounding silk towns of Passaic County employed as many as 26,000 of the total 28,263 silk workers in the state.[20] There was a somewhat greater number of women in the Lawrence textile mills, 44.6 percent to 41.6 percent in Paterson, at the time the strikes began, but the entrance of women into the silk mills was of more recent origin, and their percentage in some parts of the industry, the broad- and ribbon-silk establishments, was close to 50 percent and growing; some foresaw the day when women would make up almost the entire work force in the weaving shops.[21] Comparable figures are not available for the number of children employed in the textile mills of each city, but boys and girls under the age of sixteen were a significant part of the labor force.[22]

There was some disparity in the wages paid in the two textile centers, with the New Jersey silk workers, on average, receiving higher pay than their Massachusetts counterparts. In Lawrence, the average weekly wage was $10.49 for men over eighteen years of age and $8.18 for women; the average annual earnings of a male head of family was $400.[23] In New Jersey, the state's Bureau of Statistics reported in 1912 that broad- and ribbon-silk workers received an average yearly wage of $508.62, that workers in the dye shops were paid an average of $589.88 a year, and that the employees in the throwing mills averaged $357.79.[24]

Averages do not tell the entire story, but the bureau provided a further breakdown of wages for the three divisions. Table 1 details the range of weekly wages by sex and age for the 108 broad- and ribbon-silk shops which reported to the agency.[25]

TABLE 1. The Range of Weekly Wages by Sex and Age for 108 Broad- and Ribbon-Silk Shops

Weekly Wage	Number of Men 16+	Number of Women 16+	Number of Children −16	Total
Under $3	94	84	72	250
$3−4	72	246	313	631
$4−5	196	598	268	1,062
$5−6	302	937	87	1,326
$6−7	377	1,404	16	1,797
$7−8	453	1,798	9	2,260
$8−9	559	1,422	2	1,983
$9−10	638	845	—	1,483
$10−12	1,300	1,482	—	2,782
$12−15	3,125	2,253	—	5,378
$15−20	3,115	624	—	3,739
$20−25	665	62	—	727
Over $25	189	5	—	194
Total				23,612

Similar data available for the dye-house and throwing-mill employees indicate that the average weekly pay was somewhat lower than for workers in the weaving establishments, although still higher than that paid to the textile workers in Lawrence.[26]

The material available in the annual reports of the New Jersey Bureau of Statistics for the years before and after 1913 provides insight into what was occurring in the silk industry at the time. For example, examination of the weekly wages of the broad- and ribbon-silk workers given above shows clearly that men, on the average, received higher pay than women or those under sixteen years of age. One need not be statistically gifted to recognize what the future could hold if technological advances opened more jobs to women and children. The fact that the average yearly wage in the throwing mills, which contained the largest number of women workers, was at least $150 less than in the dye or weaving shops supports the Paterson workers' fears concerning their wages. Moreover, testimony before the Commission on Industrial Relations in 1914 suggests that in certain categories of work the annual pay for workers had already declined.[27] Despite the fact that the Paterson wages were higher than in Lawrence, the wage issue was no less a matter of concern.

A comparison of the ethnic composition of Lawrence and Paterson indicates that both cities had a large number of recent immigrants in the mills. In the former, the number of native born working in the textile industry was estimated in 1912 as 12.5 percent; in the silk center, the "English-speaking" workers accounted for 15 percent.[28] The term "English-speaking," used frequently in Paterson but nowhere clearly defined, meant essentially those of native or old-immigrant type. If this is an accurate translation of an ambiguous description, it would mean that the two textile cities were not particularly dissimilar.

What is significant about the ethnic composition of the two work forces was the mix of nationality groups in each city. Lawrence was the epitome of ethnic diversity, and the strike there involved at least twenty-five identifiable nationalities, a fact which Ettor recognized in fashioning the Central Strike Committee to assure the representation of each group. In Paterson the diversity was not as pronounced in fact or in perception. The Central Strike Committee there was organized along shop lines and the only ethnic division spoken of was between English speaking and non-English speaking. From the very beginning of the strike in Paterson, the two broad categories maintained a "shaky alliance of convenience."[29]

The ethnic split, with Italian workers comprising the bulk of the non-English speakers, was evident in work assignments, in neighborhoods, and in religious and civic organizations. To a degree not found in Lawrence, Paterson was a city "fragmented by class and nationality." The English speakers were most numerous in the ribbon branch, received the highest wages, and usually lived in better homes further removed from the mill district than the Italian workers.[30] Although it would appear that some of the local papers overemphasized the ethnic contentions between the workers during the strike, a division between the two camps did exist. Toward the end of the strike, it was the English-speaking segment in the ribbon shops which challenged the union leadership first.

In the months immediately preceeding the strikes in the two cities, the union picture in Lawrence and Paterson was markedly similar. Both cities had a history of union instability, with one textile organization after another forming, enjoying a short existence, and then fading from sight. In Lawrence, the number of textile workers in any union in January 1912 was a mere 2,800 of the 30,000 employed in the industry. Of these, 2,500 were members of ten separate independent or A.F.L. unions. Golden's U.T.W. was divided into three distinct craft locals, all representing the most skilled workers in the industry, and the largest of these, the loom fixers, had an estimated membership of only 200.[31]

The position of the U.T.W. in Paterson on the eve of the strike there was similar to that in Lawrence in January 1912. The A.F.L. textile union once had a number of Paterson locals and, as late as 1912, its Broad-Silk Local 607 had 1,888 members in good standing. Local 607 had dwindled down to virtually nothing after the early strikes at Doherty's, however, and had less than 100 members when the general strike began. In February 1913 the U.T.W.'s only strength in the New Jersey city was in the loom fixers' and twisters' local and the horizontal warpers' local, both made up of English-speaking, highly skilled, and well-paid workers.[32] In both textile cities, therefore, the U.T.W. was a minimal presence: it represented the most skilled, ignored the mass of immigrant workers, and held virtually the "same social outlook as the employers."[33]

The I.W.W. was not a strong organization in either Lawrence or Paterson in the months immediately prior to the strikes of 1912–1913, but in both the union had been active the year before. Local 20 in Lawrence was formed in 1906 out of remnants of DeLeon's S.T.&L.A., almost ceased to exist during the following depression year, then sprang to life in 1908 when it was a founding member of the N.I.U.T.W. It called a strike against the Atlantic Mills in the summer of 1911 and increased its membership to perhaps 500.[34] Following the usual course of the organization, however, the membership won in 1911 declined shortly thereafter: by January 1912 Local 20 had no more than 300 members in good standing.[35] But although the union was in a "state of disorganization" on the eve of the strike, the textile workers of Lawrence "knew of the organization's existence, its aims, and its local activities" when the first men stormed out of the mills.[36]

The prestrike history of the I.W.W. in Paterson was similar to that in Lawrence. Formed in 1906 by men with strong ties to the S.L.P., Local 152 suffered the same tenuous existence as its Massachusetts counterpart prior to 1911. It nevertheless had a fairly stable membership of about 500, and this number was increased early in February 1913 when some 400 broad-silk weavers, most from the Doherty shop, switched their allegiance from the U.T.W. According to Lessig, the membership of Local 152 was close to 900 when the general strike began.[37]

Comparing the nature, condition, and organization of the work forces in the two textile cities just prior to the strikes, there were indeed similarities. Pay was higher in Paterson, but in both cities the vast majority of workers were concerned about job conditions and the effect of technological improvements on their futures. In each city the percentage of immigrant workers was high, the mass of workers unorganized, and the I.W.W. a union not unknown to the mill hands.

But Paterson was not an exact replica of Lawrence, nor was the silk city's reputation as a hotbed of radicalism necessarily beneficial to the I.W.W. prospects there. Those less confident of the ultimate triumph of the working class under the direction of a committed revolutionary union, those more measured in their assessment of the meaning of Lawrence than the I.W.W. faithful, might have been sobered by the differences. Fresh from their success in Massachusetts, however, the union organizers harbored few doubts that they could triumph in New Jersey. Dazzled by the victory in Lawrence, always confident of the future, Flynn and the others did not pause to weigh the conditions which made a successful strike anything but certain.

When the workers of Lawrence lashed out against the two-hour wage reduction early in January 1912, their wrath was directed against twelve mills. The American Woolen Company had four of these and employed as many as 16,500 workers, or at least half of the textile operatives in the city. The other large companies in Lawrence were Pacific Mills, employing 6,000, and Arlington Mills, with some 5,000 workers. The workers' adversaries, then, were elephantine corporations with huge assets, the epitome of giantism in American industry. Although the Lawrence establishments suffered the same economic fluctuation endemic to the textile industry, they were essentially profitable concerns, well protected by high tariffs and relatively unhindered by competition from other states.[38]

The situation in Paterson was just the reverse. While it is relatively easy to enumerate and describe the companies and mills which operated along the banks of the Merrimack, it is virtually impossible to state with confidence of accuracy the number of silk firms operating in and around Silk City. If trusts were the rule in Lawrence, small shops and fragmentation were the dominant features in New Jersey. Specialization of function existed in Lawrence, but there was not the same rigid division into branches which existed in the Paterson area. There the employers were separated into distinct subsections of the silk industry, with each branch having its own employers' association and peculiar interests. Instead of the 9 employers in Lawrence, there were close to 300 separate firms in Passaic County.[39]

Of greater importance to the strikers than the division of the silk industry into three major branches (ribbon, broad-silk, and dyeing) was the separation of employers into the two rough categories of large and small establishments. In dyeing, this feature was much less pronounced than in the ribbon- and broad-silk branches, since the nature of the work done made small dye shops impractical, and better than two-thirds of the 6,000 dye-house workers were employed by two firms: Weidmann Company and the National Silk Dyeing Company. But there were nevertheless some twenty other dye shops in the city, existing on the fringes of that branch and doing work for the two giants.[40]

The exact situation in the broad-silk and ribbon-silk branches is more difficult to sketch. There were, however, approximately 118 to 120 separate mills in Paterson, of which between 55 and 60 were broad-silk establishments employing about 7,000 workers. In the ribbon-silk branch, a similar number of workers were employed by a larger number of separate owners.[41] The figures of 118 to 120 mills and 300 odd shops emphasize a significant point about the New Jersey silk industry: many mills housed any number of small concerns employing from two to forty workers. If one recognizes that the average number of workers per establishment in 1914 was 58.4 and remembers that Weidmann, National, and Doherty (to name a few of the more prominent firms) employed over 1,000 workers each, one gets an idea of the size of some of the shops. Henry Doherty, Jr., in his testimony before the Commission on Industrial Relations, estimated that the average weaving establishment in the city operated 50 looms as compared to the slightly more than 1,000 looms in his own broad-silk firm.[42]

The division in size in each of the three major branches of the industry was reflected in several ways, including membership in the employers' organizations: the Ribbon Manufacturers' Association, the Broad-Silk Manufacturers' Association, and the Master Dyers. None of these three bodies, as weak and ineffectual as they were, had the majority of the manufacturers in its branch as members. In the Broad-Silk Manufacturers' Association, only the larger firms were represented, and a good number of these had mills in Pennsylvania. Among the ribbon-silk manufacturers, the manager of the Frank & Dugan firm estimated that only about thirty-four of the shop owners were members of the narrow-silk owners' association.[43] Size was not the only determiner of which firms chose to join; at least of equal importance was the distinction which existed among employers on class and ethnic lines. Many of the owners or managers of the larger establishments had been in the city for decades, many were native born or immigrants from British textile centers, and most had begun in Paterson as weavers themselves. Henry Doherty, Sr. exemplified this type: sixty-five years of age in 1914, he had arrived in the city as a boy when there were only six hand looms in the city, had worked as a weaver, and had then founded his own company in 1900.[44]

The owners of the smaller establishments were of a different sort.

They, too, had started out as weavers in other men's shops and shared the same dreams of upward mobility which Doherty and his peers had realized. They were, however, only on the first or second rung of the ladder of entrepreneurial success in 1913. Many of their firms were only extended family shops, operating in rented space in the larger mills and existing on a shoestring in their attempt to compete with the older establishments. These small owners were also immigrants, but they had come from southern and eastern Europe and many were Jews.[45] Of different origin and faith, the aspiring small shop owners were looked down upon by the large employers, the English-speaking weavers, long-time Paterson residents, and even the city officials. Magnet, speaking from the vantage point of an English-speaking ribbon-silk weaver, called them "upstarts" and testified that they "were the worst to deal with." Rodney Miller, an industrial consultant for the National Silk Dyeing Company, echoed Magnet's statement when he told the commission that there was a tendency "among a certain branch of the Jewish element in manufacturing to exploit laborers unnecessarily." Others, including U.T.W. business agent Starr and Mayor McBride, agreed.[46]

In comparing the industrial situation of Lawrence and Paterson prior to the strikes in the two cities, a major difference was in the nature of the I.W.W.'s adversaries, Haywood wrote in May 1913: "The Paterson workers have not had to fight a concentrated trust, such as existed at Lawrence, but a gang of scattered employers, all jealous and fearful of each other. The strike undoubtedly would have ended much sooner had it not been for the desire of the richer manufacturers to see the smaller makers starved out and driven into bankruptcy, which already had occurred to a number of them."[47] Flynn, speaking on the Paterson strike after it was well over, included this factor as one of the reasons for the defeat.[48]

Another significant difference between the industrial situations in the two textile cities, and one which Flynn also emphasized in her discussion of the cause for the defeat, concerned competition from other states. Although the Lawrence corporations complained about competition from southern and other New England states, citing this as a reason they could not afford to pay fifty-six-hour wages for a fifty-four-hour week, the challenge which they faced from outside paled in comparison to that of their New Jersey counterparts. When the Paterson employers argued that they could not grant the demands put forward by the Central Strike Committee early in the strike, there was considerable substance to their argument. The silk mills of Pennsylvania did pose a genuine threat to the New Jersey industry.

In Pennsylvania, where large and more modern mills were the rule, wages were lower and hours longer than in the Passaic County textile center. Moreover, Pennsylvania in 1913 was threatening to overtake New Jersey as *the* silk state in the nation, if it had not already done so. Table 2 shows that the Pennsylvania silk industry in 1914 employed more workers in larger mills, exceeded New Jersey in the value of its product, and had become the dominant silk state at some point after 1909.[49]

TABLE 2. Silk Industry State Comparisons, 1914

Number of Establishments	Number of Workers	Value of Product	Rank in 1914	Rank in 1909
Pa. 284	44,755	$86,938,554	1	2
N.J. 368	28,263	$75,706,449	2	1

The establishment of the silk industry in eastern Pennsylvania, begun in the throwing mills before the turn of the century as technological advances allowed unskilled women and children to do that work, had spread by 1913 to include dye shops and weaving mills as well. In fact, some large dyeing and broad-silk shops in New Jersey had established annexes in that state to take advantage of the more favorable business conditions there. Those Paterson silk owners who did not have annexes, the newcomers who had the smallest shops and some of the older and larger establishments like Doherty, voiced a genuine concern when they complained that they were already at a near-ruinous competitive disadvantage. Not only was the workweek shorter in Paterson, fifty-five hours as compared to fifty-seven to sixty hours in other states, but the average wages were as much as 20 percent higher.[50] Given this situation, U.T.W. business agent Starr told the Commission on Industrial Relations, the Central Strike Committee's demand for a 25 percent increase in wages would have forced the Paterson mills out of business or prompted them to relocate in "Pennsylvania or some other place where they employ cheap labor."[51]

In the broad-silk branch of the industry, the Pennsylvania shops had the additional advantage of operating in more modern mills than in New Jersey, ones which concentrated on producing the cheaper broad silks (messalines) on multiple looms. It was the Doherty Company's attempt to compete in this area which had begun the strike activity a year prior to the general strike. Doherty believed that only by closing down three of his smaller facilities in Paterson and building the modern Lakeview facility in Clifton, where messalines would be produced on the three- and four-loom system, could his company survive.[52]

The competition which Paterson faced from Pennsylvania and the general character of the New Jersey silk industry made the 1913 strike markedly different from that waged in Massachusetts the year before. In Lawrence, the I.W.W. could focus its attack on the dominant corporation in the city, confident that if the American Woolen Company capitulated, the other textile firms in the city and across New England would fall into line. In Paterson, with its hundreds of employers, the union had to confront a beleaguered adversary fragmented by size, degree of profitability, even national origin and religion. Pennsylvania's lower wages, longer hours, and heavier reliance on women and children threatened the very existence of some of the Paterson firms if they acquiesced to the strike demands.[53]

In a very real sense, the struggle which took place in Paterson in 1913 was one of life or death for many of the owners. Believing that agreement to the strike demands without a similar capitulation by their counterparts in Pennsylvania would force them out of business or require them to relocate, the owners were determined to stand fast. Owners of the small shops could not give in and still compete with the larger establishments in the city; the larger companies which had annexes in other states did not have to give in because they were still making a profit. After the strike was over, the conviction that the competitive situation was the key to the battle was voiced by Paterson people of every persuasion. In testimony before the Commission on Industrial Relations, Doherty, Mayor McBride, U.T.W. agents Starr and Morgan, strike activists Magnet and Zuersher, and Father Stein all stated that the only solution to the problems which had confronted the city was the passage of legislation by Congress making hours and wages uniform throughout the country.[54]

The nature of the Paterson silk industry and the existence of threatening out-of-state competition made the battlegrounds of the New Jersey and Massachusetts textile strikes dissimilar. But there was another difference as well: the fact that the Paterson strike *followed* the Lawrence contest. If holding firm against perceived unreasonable and irresponsible strike demands was seen by the silk owners as crucial to the very existence of the New Jersey industry, standing resolutely against the I.W.W. threat was seen by many others as essential to the industrial peace, perhaps the very capitalist system, of the country. The victory in Lawrence, followed by the smaller success in Little Falls, had propelled the I.W.W. to a place which its long-time adversaries could never have imagined. Almost overnight, this band of hot-voiced revolutionaries threatened to become *the* labor force in the industrial centers of the East.

With the benefit of hindsight or sober reflection, the possibility of long-term success for such a union was unlikely, but the I.W.W.'s internal weaknesses and the immensity of the task which faced less revolutionary industrial unions into the 1930s could not be known at the time. What was understood was that the I.W.W. had scored a major victory over a giant corporation in Lawrence and had won significant benefits for thousands of New England textile workers. Although the success in Little Falls was of much smaller dimensions, it had continued the organization's momentum in the industry. A similar victory in Paterson, it was feared, could have enormous impact and repercussions.

During the course of the silk strike, the I.W.W. leaders made it clear that the defeat of the New Jersey silk owners would make the union a potent force throughout the country. Haywood stated the importance of victory to the union when he told a mass gathering at Haledon in June: "This is the life of the I.W.W. and if it takes years, we plan to win this strike."[55] A journalist observer of events in the city recognized this dimension of the contest and similarly emphasized the strike's importance. The I.W.W., Gregory Mason wrote in June 1913, was "fighting in Paterson . . . with an eye to the future . . . victory would lead to I.W.W. outbreaks all through the industrial centers of the East. A defeat in Paterson . . . would be a crushing blow."[56]

It is clear that both the owners and the union saw the contest as of immeasurable importance. But this is true also of the citizens of Paterson. The I.W.W.'s defeat was viewed as crucial to the industrial health of the city as well as to its national reputation. Public opinion concerning the union prior to the general strike was, if anything, even more antagonistic than it had been in the Massachusetts wool center. Longtime residents still smarted over the radical labor outbursts in the city around the turn of the century and Paterson's reputation as an anarchist stronghold; moreover, they had suffered an I.W.W. invasion of the Passaic area in 1912 and were decidedly not pleased by the prospect of another such labor explosion in their midst. Many in Paterson agreed with local businessman John Ferguson that the city would be justified to "tell the outsiders to get out of town on the next train" and with Frank & Dugan manager Moses Straus, who told the commission what he thought of the union. "The I.W.W. I don't consider an American organization," he testified. "They are un-American in their preamble and everything else."[57]

In both Lawrence and Paterson, the I.W.W. had few friends when the strikes began: the antiunion priest of Lawrence, Father James O'Reilly, had an equally antagonistic counterpart in the silk city's Father Stein; the unfriendly press in Lawrence was at least matched by most of the Paterson newspapers; Lawrence Mayor Michael Scanlon took strong action against the I.W.W. in the first days of the strike, and Mayor McBride, although professing his strong sympathy for the workers, demonstrated little even-handedness in dealing with the union. Even individuals active in the charity organizations of the two cities shared the common view that the workers were well off, had substantial accounts in savings banks, "could not have been in a tremendously impoverished condition," and had no reason to strike.[58]

If the sentiment of the two communities toward the I.W.W. was similar, two things were different: Paterson followed Lawrence and Paterson's administration was far more skilled in the handling of its strike. Both of these facts must be assigned some responsibility for the Paterson defeat. The McBride administration had an opportunity to learn from the example of the Massachusetts contest, had experienced earlier labor battles, and was supported by a large number of citizens who did "not want to have a repetition of the conditions in Lawrence."[59] As the Paterson *Guardian* commented approvingly on the day the general strike began: "Paterson is not another Lawrence."[60]

In 1913 John Brooks wrote that, in the past, I.W.W. victories had "been largely won by the blunders of [its] enemies."[61] Nothing could have confirmed this judgment better than the actions of the city officials in Lawrence. In the Massachusetts city, a new administration responded to the strike and to I.W.W. tactics with blunder after blunder. Confronted by the spontaneous violence of the first day, an apparently frightened Mayor Scanlon called for the militia on the day the walkout began and before I.W.W. organizers had even been summoned; with little sympathy for the unskilled immigrants who comprised the mass of the strikers, the militiamen proved to be "recklessly irresponsible" and provocative in their actions. The arrest of Ettor and Giovannitti on questionable charges created martyrs to the cause, focused attention on events in the city, and failed in its apparent aim to render the strike leaderless. The clash at the railroad station, which evoked a public outcry and wide sympathy for the workers, prompted the hearings which ultimately forced the American Woolen Company to capitulate.[62]

If Brooks had written later, when the struggle in New Jersey was over and there had been time for assessment, he might have added that I.W.W. defeats resulted when the union's enemies demonstrate skill in responding to its challenge. Lawrence Mayor Scanlon was the perfect example of a city official playing into the hands of the radical union; Mayor McBride showed that he was no carbon copy of his Massachusetts counterpart.

Throughout the Paterson strike, McBride demonstrated his understanding of the point made by the Paterson *Evening News* that "nothing binds men more firmly together and makes them more determined . . . than oppressive or unlawful acts of officers of the law."[63] Although there were times when the Paterson authorities skated dangerously close to making the sort of error on which the I.W.W. thrived—the arrest of Haywood and the closing of the meeting halls would be the best examples—the fine line between firm measures and outrageous punishment or oppressive tactics was never crossed for long. Haywood's imprisonment, which the New York *Call* termed "a blessing to the I.W.W.," was of short duration and he was never brought to trial; the city thus did not precipitate a reaction in the Ettor-Giovannitti mold. Turn Hall and Helvetia Hall were closed for less than a week before meetings were again held there and the potentially explosive free-speech issue defused.[64] Without any intention of applauding the Paterson authorities for the role which they played during the strike, one can recognize that they handled the I.W.W. challenge in a masterful fashion. There were few of the mistakes which marked the Lawrence strike and contributed to the victory there.

On the night of February 24, at about the same time that the I.W.W. leaders were holding the mass meeting at Turn Hall to brief the silk workers on the tactics planned for the next day, Mayor McBride met with Chief of Police Bimson and Passaic County Prosecutor Dunn at police headquarters to discuss the strike threat and plan the city's response. According to McBride, the three were determined that there "not be any digression from the proper course by either the employee or the employer" and that the city would "maintain law and order." Bimson, a veteran police officer with previous experience in Paterson labor disputes, was given the responsibility of preventing violence.[65] Although there is no evidence on what else might have been discussed that night, it is not improbable that specific strategies were sketched out at the meeting. Certainly when the strike began early the next morning, the actions of the authorities seemed well orchestrated.

Throughout the strike, the task of maintaining law and order was left entirely in the hands of the local police department. Unlike at Lawrence, where the state militia was called out at the start and played a large role throughout the struggle, militiamen never patrolled the streets of the silk city. Even though the New Jersey militia had been used during a 1902 dyers' strike in Paterson, Bimson and McBride were determined not to call for such aid. Police Captain McBride (no relation to the mayor), a veteran of twenty-eight years on the force, later stated that he had advised the chief that "there ought to be 2,000 militia" in the city, but he could not convince Bimson. According to him, the chief responded that the department could "handle the situation."[66]

When the strike began, the Paterson police force had 105 patrolmen and a total strength of 147, including secretaries, park, and truant officers.[67] For the first month of the strike these officers worked double shifts. When the contest showed no sign of ending, the city hired 35 additional men and the sheriff provided 25 special deputies, recruited and paid by Passaic County, who were assigned to night duty. In addition to these, approximately 100 O'Brien detectives were hired by the larger employers and sworn in by Sheriff Radcliff.[68] The police presence, including the private detectives, was less than 300 men. It is not true, as Renshaw has written, that "police and militia [sic] were even more numerous" in Paterson than in Lawrence.[69]

Whatever the exact number on duty, the police proved equal to the task. Most of the officers were deployed around the mills, protecting the owners' property night and day, while a floating force was available to be sent to points where picketing was particularly heavy or where incidents were expected or reported.[70] Although the arrest policy fluctuated, as mentioned earlier, at no time did the police appear reluctant to arrest pickets who refused to obey orders to disband or move along. In all, a total of 2,238 arrests were recorded during the strike or, assuming that none were arrested more than once, "one out of every eleven silk workers."[71]

The number of arrests and jail sentences served in "Sheriff Radcliff's Hotel" would appear to support the later contention that the department's heavy-handedness was even more excessive than in Lawrence. However, there seems little doubt that, from the outset, the more committed strikers actually courted arrest. U.T.W. business agent Morgan watched the police arrest as many as forty pickets at a time and told the Commission on Industrial Relations that one "would think it was arranged for a moving-picture show." In his words, the scenes were "such a burlesque, some being taken into the patrol wagons, and some jumping in the patrol wagon, and some trying to get in." If Morgan's reliability is suspect, his testimony was supported by Lessig, who spoke of the same eagerness for arrest and explained why over 1,000 strikers spent at least a few days in the county jail: "We told the people to go ahead and crowd the jail until they hadn't room, and to stop paying fines; that if we paid the $10 every time . . . the city officers would only be too glad to enrich the city treasury and that the only way to do away with that was to crowd the jail—and that they did to the queen's taste."[72] Boyd confirmed this when he wrote during the strike that "being jailed in Paterson is no longer a disgrace—it is an honor."[73]

The pack-the-jail tactic, reminiscent of the free-speech fights in the West, did not bring the city to its knees. The jail was at times very overcrowded, but most of those arrested served only a day or two and thus did not overburden either the facility or the city's coffer. More importantly, although the number of arrests in Paterson far exceeded that in Lawrence, the New Jersey officials showed better judgment than their New England brethren in their use of the arrest weapon. Most of those who served time in Passaic County were unknown silk workers. Boyd, Quinlan, and Scott were the most prominent victims of the city's heavy hand, but their treatment prompted only modest public protest and did not capture the same national attention which followed the arrest of Ettor and Giovannitti. Only the handling of Haywood, Flynn, and Reed threatened to evoke a response comparable to that which had contributed to the victory in Lawrence, and in each case, Paterson managed to escape the worst ramifications. Haywood was never tried, Flynn was not convicted for strike-related offenses, and Reed could not win the martyrdom (and publicity) which he apparently sought.[74]

While the Paterson police patrolled the mill districts to protect the owners' property, kept a tight reign on picketing activities, obliged the strikers' penchant for arrest and jail, sought to intimidate the leaders by threatening felony convictions, and showed themselves to be anything but impartial, the city avoided the blunders of the Scanlon administration. The calm, deliberate actions of Paterson authorities thus prevented the I.W.W. organizers from exploiting the explosive issue which they courted. Individual police officers appeared to be well briefed and cautioned against excessive force, and the department seemed forewarned and ready to meet whatever tactic the union devised. This latter characteristic can be explained by evidence that mass gatherings and shop sessions were carefully monitored. From almost the beginning of the strike, the county prosecutor had a stenographer present at the daily branch meetings to gather evidence which might later prove useful in judicial proceedings and to provide information to the police concerning what the union planned next. Additional intelligence came from the O'Brien agency men who were planted among the workers, pretending to be strikers or strike sympathizers.[75]

The Paterson authorities' handling of the strike was variously viewed by contemporaries but has been almost unanimously condemned by later students of the strike.[76] The picture of official mistreatment was forcefully expressed to the commission by Lessig and strike counsel

Marelli, and was also emphasized in a number of sympathetic articles of the day.[77] Not surprisingly, others in Paterson at the time saw the city's handling of the strike in a quite different light. Morgan testified that "the attitude of the police was very fair, under the circumstances," and Father Stein told the commission that the "civil authorities conscientiously did their duty, and unflinchingly did it, and did it with a great deal of wisdom."[78]

Morgan and Stein were wrong about the city's even-handedness; their failure to acknowledge that the weight of Paterson's resources was clearly on the side of the employers tells more about the U.T.W. official and the Catholic priest vis-à-vis the I.W.W. than it reflects an impartial assessment. But Father Stein was correct about the city administration's "wisdom." Mayor McBride and his associates never let the strike get out of hand and, along with Governor Fielder, ignored the calls from many sides for an external investigation of the issues. The spector of the House investigation of the Lawrence battle was probably no small factor in their preference for local arbitration or agreement.[79] Thus, although the union organizers followed almost exactly the same broad strategy and specific tactics of the Lawrence confrontation, they were unable to provoke blatant overreaction or a federal intervention. The city officials, and the owners whose position they upheld, were fortunate that there was no explosive incident which could have benefitted the strikers. A bombing, the death of a number of strikers, policemen, or innocent bystanders, or a spontaneous rampage through the streets might have provoked the sort of public outcry which the city administration was determined to prevent. But none of these occurred. There was no incident comparable to that at the Lawrence railroad depot. The matter was left to be fought out between the owners and their employees.

Although the battle did not feature an incident provocative enough to attract national attention and perhaps affect the outcome, there are differences of opinion concerning whether the strike in Paterson was violent or not. In the studies of some recent students of the strike, there emerges a picture of a contest even more violent than others which the I.W.W. waged in the East.[80] Balancing this view of the Paterson strike is the work of others who note the "total lack of violence,"[81] and who question the union's reputation for violence in general. Conlin writes:

> Haywood and some other Wobblies had an inarticulated conception of the now-familiar idea that nonviolence often frustrated the adversary into the use of violence, and the public's comparison of peaceful workers with violent employers would channel the tide of

public opinion to the workers' cause. This was exactly what happened at Lawrence and at Spokane, and the experience confirmed Wobblies in their policy. In both cities the brutality of the police and the resultant public protest were of major importance in accounting for the I.W.W. victories.[82]

If earlier I.W.W. successes can thus be attributed at least in part to the union's insistence on nonviolence coupled with the excesses of its opponents, the question of whether the Paterson strike was peaceful or not could explain why it ended in failure. Did the actions of the silk workers, either with or without union countenance, erode potential public support of the strike? Or was the strike lost even though the union's counsel of nonviolence was followed?

A reading of local newspaper accounts during the strike and of the testimony given to the Commission on Industrial Relations in 1914 can support either position.[83] The testimony of Police Captain McBride, Passaic County Prosecutor Dunn, National Dyeing Company manager Edward Lotte, and Father Stein does indeed provide evidence of violence: houses blown up, cars stoned, personal attacks on scabs and police, attempts to wreck trains, and riots in the streets. Dunn, after recounting such acts, told the commission that he "would not call it a peaceful strike" and Father Stein volunteered that "there was disorder —sad disorder."[84] But these statements concerning violence were from individuals who could not be called either sympathetic or neutral to the I.W.W.-led strike and must be considered in that context. On the other hand, some of those who testified to the peaceful nature of the contest— Lessig, Marelli, and Zuersher—were similarly witnesses with a particular bias. Zuersher's assertion that 25,000 striking clergymen "would not have been any more peaceful than the strikers themselves," must be read as the statement of a committed I.W.W. leader.[85]

None of the individuals mentioned to this point were dispassionate witnesses, and a selective use of testimony before the commission could be used to support very different pictures of the silk strike. Fortunately, there were others who testified on the question of violence whose words were not similarly suspect. Mill owner Doherty stated that "for the amount of people on strike" there was not much disorder, and dyehouse manager Lotte, although reporting instances of threat and intimidation, conceded that the strike was "peaceable." Both Starr and Morgan, whose views on the I.W.W. were clearly hostile and like Doherty and Lotte had no reason to present a tainted picture, similarly minimized the amount of violence associated with the prolonged contest. Starr testified that the strikers "conducted themselves in a very good manner," and Morgan stated that "it was very peaceful for a strike of that size." Finally, this conclusion was repeated by Paterson business-man Cooke, who told the commission that the strike was not "unusually disorderly."[86] A careful look at the entire record contained in the com-mission's final report would appear to indicate that, although there were some instances of disorder in the contest, the strike was essentially nonviolent.

There is no question that some of the city's papers did report scenes of near riot proportions, a fact especially true of the *Guardian*, but a reading of several of the papers makes one cautious. Violent outbreaks of a dimension reported in one paper would normally be expected to be covered in the other papers as well. But this was not always the case and suggests that some reports of violence were more creative than factual. I.W.W. leaders often bemoaned the slanted press treatment they received in Paterson, and there is support for their complaint from at least one source generally unfriendly to the union. Morgan was asked whether newspaper reports of violence were overdrawn, and he re-sponded that they were and that "out of a very trifling affair they [the press] would make it appear that it was a great big riot, and all that stuff." He continued that "some of the papers in particular seemed to take a great deal of delight in forcing things at Paterson."[87]

One last voice on the question of violence in Paterson is that of the *Industrial Union News*, the official organ of the Detroit I.W.W. The paper commented on the Chicago organization's conduct of the silk strike in its June 1913 number: "The anarcho-syndicalist outfit in charge at Lawrence ridiculed our idea of a peaceful strike [in Passaic in 1912] but they themselves were compelled to act peaceably. Later on the Chi-cago anarchist body succeeded in getting out the Paterson silk workers and what do we find? We find no sabotage of the mills, no violence at all, but on the other hand, we find Haywood and the other 'leaders' advising peaceful methods."[88] This account agrees with the perception of credible observers in Paterson and provides added support for the conclusion that accounts of violence were overstated by some contem-poraries and have been overused by some historians. The failure of the strike cannot be attributed to union-inspired violence which repelled would-be sympathizers.

The role which the Paterson Pageant played in the silk workers' defeat is less easily gauged. Most historians of the I.W.W. and its leader-ship of the 1913 strike have followed Flynn's account of the damaging effect of the pageant: that it detracted strikers from the picket line, in-troduced factionalism based on the jealousy of those who were not per-formers, crushed morale when the anticipated relief funds proved illusory, and prompted suspicion that the profits had been diverted into the pockets of its creators or the union organizers.[89] Recently, however, this version of the pageant and its impact has been challenged by Steve Golin. He argues that publicity was the main goal of the pageant and that, in this context, it was a success: it did publicize the strike, "tended to radicalize all those who participated in it," and offset "the power of the silk manufacturers to shape public opinion."[90]

If the pageant was promoted by Haywood and his fellow enthusiasts solely as a publicity ploy, there is no question but that it was successful. The press accounts of it were quite positive and it did attract national attention to the strike. However, it is questionable whether the fund-raising aspect was seen as inconsequential. Both before the performance and immediately thereafter, Haywood and others boosted the event as something which would provide money for relief. If Haywood did not believe this, if he knew early on that it would be a financial bust, he is guilty of a cruel hoax.

Even if publicity was the major aim from the beginning, and accepting the fact that this was achieved, Flynn's contention that the pageant hurt the cause would not be refuted. Whatever the emphasis of Haywood and the others, the workers believed that the show would make money. The local newspapers, whether in honest belief or to raise the strikers' expectations knowing they would be dashed, carried a number of stories of the relief benefits which would result. More significantly, Ebert wrote in *Solidarity* on the eve of the performance that the I.W.W. hoped "to derive the largest sum of all from the Pageant."[91] Whether realistically or not, the hard-pressed strikers expected relief aid from the extravaganza and were understandably disappointed when they were informed otherwise.

Flynn perhaps placed too much emphasis on the negative impact of the pageant, for whatever reason, but it is evident that even among the strike leaders—Haywood and Quinlan in particular—enthusiasm for the struggle seemed to diminish shortly after the performance. Historians who accept and repeat her analysis are correct that the dramatic reenactment did more harm than good.[92]

Flynn's suggestion that the strike might also have been damaged by the presence of agents provocateur has considerably less merit, if indeed it can be taken seriously at all. In the speech on Paterson which she gave before the New York Civic Club in late January 1914, the I.W.W. organizer made no mention of the possibility that the strike had been sabotaged by agents posing as supporters. It was not until she wrote her autobiography that she named Boyd as either an "irresponsible extremist or a provocateur," noting that his fiery speeches attacking the flag and advocating sabotage turned public sentiment against the strike.[93]

Flynn offered no proof of Boyd's allegedly sinister motive, and in fact her statement is couched more as a suspicion than a charge, but she had earlier attributed the defeat to subversive influences. In 1926 she told an interviewer that "local leaders, some of them spies, came to terms with the manufacturers over the heads of the strike committee."[94] Most students of the strike have not given much credence to her allegations, but Renshaw wrote that Boyd "may have been" an agent provocateur and Conlin stated that it was "likely" that Boyd sought to provoke antiunion reaction. No other writers have entertained the notion, and two, Dubofsky and Peter Carlson, confused Boyd with New Jersey S.P.A. Chairman Killingbeck.[95]

What prompted Flynn to write that Boyd might have been an agent and to assert that some of the leaders (unspecified) were spies were apparently incidents which occurred after the strike was history. In the case of Boyd, Flynn's suspicions can be attributed to the Englishman's actions while in prison.

Boyd was arrested on June 24, 1913, on charges stemming from his inflammatory remarks at the time of Haywood's arrest in late March. After waiving his right to a jury trial, he finally appeared before Judge Klenert in the Court of Quarter Sessions on September 29. Boyd admitted the words attributed to him at the Turn Hall meeting six months before, and was found guilty of violating the New Jersey law which made it a high misdemeanor to advocate, encourage, or incite destruction of property. Unlike the earlier trials of Quinlan and Flynn, there were few spectators in the court—of the strike leaders, only Lessig and Quinlan were present to give Boyd their support.[96]

The conviction was immensely popular with the editorial writers in the more conservative papers. The New York *Times* enthused that it would "go far to discourage the assaults against property by members of that lawbreaking party," the I.W.W., and observed that Boyd "richly deserved" the heavy penalty which the law provided. The Paterson *Evening News* applauded the conviction with equal enthusiasm, labeling Boyd as "that type of loud-mouth labor agitator who make a profession of stirring up trouble."[97]

Boyd was fined $500 and sentenced to a term of from one to seven years in Trenton State Prison. Ashley, Reed, Dodge, Quinlan, and Lessig were present when the sentence was handed down and, prepared for the outcome, were able to provide bail, pending appeal.[98] At this time, Boyd's stock was high among I.W.W. leaders and the New York circle of intellectuals with whom he had worked on the pageant and the Children's Committee. The radical press rallied to his support and condemned his conviction and sentence: *Solidarity*, *Mother Earth*, *The Masses*, and the New York *Call* were able to set aside their other differences and unite behind him. A Boyd Defense Fund was established, headed by the indefatigable Ashley and supported by Flynn, *The Masses*, and the *Call*.[99] But on July 27, 1914, despite all efforts, the New Jersey Supreme Court handed down its decision on the appeal, sustaining Judge Klenert. A number of delaying tactics kept the writer from beginning his sentence for seven additional months, but on May 23, 1915, he entered Trenton State Prison.[100]

Boyd began his sentence more than two years after he had stood before the striking silk workers in Paterson to protest Haywood's arrest and to urge the use of extreme methods. During that period, he apparently had occasion to reflect on his actions and to reassess the radical union to which he had given support. He had become a close friend of Reed and acted as Reed's confidant, secretary, and traveling companion. According to Hicks, Reed's biographer, the Englishman had become disillusioned with socialism and no longer had any association with the I.W.W. In addition, if Steiger can be credited, Boyd had come to believe that he had been used by the union agitators in Paterson. In his *Memoirs of a Silk Striker*, the New York weaver wrote that Boyd and his wife appealed to him for defense funds and, during their conversation, Boyd charged that Haywood and Flynn had advised him on what to say in the speeches which had resulted in his arrest and later conviction.[101]

The truth of Boyd's statement, or rather Steiger's relating of it, is doubtful, but it is certain that Reed's friend regretted his words. Two days after Boyd entered prison, he appealed to the New Jersey Court of Pardons for clemency, renouncing the views expressed in his speeches.[102] When the pardon request was denied a month later, *Solidarity* welcomed the rejection and urged I.W.W. members to make an issue of the courts' handling of Boyd, but the reaction of the radical community on the petition was generally that expressed in *Mother Earth*. The anarchist monthly called the writer's request for clemency "a document so cringing and slimy" that further comment was unnecessary and dismissed the imprisoned Englishman as a "yellow cur."[103]

It is Boyd's disavowal of his earlier sentiments, his unwillingness to become a martyr to serve I.W.W. purposes, which best explains Flynn's later suspicions. Nothing in his earlier actions or connected to his treatment by the state of New Jersey supports the innuendo in her autobiography. Hicks wrote of Boyd's close association with Reed, whom he first met in Paterson: "Boyd was perhaps the first thoroughly informed Marxist Reed had known. Though he was only two years older than Reed, he had been brought up in the radical movement, had been an active revolutionary for more than a decade, and had read and re-read the classics of Marxism."[104] The evidence, then, points to long-held radical beliefs which would have made him an unlikely recruit as a provocateur by the New Jersey owners.

If Boyd was an agent provocateur, he paid heavily for his work. He was not treated gently by the New Jersey authorities whom he allegedly served as an ally of the Paterson police and manufacturers. With the exception of Quinlan, no one served more months in prison.

When Flynn gave her interview to Harber Allen in 1926, she used the plural in speaking about "local leaders, some of them spies," who had caused the defeat in Paterson. Boyd was clearly one of those she referred to, and, although she never clearly identified the others, one might well have been Lessig. Once again Steiger provides some clue to this representation, alleging in his Memoirs that Lessig and Koettgen had been in New York late in July 1913 as participants in a socialist scheme to reach a settlement "behind the backs of the national union organizers."[105]

If Lessig were a spy for the New Jersey owners, he maintained his cover long after 1913. He remained active in Paterson Local 152 after the strike ended and in 1914 was in Massachusetts as the secretary of the N.I.U.T.W. His testimony before the Commission on Industrial Relations gave no hint of any disillusionment with the union nor any deviation from its revolutionary doctrines.

In 1924 Lessig was back in Paterson and involved in a strike called by the Associated Silk Workers (A.S.W.), standing once again with some of the same men who had been active in the struggle a decade earlier. As that strike wore on, however, Lessig apparently encouraged the A.S.W. to pass a resolution supporting settlement on a shop-by-shop basis, a recommendation which led some of the striking weavers to believe he had deserted them.[106] In June 1925 charges were made, reportedly by "a representative of the Department of Justice," that Lessig was employed by a private detective agency and had been spying on the workers.[107]

Like Boyd's recantation in his clemency appeal, Lessig's advocacy of shop-by-shop settlement in a later strike and the charges leveled against him at that time might well have been the sole basis for Flynn's veiled statements. But again as with Boyd, there is no evidence on Lessig to support the charge that he was an agent or spy in 1913 and more to suggest that he was not. Much as Flynn may have wished to place the blame for the defeat in Paterson on traitors within, treachery by either Boyd or Lessig cannot be included in a summary of contributing causes. If the two men were guilty of anything, it was in later deviating from the principles and tactics which Flynn upheld to the end.

The major causes for the failure of the New Jersey silk strike of 1913 were the nature of the industry in Paterson and the skill with which the city officials contained the strike without prompting a loud public outcry or an external investigation. The I.W.W. used virtually the same tactics among similar workers which had been successful in Lawrence—establishing a representative coordinating committee, adhering to the policy of nonviolence, demonstrating creativity in upholding worker morale, organizing an evacuation of the strikers' children, and the rest—but in the New Jersey battle they did not work. The union leaders were hard pressed, apparently incapable, of coming up with something which would bring success. The Paterson Pageant, the only novel twist in the silk strike, might have been planned as the cause célèbre to match the Lawrence "Children's Crusade," [108] but it failed in this and probably hurt more than it helped. Clearly it did not generate the sort of public sympathy which might have led to victory. Mayor McBride and his officers refused to commit the kind of blunders which had been instrumental in bringing success in Massachusetts: I.W.W. nonviolence did not succeed in placing the villain's mantle squarely on the heads of the owners and public officials as it had in Lawrence.

In a sense, both sides were governed by the experience of the 1912 New England textile strike. The union followed a game plan which had worked before and which the leaders were confident would work again; the city learned that overreaction could bring the very results which it sought to avoid. In following the tactics of Lawrence, the I.W.W. organizers refused to acknowledge that there were important differences between the industries of the two textile centers and to make adjustments accordingly. It is this inflexibility, rather than any inherent faults in the union's founding principles, which can be questioned.

In Paterson the strike leaders organized and orchestrated a general strike against an industry in decline and one in which the opposition was fragmented by function, size, and profitability. There were no trusts, no one dominant opponent like the American Woolen Company. The largest of the Paterson firms, particularly in the dyeing and broadsilk branches, had annexes in Pennsylvania and could not be forced to capitulate as long as the out-of-state facilities continued to produce. The smallest shops, some employing less than a handful of workers, were marginal operations which could make a profit only by a near ruthless exploitation of their employees. There was virtually nothing that the two extremes of employers had in common except their unwillingness or inability to meet the I.W.W. demands. Given this situation, there were only two strategies which might have turned the tide in favor of the silk workers: exploiting the divisiveness of the opposition to push early on for a shop-by-shop settlement or expanding the strike to shut down the Pennsylvania mills.

To the very end the I.W.W. organizers refused every call for individual shop agreements, preferring the promise of a total victory in Paterson to the possibility of winning at least modest gains for a portion of the workers. When the Central Strike Committee finally disregarded the union's advice and called a vote on the question, it was too late: signs of defeat were too evident to make much difference and only a small portion of the workers even bothered to vote.

The I.W.W. leaders did attempt to spread the strike to the Pennsylvania shops, sending organizers who succeeded in getting some of the silk workers out for a time, but the union was never really successful in this effort. According to Fred W. Thompson, this failure to achieve industrywide solidarity was a major cause of the Paterson defeat. Conceding that "there had not been the necessary preparation" for a strike in the Pennsylvania silk towns, the I.W.W.'s historian concluded that the union "could not win in the old silk center against modern technology in other towns, with the better looms owned by the same interests."[109] More recent and impartial students of the 1913 strike agree, for example, Howard Levin: "The I.W.W. was . . . never able to organize the workers in Pennsylvania plants and so these mills continued to produce moderate amounts of cheap silk. The production of these mills played an important role in the eventual failure of the strike."[110]

Although the I.W.W. organizers' attempt to expand the strike into Pennsylvania indicates that they were aware of the importance of those shops to the New Jersey struggle, their failure to do so did not prompt them to moderate or modify their demands on the Paterson owners. This intransigence cost the New Jersey workers dearly. Blind to or uncaring about the constraints placed on the Paterson employers by competition from other states, Haywood and the others refused to acknowledge that the technologically backward owners could not back down. The four-loom issue, the spark which had ignited the general strike, was not simply another instance of exploitation—it was, in the absence of industrywide standards, the only way in which the broad-silk shops could hope to save themselves. The owners of Paterson saw the strike quite literally as a fight for survival.

The union's steadfast refusal to accept shop-by-shop settlement when such a divide and conquer tactic might have been rewarding, its inability to shut down the Pennsylvania silk mills, and its refusal to recognize that the owners believed they had little room to negotiate or compromise are points on which the I.W.W. can be faulted. In addition, the union can be blamed for the specific demands which the Central Strike Committee handed to the employers: "Unfortunately, Wobblies did not necessarily give the strikers wise counsel. Paterson's workers had sought to earn a few cents more and work a few minutes less each day. But to Miss Flynn and Haywood, among others, . . . these few material gains were not enough."[111] By almost any standard, and certainly in light of the conditions in the silk industry in New Jersey, the demands were extreme and almost impossible to meet.

Some I.W.W. enthusiasts argued after the strike was over that the union erred in acting too much as a conventional union and not enough as a revolutionary body which it was. The strike was over "bread and butter" gains, in the broadest sense of the term. But a close look at what the I.W.W. sought for the workers in the three branches of the industry indicates that the union did not completely eschew its revolutionary genesis and that Panken was correct in attacking the strike leaders as unrealistic.[112]

The demands for a forty-four-hour week to replace the fifty-five hours then the norm in New Jersey, for substantial increases in the minimum wage in all three branches of the industry, for the restoration of the 1894 price list for ribbon workers, and for the abolition of the multiple-loom system in the broad-silk shops were not moderate ones. The I.W.W.'s insistence on obtaining them in every shop would make it appear that the union did not merely wish to improve the workers' lot, but that it sought a big victory. If the union could pull it off, could achieve such gains for over 25,000 silk workers, it would mean a success of enormous proportions. Following the victories in Lawrence and in Little Falls, the I.W.W. would then have to be recognized as a potent force in the country and as a genuine threat to A.F.L. hegemony. The I.W.W., as well as the silk city's employers, was playing for high stakes in Paterson and was not prepared to compromise or retreat.

The I.W.W. fought in the New Jersey silk center as both a union and a revolutionary body devoted to the ultimate overthrow of the capitalist system. This duality, present within the organization from its founding, played a role in the strike's failure. In Lawrence and Little Falls, union organizers were called to assume the leadership of strikes already underway to protest a loss in wages which followed legislation reducing the maximum workweek. In the two successful textile strikes, I.W.W. leaders functioned more as "bread and butter" unionists seeking realizable goals for the workers involved. The Paterson contest differed from these earlier battles in that the I.W.W. essentially created the general strike, using the year-long agitation against the multiple-loom system in the broad-silk branch as a springboard to call out the workers in the ribbon shops and dye houses. The demands were extreme, as noted above, and victory over the employing class seemed to take precedence over gaining improvements for the workers on the job. This emphasis on broader revolutionary goals, on the strike as a school to educate workers in the class struggle, eventually stiffened the back of the union's adversaries and alienated potential supporters, particularly within the S.P.A.

In both Lawrence and Little Falls, socialists played a major role in the successful strike: providing relief funds, helping in the children's evacuation, urging a congressional investigation, and the like. But in Paterson, the relationship between the two bodies was strained and eventually broken. The most heated round in the confrontation did not come until the strike was virtually over, but the tension was evident almost from the beginning and prevented the marshaling of the united front which might have been beneficial. Either because the leaders were confident that they did not need the help of the party or because they believed the party would help no matter what the union did or said, the prospect for victory was not improved by this. It is not purely coincidental that the socialist ribbon workers of New York City were the first workers to break with the I.W.W. and seek an independent settlement.

The long battle between the silk employers of Paterson and the I.W.W. was a fight between two determined adversaries. The owners, supported by the city administration and given moral encouragement by conservatives across the country, were not prepared to capitulate to an organization which preached revolution and was seen after Lawrence as a genuine threat. The I.W.W., buoyed by its textile victories of the year before, saw similar success in the silk city as a triumph for its brand of radical unionism and as a giant step toward permanency and the realization of its ultimate goal. It was for this reason that the union violated its own stricture against waging long strikes. Given the crucial importance which both sides assigned to the struggle, the antagonists seemed willing to fight it out "until Hell freezes over." The workers themselves were like pathetic spectators in a war between the two. The strike only came to an end when a portion of them, seeing nothing ahead but continued hardship for themselves and their families, broke with the union and sought to salvage whatever modest gains the employers would concede. When the ribbon workers in New York finally came to their own terms and fractured the tenuous solidarity which the I.W.W. had maintained, the rush back to the mills began. The union tried to keep the strike going, and never openly concurred that it was over, but the silk workers finally accepted the inevitable. In this sense,

Ettor was correct in stating that hunger had driven the workers back to the mills.[113]

It is ironic that the 1913 silk strike, viewed as a life or death struggle by each side, ended with the defeat of both. The I.W.W. after Paterson was never again the threat it had been in the East; whatever promise it had was dashed by its loss in New Jersey. The silk owners of Passaic County, the technical victors in the long contest, had little opportunity to savor their triumph. The decline of the city which was once hailed as the "Lyons of America," already begun by the turn of the century, was accelerated by the strike. Both the I.W.W. and city of Paterson would never again be the same.

The Paterson strike of 1913 played a part in the redirection of the I.W.W. and helped turn a number of the union's early enthusiasts onto new paths. But the silk strike was no less significant to the New Jersey city's later fortunes. Time would show that the costs born by Silk City and its inhabitants were even greater than most recognized or acknowledged when the contest ended. Students of Paterson and of the silk industry in the United States agree that the I.W.W.-led general strike dealt a blow to the New Jersey silk center from which it never fully recovered. The domestic textile industry prospered during World War I and the Paterson manufacturers shared in that boom period, but following the armistice the local industry's path was inexorably downward. The prosperity of the war years proved only a brief respite from the long-standing problems of the New Jersey silk owners which had been exacerbated by the general strike.[114]

In the years before the war, the strike's impact on Paterson could be measured in the declining number of silk operatives and shops within or in close proximity to the city. An exodus of textile workers began during the strike itself—estimated at fully 10 percent of Paterson's 25,000 silk workers—which was not reversed by the reopening of the mills.[115] The prosperity of 1919 checked the tide for a time, but during the subsequent ten years, the departure of silk workers reached near flood proportions. By 1929 the number of Paterson residents employed in the industry had fallen to 16,368 and the New Jersey city could claim a mere one-eighth of the silk workers in the country.[116]

The reduction in the Paterson silk industry's work force was at first accompanied by a corresponding decline in the number of silk establishments in the city. As a result of the New Jersey broad-silk weavers' stubborn resistance to the extension of the multiple loom system, the industrywide demand for shorter hours and higher wages, and the general propensity of the employees in every branch to translate their grievances into frequent work stoppages, a number of Paterson's establishments began to move all or part of their operations elsewhere. Some firms simply went out of existence entirely.

Although a number of the smaller firms in Paterson failed and some of the larger ones relocated to the more halcyon silk cities of eastern Pennsylvania in 1913 and 1914, the total number of silk establishments in the New Jersey city was reduced for a period of only a year or two. In 1919 there were almost twice as many shops operating in the mills along the Passaic than there had been five years earlier. A superficial glance might suggest that the proliferation of shops from 291 to 574 during this period was an indication of recovery and expansion in the Paterson industry. Just the reverse is true. Beginning a few years after the 1913 strike, the New Jersey industry underwent an evident and substantial change, marked by the appearance of numerous small "cockroach" shops.

As larger firms either left the business or moved elsewhere, rental space became available in the dreary brick behemoths which sprawled near the Passaic River. Almost any amount of floor space could be rented and each year ambitious weavers, supported by the labor of their wives and children, moved into the vacated areas. In place of the larger firms, which had occupied whole floors or an entire mill building in earlier years, family-sized shops crowded into the structures in hive-like fashion. Many of the former mill owners and occupants, grateful that the family-loom operation afforded them the opportunity to escape the labor problems and financial reverses which had plagued them in Paterson, aided the transformation of the local industry by selling their equipment to the individual weavers on easy terms.

The Lakeview mill of the Henry Doherty Company, whose effort to introduce the multiple loom system had precipitated the labor problems of 1912–1913, proved to be the last new facility built in the Passaic County area. Instead of adopting Doherty's solution of constructing large and modern plants to meet the competition from firms in Pennsylvania, the New Jersey silk industry, which had always defied the centripetal tendencies of other industries in the age of trustification, reverted to the retrograde form of small and highly competitive shops. Neither the small shop owners nor those few who worked for them benefited from the new form of organization. Profits were marginal and losses were prevented only by an exploitation of employees which far exceeded that of 1913.[117]

By the end of the 1920s, the silk industries in New Jersey and Pennsylvania were strikingly dissimilar. In the former state, cockroach shops dominated, with more firms employing from 6 to 20 workers than any other number and with 75 percent of the establishments having less than 50 employees; only 2 New Jersey silk companies employed a work force of over 500. In contrast, Pennsylvania contained 14 silk firms employing over 500 operatives, with establishments employing from 101 to 250 workers the most numerous. Paterson still carried the proud title of "Silk City" as the country entered the depression decade, but the sobriquet was more a reflection of what had been than an accurate contemporary description. Where 25,000 silk workers had toiled in almost 300 establishments in the city and its environs in 1913, only somewhat over 16,000 labored in the more than 700 shops extant in 1930. In that latter year, Paterson was home to 42 percent of all silk firms in the United States, but it produced only 14 percent of the country's total value of silk products. The city most identified with the American silk industry clearly had yielded dominance to the textile centers along the Susquehanna, Schuylkill, and Lehigh Rivers of Pennsylvania.[118] Moreover, the fortunes of the city continued to worsen after 1930. In 1938 Paterson reported only 6,441 silk workers. In addition to these workers, 456 firms, having an average of 14 operatives per establishment, were what remained of the once thriving silk city in New Jersey.[119]

No single factor was responsible for the decline of the industry in Paterson. The general strike of 1913, however, played a role in the decaying process of the venerable industrial center. The New Jersey manufacturers had been threatened since the 1890s by their competitors in other states and might have been overwhelmed without the intrusion of the I.W.W., but the prolonged struggle of the weavers and dye-house workers in 1913 at least expedited the decline. Journalist Mel Most, in his account in the *Bergen* (New Jersey) *Record* in 1973, assigns the principal blame for the city's subsequent economic and social ills to the strike. The contemporary accounts of the violence of the general strike—which he concludes were "more hysterical than historical"— gave the city a reputation as a hotbed of revolutionary sentiment which it could not overcome and served to repel industries which might have taken the place of silk. Stories of the "near revolution of 1913" had little substance, but they "ended the rise of Paterson as an industrial center." The final legacy of the heroic struggle between two determined antagonists in 1913 was the creation of "a myth that killed Silk City."[120]

Appendix

Chronology of the Strike

Feb. 19: General strike is announced for February 25 at Turn Hall meeting.
    25: Strike begins; 6,000 leave the mills at 8 a.m. Flynn, Tresca, and Quinlan are arrested at Turn Hall meeting.
    27: General Strike Committee is organized. Socialist Killingbeck is arrested.
    28: *Weekly Issue* office is raided; Editor Scott is arrested; dyers' helpers join the strike en masse.
Mar. 2: First meeting is held at Barber's Grove in Haledon.
    7: Ribbon-Silk workers join the strike; Haywood arrives in Paterson.
    11: Official strike demands are presented to the employers.
    13: Manufacturers issue their "ultimatum" on strike demands.
    17: Flag Day celebrated in Paterson.
    27: The majority of silk workers in the New York City area strike.
    30: Haywood and Lessig are arrested at Lafayette Oval and are charged with disorderly conduct and unlawful assembly.
    31: Boyd delivers speech at Turn Hall; A.F.L Local Trade Council is asked to call a twenty-four-hour sympathy strike; Mayor McBride responds to questions on his position.
Apr. 1: A.F.L. Council rejects I.W.W. request for sympathy strike.
    3: Clergymen's committee meets with representatives of strikers.
    9: Aldermen meet at the Paterson High School Auditorium.
    15: Strike counsel Marelli asks for a federal investigation; Quinlan urges petition to Congress for study of silk tariff.
    19: Modestino dies.
    21: A.F.L. meets at the Armory.
    22: Funeral of Modestino is held.
    23: A.F.L. opens recruiting drive at the Labor Institute.
    26: Flynn, Tresca, and Quinlan are arrested for their speeches on Feb. 25.
    28: Reed is arrested for disorderly conduct and sentenced to twenty days by Recorder Carroll; Haywood is arrested at Passaic Railroad Station.
May 1: First contingent of children "evacuated" to New York City homes.
    3: Mayor McBride appoints a Committee of Twenty-five.
    7: First trial of Quinlan begins.
    10: Quinlan jury reports deadlock and is dismissed.
    11: Rocks found on Erie tracks.
    12: Second Quinlan trial begins.
    14: Quinlan is convicted.

16: Socialists sponsor protest meeting at Lafayette Oval; Haywood announces plans for a strike pageant in New York City.

17: Editor Scott is arrested; A.F.L. abandons effort to enroll silk workers in the U.T.W.

19: Police order the closing of Turn Hall and Helvetia Hall.

21: Strike counsel Marelli petitions for a "foreign jury" in I.W.W. trials.

23: Mayor McBride's committee acknowledges failure and disbands.

29: S.P.A. of Passaic urges a federal investigation.

June 3: Scott is convicted under the 1902 New Jersey antianarchist statute for his February 28 editorial.

7: Pageant is held at Madison Square Garden in New York City.

13: Haywood announces that pageant will bring $5,000 for relief.

17: Reed and Haywood speak at a meeting of strikers; Haywood states that the pageant lost money.

19: Central Strike Committee instructs delegates to hold referendum on whether to accept shop-by-shop settlements.

24: Financial statement on the pageant is presented by Boyd and Ashley; Boyd is arrested for his speech on March 31.

26: Strikers vote not to endorse shop-by-shop settlement plan.

29: Madonna is shot and killed in apparent striker-scab confrontation.

30: Flynn trial begins before a "foreign" (Hudson County) jury.

July 3: Flynn jury announces deadlock and is dismissed. Quinlan is sentenced to two to seven years on May 14 conviction; Scott is arraigned on libel charge.

5: Madonna funeral is held.

15: *Evening News* estimates that one-fourth (6,000) of the strikers returned to work.

17: I.W.W. leaders deny that the strike is broken.

18: Ribbon-shop committee endorses shop-by-shop settlement; Central Strike Committee advises workers to return to shops which agree to a wage increase and shorter hours.

19: Strikers reach an agreement at Smith & Kauffman in New York City.

22: Mayor of Haledon indicted by Passaic County Grand Jury; Flynn tells strikers to make best settlement they can.

23: Dyers' Helpers meet and vote to end strike; relief facilities in Paterson are closed for lack of funds; ribbon-silk weavers vote to remain out unless shop agrees to follow the Smith & Kauffman settlement.

24: Dyers' meet at Turn Hall; I.W.W. asks reconsideration of their vote to return to work.

25: I.W.W. calls off Haledon meeting scheduled for Sunday, July 27.

26: Panken letter is published in the New York *Call.*

28: Central Strike Committee agrees not to call off the strike officially; Flynn gives this date as the one for the end of the strike.

30: City dismisses special police hired during the strike.

Aug. 3: Paterson children return to the city.

22: Ribbon weavers at Johnson & Cowdin agree to return to work.

Notes

Preface

1. Joseph R. Conlin, *Bread and Roses Too, Studies of the Wobblies* (Westport, Conn., 1969); Melvyn Dubofsky, *We Shall Be All: A History of the I.W.W.* (Chicago, 1969); Philip S. Foner, *History of the Labor Movement in the United States*, vol. 4: *The Industrial Workers of the World, 1905–1917* (New York, 1965); Patrick Renshaw, *The Wobblies: The Story of Syndicalism in the United States* (New York, 1967).

2. Graham Adams, *Age of Industrial Violence, 1910–1915: The Activities and Findings of the United States Commission on Industrial Relations* (New York, 1966).

3. Joyce L. Kornbluh, ed., *Rebel Voices: An I.W.W. Anthology* (Ann Arbor, Mich., 1964).

4. See, for example, Steve Golin, "Defeat Becomes Disaster: The Paterson Strike of 1913 and the Decline of the I.W.W.," *Labor History*, 24 (Spring 1983), 223–238; Steve Golin, "The Paterson Pageant: Success or Failure?" *Socialist Review*, 69 (May-June 1983), 45–78; Howard Levin, "Paterson Silk Workers' Strike," *King's Crown Essays*, 9 (Winter 1961–1962), 44–64; Linda Nochlin, "The Paterson Strike Pageant of 1913," *Art in America* (May-June 1974), 64–68; James D. Osborne, "Paterson: Immigrant Strikers and the War of 1913," in Joseph R. Conlin, ed., *At the Point of Production: The Local History of the I.W.W.* (Westport, Conn., 1981), 61–78; Eugene M. Tobin, "Direct Action and Conscience: The 1913 Paterson Strike as Example of the Relationship Between Labor Radicals and Liberals," *Labor History*, 20 (Winter 1979), 73–88; and Robert H. Zeiger, "Robin Hood in the Silk City: The I.W.W. and the Paterson Silk Strike of 1913," *New Jersey Historical Society Proceedings*, 84 (July 1966), 182–195.

5. Joseph R. Conlin, *Big Bill Haywood and the Radical Union Movement* (Syracuse, 1969); and Peter Carlson, *Roughneck: The Life and Times of Big Bill Haywood* (New York, 1983).

6. William D. Haywood, *Bill Haywood's Book: The Autobiography of Big Bill Haywood* (New York, 1929).

7. Elizabeth Gurley Flynn, *I Speak My Own Piece: Autobiography of the "Rebel Girl"* (New York, 1955). For a brief account of Flynn's entire life, see Helen C. Camp's biography in *Notable American Women—The Modern Period* (Cambridge, Mass., 1980), 242–246.

8. See, for example, Max Eastman, *Heroes I Have Known* (New York, 1942) on Tresca; Patrick Quinlan, "Glorious Paterson," *International Socialist*

Review, 14 (December 1913), 355–357; Patrick Quinlan, "The Paterson Strike and After," *New Review*, 2 (January 1914), 26–33; Ewald Koettgen, "Making Silk," *International Socialist Review*, 14 (March 1914), 551–556; Ewald Koettgen, "No Grievances At All!" *The Pageant of the Paterson Strike* (New York, 1913), 9–11; Frederick S. Boyd, "The General Strike in the Silk Industry," *The Pageant of the Paterson Strike* (New York, 1913), 3–8.

9. Mabel Dodge Luhan, *Intimate Memoirs*, vol. 3: *Movers and Shakers* (New York, 1936); Hutchins Hapgood, *A Victorian in the Modern World* (New York, 1939); and Max Eastman, *Enjoyment of Living* (New York, 1948).

10. Upton Sinclair, *American Outpost: A Book of Reminiscences* (New York, 1932); Mary Heaton Vorse, *A Footnote to Folly* (New York, 1935); Lincoln Steffens, *Autobiography* (New York, 1931); and Margaret Sanger, *An Autobiography* (New York, 1938).

11. John Reed, "Almost Thirty," *New Republic*, 86 (April 15-April 29, 1936), 267–270, 332–336; Granville Hicks, *John Reed: The Making of a Revolutionary* (New York, 1936); Richard O'Connor and Dale L. Walker, *The Lost Revolutionary: A Biography of John Reed* (New York, 1967); and Robert Rosenstone, *Romantic Revolutionary: A Biography of John Reed* (New York, 1975). Sketches of Reed also abound in the memoirs of his New York circle and in the numerous works on the Greenwich Village Rebels. During the strike, Reed published two accounts of the battle in Paterson: "Sheriff Radcliff's Hotel," *Metropolitan Magazine*, 38 (September 1913), 14–16, 59–60; and "War in Paterson," *The Masses*, 4 (June 1913), 14–17.

12. The bibliography gives a complete record of primary and secondary works about the strike and its connection with the labor and socialist movements of the day.

13. Witter Bynner, *Cake* (New York, 1926); Max Eastman, *Venture* (New York, 1927); Carl Van Vechten, *Peter Whiffle* (New York, 1922); and Harry Kemp, *More Miles* (New York, 1926).

14. Although the strike was never officially called off by the I.W.W.—or even recognized as having ended—the date usually given is July 28.

15. U. S. Commission on Industrial Relations, *Final Report and Testimony on Industrial Relations*, 64th Congress, 1st Session, Senate Document #451 (Washington, 1916).

16. Even within the ranks of those in the camp of supporters during the life of the contest, differences are evident. The New York *Call, Solidarity, Appeal to Reason*, and the *International Socialist Review* differ in their degree of enthusiasm and on specific incidents of the strike. After the strike ended, in fact, some of these turned into the I.W.W.'s sharpest critics. The same differences appear in the treatment of the strike found in the Paterson newspapers, with the *Evening News* the most sympathetic and the *Press* and *Guardian* the most hostile.

17. Patrick Renshaw, in the chapter on the Lawrence and Paterson strikes in *The Wobblies*, relies most heavily on accounts by Flynn, *Solidarity*, and sympathetic accounts in the *International Socialist Review*; James Osborne, in emphasizing the violent nature of the strike and the anti-Italian sentiments among

the native-born strikers, relies heavily on the Paterson *Guardian* and the testimony of those in whose interest it was to emphasize this aspect.

Chapter 1. The Industrial Workers of the World

1. J. Ramsey MacDonald, *Syndicalism* (London, 1912), p. 36.

2. Melvyn Dubofsky, "The Origins of Western Working Class Radicalism, 1890–1905," *Labor History*, 7 (Spring 1966), 153–154.

3. Charles A. Madison, *American Labor Leaders* (New York, 1962), pp. 264–266; William M. Dick, *Labor and Socialism in America: The Gompers Era* (New York, 1972), pp. 92–93.

4. Dick, *Labor and Socialism*, pp. 92–97.

5. Vernon H. Jensen, *Heritage of Conflict* (Ithaca, N. Y., 1950), pp. 160–161.

6. Vincent St. John, *The I.W.W.: Its History, Structure and Methods* (Chicago, 1914), p. 3; *Appeal to Reason*, January 28, 1905; Jensen, *Heritage*, p.164.

7. The signers were W. J. Pinkerton, Algie M. Simons, Thomas J. Hagerty, William E. Trautmann, Charles M. Moyer, George Estes, William D. Haywood, William Shurtless, M. E. White, Thomas J. DeYong, Charles O. Sherman, Fred D. Henion, "Mother" Jones, Frank M. McCabe, John M. O'Neill, Frank Bohm, Daniel McDonald, John Guild, Joseph Schmitt, W. L. Hall, Ernest Unterman, W. J. Bradley, Frank Krafft, A. J. Swing, J. E. Fitzgerald, and Clarence Smith. Samuel Gompers, "Trade Unions To Be Smashed Again," *American Federationist*, 12 (March 1905), 139–140.

8. Gompers, "Trade Unions To Be Smashed," p. 139.

9. H. Wayne Morgan, *Eugene V. Debs* (Syracuse, N. Y., 1962), p. 89; Marc Karson, *American Labor Unions and Politics, 1900–1918* (Carbondale, Ill., 1958), pp. 153–154.

10. Karson, *American Labor Unions*, pp. 153–154; Dick, *Labor and Socialism*, pp. 100–101; Victor Berger, *Broadsides* (Milwaukee, 1912), pp. 162–165.

11. Foster Rhea Dulles, *Labor in America* (New York, 1955), p. 210; Dick, *Labor and Socialism*, pp. 99–100; David A. Shannon, *The Socialist Party of America* (New York, 1950), p. 1.

12. David DeLeon, "The Chicago Convention," *Daily People*, June 27, 1907. Reprinted in *Industrial Unionism, Selected Editorials of Daniel DeLeon* (New York, 1920), vol. 1, pp. 26–28.

13. St. John, *I.W.W.*, pp. 4–5; Dubofsky, "Origins," p. 153; Dick, *Labor and Socialism*, p. 48; James Weinstein, *The Decline of Socialism in America, 1912–1925* (New York, 1967), p. 33.

14. Max Nomad, *Rebels and Renegades* (New York, 1932), p. 356; George G. Groat, *An Introduction to the Study of Organized Labor* (New York, 1916), p. 432; Jensen, *Heritage*, p. 170; Paul F. Brissenden, *The I.W.W.: A Study of American Syndicalism* (New York, 1919), p. 84; Madison, *American Labor Leaders*, p. 267.

15. *Proceedings of the First Convention of the Industrial Workers of the World* (New York, 1905), pp. 1, 153.

16. Ibid., p. 119.

17. Jean Y. Tussey, ed., *Eugene V. Debs Speaks* (New York, 1970), pp. 115, 118.

18. *Proceedings of the First Convention*, pp. 161–162.

19. Philip S. Foner, *History of the Labor Movement in the United States*, vol. 4: *The Industrial Workers of the World, 1905–1917* (New York, 1965), pp. 115, 135; Testimony of Vincent St. John, U. S. Commission on Industrial Relations, *Final Report and Testimony on Industrial Relations*, 64th Congress, 1st Session, Senate Document #451 (Washington, 1916), vol. 2, pp. 1446, 1449, 1452.

20. Patrick Renshaw, *The Wobblies: The Story of Syndicalism in the United States* (New York, 1967), pp. 59–60.

21. Samuel Gompers, "Those 'World Redeemers' At Chicago—Their Plight," *American Federationist*, 12 (August 1905), 514–516.

22. Karson, *American Labor Unions*, p. 162.

23. Ira Kipnis, *The American Socialist Movement, 1897–1912* (New York, 1952), p. 292; Joseph R. Conlin, ed., *The American Radical Press, 1880–1960* (Westport, Conn., 1974), p. 82; Shannon, *Socialist Party*, p. 18; Algie M. Simons, "The Industrial Workers of the World," *International Socialist Review*, 6 (August 1905), 65–66.

24. *Appeal to Reason*, August 5, 1905.

25. Eugene V. Debs, "The Industrial Convention," *International Socialist Review*, 6 (August 1905), p. 85.

26. Joseph R. Conlin, *Big Bill Haywood and the Radical Union Movement* (Syracuse, N. Y., 1969), p. 120; St. John, *I.W.W.*, p. 7.

27. James P. Cannon, *The I.W.W.: The Great Anticipation* (New York, 1956), p. 13.

28. Selig Perlman and Philip Taft, *History of Labor in the United States, 1896–1932* (New York, 1935), pp. 232–233; Dulles, *Labor in America*, p. 212.

29. Morgan, *Debs*, pp. 88–89.

30. Algie M. Simons, "Socialism in the Present Campaign," *International Socialist Review*, 7 (October 1906), 243.

31. Melvyn Dubofsky, *We Shall Be All* (Chicago, 1969), p. 132.

32. Ray Ginger, *The Bending Cross* (New Brunswick, N.J., 1949), p. 224; Conlin, *Big Bill*, pp. 77–78.

33. Brissenden, *I.W.W.*, p. 175; Jensen, *Heritage*, p. 238; Peter Carlson, *Roughneck: The Life and Times of Big Bill Haywood* (New York, 1983), pp. 105–106, 147–149.

34. William D. Haywood, *Bill Haywood's Book: The Autobiography of Big Bill Haywood* (New York, 1929), p. 202; Carlson, *Roughneck*, p. 98.

35. *Appeal to Reason*, June 1, 1907.

36. Conlin, *Big Bill*, pp. 84–85; Carlson, *Roughneck*, pp. 151–152.

37. Philip Taft, *Organized Labor in American History* (New York, 1964), p. 291; Karson, *American Labor Unions*, pp. 169–170; Perlman and Taft, *History*, p. 235; Cannon, *Great Anticipation*, pp. 20–22.

38. *Industrial Union News*, January 1912. Flynn later described St. John as

"A quiet little man with the taciturnity of the true pioneer, a grim fighter and a dead shot." Harber Allen, "The Flynn," *American Mercury*, 9 (December 1926), 428.

39. Conlin, *Big Bill*, p. 122.

40. Cannon, *Great Anticipation*, p. 17; For this view see Madison, *American Labor Leaders*, p. 271; Foner, *History*, vol. 4, p. 170; Perlman and Taft, *History*, p. 236; Dick, *Labor and Socialism*, p. 104.

41. Karson, *American Labor Unions*, p. 172; Brissenden, *I.W.W.*, p. 228.

42. Foner, *History*, vol. 4, p. 123; Groat, *Introduction*, p. 433.

43. William Preston, *Aliens and Dissenters: Federal Suppression of Radicals, 1903–1933* (Cambridge, Mass., 1953), p. 43; Perlman and Taft, *History*, p. 236; Renshaw, *Wobblies*, p. 87. A more recent study of the Spokane fight contends that it was not the victory it is usually depicted. See Glen J. Broyles, "The Spokane Free Speech Fight, 1909–1910: A Study in I.W.W. Tactics," *Labor History*, 19 (Spring 1978), 238–252.

44. Foner, *History*, vol. 4, p. 121.

45. Louis Duchez, "Victory at McKees Rocks," *International Socialist Review*, 10 (October 1909), p. 291; *Appeal to Reason*, September 25, 1909; James Duncan, "Victory at McKees Rocks," *American Federationist*, 16 (October 1909), 877.

46. Dubofsky, *We Shall Be All*, p. 208.

47. Perlman and Taft, *History*, p. 265.

Chapter 2. Lawrence

1. Paul F. Brissenden, *The I.W.W.: A Study of American Syndicalism* (New York, 1919), pp. 213–214; Robert Brooks, "The United Textile Workers of America" (Unpublished Ph.D. Dissertation, Yale, 1935), pp. 182–183.

2. Fred W. Thompson, *The I.W.W.: Its First Fifty Years* (Chicago, 1955), pp. 35–36, 53; *Industrial Union Bulletin*, March 2 and April 27, 1907.

3. Thompson, *I.W.W.*, pp. 36–37, 53; *Industrial Union Bulletin*, December 12, 1908; Melvyn Dubofsky, *We Shall Be All* (Chicago, 1969), pp. 126–127.

4. *Solidarity*, March 26, 1910; *Industrial Worker*, April 2, 1910.

5. *Solidarity*, September 17, 1910; Leo Wolman, "The Extent of Labor Organization in the United States in 1910," *Quarterly Journal of Economics*, 30 (May 1916), 610.

6. *Solidarity*, July 8, 1911.

7. Lorin F. DeLand, "The Lawrence Strike: A Study," *Atlantic Monthly*, 109 (May 1912), 694; Maurice B. Dorgan, *History of Lawrence, Massachusetts* (Lawrence, Mass., 1924), pp. 52–53, 113; Justus Ebert, *The Trial of a New Society* (Cleveland, 1913), pp. 12–16.

8. Mass. Bureau of Statistics, *Thirteenth Annual Report on Strikes and Lockouts, 1912* (Boston, 1913), pp. 32–33, 38.

9. Henry F. Bedford, *Socialism and the Workers in Massachusetts, 1886–1912* (Amherst, Mass., 1966), p. 248; Leslie H. Marcy and Frederick S. Boyd,

"One Big Union Wins," International Socialist Review, 12 (April 1912), 617; Donald B. Cole, Immigrant City: Lawrence, Massachusetts (Chapel Hill, N.C., 1963), pp. 134–135.

10. United Textile Workers of America, Proceedings of the Eleventh Convention (1911), p. 50.

11. Richard Abrams, Conservatism in a Progressive Era: Massachusetts Politics, 1900–1912 (Cambridge, Mass., 1964), p. 275; Thompson, I.W.W., p. 54; Solidarity, February 4, 1911.

12. Solidarity, March 18 and July 1, 1911.

13. Thompson, I.W.W., pp. 54–55; Solidarity, October 21 and November 18, 1911; Industrial Worker, November 23, 1911.

14. Mass. Bureau of Statistics, Thirteenth Annual Report, pp. 22–23; Ebert, Trial, p. 37.

15. John N. Cole, "The Issue At Lawrence—The Manufacturers' Point of View: A Reply," Outlook, 100 (February 24, 1912), 405; Harry Emerson Fosdick, "After the Strike—In Lawrence," Outlook, 101 (June 15, 1912), 343.

16. Mass. Bureau of Statistics, Thirteenth Annual Report, pp. 21–22.

17. Ibid., p. 22.

18. Mary Heaton Vorse, "The Trouble at Lawrence," Harper's Weekly, 56 (March 16, 1912), 10; Mary K. O'Sullivan, "The Labor War at Lawrence," Survey, 28 (April 6, 1912), 72.

19. Mass. Bureau of Statistics, Thirteenth Annual Report, p. 24.

20. Dorgan, Lawrence, p. 152; "Two Hours, Reduced Wages, and a Strike," Survey, 27 (January 27, 1912), 1633.

21. Fred E. Beal, Proletarian Journey (New York, 1937), pp. 38, 40–41.

22. Fosdick, "After the Strike," p. 344.

23. Thompson, I.W.W., p. 55; Ebert, Trial, pp. 33, 36; William D. Haywood, Bill Haywood's Book: The Autobiography of Big Bill Haywood (New York, 1929), p. 246; Elizabeth Gurley Flynn, I Speak My Own Piece: Autobiography of the "Rebel Girl" (New York, 1955), p. 117.

24. Dorgan, Lawrence, p. 152; Mary E. Marcy, "The Battle for Bread at Lawrence," International Socialist Review, 12 (March 1912), 535; "Two Hours, Reduced Wages," pp. 1633–1634; Thompson, I.W.W., pp. 55–56; Mass. Bureau of Statistics, Thirteenth Annual Report, p. 27.

25. Mass. Bureau of Statistics, Thirteenth Annual Report, p. 25; Marcy and Boyd, "One Big Union Wins," p. 617.

26. "Lawrence Strike Raises a Big Question in Immigration," Square Deal, 10 (April 1912), 264; Beal, Proletarian Journey, pp. 43–44; Cole, Immigrant City, p. 184; Ebert, Trial, p. 42; Solidarity, June 15, 1912.

27. U. S. Congress, House, The Strike at Lawrence, Massachusetts, Hearings before the Committee on Rules of the House of Representatives . . . 1912, 62d Congress, 2d Session, House Document #671, p. 292.

28. Marcy, "The Battle for Bread," p. 542; Mass. Bureau of Statistics, Thirteenth Annual Report, p. 27; U. S. Congress, House, Strike at Lawrence, p. 302.

29. Lewis E. Palmer, "A Strike for Four Loaves of Bread," Survey, 27 (February 3, 1912), 1692.

30. "Statements by People Who Took Part," *Survey*, 28 (April 6, 1912), 76–77; Walter Merriam Pratt, "The Lawrence Revolution," *New England Magazine*, 46 (March 1912), 7.

31. Joseph R. Conlin, *Big Bill Haywood and the Radical Union Movement* (Syracuse, N. Y., 1969), p. 134; Dorgan, *Lawrence*, p. 153; "Ettor in Jail: Strike Goes On," *Survey*, 27 (February 10, 1912), 1726.

32. Ebert, *Trial*, pp. 71, 74–75; Haywood, *Book*, p. 247; Peter Carlson, *Roughneck* (New York, 1983), pp. 163–166.

33. Beal, *Proletarian Journey*, p. 47.

34. Vorse, "Trouble at Lawrence," p. 56; Mass. Bureau of Statistics, *Thirteenth Annual Report*, p. 26.

35. U.T.W., *Proceedings of the Twelfth Convention* (1912), pp. 20–21.

36. "Larger Meaning of the Lawrence Strike," *Current Literature*, 52 (April 1912), 383.

37. "Children of a Strike," *Survey*, 27 (February 24, 1912), 1792.

38. O'Sullivan, "Labor War," p. 72; U. S. Congress, House, *Strike at Lawrence*, p. 126.

39. Walter E. Weyl, "It Is Time To Know," *Survey*, 28 (April 6, 1912), 65; Madison, *American Labor Leaders* (New York, 1962), p. 275.

40. Ira Kipnis, *The American Socialist Movement, 1897–1912* (New York, 1952), p. 332.

41. Bedford, *Socialism in Massachusetts*, pp. 245, 257–258.

42. "Children of a Strike," *Survey*, 27 (February 24, 1912), 1791.

43. C. C. Carstens, "The Children's Exodus from Lawrence," *Survey*, 28 (April 6, 1912), 70.

44. U. S. Congress, House, *Strike at Lawrence*, p. 100.

45. Carstens, "Children's Exodus," pp. 70–71.

46. William D. Haywood, "When the Kiddies Came Home," *International Socialist Review*, 12 (May 1912), 716.

47. U. S. Congress, House, *Strike at Lawrence*, pp. 226–228.

48. "Lawrence Strike: A Review," *Outlook*, 100 (March 9, 1912), 535; U. S. Congress, House, *Strike at Lawrence*, p. 231.

49. Carstens, "Children's Exodus," p. 71; U. S. Congress, House, *Strike at Lawrence*, pp. 369–370.

50. "The Embargo on Strike Children," *Survey*, 27 (March 2, 1912), 1822.

51. "The Lesson of Lawrence," *The Masses*, 3 (April 1912), 3; "The Embargo on Strike Children," p. 1822.

52. *Appeal to Reason*, March 2, 1912.

53. *New York Call*, February 27, 1912.

54. Richard Washburn Child, "Who's Violent?" *Collier's*, 49 (June 29, 1912), 13.

55. Ebert, *Trial*, p. 78.

56. Sally M. Miller, *Victor Berger and the Promise of Constructive Socialism, 1910–1920* (Westport, Conn., 1973), pp. 96–97; Haywood, *Book*, p. 249.

57. *New York Call*, February 28, 1912.

58. *Mother Earth*, 6 (February 1912), 357.

59. U. S. Congress, House, *Strike at Lawrence*, p. 9; Ellen Wetherell, "Before Congress," *International Socialist Review*, 12 (March 1912), 631–632.

60. U. S. Congress, House, *Strike at Lawrence*, p. 9; Robert A. Woods, "The Clod Stirs," *Survey*, 27 (March 16, 1912), 1929; Constance D. Leupp, "The Lawrence Strike Hearings," *Survey*, 27 (March 23, 1912), 1953; Cole, *Immigrant City*, p. 8.

61. Mass. Bureau of Statistics, *Thirteenth Annual Report*, p. 26; Fosdick, "After the Strike," pp. 343–344.

62. Carl Hovey, "Haywood and Haywoodism," *Metropolitan Magazine*, 37 (June 1912), 49.

63. *Solidarity*, March 23, 1912.

64. Fosdick, "After the Strike," p. 346; "The Lawrence Strike: A Review," p. 536; "After the Battle," *Survey*, 28 (April 6, 1912), 2; Deland, "Lawrence," p. 705; Hugh H. Lusk, "Industrial War," *Forum*, 48 (November 1912), 563; Walter E. Weyl, "It Is Time To Know," *Survey*, 28 (April 6, 1912), 66–67; Walter V. Woehlke, "I.W.W.," *Outlook*, 101 (July 6, 1912), 536.

65. "New Labor Movement," *Literary Digest*, 44 (April 6, 1912), 677.

66. Hezekiah N. Duff, "What of the Year 1913?" *Square Deal*, 11 (January 1913), 487.

67. Foster Rhea Dulles, *Labor in America* (New York, 1955), p. 219; *Industrial Worker*, March 28, 1912; *Solidarity*, March 30, 1912; Beal, *Proletarian Journey*, p. 54; "Lawrence and the Industrial Workers of the World," *Survey*, 28 (April 6, 1912), 79–80; Brissenden, *I.W.W.*, p. 292.

68. Marcy and Boyd, "One Big Union Wins," p. 630.

69. Ray Stannard Baker, "Revolutionary Strike," *American Magazine*, 74 (May 1912), 19; *Mother Earth*, 7 (April 1912), 37; *The Agitator*, March 15, 1912; Phillips Russell, "Strike Tactics," *New Review*, 1 (March 29, 1913), 407; William E. Bohn, "The Industrial Workers of the World," *Survey*, 28 (May 4, 1912), 220–221; H. Scott Bennett, "Two Kinds of Unionism," *International Socialist Review*, 13 (August 1912), 135; Ralph Chaplin, *Wobbly: The Rough and Tumble Story of a Radical* (Chicago, 1948), p. 135; Justus Ebert, *The I.W.W. in Theory and Practice* (Chicago, 1920), p. 48; Eugene V. Debs, "A Plea For Solidarity," *International Socialist Review*, 14 (March 1914), 536.

70. William D. Haywood, "The Fighting I.W.W., *International Socialist Review*, 13 (September 1912), 247.

71. Thompson, *I.W.W.*, p. 59; Bedford, *Socialism In Massachusetts*, p. 273.

72. Ed DeLaney and M. T. Rice, *The Bloodstained Trail: A History of Militant Labor in the United States* (Seattle, 1927), p. 70; Robert A. Bakeman, "Little Falls—A Capitalist City Stripped of its Veneer," *New Review*, 1 (February 8, 1913), 168; Robert E. Snyder, "Women, Wobblies, and Workers' Rights: The 1912 Textile Strike in Little Falls, New York," *New York History*, 60 (January 1979), 29–57.

73. Haywood, *Book*, p. 257; Foner, *History*, p. 351; U.T.W., *Proceedings of the Thirteenth Convention* (1913), p. 35.

74. New York *Call*, January 3, 4, 1913; Bakeman, "Little Falls," p. 174.

75. Katherine Anthony, "The Waiters' Strike," *Survey*, 28 (May 25, 1912),

330–331; *Solidarity*, June 15, 1912; New York *Call*, June 26, October 23, December 19, 1912 and January 1, 2, 1913; Frank Bohn, "The Strike of the New York Hotel and Restaurant Workers," *International Socialist Review*, 13 (February 1913), 621.

76. New York *Times*, January 27, 1913.

Chapter 3. Unrest in the Silk Industry

1. U.T.W., *Proceedings of the First Convention* (1901), p. 2; U.T.W., *Proceedings of the Second Convention* (1902), p. 43; U.T.W., *Proceedings of the Third Convention* (1903), p. 18.

2. Robert Brooks, "The United Textile Workers of America" (Unpublished Ph.D. Dissertation, Yale, 1935), p. 255; U.T.W. *Proceedings of The Third Convention*, p. 30; U.T.W., *Proceedings of the Fifth Convention* (1905), p. 27; U.T.W., *Proceedings of the Seventh Convention* (1907), p. 41; U.T.W., *Proceedings of the Eighth Convention* (1908), pp. 26–27, 45.

3. U.T.W., *Proceedings of the Ninth Convention* (1909), pp. 4, 18–19, 23.

4. Ibid., pp. 12, 24–26; James E. Wood, "History of Labor in the Broad-Silk Industry of Paterson, New Jersey, 1879–1940," (Unpublished Ph.D. Dissertation, University of California, 1942), pp. 225–228.

5. *Solidarity*, December 23, 1911.

6. *The Bulletin*, 1 (September 1906), 14; *Industrial Union Bulletin*, January 10, March 9, 16, 23, 1907.

7. Fred W. Thompson, *The I.W.W.: Its First Fifty Years* (Chicago, 1955), p. 36; *Industrial Union Bulletin*, April 6, 13, May 25, 1907.

8. *Industrial Union Bulletin*, July 20, 1907 and January 25, May 9, 16, 1908. The ten Paterson delegates were Frank Werlick, William Glanz, Louis Smith, F. Fiorina, F. Gallo, A. Guabello, A. Bock, A. Bethold, F. Domo, and M. Durkin. Adolph Seyer and Emil Landgraf attended as alternates.

9. *Industrial Worker*, April 2, 1910; *Solidarity*, August 13, 1910.

10. William Glanz to William E. Trautmann, April 19, 1908. Reprinted in *Industrial Union Bulletin*, May 8, 1908.

11. Thompson, *I.W.W.*, p. 37.

12. Rudolph Katz, "With DeLeon," *Daniel DeLeon, The Man and His Work; A Symposium*, 4th ed. (New York, 1934), p. 153; *Industrial Union News*, January 1912.

13. Testimony of Rudolph Katz, U. S. Commission on Industrial Relations, *Final Report and Testimony on Industrial Relations*, 64th Congress, 1st Session, Senate Document #451 (Washington, 1916), vol. 3, p. 2473; *Industrial Union News*, January 1913.

14. *Industrial Union News*, January 1912.

15. Paul F. Brissenden, *The I.W.W.: A Study of American Syndicalism* (New York, 1919), p. 230.

16. *Industrial Union Bulletin*, February 20, 27, 1909.

17. Leo Wolman, "The Extent of Labor Organization in the United States in 1910," *Quarterly Journal of Economics*, 30 (May 1916), 610.

18. N.J., *33rd Annual Report of the Bureau of Statistics of Labor and Industries* (1910), pp. 263–264, 267–269.

19. Wood, "Broad-Silk Industry," pp. 228–229; U.T.W., *Proceedings of the Tenth Convention* (1910), pp. 27–28; New York *Times*, July 4, 1913; Testimony of Thomas F. Morgan, U. S. Commission on Industrial Relations, *Final Report*, vol. 3, p. 2422.

20. "The Strike of the Jersey Silk Workers," *Survey*, 30 (April 19, 1913), 81.

21. N.J., *36th Annual Report* (1913), pp. 187–188.

22. U. S. Bureau of the Census, *Census of Manufacturing: 1914, The Silk Industry* (Washington, 1917), p. 10; *Industrial Union News*, June 1912.

23. N.J., *36th Annual Report* (1913), p. 188; Gregory Mason, "Industrial War in Paterson," *Outlook*, 104 (June 17, 1913), 286–287.

24. Testimony of Henry Doherty, Jr., U. S. Commission on Industrial Relations, *Final Report*, vol. 3, pp. 2432–2433; Wood, "Broad-Silk Industry," p. 232.

25. Testimony of Doherty, Jr., U. S. Commission on Industrial Relations, *Final Report*, vol. 3, pp. 2433–2434; "Strike of the Jersey Silk Workers," pp. 81–82; Mason, "Industrial War," pp. 286–287.

26. N.J., *35th Annual Report* (1912), p. 294; *Solidarity*, December 23, 1911; U.T.W., *Proceedings of the Eleventh Convention* (1911), p. 80.

27. Testimony of James Starr, U. S. Commission on Industrial Relations, *Final Report*, vol. 3, p. 2615; U.T.W., *Proceedings of the Twelfth Convention* (1912), pp. 33–34; *Industrial Union News*, February 1912.

28. Wood, "Broad-Silk Industry," pp. 234–235.

29. Paterson *Press*, November 11, 1911.

30. Ibid., November 21, 1911.

31. New York *Call*, December 6, 1911.

32. *Solidarity*, December 2, 23, 1911; Testimony of Katz, U. S. Commission on Industrial Relations, *Final Report*, vol. 3, p. 2483.

33. Wood, "Broad-Silk Industry," p. 235.

34. Ibid., p. 238; *Industrial Union News*, February and March, 1912; Testimony of Starr, U. S. Commission on Industrial Relations, *Final Report*, vol. 3, p. 2626; New York *Call*, February 13, 1912.

35. *Industrial Union News*, June 1912; Wood, "Broad-Silk Industry," p. 236; Brooks, "U.T.W.," p. 222.

36. *Industrial Union News*, March 1912; Paterson *Press*, February 20, 1912.

37. N.J., *35th Annual Report* (1912), p. 230; Paterson *Press*, February 20, 1912.

38. Wood, "Broad-Silk Industry," p. 239; Paterson *Press*, February 23, 1912; New York *Call*, February 24, 1912.

39. Paterson *Press*, February 26, 27, 1912; New York *Call*, February 27, 1912; N.J., *35th Annual Report* (1912), p. 230.

40. New York *Call*, February 27, 28, 1912; Paterson *Press*, February 28, 1912; Testimony of Katz, U. S. Commission on Industrial Relations, *Final Report*, vol. 3, p. 2474.

41. *Industrial Union News*, March 1912.

42. Paterson *Press*, February 29, March 1, 1912; New York *Call*, February 28, 9, March 1, 1912.

43. Paterson *Press*, March 2, 3, 4, 1912; New York *Call*, March 5, 1912.

44. *Industrial Union News*, April 1912.

45. *Solidarity*, March 1, 1913.

46. Mary Brown Sumner, "Broad-Silk Weavers of Paterson," *Survey*, 27 (March 16, 1912), 1932–1933.

47. Philip Newman, "The First I.W.W. Invasion of New Jersey," *Proceedings of the New Jersey Historical Society*, 58 (October 1940), 277.

48. Paterson *Press*, March 7, 21, 1912; Katz, "With DeLeon," p. 159.

49. New York *Call*, March 11, 1912; Paterson *Press*, March 14, 21, 1912.

50. New York *Call*, March 11, 12, 13, 20, 23, April 4, 1912; N.J., *35th Annual Report* (1912), p. 239.

51. N.J., *35th Annual Report* (1912), p. 235; Michael H. Ebner, "The Passaic Strike of 1912 and the Two I.W.W.s," *Labor History*, 11 (Fall 1970), 453–455; Brooks, "U.T.W.," p. 222.

52. Ebner, "The Passaic Strike," pp. 458–459.

53. Ibid., p. 460; New York *Call*, March 30, April 1, 1912.

54. New York *Call*, April 3, 1912.

55. Ibid., April 5, 1912.

56. Ibid., April 6, 8, 1912.

57. *Solidarity*, April 6, 1912.

58. *Industrial Union News*, May 1912.

59. New York *Call*, April 10, 1912.

60. N.J., *35th Annual Report* (1912), p. 238.

61. New York *Call*, April 12, 1912; Ebner, "The Passaic Strike," pp. 464–465.

62. *Solidarity*, April 20, October 26, 1912; *Industrial Union News*, May 1912; "Rumored Split in the Ranks of the Workers of the World," *Square Deal*, 11 (August 1912), 65–68; "Silencing Industrial Workers," *Literary Digest*, 44 (April 20, 1912), 800; Ebner, "The Passaic Strike," p. 466.

63. *Industrial Union News*, May 1912.

64. N.J., *35th Annual Report* (1912), p. 231.

65. *Solidarity*, April 6, 13, 27, 1912; New York *Call*, May 9, 1912.

66. New York *Call*, May 9, 10, 13, 14, 18, 23, 24, 1912; *Industrial Union News*, June 1912.

67. New York *Call*, June 1, 7, August 13, 1912; *Industrial Union News*, July 1912; Katz, "With DeLeon," p. 161; *Solidarity*, June 29, 1912.

68. *Solidarity*, June 8, 29, 1912.

69. Ibid., September 14, 1912.

70. New York *Call*, November 19, 1912; *Solidarity*, November 23, 1912; Patrick Quinlan, "The Paterson Strike and After," *New Review*, 2 (January 1914), 27–28.

71. Quinlan, "The Paterson Strike," p. 28; William D. Haywood, "The Rip in the Silk Industry," *International Socialist Review*, 13 (May 1913), 783; Paterson

Evening News, January 10, 24, 1913; Testimony of Adolph Lessig, U. S. Commission on Industrial Relations, *Final Report*, vol. 3, p. 2453.

72. Testimony of Lessig, U. S. Commission on Industrial Relations, *Final Report*, vol. 3, p. 2454.

73. N.J., *36th Annual Report* (1913), p. 175; Paterson *Evening News*, January 24, 1913; Paterson *Sunday Chronicle*, January 26, 1913.

74. Testimony of Doherty, Jr., U. S. Commission on Industrial Relations, *Final Report*, vol. 3, p. 2436; Paterson *Guardian*, January 27, 28, 1913; Paterson, *Evening News*, January 27, 1913; N.J., *36th Annual Report* (1913), p. 175.

75. Paterson *Evening News*, January 31, 1913.

76. N.J., *36th Annual Report* (1913), p. 177; Quinlan, "The Paterson Strike," p. 28; Paterson *Morning Call*, February 19, 1913.

77. Paterson *Evening News*, February 21, 24, 1913; New York *Call*, February 22, 1913; Paterson *Guardian*, February 24, 1913.

Chapter 4. Launching the General Strike

1. Elizabeth Gurley Flynn, *I Speak My Own Piece: Autobiography of the "Rebel Girl"* (New York, 1955), p. 143; New York *Call*, February 25, 1913.

2. Testimony of Adolph Lessig, U. S. Commission on Industrial Relations, *Final Report and Testimony on Industrial Relations*, 64th Congress, 1st Session, Senate Document #451 (Washington, 1916), vol. 3, pp. 2452–2453; Elizabeth Gurley Flynn, "The Truth About the Paterson Strike," Typescript in Labadie Collection, University of Michigan, p. 4; New York *Call*, February 25, 1913.

3. Paterson *Evening News*, February 25, 1913; New York *Times*, February 26, 1913; Paterson *Guardian*, February 25, 1913.

4. Paterson *Guardian*, February 25, 1913; Paterson *Morning Call*, February 26, 1913; Passaic *Weekly Issue*, February 28, 1913, as reprinted in the New York *Times*, June 4, 1913; New York *Call*, February 27, 1913.

5. New York *Times*, February 27, 1913; *Solidarity*, March 15, 1913.

6. Paterson *Evening News*, March 4, 1913.

7. Flynn, *I Speak*, p. 147.

8. Paterson *Evening News*, February 27, 28, 1913; New York *Times*, February 27, 1913.

9. Paterson *Evening News*, February 26, 27, March 1, 1913; Paterson *Guardian*, March 1, 1913; N.J., *36th Annual Report of the Bureau of Statistics of Labor and Industries* (1913), pp. 186–188.

10. Paterson *Guardian*, February 27, March 1, 1913; Paterson *Evening News*, March 1, 1913; Testimony of Alexander Scott, U. S. Commission on Industrial Relations, *Final Report*, vol. 3, p. 2519; Philip C. Newman, *The Labor Legislation of New Jersey* (Washington, 1943), p. 39.

11. New York *Call*, November 7, 1912, and March 3, 1913; Paterson *Evening News*, March 3, 1913.

12. New York *Times*, March 4, 1913; New York *Call*, March 4, 1913; Paterson *Evening News*, March 4, 1913.

13. Paterson *Guardian*, March 5, 6, 1913; Paterson *Evening News*, March 8, 1913; New York *Call*, March 8, 1913.

14. Testimony of Andrew F. McBride, U. S. Commission on Industrial Relations, *Final Report*, vol. 3, p. 2553; Testimony of Thomas F. Morgan, ibid., p. 2416; Testimony of Louis Magnet, ibid., p. 2574; F. G. R. Gordon, "A Labor Man's Story of the Paterson Strike," *National Civic Federation Review*, 4 (December 1, 1913), 16.

15. Testimony of Michael Dunn, U. S. Commission on Industrial Relations, *Final Report*, vol. 3, p. 2550; Testimony of James Cooke, ibid., p. 2608; N.J., *36th Annual Report* (1913), p. 176.

16. Testimony of Lessig, U. S. Commission on Industrial Relations, *Final Report*, vol. 3, p. 2454; Flynn, "The Truth," p. 4.

17. Leo Mannheimer, "Darkest New Jersey," *Independent*, 74 (May 29, 1913), 1191–1192; Inis Weed and Louis Carey, "I Make Cheap Silk," *The Masses*, 5 (November 1913), 7.

18. John H. Steiger, *The Memoirs of a Silk Striker: An Exposure of the Tactics and Principles of the I.W.W.* (New York, 1914), p. 7; Testimony of Edward Zuersher, U. S. Commission on Industrial Relations, *Final Report*, vol. 3, p. 2577; Testimony of Magnet, ibid., pp. 2572–2573.

19. Paterson *Evening News*, February 25, 1913.

20. Paterson *Guardian*, March 7, 1913; Paterson *Evening News*, March 7, 1913.

21. Paterson *Evening News*, March 10, 1913.

22. Flynn, "The Truth," pp. 6–7.

23. Paterson *Evening News*, March 11, 1913; William D. Haywood, "The Rip in the Silk Industry," *International Socialist Review* (May 1913), 784; N.J., *36th Annual Report* (1913), p. 183.

24. Paterson *Evening News*, March 11, 1913.

25. Fred W. Thompson, "The Way of the Wobbly," *Twenty-Five Years of Industrial Unionism* (Chicago, 1930), p. 45; *Solidarity*, April 19, 1913; Flynn, "The Truth," p. 5.

26. *Solidarity*, March 8, 1913; New York *Call*, February 28, 1913; Flynn, "The Truth," p. 4; Testimony of Lessig, U. S. Commission on Industrial Relations, *Final Report*, vol. 3, p. 2457; Testimony of Zuersher, ibid., p. 2602.

27. Testimony of Lessig, U. S. Commission on Industrial Relations, *Final Report*, vol. 3, p. 2457; Testimony of Zuersher, ibid., p. 2602.

28. William D. Haywood, *Bill Haywood's Book: The Autobiography of Big Bill Haywood* (New York, 1929), p. 7.

29. Ibid., pp. 8–64; David H. Grover, *Debaters and Dynamiters: The Story of the Haywood Trial* (Corvallis, Ore., 1964), p. 286; Melvyn Dubofsky, *We Shall Be All* (Chicago, 1969), pp. 237–238; Elizabeth Gurley Flynn, *Debs, Haywood, Ruthenberg* (New York, 1939), p. 147. For a full treatment of the various phases of Haywood's career, see Joseph R. Conlin, *Big Bill Haywood and the Radical Union Movement* (Syracuse, N. Y., 1969).

30. "About Haywood," *Literary Digest*, 46 (June 14, 1913), 1352; Andre Tridon, "Haywood," *New Review*, 1 (May 1913), 502–503.

31. Frank Walsh, "My Impressions of the Witnesses and Their Testimony," *Solidarity*, July 31, 1915.

32. Max Eastman, *Enjoyment of Living* (New York, 1948), p. 449. Haywood's most recent biographer agrees with Eastman's assessment, writing: Haywood's "synthesis of ... theories resulted in an undigested philosophy that was idealistic, but was also naive and possibly undemocratic. Haywood's beliefs were a jumble of contradictions." Peter Carlson, *Roughneck: The Life and Times of Big Bill Haywood* (New York, 1983), pp. 194–195.

33. Eastman, *Enjoyment*, p. 448; Emma Goldman, *Living My Life* (New York, 1931), p. 489.

34. J. Ramsey MacDonald, *Syndicalism* (London, 1912), pp. 36–37.

35. Flynn, *Debs, Haywood, Ruthenberg*, p. 26.

36. James P. Cannon, *Notebook of an Agitator* (New York, 1958), p. 61.

37. Conlin, *Big Bill*, pp. 210–211.

38. "Haywood's Battle in Paterson," *Literary Digest*, 46 (May 10, 1913), 1044.

39. Haywood, *Book*, p. 272; Margaret Sanger, *An Autobiography* (New York, 1938), p. 84.

40. Andre Tridon, *The New Unionism* (New York, 1913), p. 113; "E. G. Flynn: Labor Leader," *Outlook*, 111 (December 15, 1915), 905.

41. Helen C. Camp, "Elizabeth Gurley Flynn," *Notable American Women—The Modern Period* (Cambridge, Mass., 1980), p. 243; Flynn, *I Speak*, pp. 30, 33, 36; Tridon, *New Unionism*, p. 113; Goldman, *Living My Life*, p. 489.

42. Flynn, *I Speak*, pp. 68–69, 75, 104; William Z. Foster, *Pages From a Worker's Life* (New York, 1939), pp. 231–232.

43. Flynn, *I Speak*, p. 103.

44. Max Eastman, *Heroes I Have Known* (New York, 1942), pp. 19–21, 36; New York *Times*, January 12, 1943; Flynn, *I Speak*, pp. 135, 324.

45. New York *Times*, May 8, 1913; Eastman, *Heroes*, p. 17; Testimony of Dunn, U. S. Commission on Industrial Relations, *Final Report*, vol. 3, p. 2551.

46. Eastman, *Heroes*, p. 21.

47. Flynn, *I Speak*, p. 136.

48. John Beffel, "Patrick L. Quinlan," Typescript in Labadie Collection; *Solidarity*, June 14, 1913.

49. C. Desmond Greaves, *The Life and Times of James Connolly* (London, 1961), pp. 155–156, 160, 163–164.

50. Beffel, "Quinlan"; *Solidarity*, June 14, 1913.

51. *Appeal to Reason*, January 22, 1916.

52. Testimony of Lessig, U. S. Commission on Industrial Relations, *Final Report*, vol. 3, pp. 2453, 2455, 2469, 2471.

53. Testimony of Zuersher, ibid., p. 2586.

54. Testimony of Magnet, ibid., pp. 2572–2576; Flynn, "The Truth," p. 9.

55. New York *Call*, July 22, 1913; Paterson *Evening News*, July 23, 1913.

56. Paterson *Guardian*, March 8, 1913.

57. Paterson *Evening News*, March 12, 1913.

58. Ibid., March 14, 1913.

59. Ibid., March 12, 13, 14, 1913.

60. Testimony of Henry F. Marelli, U. S. Commission on Industrial Relations, *Final Report*, vol. 3, p. 2538.

61. Paterson *Morning Call*, March 13, 1913.

62. Paterson *Guardian*, March 14, 1913.

63. Testimony of John L. Matthews, U. S. Commission on Industrial Relations, *Final Report*, vol. 3, pp. 2583–2584.

64. Paterson *Evening News*, March 11, 12, 1913; New York *Call*, March 12, 1913.

65. New York *Times*, April 19, 1913; Mannheimer, "Darkest New Jersey," p. 1190.

66. Alexander Scott, "What the Reds Are Doing in Paterson," *International Socialist Review*, 13 (June 1913), 852–856.

67. *Industrial Union News*, April, May, June 1913; Testimony of Lessig, U. S. Commission on Industrial Relations, *Final Report*, vol. 3, p. 2456.

68. Paterson *Evening News*, March 17, 1913; Haywood, *Book*, p. 262; *Solidarity*, March 29, 1913; New York *Call*, March 25, 1913.

69. Paterson *Evening News*, March 13, 21, 1913; Robert J. Wheeler, "The Allentown Silk Dyers' Strike," *International Socialist Review*, 13 (May 1913), 820–821.

70. New York *Call*, March 19, 20, 1913; *Solidarity*, April 26, 1913.

71. New York *Call*, March 18, 19, 21, 26, 28, 1913; New York *Times*, March 19, 1913; Steiger, *Memoirs*, pp. 14–17.

72. Ernest T. Hiller, *The Strike: A Study in Collective Action* (Chicago, 1928), p. 10.

73. Flynn, "The Truth," p. 14.

74. Phillips Russell, "Strike Tactics," *New Review*, 1 (March 29, 1913), 407–408.

75. New York *Call*, July 4, 1913.

76. Flynn, "The Truth," p. 13.

77. Hiller, *The Strike*, pp. 79–94.

78. Paterson *Evening News*, March 18, 1913; New York *Call*, March 19, 1913.

79. Paterson *Evening News*, March 17, 18, 1913; New York *Call*, March 19, 1913.

80. N.J., *36th Annual Report* (1913), pp. 191–192.

81. New York *Times*, March 20, 1913.

82. Paterson *Evening News*, March 19, 1913; Paterson *Morning Call*, March 20, 1913; New York *Call*, March 20, 1913.

83. Paterson *Evening News*, March 20, 1913.

84. Paterson *Evening News*, March 20, 21, 1913; Paterson *Guardian*, March 21, 1913.

85. Paterson *Guardian*, March 25, 1913; *Evening News*, March 25, 27, 1913; Paterson *Morning Call*, March 28, 1913.

Chapter 5. "Until Hell Freezes Over"

1. New York *Call*, March 26, 1913; Paterson *Morning Call*, March 25, 1913; Paterson *Guardian*, March 25, 1913; Paterson *Evening News*, March 27, 1913.

2. Paterson *Evening News*, March 26, 27, 1913.

3. "City Officials Adopt Repressive Measures," *Survey*, (April 19, 1913), 82; New York *Call*, March 12, 1913; Paterson *Evening News*, March 13, 15, 17, 1913.

4. Paterson *Evening News*, March 28, 1913; New York *Call*, March 29, 1913.

5. New York *Call*, March 31, 1913; New York *Times*, March 31, 1913; Paterson *Guardian*, March 31, 1913; Phillips Russell, "The Arrest of Haywood and Lessig," *International Socialist Review*, 13 (May 1913), 789.

6. Patrick F. Gill and Redmond S. Brennan, "Report on the Inferior Courts and Police of Paterson," Typescript in the Paterson Free Public Library, 1914, Part 2, pp. 2–3, 6–7, 10.

7. Paterson *Evening News*, April 1, 1913.

8. Ibid., April 7, 1912; New York *Call*, April 2, 1912.

9. Elizabeth Gurley Flynn, *I Speak My Own Piece: Autobiography of the "Rebel Girl"* (New York, 1955), p. 149; Joseph R. Conlin, "The I.W.W. and the Question of Violence," *Wisconsin Magazine of History*, 51 (Spring 1968), 324; Paterson *Evening News*, September 29, 1913.

10. Flynn, *I Speak*, p. 144.

11. *Solidarity*, October 11, 1913; Granville Hicks, *John Reed: The Making of a Revolutionary* (New York, 1936), p. 110; F. S. Boyd to the Editor, *Survey*, 27 (February 17, 1912), 1786. Both Dubofsky and Carlson state erroneously that Boyd was arrested for reading the free speech clause of the New Jersey Constitution. This incident, which Dubofsky dates on February 26, involved Killingbeck and not Boyd. The Englishman spoke for the first time in Paterson on March 31 and his comments on that occasion prompted his arrest and later conviction.

12. Paterson *Evening News*, March 31, 1913.

13. Elizabeth Gurley Flynn, *Sabotage* (Chicago, 1916), p. 5.

14. Paterson *Guardian*, April 1, 1913.

15. New York *Call*, June 10, 1913; Paterson *Guardian*, April 1, 1913; Paterson *Evening News*, April 1, 1913.

16. Paterson *Evening News*, April 2, 1913; Flynn, *I Speak*, p. 149; Flynn, *Sabotage*, p. 23.

17. Paterson *Evening News*, April 3, 7, 1913.

18. Paterson *Guardian*, April 2, 1913.

19. Paterson *Evening News*, April 1, 1913.

20. Ibid., April 4, 1913.

21. Ibid., April 5, 1913.

22. Testimony of Anthony H. Stein, U. S. Commission on Industrial Relations, *Final Report and Testimony on Industrial Relations* 64th Congress, 1st Session, Senate Document #451 (Washington, 1916), vol. 3, pp. 2576–2577; Paterson *Evening News*, April 3, 1913; Paterson *Guardian*, April 4, 1913.

23. Paterson *Evening News*, April 7, 1913.

24. Paterson *Guardian*, April 8, 1913; Paterson *Evening News*, April 8, 9, 1913.

25. Paterson *Evening News*, April 9, 1913; Paterson *Guardian*, April 9, 1913; "City Officials Adopt Repressive Measures," p. 83.

26. New York *Call*, April 10, 1913; Paterson *Evening News*, April 10, 1913; Testimony of Stein, U. S. Commission on Industrial Relations, *Final Report*, vol. 3, p. 2576; Testimony of James Starr, ibid., p. 2617.

27. New York *Call*, April 11, 1913.

28. Paterson *Morning Call*, April 11, 1913; Paterson *Evening News*, April 11, 12, 14, 15, 1913; New York *Call*, April 12, 16, 1913.

29. Paterson *Evening News*, April 18, 1913; New York *Times*, April 18, 1913; New York *Call*, April 18, 1913; Testimony of Michael Dunn, U. S. Commission on Industrial Relations, *Final Report*, vol. 3, pp. 2548–2549.

30. Paterson *Evening News*, April 19, 1913.

31. John Steiger, *The Memoirs of a Silk Striker: An Exposure of the Tactics and Principles of the I.W.W.* (New York, 1914), pp. 120–121; Paterson *Evening News*, April 22, 23, 1913.

32. "Double Labor War at Paterson, New Jersey," *Outlook*, 104 (May 3, 1913), 11.

33. N.J., *36th Annual Report of the Bureau of Statistics of Labor and Industries* (1913), p. 194.

34. Ibid., p. 181; Testimony of Thomas F. Morgan, U. S. Commission on Industrial Relations, *Final Report*, vol. 3, p. 2414; Testimony of Starr, ibid., pp. 2612–2614.

35. Testimony of Morgan, U. S. Commission on Industrial Relations, *Final Report*, vol. 3, p. 2416; Testimony of Starr, ibid., p. 2617; Paterson *Evening News*, March 28, 29, 1913.

36. Paterson *Evening News*, April 2, 1913; Paterson *Guardian*, April 1, 1913; Testimony of Starr, U. S. Commission on Industrial Relations, *Final Report*, vol. 3, p. 2617.

37. Paterson *Evening News*, April 2, 1913.

38. Paterson *Guardian*, April 18, 1913; Paterson *Evening News*, April 19, 1913; New York *Times*, April 20, 1913.

39. Paterson *Guardian*, April 19, 1913; Paterson *Evening News*, April 21, 1913.

40. Paterson *Guardian*, April 22, 1913; New York *Call*, April 22, 1913; *Solidarity*, May 3, 1913.

41. William D. Haywood, "On the Paterson Picket Line," *International Socialist Review*, 13 (June 1913), 849–850; Flynn, *I Speak*, p. 153; Paterson *Evening News*, April 22, 1913; Robert Brooks, "The United Textile Workers of America" (Unpublished Ph.D. Dissertation, Yale, 1935), p. 119; William D. Haywood, *Bill Haywood's Book: The Autobiography of Big Bill Haywood* (New York, 1929), p. 268.

42. New York *Times*, April 22, 1912; *Solidarity*, May 3, 1913; New York

Call, April 22, 1913; "The I.W.W. Suffers," *Square Deal,* 12 (May 1913), 383; Paterson *Morning Call,* April 22, 1913.

43. Alexander Scott, "What the Reds Are Doing in Paterson," *International Socialist Review,* 13 (June 1913), 855; Haywood, "On the Picket Line," p. 850.

44. Paterson *Evening News,* April 22, 28, 1913; New York *Times,* April 28, 1913; New York *Call,* April 29, 1913.

45. Paterson *Evening News,* April 29, 1913; New York *Call,* April 30, 1913; New York *Times,* April 29, 1913.

46. Paterson *Evening News,* April 23, 24, 1913; New York *Call,* April 26, 1913; Paterson *Guardian,* April 26, 1913; U.T.W., *Proceedings of the Thirteenth Convention* (1913), p. 24; Testimony of Morgan, U. S. Commission on Industrial Relations, *Final Report,* vol. 3, p. 2420.

47. *Solidarity,* May 17, 1913; New York *Times,* May 18, 1913; Paterson *Guardian,* May 17, 1913.

48. Testimony of Morgan, U. S. Commission on Industrial Relations, *Final Report,* vol. 3, p. 2420; U.T.W., *Proceedings of Thirteenth Convention* (1913), pp. 20, 24, 49, 61, 64.

49. Paterson *Evening News,* April 25, 26, 28, 1913; Paterson *Guardian,* April 26, 1913; New York *Times,* April 26, 28, 29, May 1, 1913; New York *Call,* April 29, 1913; Peter Carlson, *Roughneck: The Life and Times of Big Bill Haywood* (New York, 1983), pp. 214–215.

50. New York *Times,* April 19, 1913; New York *Call,* April 22, 1913; Paterson *Evening News,* April 19, 1913; Testimony of James W. Cooke, U. S. Commission on Industrial Relations, *Final Report,* vol. 3, p. 2611; Paterson *Guardian,* April 24, 1913.

51. New York *Call,* April 30, 1913; New York *Times,* April 30, May 1, 1913; Paterson *Evening News,* May 1, 1913; Paterson *Guardian,* May 1, 1913.

52. New York *Call,* May 2, 7, 12, 1913; N.J., *36th Annual Report* (1913), pp. 180–181.

53. Paterson *Evening News,* May 5, 1913. Mayor McBride later testified that he had formed his committee "about a month after the strike began" (in late March). Whatever the reason for this error, it is clear that his testimony on this episode is flawed. Testimony of Andrew F. McBride, U. S. Commission on Industrial Relations, *Final Report,* vol. 3, p. 2555.

54. William Nelson and Charles Shriner, *History of Paterson and Its Environs* (New York, 1928), vol. 3, p. 208; *Appeal to Reason,* July 26, 1913.

55. Paterson *Evening News,* March 26, 27, 28, April 1, 1913.

56. In addition to Griggs, those named to the committee were: Dr. F. E. Agnew, Passaic County Surrogate Frederick Beggs, retired businessman Arthur W. Bishop, former Mayor Christian Braun, hardware merchant J. W. Cleveland, grocer Richard B. Conklin, County Counsel J. Willard DeYoe, undertaker William M. Dufford, William T. Fanning, Reverend David S. Hamilton, retired builder David Henry, former Judge George S. Hilton, former vice president's son Garret A. Hobart, Jr., Rabbi A. S. Isaacs, Dr. Walter B. Johnson, Board of Trade acting President E. H. Lambert, builder Michael Lynch, Reverend Clarence E. MacCartney, Reverend Dean McNulty, former Judge Francis Scott,

Dr. Francis H. Todd, lawyer E. R. Weiss, Superintendent of Schools John R. Wilson, and builder Nicholas Tanis. Paterson *Morning Call*, May 5, 1913; New York *Call*, May 5, 1913; Testimony of Andrew F. McBride, U. S. *Commission on Industrial Relations*, vol. 3. p. 2555.

57. Paterson *Evening News*, May 5, 1913; New York *Times*, May 5, 6, 1913.

58. Paterson *Evening News*, May 7, 8, 1913; Paterson *Morning Call*, May 7, 1913; *Solidarity*, May 10, 1913.

59. Paterson *Evening News*, May 8, 10, 13, 23, 1913; Testimony of Andrew F. McBride, U. S. Commission on Industrial Relations, *Final Report*, vol. 3, p. 2555.

60. New York *Times*, May 8, 1913.

61. Ibid., May 8, 9, 10, 11, 1913; Testimony of Henry F. Marelli, U. S. Commission on Industrial Relations, *Final Report*, vol. 3, pp. 2540–2541.

62. Paterson *Sunday Chronicle*, May 11, 1913.

63. Paterson *Guardian*, May 10, 12, 1913; New York *Call*, May 12, 1913; *Solidarity*, May 17, 1913; New York *Times*, May 13, 1913.

64. New York *Call*, May 13, 1913; New York *Times*, May 13, 1913.

65. New York *Times*, May 14, 15, 1913; New York *Call*, May 14, 15, 1913.

66. "Labor and the Law," *Nation*, 96 (May 22, 1913), 515–516; New York *Times*, May 16, 1913; Paterson *Evening News*, May 14, 1913.

67. New York *Times*, May 15, 1913; New York *Call*, May 15, 1913; "The Strike of the Jersey Silk Weavers," *Survey*, 30 (May 31, 1913), 300. Quinlan's conviction prompted considerable outrage from many New York liberals and served to generate financial support for relief purposes and Quinlan's appeal. See Eugene M. Tobin, "Direct Action and Conscience: The 1913 Paterson Strike as Example of the Relationship between Labor Radicals and Liberals," *Labor History*, 20 (Winter 1979), 73–78.

68. Paterson *Evening News*, May 16, 1913; New York *Times*, May 16, 1913; New York *Call*, May 17, 1913; Paterson *Guardian*, May 17, 1913.

69. New York *Times*, May 18, 1913.

70. Paterson *Evening News*, May 19, 1913; Paterson *Guardian*, May 19, 1913; New York *Times*, May 19, 1913.

71. Paterson *Evening News*, May 19, 20, 21, 1913; Testimony of Andrew J. McBride, U. S. Commission on Industrial Relations, *Final Report*, vol. 3, pp. 2565–2566.

72. Paterson, *Evening News*, May 14, 1913; *Solidarity*, May 13, 1913; New York *Call*, May 23, 1913.

73. Paterson *Guardian*, May 22, 23, 1913; Paterson *Evening News*, May 21, 1913.

74. Paterson *Evening News*, May 16, 20, 24, 1913; New York *Call*, May 20, 27, 1913; New York *Times*, May 20, 21, 25, 1913.

75. New York *Call*, May 30, 1913.

76. Philip C. Newman, *The Labor Legislation of New Jersey* (Washington, 1943), p. 39; "What Is Hostility to Government?" *Outlook*, 104 (June 21, 1913), 351.

77. New York *Times*, June 4, 1913; New York *Call*, June 4, 1913.

78. Newman, *Labor Legislation*, p. 39; "The Conviction of Alexander Scott," *International Socialist Review*, 14 (July 1913), 10.

79. New York *Call*, June 4, 1913; "The Conviction of Alexander Scott," p. 11; "Freedom of Press at Issue in Paterson," *Survey*, 30 (June 14, 1913), 368; "What Is Hostility to Government?" p. 351; "New Jersey's Journalistic Perils," *Literary Digest*, 46 (June 21, 1913), 1366–1367.

80. New York *Times*, June 8, 14, 1913.

81. "An Investigation of the Paterson Troubles Urged," *Survey*, 30 (June 14, 1913), 368; Paterson *Evening News*, June 5, 1913. Presented by Frederick C. Howe, it was signed by John B. Andrews, Howard B. Woolston, Lillian D. Wald, Henry Moskowitz, John Haynes Holmes, Leo Mannheimer, Delos F. Wilcox, John A. Fitch, Gaylord S. White, Bolton Hall, J. Aspinwall Hodge, John P. Peters, Percy S. Grant, Owen R. Lovejoy, Paul U. Kellogg, Burdette G. Lewis, Howard Bradstreet, John Collier, Amos Pinchot, Theodore Kelley, J. Howard Melish, Hutchins Hapgood, John L. Elliott, Gilbert N. Roe, Graham R. Taylor, and Sam A. Lewisohn.

82. Ralph Chaplin, "How the I.W.W. Defends Labor," *Twenty-Five Years of Industrial Unionism* (Chicago, 1930), p. 23.

83. Elizabeth Gurley Flynn, "The Truth About the Paterson Strike," Typescript in Labadie Collection, University of Michigan, p. 3.

Chapter 6. The Pageant

1. Graham Adams, *Age of Industrial Violence, 1910–1915: The Activities and Findings of the United States Commission on Industrial Relations* (New York, 1966), pp. 25–27; "Movement Under Way for Industrial Commission," *Survey*, 27 (March 2, 1912), 1821.

2. John Bates Clark, "A Commission on Industrial Relations," *Survey*, 28 (July 6, 1912), 493–494.

3. David A. Shannon, *Socialist Party of America* (New York, 1955), p. 8; Morris Hillquit, *Loose Leaves From A Busy Life* (New York, 1971), p. 55.

4. Shannon, *Socialist Party*, p. 58.

5. Gladys Boone, *The Women's Trade Union Leagues in Great Britain and the United States of America* (New York, 1968), pp. 77–80.

6. John G. Brooks, *American Syndicalism: The I.W.W.* (New York, 1913), pp. 106, 109; Emma Goldman, "Syndicalism: Theory and Practice," *Mother Earth*, 7 (January 1913), 373–374.

7. "Direct Action As a Weapon," *Independent*, 74 (January 9, 1913), 71.

8. Brooks, *American Syndicalism*, p. 105.

9. Van Wyck Brooks, *The Confident Years: 1885–1915* (New York, 1952), pp. 478–479.

10. Granville Hicks, *John Reed: The Making of a Revolutionary* (New York, 1936), p. 92; Art Young, *On My Way* (New York, 1928), pp. 274–275; Max Eastman, *Enjoyment of Living* (New York, 1948), pp. 390, 394; Daniel Aaron, *Writers on the Left* (New York, 1961), pp. 20–21. The most recent and complete account of *The Masses* group is Leslie Fishbein, *Rebels in Bohemia* (Chapel Hill, N. C., 1982).

11. Eastman, *Enjoyment of Living*, pp. 394, 398, 400.

12. Aaron, *Writers on the Left*, p. 21; James B. Gilbert, *Writers and Partisans: A History of Literary Radicalism in America* (New York, 1968), p. 29.

13. Contributing editors in literature included Louis Untermeyer, Howard Brubaker, Vorse, Robert Carlton Brown, Arthur Bullard, Dell, Frank Bohn, and William English Walling; contributing editors in art were John Sloan, Young, K. R. Chamberlain, Maurice Becker, Cornelia Barns, Alice and Charles Winter, George Bellows, H. J. Glintenkamp, Glenn O. Coleman, and Stuart Davis. Among others on the staff were Eugene Wood, Ellis O. Jones, Inez Haynes Gillmore, H. J. Turner, William Washburn Nutting, Edmond McKenna, G. S. Sparks, John Barber, Robert Minor, Boardman Robinson, Helen Marot, and Arturo Giovannitti. Eastman, *Enjoyment of Living*, pp. 553–554n.

14. Julian Street, "A Soviet Saint," *Saturday Evening Post*, 203 (September 13, 1930), 8–9; Robert Hallowell, "John Reed," *New Republic*, 24 (November 17, 1920), 298; Orrick Johns, *Time of Our Lives: The Story of My Father and Myself* (New York, 1937), p. 236. These characterizations of Reed are captured in the title of his most recent biography: Robert Rosenstone, *Romantic Revolutionary: A Biography of John Reed* (New York, 1975).

15. Walter Lippmann, "Legendary John Reed," *New Republic*, 1 (December 26, 1914), 15.

16. Margaret Sanger, *An Autobiography* (New York, 1938), p. 70; Floyd Dell, *Homecoming, An Autobiography* (New York, 1933), pp. 327–328; Street, "Soviet Saint," p. 65.

17. Hutchins Hapgood, *A Victorian in the Modern World* (New York, 1939), p. 318.

18. Kenneth S. Lynn, "The Rebels of Greenwich Village," *Perspectives in American History*, 8 (1974), 368–369.

19. Gilbert, *Writers and Partisans*, pp. 25–26.

20. Allen Churchill, *The Improper Bohemians: A Re-creation of Greenwich Village in its Heyday* (New York, 1959), p. 15; Christopher Lasch, *The New Radicalism in America, 1889–1963: The Intellectual As a Social Type* (New York, 1965), p. 104.

21. Mabel Dodge Luhan, *Intimate Memoirs*, vol. 3, *Movers and Shakers* (New York, 1936), pp. 5–6

22. Ibid., pp. 10, 17, 20.

23. Churchill, *Improper Bohemians*, pp. 42–43; Luhan, *Movers and Shakers*, pp. 16–23.

24. Luhan, *Movers and Shakers*, pp. 17–18, 47.

25. Hapgood, *A Victorian*, p. 347.

26. Eastman, *Enjoyment of Living*, p. 425.

27. Hapgood, *A Victorian*, p. 348; Luhan, *Movers and Shakers*, p. 47.

28. Luhan, *Movers and Shakers*, p. 23.

29. Lincoln Steffens, *Autobiography* (New York, 1931), p. 634; Eastman, *Enjoyment of Living*, pp. 427, 424; Hapgood, *A Victorian*, pp. 314, 202–203; Emma Goldman, "Intellectual Proletarians," *Mother Earth*, 8 (February 1914), 369.

30. Luhan, *Movers and Shakers*, pp. 57–58, 66, 69.

31. Lasch, *New Radicalism*, p. 128.

32. Luhan, *Movers and Shakers*, pp. 233, 140, 83.

33. Max Eastman, *Venture* (New York, 1927), pp. 209–210.

34. Sanger, *Autobiography*, pp. 73–74.

35. Hapgood, *A Victorian*, p. 350; Luhan, *Movers and Shakers*, p. 187; William D. Haywood, *Bill Haywood's Book: The Autobiography of Big Bill Haywood* (New York, 1929), p. 262. Melvyn Dubofsky and Graham Adams both place this meeting at the Dodge apartment, as does Reed biographer Granville Hicks. Melvyn Dubofsky, *We Shall Be All: A History of the I.W.W.* (Chicago, 1969), p. 279; Adams, *Age of Industrial Violence, 1910–1915*, p. 93; Hicks, *John Reed*, p. 96. I have accepted the alternative version because Dodge, who loved to be in the center of things, would most probably have put the scene in her home if it had in fact occurred there; and because Haywood, in his autobiography, describes the meeting in "the home of a New York friend of mine," a term more appropriate to his mistress than to Dodge by the time Haywood wrote. The most recent article on the pageant and the latest biography of Haywood both place the event in the home of B. Shostac. Steve Golin, "The Paterson Pageant: Success or Failure?" *Socialist Review*, 69 (May–June 1983), 47; Peter Carlson, *Roughneck: The Life and Times of Big Bill Haywood* (New York, 1983), pp. 217–218.

36. Luhan, *Movers and Shakers*, pp. 188–189. Reed biographer Rosenstone questions this account, which is repeated in Hapgood's autobiography published three years after *Movers and Shakers*, but is unable to uncover solid evidence to support any alternative scenario. He acknowledges that "the origins of the idea for the pageant are difficult to pin down." Rosenstone, *Romantic Revolutionary*, p. 126n. Rosenstone apparently agrees with Hicks's account: the idea for the pageant followed Reed's arrest and four-day detainment in the County Jail. Hicks places the genesis of the pageant idea "in the middle of May," and Rosenstone points out that the first mention of a pageant in the press was in the New York *Times* on May 22, almost a month after Reed's arrest. Hicks, *John Reed*, p. 101; Rosenstone, *Romantic Revolutionary*, p. 127n. Rosenstone, however, is incorrect concerning press mention of the pageant. In fact, on May 16 Haywood told a mass gathering of strikers the plan, most probably after he had discussed it with his associates and the Central Strike Committee, and provided enough detail to suggest that some planning had already gone into the dramatization. This and the fact that Reed was in jail for four days does give at least some support to Dodge's contention that Reed went to Paterson for the first time after the gathering at Shostac's apartment. Paterson *Evening News*, May 16, 1913; New York *Times*, May 17, 1913; New York *Call*, May 17, 1913.

37. Richard O'Connor and Dale L. Walker, *The Lost Revolutionary: A Biography of John Reed* (New York, 1967), p. 73.

38. Linda Nochlin, "The Paterson Strike Pageant of 1913," *Art in America*, 62 (May–June 1974), 67.

39. *Survey*, 29 (March 15, 1913), 826.

40. Haywood, *Book*, p. 262.

41. Testimony of Andrew J. McBride, U. S. Commission on Industrial Relations, *Final Report and Testimony on Industrial Relations*, 64th Congress, 1st Session, Senate Document #451 (Washington 1916), vol. 3, pp. 2559–2560; John Reed, "Sheriff Radcliff's Hotel," *Metropolitan Magazine*, 38 (September 1913), 14; Hicks, *John Reed*, p. 28.

42. John Reed, "Almost Thirty," *New Republic*, 86 (April 29, 1936), 335.

43. John Reed, "War in Paterson," *The Masses*, 4 (June 1913), 14–17; Testimony of Andrew J. McBride, U. S. Commission on Industrial Relations, *Final Report*, vol. 3, p. 2560; O'Connor and Walker, *Lost Revolutionary*, p. 78; Aaron, *Writers on the Left*, p. 17.

44. Hapgood, *A Victorian*, p. 353; Eastman, *Enjoyment of Living*, p. 447.

45. Hapgood, *A Victorian*, p. 355.

46. Luhan, *Movers and Shakers*, p. 200.

47. Street, "Soviet Saint," p. 203; Nochlin, "Paterson Pageant," p. 65.

48. Paterson *Evening News*, May 19, 1913.

49. Luhan, *Movers and Shakers*, pp. 200–204; Upton Sinclair, *American Outpost: A Book of Reminiscences* (New York, 1932), pp. 263, 79.

50. New York *Call*, May 29, 1913; Hicks, *John Reed*, p. 101.

51. New York *Call*, June 26, 1913; Paterson *Evening News*, June 25, 1913; Phillips Russell, "The World's Greatest Labor Play: The Paterson Strike Pageant," *International Socialist Review*, 14 (July 1913), 8.

52. John H. Steiger, *The Memoirs of a Silk Striker: An Exposure of the Principles and Tactics of the I.W.W.* (New York, 1914), pp. 43–44; New York *Call*, June 26, 1913; Russell, "Labor Play," pp. 8–9; Paterson *Evening News*, June 25, 1913.

53. Paterson *Evening News*, May 27, 1913.

54. Paterson *Guardian*, June 5, 1913.

55. *Solidarity*, June 7, 1913.

56. *Industrial Worker*, June 12, 1913.

57. New York *Call*, June 7, 1913.

58. Paterson *Evening News*, June 7, 1913; Paterson *Guardian*, June 7, 1913; Haywood, *Book*, p. 263; Sinclair, *American Outpost*, p. 263.

59. Russell, "Labor Play," p. 7; New York *Times*, June 8, 25, 1913; Hicks, *John Reed*, p. 102; Paterson *Evening News*, June 9, 1913.

60. New York *Times*, June 8, 1913.

61. Ibid.; Paterson *Evening News*, June 9, 1913.

62. "The Pageant As a Form of Propaganda," *Current Opinion*, 55 (July 1913), 32; "The Paterson Strike Pageant," *Independent*, 74 (June 19, 1913), 1407.

63. "Pageant of the Paterson Strike," *Survey*, 30 (June 28, 1913), 428.

64. Paterson *Morning Call*, June 9, 1913; Paterson *Guardian*, June 9, 1913; New York *Times*, June 9, 1913; "A Wave of Love in Henry Street," *Survey*, 30 (June 28, 1913), 427–428.

65. New York *Times*, June 8, 1913; Paterson *Morning Call*, June 9, 1913; Paterson *Evening News*, June 9, 1913; "Pageant of the Paterson Strike," *Survey*, 30 (June 28, 1913), 428.

66. Steiger, *Memoirs*, p. 49.

67. Paterson *Guardian*, June 13, 1913; Paterson *Evening News*, June 14, 1913; New York *Times*, June 14, 1913.

68. Paterson *Evening News*, June 14, 18, 1913; New York *Times*, June 24, 1913.

69. New York *Times*, June 25, 1913; Paterson *Evening News*, June 25, 1913; New York *Call*, June 26, 1913.

70. Paterson *Evening News*, June 25, 1913; New York *Call*, January 21, 1919; Emma Goldman, *Living My Life* (New York, 1931), p. 676; Sanger, *Autobiography*, p. 71; William D. Haywood, "On the Picket Line at Little Falls, New York," *International Socialist Review*, 13 (January 1913), 522; Madeline Gray, *Margaret Sanger* (New York, 1979), p. 55.

71. Paterson *Evening News*, June 25, July 11, 1913.

72. Steiger, *Memoirs*, p. 112.

73. Mel Most, "The 1913 Silk Strike Terror—The Hoax That Killed Silk City," *Bergen Record*, September 30, 1973.

74. Steiger, *Memoirs*, p. 56.

75. Paterson *Evening News*, June 25, 1913; New York *Call*, June 26, 1913.

76. New York *Times*, June 27, 1913.

77. Steiger, *Memoirs*, p. 61. Whether the pageant was "a failure" is the subject of Golin, "The Paterson Pageant: Success or Failure?" and is discussed in a later chapter.

78. Hapgood, *A Victorian*, p. 580.

79. Hicks, *John Reed*, pp. 106–107.

80. John Stuart, "The Education of John Reed," in *The Education of John Reed, Selected Writings* (New York, 1955), p. 18.

81. Reed, "Almost Thirty," p. 268.

82. Luhan, *Movers and Shakers*, pp. 145–147, 249.

83. Ibid., p. 303.

84. Ibid., pp. 341–344, 347.

85. Flynn to Agnes Inglis, July 1950, Labadie Collection, University of Michigan; Agnes Meyer, *Out of These Roots* (Boston, 1953), p. 102.

86. Sanger, *Autobiography*, pp. 85, 96.

87. Carlson, *Roughneck*, p. 221 and Gray, *Sanger*, p. 39 both refer to Ashley at this time as Haywood's "lover." Goldman, *Living My Life*, p. 676.

88. Elizabeth Gurley Flynn, *I Speak My Own Piece: Autobiography of the "Rebel Girl"* (New York, 1955), p. 169.

89. Hapgood, *A Victorian*, p. 581.

Chapter 7. Demobilization

1. New York *Times*, June 9, 1913; Paterson *Evening News*, June 9, 1913; *Solidarity*, June 14, 1913.

2. Paterson *Guardian*, June 13, 1913; New York *Times*, June 24, 1913.

3. Elizabeth Gurley Flynn, "The Truth About The Paterson Strike," Typescript in the Labadie Collection, University of Michigan, p. 19.

4. Joseph R. Conlin, *Big Bill Haywood and the Radical Union Movement*

(Syracuse, N. Y., 1969), p. 141; Melvyn Dubofsky, *We Shall Be All: A History of the I.W.W.* (Chicago, 1969), p. 280. An opposing view, arguing the pageant was a success, appears in Steve Golin, "The Paterson Pageant: Success or Failure?" *Socialist Review*, 69 (May–June 1983), 45–78. The role of the Madison Square Garden reenactment is discussed in full in a subsequent chapter concerning the strike's failure.

5. Ernest T. Hiller, *The Strike: A Study in Collective Action* (Chicago, 1928), pp. 95–96.

6. Paterson *Guardian*, June 10, 1913; Paterson *Evening News*, June 12, 1913.

7. Paterson *Guardian*, June 11, 1913.

8. New York *Times*, June 14, 1913.

9. Paterson *Evening News*, June 5, 1913; New York *Call*, June 6, 1913.

10. Paterson *Morning Call*, June 6, 1913; Paterson *Evening News*, June 6, 1913.

11. Flynn, "The Truth," p. 23.

12. Paterson *Evening News*, June 11, 13, 1913.

13. Ibid., June 16, 1913.

14. Ibid., June 17, 1913.

15. Paterson *Morning Call*, June 18, 1913.

16. Paterson *Evening News*, June 18, 19, 1913; Paterson *Morning Call*, June 19, 1913.

17. Paterson *Morning Call*, June 20, 1913; Paterson *Guardian*, June 20, 1913; Paterson *Evening News*, June 20, 1913; New York *Call*, June 21, 1913.

18. Paterson *Evening News*, June 20, 1913.

19. New York *Times*, June 23, 1913.

20. Paterson *Morning Call*, June 24, 1913; Paterson *Evening News*, June 24, 1913.

21. Paterson *Morning Call*, June 23, 1913; Paterson *Evening News*, June 24, 25, 27, 28, 1913; Paterson *Guardian*, June 28, 1913; New York *Call*, June 28, 1913; Testimony of Edward Zuersher, U. S. Commission on Industrial Relations, *Final Report and Testimony on Industrial Relations*, 64th Congress, 1st Session, Senate Document #451 (Washington, 1916), vol. 3, p. 2603.

22. *Solidarity*, June 28 and July 5, 1913; Paterson *Guardian*, June 27, 1913; Paterson *Evening News*, June 27, 1913.

23. Testimony of Zuersher, U. S. Commission on Industrial Relations, *Final Report*, vol. 3, p. 2603.

24. Flynn, "The Truth," pp. 21–23.

25. Paterson *Evening News*, June 28, 1913.

26. New York *Times*, July 1, 6, 1913; New York *Call*, July 5, 1913.

27. New York *Times*, May 23, 24, 1913.

28. *Solidarity*, June 21, 1913.

29. New York *Times*, July 1, 1913.

30. New York *Times*, July 1, 2, 3, 1913; Paterson *Evening News*, July 3, 4, 5, 7, 1913.

31. New York *Times*, July 4, 1913; Paterson *Evening News*, July 3, 1913; New York *Call*, July 4 and August 12, 1913.

32. Paterson *Evening News*, July 3, 5, 1913.

33. Ibid., July 16, 24, 25, 1913; New York *Call*, July 15, 17, 19, 22, 25, 1913; New York *Times*, July 23, 1913.

34. Paterson *Evening News*, July 1, 2, 5, 1913.

35. Ibid., July 7, 1913.

36. Ibid., July 7, 1913; Paterson *Morning Call*, July 7, 1913; New York *Call*, July 8, 1913.

37. New York *Call*, July 9, 12, 1913.

38. Paterson *Evening News*, July 14, 16, 1913.

39. John F. Steiger, *The Memoirs of a Silk Striker: An Exposure of the Principles and Tactics of the I.W.W.* (New York, 1914), pp. 15–17.

40. Patrick Quinlan, "Silk, Starvation and Solidarity," *Appeal to Reason*, August 16, 1913.

41. Steiger, *Memoirs*, pp. 74–76.

42. Ibid., pp. 76–77; Paterson *Evening News*, July 18, 1913.

43. Paterson *Evening News*, July 18, 1913.

44. Steiger, *Memoirs*, pp. 70–72.

45. Paterson *Guardian*, July 18, 1913.

46. Paterson *Morning Call*, July 19, 1913; Paterson *Evening News*, July 19, 1913.

47. Paterson *Morning Call*, July 19, 1913.

48. New York *Call*, July 19, 21, 1913.

49. Paterson *Evening News*, July 21, 22, 1913.

50. Ibid., July 23, 1913.

51. Paterson *Evening News*, July 23, 24, 25, 1913; New York *Times*, July 23, 1913; Paterson *Morning Call*, July 25, 1913.

52. Paterson *Evening News*, July 24, 26, 28, 29, 30, 1913.

53. New York *Call*, July 29, 1913; *Solidarity*, July 19, 26 and August 2, 1913.

54. Paterson *Evening News*, July 22, 23, 24, 1913.

55. Ibid., July 31 and August 1, 1913.

56. Paterson *Evening News*, August 4, 12, 15, 1913; Paterson *Guardian*, August 14, 15, 1913.

57. Paterson *Guardian*, August 20, 22, 1913; Paterson *Evening News*, August 25, 1913.

58. Paterson *Evening News*, July 24, 30, 1913.

59. Ibid., July 24, August 1, 1913.

60. Ibid., August 1, 20, 1913; New York *Call*, August 2, 1913.

61. Paterson *Evening News*, August 4, 7, 9, 1913; *Solidarity*, August 9, 16, 1913; Testimony of Adolph Lessig, U. S. Commission on Industrial Relations, *Final Report*, vol. 3, p. 2464.

Chapter 8. The Bitter Aftermath

1. New York *Call*, July 29, 1913.

2. Ibid.; Graham Adams, *Age of Industrial Violence, 1910–1915: The Ac-*

tivities and Findings of the United States Commission on Industrial Relations (New York, 1966), p. 97; Patrick Renshaw, *The Wobblies: The Story of Syndicalism in the United States* (New York, 1967), p. 155; Joseph R. Conlin, *Big Bill Haywood and the Radical Union Movement* (Syracuse, N. Y., 1969), p. 143; Melvyn Dubofsky, *We Shall Be All: A History of the I.W.W.* (Chicago, 1969), p. 283.

3. Mary E. Marcy, "The Paterson Strike," *International Socialist Review*, 14 (October 1913), 177.

4. "Haywood and the I.W.W.," *International Socialist Review*, 14 (November 1913), 277.

5. *Solidarity*, August 30, 1913.

6. *Mother Earth*, 8 (August 1913), 162; Alexander Berkman, "The I.W.W. Convention," *Mother Earth*, 8 (October 1913), 233–234.

7. Patrick Quinlan, "The Paterson Strike and After," *New Review*, 2 (January 1914), pp. 30–31; Wilson Killingbeck, "Strike Lost," *New York Call*, July 28, 1913.

8. *New York Times*, July 25, 1913.

9. Samuel Gompers, "The I.W.W. Strikes," *American Federationist*, 20 (August 1913), 622–623.

10. Ralph Chaplin, *Wobbly: The Rough and Tumble Story of a Radical* (Chicago, 1948), pp. 142–143.

11. David A. Shannon, *The Socialist Party of America* (New York, 1955), p. 11

12. *New York Call*, March 14, 1912; Vida Scudder, "For Justice Sake," *Survey*, 28 (April 6, 1912), 77–79; Justus Ebert, *The Trial of a New Society* (Cleveland, 1913), p. 75; Philip S. Foner, *History of the Labor Movement in the United States*, volume 4: *The Industrial Workers of the World, 1905–1917* (New York, 1965), p. 401; Ira Kipnis, *The American Socialist Movement, 1897–1912* (New York, 1952), pp. 331–332; Henry F. Bedford, *Socialism and the Workers in Massachusetts, 1886–1912* (Amherst, Mass., 1966), p. 257.

13. William M. Dick, *Labor and Socialism in America: The Gompers Era* (Port Washington, N. Y., 1972), pp. 105–106.

14. Eugene V. Debs, "Sound Socialist Tactics," *International Socialist Review*, 12 (February 1912), 481.

15. Sally M. Miller, *Victor Berger and the Promise of Constructive Socialism, 1910–1920* (Westport, Conn., 1973), pp. 103–104; Marc Karson, *American Labor Unions and Politics, 1900–1918* (Carbondale, Ill., 1958), p. 196; William Z. Foster, *History of the Communist Party of the United States* (New York, 1952), p. 122; William D. Haywood, *Bill Haywood's Book: The Autobiography of Big Bill Haywood* (New York, 1929), p. 257.

16. Foner, *History*, vol. 4, p. 408; Eugene V. Debs, "This Is Our Year," *International Socialist Review*, 13 (July 1912), 17.

17. *New York Call*, December 4, 1912.

18. Miller, *Berger*, p. 108; H. Wayne Morgan, *Eugene V. Debs: Socialist For President, 1900–1924* (Syracuse, N. Y., 1962), pp. 144–145; "The Recall of Haywood," *Independent*, 74 (March 6, 1913), 490.

19. William Z. Foster, *Pages From A Worker's Life* (New York, 1939), p. 269; Foster, *History of the Communist Party*, p. 123.

20. See, for example, Morgan, *Debs*, pp. 145–146; Karson, *Labor and Politics*, p. 197; Joseph R. Conlin, "The I.W.W. and the Socialist Party," *Science and Society*, 31 (Winter 1967), p. 35; Dick, *Labor and Socialism*, p. 107; Shannon, *Socialist Party of America*, p. 78; Kipnis, *American Socialist Movement*, p. 418; and Daniel Bell, "The Background and Development of Marxian Socialism in the United States," in Donald Drew Egbert and Stow Persons, eds., *Socialism and American Life* (Princeton, 1952), vol. 1, p. 291. James Weinstein challenges this view in *The Decline of Socialism in America, 1912–1925* (New York, 1967), as does Miller, *Berger*, p. 109.

21. Conlin, *Big Bill*, p. 166.

22. William Preston, *Aliens and Dissenters: Federal Suppression of Radicals, 1903–1963* (Cambridge, Mass., 1963), p. 36.

23. Kipnis, *American Socialist Movement*, p. 334.

24. Paterson *Guardian*, February 26, 27, 1913; Paterson *Evening News*, February 26, 28 and March 1, 21, 26, 27, 1913; New York *Call*, March 3, 13, 1913.

25. Paterson *Evening News*, April 9, 1913.

26. New York *Call*, May 28, 30, 1913; Paterson *Sunday Chronicle*, June 8, 1913; "Recall the Recall," *New Review*, 1 (April 12, 1913), 451–452; "Democracy on Trial," *New Review*, 1 (July 1913), 614–615.

27. *Labor's Who's Who*, p. 181; New York *Times*, February 5, 1968. Panken became, in 1917, the first socialist judge elected in New York City and, after appointment by Mayor Fiorello LaGuardia in 1934, served for twenty years on the bench of the Domestic Relations Court in that city.

28. New York *Call*, July 26, 1913.

29. Paterson *Evening News*, March 21, 1913; New York *Call*, July 26, 1913; Haywood, *Book*, p. 268; Joseph Ettor, "An Open Letter to Jacob Panken," *Solidarity*, August 9, 1913; Ewald Koettgen, "What A Lawyer Doesn't Know," *Solidarity*, August 23, 1913.

30. New York *Call*, July 26, 1913.

31. Killingbeck, "Strike Lost," New York *Call*, July 28, 1913.

32. New York *Call*, August 12, 1913.

33. Ibid., August 20, 1913.

34. Ibid., August 19, 1913.

35. Foner, *History*, vol. 4, p. 141.

36. John H. Steiger, *The Memoirs of a Silk Striker: An Exposure of the Principles and Tactics of the I.W.W.* (New York, 1914), pp. 3, 26–31. Charges of exorbitant fees paid to the I.W.W. organizers were common during this and other strikes. In fact, the national union leaders in Paterson received $3 per diem or $18 a week, plus their travel expenses to and from New York City. Koettgen, the local full-time organizer, received $18 per week. Testimony of Edward Zuersher, U. S. Commission on Industrial Relations, *Final Report and Testimony on Industrial Relations*, 64th Congress, 1st Session, Senate Document #451 (Washington, 1916), vol. 3 pp. 2594, 2602.

37. Steiger, *Memoirs*, p. 102.

38. *Mother Earth*, 8 (August 1913), 162.

39. *Solidarity*, August 9, 1913.

40. Ibid., August 23, 1913.

41. Frank Dawson, "Strikes and Strikes," *Solidarity*, August 23, 1913; Giovanni DiGregorio, "Reflections Upon Paterson Strike," *Solidarity*, August 30, 1913.

42. Elizabeth Gurley Flynn, "The Truth About the Paterson Strike," Typescript in Labadie Collection, University of Michigan, pp. 1, 9–10, 12.

43. Ibid., pp. 8–10.

44. Ibid., pp. 5–6

45. Ibid., pp. 17–18.

46. Ibid., p. 29.

47. Ibid., pp. 1–2.

48. New York *Call*, March 21, 1914.

49. *Stenographic Report of the Eighth Convention of the Industrial Workers of the World* (Chicago, 1913), p. 36.

50. Ibid., p. 29.

51. Dubofsky, *We Shall Be All*, p. 288.

52. Ibid., pp. 82, 144–145.

53. *Solidarity*, August 23, 1913.

54. Paul F. Brissenden, *The I.W.W.: A Study of American Syndicalism* (New York, 1919), pp. 306–307.

55. *Report of the Eighth Convention*, p. 20.

56. *Solidarity*, September 27, 1913.

57. *Report of the Eighth Convention*, pp. 64–65.

58. Ibid., pp. 105–107.

59. Ibid., pp. 83, 116, 118.

60. Ibid., p. 65.

61. Ibid., p. 117.

62. Ben L. Reitman, "Impressions of the Chicago Convention," *Mother Earth*, 8 (October 1913), 241–242.

63. Alexander Berkman, "The I.W.W. Convention," *Mother Earth*, 8 (October 1913), 233–234.

64. Ewald Koettgen, "The I.W.W. Convention," *International Socialist Review*, 14 (November 1913), 275–276.

65. Robert F. Hoxie, "The Truth About the I.W.W.," *Journal of Political Economy*, 21 (November 1913), 785–797; "Trade Unionism in the United States: General Character and Types," ibid., 22 (March–May 1914), 201–217, 464–481.

66. Hoxie, "The Truth," pp. 785–787.

67. *Report of the Eighth Convention*, p. 30.

68. Hoxie, "The Truth," p. 791.

69. Ibid., p. 797.

70. Robert F. Hoxie, *Trade Unionism in the United States* (New York, 1920), pp. 151–152; Hoxie, "The Truth," p. 789.

71. Sidney Lens, *The Labor Wars* (New York, 1974), pp. 217–222.

72. *Syndicalist*, April 15, 1913.

73. Ibid., July 1, 1913.

74. Emmet Larkin, *James Larkin—Irish Labor Leader, 1876–1947* (Cambridge, Mass., 1965), p. 7; Paterson *Evening News*, August 4, 1913; *Solidarity*, August 9, 16, 1913.

75. Thomas Mann, "A Plea for Solidarity," *International Socialist Review*, 14 (January 1914), 392–393.

76. Eugene V. Debs, "A Plea for Solidarity," *International Socialist Review*, 14 (March 1914), 535–536.

77. Ibid., p. 538.

78. William D. Haywood, "An Appeal for Industrial Solidarity," *International Socialist Review*, 14 (March 1914), 544–545.

79. Joseph J. Ettor, "I.W.W. vs. A.F. of L.," *New Review*, 2 (May 1914), 280, 284–285.

80. Karson, *Labor and Politics*, p. 198; Philip Taft, *Organized Labor In American History* (New York, 1964), p. 296; *Solidarity*, October 3, 1914.

81. Taft, *Organized Labor*, pp. 296–297; Philip Taft, "The I.W.W. In The Grain Belt," *Labor History*, 1 (Winter 1960), 53–67.

82. *Proceedings of the Tenth Convention of the Industrial Workers of the World* (Chicago, 1917), pp. 63–64.

83. Ibid., pp. 39–40.

84. Fred W. Thompson, *The I.W.W.—Its First Fifty Years* (Chicago, 1955), pp. 62–63.

Chapter 9. The Crucial Test

1. Philip S. Foner, *History of the Labor Movement in the United States*, vol. 4: *The Industrial Workers of the World, 1905–1917* (New York, 1965), p. 369; Melvyn Dubofsky, *We Shall Be All: A History of the I.W.W.* (Chicago, 1969), pp. 284–285; Robert L. Tyler, *Rebels of the Woods: The I.W.W. in the Pacific Northwest* (Eugene, Ore., 1967), p. 9.

2. Foner, *History*, vol. 4, p. 471n; Tyler, *Rebels*, p. 9.

3. Tyler, *Rebels*, p. 21.

4. Foner, *History*, vol. 4, p. 136.

5. Sidney Lens, *Radicalism in America* (New York, 1969), p. 24.

6. Ibid., p. 211; Donald Drew Egbert and Stowe Persons, eds., *Socialism and American Life* (Princeton, N.J., 1952), p. 161.

7. Testimony of Moses H. Straus, U. S. Commission on Industrial Relations, *Final Report and Testimony on Industrial Relations*, 64th Congress, 1st Session, Senate Document #451 (Washington, 1916), vol. 3, pp. 2490–2491.

8. John Brooks, *American Syndicalism: The I.W.W.* (New York, 1913), p. 175.

9. David J. Saposs, *Left Wing Unionism: A Study of Radical Policies and Tactics* (New York, 1926), p. 143.

10. Dubofsky, *We Shall Be All*, p. 482. See also Foner, *History*, vol. 4, p. 144, and Saposs, *Left Wing Unionism*, p. 144.

11. Shichiro Matsui, *The History of the Silk Industry in the United States* (New York, 1930), p. 216.

12. Dubofsky, *We Shall Be All*, p. 482.

13. William D. Haywood, "An Appeal For Industrial Solidarity," *International Socialist Review*, 14 (March 1914), 544.

14. Saposs, *Left Wing Unionism*, p. 138; Selig Perlman and Philip Taft, *History of Labor in the United States, 1896–1932*, vol. 4 of John R. Commons et al., *Labor Movements* (New York, 1935), p. 280.

15. Robert R. R. Brooks, "The United Textile Workers of America" (Unpublished Ph.D. Dissertation, Yale University, 1935), pp. 275–276.

16. Foner, *History*, vol. 4, p. 369; Howard Levin, "Paterson Silk Workers' Strike," *King's Crown Essays*, 9 (Winter 1961–1962), 48; Robert E. Snyder, "Women, Wobblies, and Workers' Rights: The 1912 Textile Strike in Little Falls, New York," *New York History*, 60 (January 1979), 29–57.

17. Dubofsky, *We Shall Be All*, p. 264.

18. Martin C. Mooney, "The Industrial Workers of the World and the Immigrants of Paterson and Passaic, New Jersey, 1907–1913" (Unpublished M. A. Thesis, Seton Hall University, 1969), p. 60.

19. Dubofsky, *We Shall Be All*, p. 229; Donald C. Cole, *Immigrant City: Lawrence, Massachusetts* (Chapel Hill, N. C., 1963), p. 113.

20. U. S. Bureau of the Census, *Census of Manufacturing, 1914: The Silk Industry* (Washington, 1917), p. 5.

21. Mass. Bureau of Statistics, *Thirteenth Annual Report on Strikes and Lockouts, 1912* (Boston, 1913), p. 32; N.J., *36th Annual Report of the Bureau of Statistics and Industries of New Jersey for the Year Ending October 31st, 1913* (Paterson, 1914), p. 21; Testimony of Thomas F. Morgan, U. S. Commission on Industrial Relations, *Final Report*, vol. 3, p. 2429; Testimony of Edward F. L. Lotte, ibid., p. 2451; Testimony of Straus, ibid., p. 2492.

22. Mass. Bureau of Statistics, *Thirteenth Annual Report*, p. 32; N.J., *36th Annual Report*, p. 21.

23. W. Jett Lauck, "The Significance of the Situation at Lawrence," *Survey*, 27 (February 17, 1912), 1773.

24. N.J., *36th Annual Report*, p. 78.

25. Ibid., p. 113.

26. Ibid., pp. 113–114.

27. Testimony of Morgan, U. S. Commission on Industrial Relations, *Final Report*, vol. 3, p. 2425.

28. Lauck, "Significance," p. 27; Testimony of Morgan, U. S. Commission on Industrial Relations, *Final Report*, vol. 3, p. 2423.

29. Dubofsky, *We Shall Be All*, p. 270.

30. Nancy Fogelson, "They Paved the Street With Silk: New Jersey Silk Workers, 1913–1924," *New Jersey History*, 97 (Autumn 1979), 139; Testimony of Andrew J. McBride, U. S. Commission on Industrial Relations, *Final Report*, vol. 3, p. 2560.

31. Mass. Bureau of Statistics, *Thirteenth Annual Report*, p. 23; Justus Ebert, *The Trial of a New Society* (Cleveland, 1913), p. 37; Cole, *Immigrant City*, p. 135; Philip Taft, *Organized Labor in American History* (New York, 1964), p. 292.

32. Testimony of Morgan, U. S. Commission on Industrial Relations, *Final Report*, vol. 3, pp. 2413, 2419.

33. Richard Abrams, *Conservatism in a Progressive Era: Massachusetts Politics, 1902–1912* (Cambridge, Mass., 1964), p. 275.

34. Fred W. Thompson, *The I.W.W.: Its First Fifty Years* (Chicago, 1955), p. 54; *Solidarity*, November 18, 1911.

35. Mass. Bureau of Statistics, *Thirteenth Annual Report*, pp. 22–23; Leslie H. Marcy and Frederick S. Boyd, "One Big Union Wins," *International Socialist Review*, 12 (April 1912), 617.

36. Ebert, *Trial*, p. 37; Dubofsky, *We Shall Be All*, p. 234.

37. Testimony of Adolph Lessig, U. S. Commission on Industrial Relations, *Final Report*, vol. 3, p. 2453.

38. Maurice B. Dorgan, *History of Lawrence, Massachusetts* (Lawrence, Mass., 1924), p. 113; Ebert, *Trial*, pp. 12–16; Dubofksy, *We Shall Be All*, p. 229; Foner, *History*, vol. 4, pp. 307, 309.

39. U. S. Bureau of the Census, *Silk*, p. 5.

40. Testimony of Lotte, U. S. Commission on Industrial Relations, *Final Report*, vol. 3, pp. 2444–2445.

41. Testimony of Morgan, ibid., pp. 2414, 2427, 2419.

42. Testimony of Doherty, ibid., p. 2432; Ruth Tierney, "The Decline of the Silk Industry in Paterson, New Jersey" (Unpublished M.A. Thesis, Cornell University, 1938), p. 125.

43. Testimony of Doherty, U. S. Commission on Industrial Relations, *Final Report*, vol. 3, p. 2437; Testimony of Straus, ibid., p. 2491; Testimony of Ralph Rosenheim, ibid., p. 2624.

44. Doherty, ibid., pp. 2432, 2440.

45. Fogelson, "They Paved the Streets With Silk," p. 140.

46. Testimony of Magnet, U. S. Commission on Industrial Relations, *Final Report*, vol. 3, p. 2573; Testimony of Rodney Miller, ibid., p. 2497; Testimony of John W. Ferguson, ibid., p. 2579; Testimony of James Starr, ibid., p. 2613; Testimony of Andrew F. McBride, ibid., p. 2553.

47. William D. Haywood, "The Rip in the Silk Industry," *International Socialist Review*, 13 (May 1913), 785.

48. Elizabeth Gurley Flynn, "The Truth About The Paterson Strike," Typescript in the Labadie Collection, University of Michigan Library.

49. U. S. Bureau of the Census, *Silk*, p. 5.

50. U. S. Bureau of Labor Statistics, *Wages and Hours in the Cotton, Woolen and Silk Industries*, Document #128 (Washington, 1913), p. 206; Dubofsky, *We Shall Be All*, pp. 267–268; Testimony of Morgan, U. S. Commission on Industrial Relations, *Final Report*, vol. 3, p. 2428.

51. Testimony of Starr, U. S. Commission on Industrial Relations, *Final Report*, vol. 3, p. 2617.

52. Testimony of Doherty, ibid., pp. 2432–2433.

53. Foner, *History*, vol. 4, p. 370.

54. Testimony of Doherty, U. S. Commission on Industrial Relations, *Final Report*, vol. 3, p. 2444; Testimony of Andrew F. McBride, ibid., p. 2557; Testimony of Starr, ibid., pp. 2627–2628; Testimony of Magnet, ibid., p. 2576; Testimony of Zuersher, ibid., p. 2606; Testimony of Anthony H. Stein, ibid., p. 2577.

55. Paterson, *Evening News*, June 9, 1913.

56. Gregory Mason, "Industrial War in Paterson," *Outlook*, 104 (June 17, 1913), 285.

57. Testimony of Ferguson, U. S. Commission on Industrial Relations, *Final Report*, vol. 3, p. 2581; Testimony of Straus, ibid., p. 2490.

58. Testimony of Cooke, ibid., p. 2608.

59. Testimony of Ferguson, ibid., p. 2580.

60. Paterson *Guardian*, February 25, 1913.

61. Brooks, *American Syndicalism*, p. 31.

62. Patrick Renshaw, *Wobblies: The Story of Syndicalism in the United States* (New York, 1967), p. 140; Dubofsky, *We Shall Be All*, p. 229; Foner, *History*, vol. 4, p. 325.

63. Paterson *Evening News*, April 7, 1913.

64. New York *Call*, April 2, 1913; Paterson *Evening News*, May 24, 1913.

65. Testimony of Andrew F. McBride, U. S. Commission on Industrial Relations, *Final Report*, vol. 3, 2556.

66. Testimony of Andrew J. McBride, ibid., pp. 2564–2565.

67. *Annual Report of the City Officers of the City of Paterson, 1913* (Paterson, 1913), pp. 293–294, 309–312.

68. Testimony of Andrew J. McBride, U. S. Commission on Industrial Relations, *Final Report*, vol. 3, pp. 2564, 2558; *Annual Report of the City Officers*, xi.

69. Renshaw, *The Wobblies*, p. 151.

70. Testimony of Lotte, U. S. Commission on Industrial Relations, *Final Report*, vol. 3, p. 2446.

71. Testimony of Andrew J. McBride, ibid., p. 2572; Patrick F. Gill and Redmond S. Brennan, "Report on the Inferior Courts and Police of Paterson," Typescript in the Paterson Public Library, Part 2, p. 11. Mayor McBride detailed the number of arrests by month: February, 119; March, 281; April, 628; May, 591; June, 374; July, 245.

72. Testimony of Morgan, U. S. Commission on Industrial Relations, *Final Report*, vol. 3, p. 2421; Testimony of Lessig, ibid., p. 2462; Testimony of Henry F. Marelli, ibid., 2535.

73. Frederick S. Boyd, "The General Strike in the Silk Industry," *The Pageant of the Paterson Strike* (New York, 1913), p. 6.

74. Police Captain McBride testified that Reed, upon warning by a police officer that he would be arrested if he did not move along, responded: "I came here for that purpose." The Captain stated that the department had "more inquiries about [Reed] than about Haywood all through the strike." Testimony of Andrew J. McBride, U. S. Commission on Industrial Relations, *Final Report*, vol. 3, p. 2560.

75. Ibid., pp. 2565, 2569–2570.

76. Foner, for example, cites "the brutal suppression of [the strikers'] democratic rights" as a major cause for the defeat, noting the mass arrests and the use of the courts to "drive them back to work." Foner, *History*, vol. 4, pp. 360, 370–371.

77. See, for example, Testimony of Marelli, U. S. Commission on Industrial Relations, *Final Report*, vol. 3, p. 2543; Testimony of Lessig, ibid., pp. 2462–2463; "City Officials Adopt Repressive Measures," *Survey*, 30 (April 19, 1913), 82; and "Paterson," *New Review*, 1 (June 1913), 545.

78. Testimony of Morgan, U. S. Commission on Industrial Relations, *Final Report*, vol. 3, p. 2421; Testimony of Stein, ibid., p. 2578.

79. Among those pressing for a federal investigation were the Businessman's Committee of Forty, which appealed to U.S. Senator William Hughes and Congressman Robert S. Bremmer; the S.P.A.; Paterson Alderman Rogers; and strike attorney Marelli, whose request Haywood termed "a good thing." The Paterson *Press*, the Board of Trade, and the New Jersey House of Representatives were among those who urged a state investigation.

80. Renshaw writes that there were the "same violent scenes as [in] Lawrence," and Adams contends that "explosions destroyed property" and that "both sides battled openly with clubs and guns." The most recent and emphatic emphasis on the violent nature of the strike is found in articles by James D. Osborne. In his view the 1913 strike fit into the "tradition of industrial disorder in the city" but with two important differences: a change in the city authorities' attitude of being "traditionally responsive to workingmen's pressure" and the hostility shown toward the Italian workers. The result was the "sensational disorder of 1913." Although Osborne acknowledges that the I.W.W. leaders cautioned against violence and boasted of the nonviolent nature of the strike, he concludes that "the strikers' behavior mocked this sentiment. Once on the streets, they acted on their own initiative. Crowds gathered to jeer and hoot. Scabs were beaten up; their houses were stoned and even bombed. Mill property also was attacked; attempts were made to blow up mills, and more commonly, factory windows were smashed." Renshaw, *The Wobblies*, p. 151; Graham Adams, *Age of Industrial Violence, 1910–1915: The Activities and Findings of the United States Commission on Industrial Relations* (New York, 1966), p. 75; James D. Osborne, "Italian Immigrants and the Working Class in Paterson: The Strike of 1913 in Ethnic Perspective," in Paul A. Stellhorn, ed., *New Jersey's Ethnic Heritage* (Trenton, 1978), pp. 11–34; and Osborne, "Paterson: Immigrant Strikers and the War of 1913," in Joseph R. Conlin, ed., *At the Point of Production: The Local History of the I.W.W.* (Westport, Conn., 1981), pp. 61–78.

81. Foner, *History*, vol. 4, p. 358.

82. Joseph R. Conlin, "The I.W.W. and the Question of Violence," *Wisconsin Magazine of History*, 51 (Spring 1968), 320.

83. Osborne relies heavily on the commission report, which he contends "contains abundant evidence" of violence. In addition, he maintains that "all

leading historians of the strike have ignored the local Paterson press," an oversight which "has led to the woeful ignoring of violence perpetrated by silk workers." Osborne, "Italian Immigrants," p. 176, n. 19.

84. Testimony of Andrew J. McBride, U. S. Commission on Industrial Relations, *Final Report*, vol. 3, pp. 2562–2564; Testimony of Dunn, ibid., pp. 2548–2552; Testimony of Lotte, ibid., p. 2446; Testimony of Stein, ibid., p. 2578. Osborne used all of these to support his point on violence.

85. Testimony of Lessig, ibid., p. 2458–2459; Testimony of Marelli, ibid., p. 2453; Testimony of Zuersher, ibid., pp. 2593–2594.

86. Testimony of Doherty, ibid., p. 2438; Testimony of Lotte, ibid., p. 2446; Testimony of Starr, ibid., p. 2614; Testimony of Morgan, ibid., p. 2420; Testimony of Cooke, ibid., p. 2609.

87. Testimony of Morgan, ibid., p. 2420.

88. *Industrial Union News*, June 1913.

89. Elizabeth Gurley Flynn, *I Speak My Own Piece: Autobiography of the "Rebel Girl"* (New York, 1955), p. 169; Mary Heaton Vorse, *A Footnote To Folly* (New York, 1935), p. 53.

90. Golin contends that the pageant was a success, that Flynn blamed it for the strike's defeat out of her own jealousy of Haywood's connection to it or her wish to find scapegoats, and that her account is without substantiation. According to Golin, there was no confirming evidence that the show prompted jealousy on the part of strikers or that picketing slackened off because of it. Those who have accepted Flynn's charge that the pageant's financial losses prompted the stampede back to the mills is, he asserted, a direct consequence of a misreading of the intent of the Madison Square Garden performance; only if one views the pageant as primarily a fund raiser, can one accept Flynn's view that it was a failure. Golin refused to accept this reading and argued that the pageant was essentially a publicity tactic and that it was not performed in the expectation it would raise substantial funds for relief. Noting the meetings held in New York to determine whether the show should be canceled because of the enormous expenses involved, he contended that the pageant's New York supporters decided to go on even though they knew the show would lose money. Steve Golin, "The Paterson Pageant: Success or Failure?" *Socialist Review*, 69 (May–June 1983), 49, 51, 65–69, 72.

91. *Solidarity*, June 7, 1913.

92. See, for example, Daniel Aaron, *Writers On The Left* (New York, 1961), p. 35; Adams, *Age of Industrial Violence*, pp. 96–97; Peter Carlson, *Roughneck: The Life and Times of Big Bill Haywood* (New York, 1983), p. 220; Dubofsky, *We Shall Be All*, pp. 280–281; Foner, *History*, vol. 4, pp. 366–367; Renshaw, *The Wobblies*, p. 116; Robert A. Rosenstone, *Romantic Revolutionary: A Biography of John Reed* (New York, 1975), p. 131; Fogelson, "They Paved the Streets," p. 138; Joseph R. Conlin, *Big Bill Haywood and the Radical Union Movement* (Syracuse, 1969), p. 142.

93. Flynn, *I Speak*, p. 149.

94. Harber Allen, "The Flynn," *American Mercury*, 9 (December 1926), 431.

95. Renshaw, *Wobblies*, p. 144; Conlin, "I.W.W. and the Question of Violence," p. 324; Carlson, *Roughneck*, p. 216; Dubofsky, *We Shall Be All*, p. 277.

96. Paterson *Evening News*, September 24, 29, 1913; New York *Call*, September 30, 1913.

97. New York *Times*, October 2, 1913; Paterson *Evening News*, September 30, 1913.

98. New York *Times*, October 2, 1913; New York *Call*, October 4, 1913.

99. New York *Call*, October 4, 1913; *Mother Earth*, 8 (October 1913), 227–228; *Solidarity*, October 11, 1913; "Free Speech on Trial," *The Masses*, 5 (November 1913), 14.

100. New York *Call*, July 28, 1914; New York *Times*, March 25, 1915.

101. Granville Hicks, *John Reed: The Making of a Revolutionary* (New York, 1936), p. 181; John H. Steiger, *The Memoirs of a Silk Striker: An Exposure of the Principles and Tactics of the I.W.W.* (New York, 1914), p. 94.

102. Accompanying his recantation and supporting his appeal was a petition signed by Theodore Roosevelt, Herbert Croly, Carl Hovey, Finley Peter Dunne, Fred C. Howe, Reverend Percy Stickney Grant, Lippmann, Steffens, and Reed. *Solidarity*, April 3, 1915; "The Recantation of Frederick Sumner Boyd," *Mother Earth*, 10 (April 1915), 80.

103. *Mother Earth*, 10 (April 1915), 68–69.

104. Hicks, *Reed*, p. 111.

105. Steiger, *Memoirs*, p. 72; *Solidarity*, August 9, 1913. Golin's article on the Paterson strike's aftermath notes that Flynn and Lessig were at odds as early as June 1913 and that Flynn, in her autobiography, "attacked Lessig's integrity, accusing him of having been a company agent in a later strike." Golin, "Defeat Becomes Disaster," p. 236. Flynn, however, did not accuse Lessig of this later "treachery" directly. Instead, she wrote: "I stayed over in Paterson quite often, usually at the home of A. Lessig, one of the local leaders (accused in a later strike of being a company agent)." Flynn, *I Speak*, p. 166. As in the case of her comments concerning Boyd, Flynn intimated rather than made an unambiguous charge.

106. Fogelson, "They Paved the Streets with Silk," pp. 141–144.

107. New York *Times*, June 25, 1935.

108. Dubofsky, *We Shall Be All*, p. 279.

109. Thompson, *The I.W.W.*, pp. 60–61.

110. Levin, "Paterson Silk Workers' Strike," pp. 55–56.

111. Dubofsky, *We Shall Be All*, pp. 284–285.

112. New York *Call*, July 26, 1913.

113. *Solidarity*, August 9, 1913.

114. John A. Carpenter, "The Industrial Development of Paterson, New Jersey, 1792–1913" (Unpublished M. A. Thesis, Columbia University, 1947), p. 75; Mel Most, "The 1913 Silk Strike Terror—The Hoax That Killed Silk City," *Bergen Record* (September 30, 1973), 6.

115. New York *Times*, September 11, 1913; Most, "Silk Strike Terror," p. 6.

116. Grace Hutchins, *Labor and Silk* (New York, 1929), pp. 25–26.

117. Morris William Garber, "The Silk Industry of Paterson, New Jersey, 1840–1913" (Unpublished Ph.D. Dissertation, Rutgers University, 1969), p. 276; Ruth Tierney, "Decline of Silk," p. 23; Matsui, *History of the Silk Industry*, p. 40.

118. Tierney, "Decline of Silk," p. 125; Matsui, *History of the Silk Industry*, p. 39; Hutchins, *Labor and Silk*, pp. 25–26. Tierney provides the following chart on the changing nature of the Paterson silk industry:

Proliferation of Shops in Paterson, 1913–1927

Year	Shops	Workers	Average workers per shop
1914	291	16,992	58.4
1919	574	21,836	38.0
1921	593	16,666	28.1
1923	614	16,830	29.4
1925	691	16,368	23.7
1927	704	14,628	20.8

119. Tierney, "Decline of Silk," p. 125.

120. Most, "Strike Terror," pp. 6, 11, 13.

Bibliography

I. PRIMARY SOURCES

A. Government Publications

Annual Report of the City Officers of the City of Paterson, 1913. Paterson: C. M. Herrick, 1913.

Massachusetts Bureau of Statistics. *13th Annual Report on Strikes and Lockouts, 1912*. Boston: Wright & Potter Printing Co., 1913.

New Jersey. *33rd Annual Report of the Bureau of Statistics of Labor and Industries for the Year Ending October 31st, 1910*. Paterson: News Printing Co., 1910.

_____. *34th Annual Report of the Bureau of Statistics of Labor and Industries for the Year Ending October 31st, 1911*. Camden: Sinnickson Chew & Sons Co., 1912.

_____. *35th Annual Report of the Bureau of Statistics of Labor and Industries for the Year Ending October 31st, 1912*. Camden: Sinnickson Chew & Sons Co., 1913.

_____. *36th Annual Report of the Bureau of Statistics and Industries of New Jersey for the Year Ending October 31st, 1913*. Paterson: News Printing Co., 1914.

_____. *37th Annual Report of the Bureau of Industrial Statistics for the Year Ending October 31st, 1914*. Camden: S. Chew & Sons Co., 1915.

_____. *38th Annual Report of the Bureau of Industrial Statistics for the Year Ending October 31st, 1915*. Camden: S. Chew & Sons Co., 1916.

_____. *39th Annual Report of the Bureau of Industrial Statistics for the Year Ending October 31st, 1916*. Trenton: MacCrellish & Quigley Co., 1917.

_____. *Manual of the Legislature of New Jersey, 1912–1913*. Trenton: Thomas F. Fitzgerald, 1913.

New Jersey Commission on Immigration. *Report*. Trenton: MacCrellish & Quigley, 1914.

United States Bureau of the Census. *Census of Manufacturing: 1914, The Silk Industry*. Washington: Government Printing Office, 1917.

United States Bureau of Labor Statistics. *Wages and Hours in the Cotton, Woolen and Silk Industries*. Document #128. Washington: Government Printing Office, 1913.

United States Commission on Industrial Relations. *Final Report and Testimony* on *Industrial Relations*. vols. 2, 3, 9. 64th Congress, 1st Session, Senate Document #451. Washington: Government Printing Office, 1916.

United States Congress. House. *The Strike at Lawrence, Massachusetts, Hearings before the Committee on Rules of the House of Representatives on House Resolutions 409 and 433, March 2–7, 1912.* 62d Congress, 2d Session, House Document #671. Washington: Government Printing Office, 1912.

————. Senate. *Immigrants in Industries. Part 5: Silk Goods Manufacturing and Dyeing.* 61st Congress, 2d Session, Senate Document #633. Washington: Government Printing Office, 1911.

United States Industrial Commission. *The Silk Industry in America, as Represented to the United States Industrial Commission at a Hearing at the Fifth Avenue Hotel, New York, May 22, 1901.* Washington: Government Printing Office, 1901.

B. Union Proceedings and Publications

American Federation of Labor. *Report of the Proceedings of the Thirty-Second Annual Convention.* Washington: Law Reporter Printing Co., 1912.

————. *Report of the Proceedings of the Thirty-Third Annual Convention.* Washington: Law Reporter Printing Co., 1913.

————. *Report of the Proceedings of the Thirty-Fourth Annual Convention.* Washington: Law Reporter Printing Co., 1914.

American Federationist, 1905–1920.

Industrial Union Bulletin, 1907–1909.

Industrial Union News, 1912–1924.

Industrial Worker, 1910–1913.

Industrial Workers of the World. *Proceedings of the First Convention of the Industrial Workers of the World.* New York: Merit Publishers, 1969.

————. "Stenographic Report of the Seventh Annual Convention of the Industrial Workers of the World, Chicago: September 16, 26, 1912."

————. "Stenographic Report of the Eight Annual Convention of the Industrial Workers of the World, Chicago: September 15–29, 1913."

————. *Proceedings of the Tenth Convention of the Industrial Workers of the World Held at Chicago, Illinois, November 20 to December 1, 1916.* Chicago: Published by the I.W.W., 1917.

Solidarity, 1909–1917.

United Textile Workers. *Proceedings of the First–Sixteenth Annual Conventions* (1900–1916).

C. Newspapers

Appeal to Reason, 1903–1916.

New York *Call,* 1912–1919.

New York *Times,* 1913–1920.

Paterson *Evening News,* 1910–1919.

Paterson *Guardian,* 1913–1915.

Paterson *Morning Call,* 1913–1916.

Paterson *Press,* 1911–1914.
Paterson *Press-Guardian,* 1915–1919.
Paterson *Sunday Chronicle,* 1913–1916.

D. Magazines and Journals
Atlantic Monthly
Collier's
Forum
Harper's Weekly
Independent
International Socialist Review
Journal of Political Economy
Life and Labor
Literary Digest
The Masses
Metropolitan Magazine
Mother Earth
National Civic Federation Review
Nation
New Republic
New Review
North American Review
Outlook
Rebel Worker
Survey
Square Deal
Syndicalist
Voice of the People
World's Work

E. Memoirs, Letters, Collected Writings, and Speeches
Beal, Fred E. *Proletarian Journey.* New York: Hillman-Curl, 1937.
Berger, Victor. *Broadsides.* Milwaukee: The Social-Democratic Publishing Company, 1912.
Cannon, James P. *Notebook of an Agitator.* New York: Pioneer Publishers, 1958.
Chaplin, Ralph. *Wobbly: The Rough and Tumble Story of a Radical.* Chicago: University of Chicago Press, 1948.
Debs, Eugene V. *Eugene V. Debs Speaks.* Jean Y. Tussey, ed. New York: Pathfinder Press, 1970.
DeLeon, Daniel. *Socialist Reconstruction of Society.* New York: New York Labor News Co., 1920.
———. *Speeches and Editorials.* 2 vols. New York: New York Labor News Co., 1920.
Dell, Floyd. *Homecoming, An Autobiography.* New York: Farrar & Rhinehart, 1933.

Eastman, Max. *Enjoyment of Living.* New York: Harper & Brothers, 1948.

Flynn, Elizabeth Gurley. *I Speak My Own Piece: Autobiography of the "Rebel Girl."* New York: International Publishers Co., 1955.

Foster, William Z. *Pages from a Worker's Life.* New York: International Publishers Co., 1939.

Glaspell, Susan. *The Road to the Temple.* New York: Frederick A. Stokes Co., 1941.

Goldman, Emma. *Living My Life.* New York: Alfred A. Knopf, 1931.

Gompers, Samuel. *Seventy Years of Life and Labor.* 2 vols. New York: Augustus M. Kelley Publishers, 1925.

Hapgood, Hutchins. *A Victorian in the Modern World.* New York: Harcourt, Brace and Co., 1939.

Hapgood, Norman. *The Changing Years.* New York: Farrar & Rhinehart, 1930.

Harriman, Mrs. J. Borden. *From Pinafores to Politics.* New York: Henry Holt and Co., 1923.

Haywood, William D. *Bill Haywood's Book: The Autobiography of Big Bill Haywood.* New York: International Publishers Co., 1929.

Hillquit, Morris. *Loose Leaves from a Busy Life.* New York: Da Capo Press, 1971.

Johns, Orrick. *Time of Our Lives: The Story of My Father and Myself.* New York: Stackpole Sons, 1937.

Jones, Mary Harris. *Autobiography of Mother Jones.* Charles H. Kerr & Co., 1925.

Luhan, Mabel Dodge. *Intimate Memoirs.* Vol. 3: *Movers and Shakers.* New York: Harcourt, Brace and Co., 1936.

Meyer, Agnes E. *Out of These Roots.* Boston: Little, Brown and Co., 1953.

Poole, Ernest. *The Bridge, My Own Story.* New York: Macmillan Co., 1940.

Reed, John. *The Education of John Reed, Selected Writings.* John Stuart, ed. New York: International Publishers Co., 1955.

Sanger, Margaret H. *An Autobiography.* New York: W. W. Norton & Co., 1938.

Scudder, Vida D. *On Journey.* New York: E. P. Dutton & Co., 1937.

Sinclair, Upton. *American Outpost: A Book of Reminiscences.* New York: Farrar & Rhinehart, 1932.

_____. *The Autobiography of Upton Sinclair.* New York: Harcourt, Brace & World, 1962.

Steffens, Lincoln. *Autobiography.* New York: Harcourt, Brace and Co., 1931.

_____. *The Letters of Lincoln Steffens.* Ella Winter and Granville Hicks, eds. 2 vols. New York: Harcourt, Brace and Co., 1938.

_____. *The World of Lincoln Steffens.* Ella Winter and Herbert Shapiro, eds. New York: Hill and Wang, 1963.

Steiger, John H. *The Memoirs of a Silk Striker: An Exposure of the Principles and Tactics of the I.W.W.* New York: Privately Printed, 1914.

Vorse, Mary Heaton. *A Footnote To Folly.* New York: Farrar & Rhinehart, 1935.

Young, Art. *On My Way.* New York: Horace Liveright, 1928.

F. Books and Articles

"About Haywood," *Literary Digest* (June 14, 1913), 1352–1354.

"Acquittal of the I.W.W. Leaders," *Literary Digest*, 45 (December 7, 1912), 1049–1050.

"After the Battle," *Survey*, 28 (April 6, 1912), 1–2.

"Aftermath of the Paterson Strike," *Outlook*, 105 (November 29, 1913), 679.

"After the Strike—In Lawrence," *Outlook*, 101 (June 15, 1912), 340–346.

"Akron and the I.W.W.," *Collier's*, 51 (June 21, 1913), 31.

Anthony, Katharine. "The Waiters' Strike," *Survey*, 28 (May 25, 1912), 330–331.

"At His Old Tricks Again," *Square Deal*, 10 (March 1912), 191–192.

"Attention! Organized Labor," *American Federationi' t*, 12 (May 1905), 277.

Bakeman, Robert A. "Little Falls—A Capitalist City Stripped of Its Veneer," *New Review*, 1 (February 8, 1913), 167–174.

Baker, Ray Stannard. "Revolutionary Strike," *American Magazine*, 74 (May 1912), 18–30c.

Beal, Fred E. *Proletarian Journey*. New York: Hillman-Curl, 1937.

Bennett, H. Scott. "Two Kinds of Unionism," *International Socialist Review*, 13 (August 1912), 135–136.

Berkman, Alexander. "The I.W.W. Convention," *Mother Earth*, 8 (October 1913), 232–233.

"Big All-Inclusive Labor Trust—The Aim of the I.W.W.," *Review of Reviews*, 46 (November 1912), 613–615.

Bohn, Frank. "Is the I.W.W. To Grow?" *International Socialist Review*, 12 (July 1911), 42–44.

———. "The Strike of the New York Hotel and Restaurant Workers," *International Socialist Review*, 13 (February 1913), 620–621.

———. "Voting, Fighting, Educating!" *International Socialist Review*, 14 (December 1913), 363–367.

Bohn, William E. "The Industrial Workers of the World," *Survey*, 28 (May 4, 1912), 220–225.

Boyd, Frederick Sumner. "The General Strike in the Silk Industry," *The Pageant of the Paterson Strike* (New York: Success Press, 1913), 3–8.

Boyle, James. *The Minimum Wage and Syndicalism*. Cincinnati: Stewart & Kidd Co., 1913.

———. "Syndicalism, The Latest Manifestation of Labor's Unrest," *Forum*, 48 (August 1912), 223–233.

Brooks, John G. *American Syndicalism: The I.W.W.* New York: Macmillan Co., 1913.

———. "The Real Trouble with the Industrial Workers of the World," *Survey*, 31 (October 25, 1913), 87–88.

———. "The Shadow of Anarchy," *Survey*, 28 (April 6, 1912), 80–82.

Cannon, James P. *The I.W.W.: The Great Anticipation*. New York: Pioneer Publishers, 1956.

Carstens, C. C. "The Children's Exodus from Lawrence," *Survey*, 28 (April 6, 1912), 70–71.

"Chairman Walsh," *The Masses*, 6 (September 1915), 10.

Chaney, William. "Working Class Politics, From Debs' Chicago Speech," *International Socialist Review*, 11 (November 1910), 257–261.

Chaplin, Ralph. "How the I.W.W. Defends Labor," *Twenty-Five Years of Industrial Unionism.* Chicago: I.W.W. Publishing Bureau, 1930.

Child, Richard Washburn. "Industrial Revolt at Lawrence," *Collier's*, 48 (March 9, 1912), 13–15.

———. "Who's Violent?" *Collier's*, 49 (June 29, 1912), 12–13, 22.

"Children of a Strike," *Survey*, 27 (February 24, 1912), 1791–1794.

"City Officials Adopt Repressive Measures," *Survey*, 30 (April 19, 1913), 82–83.

Clark, John B. "A Commission on Industrial Relations," *Survey*, 28 (July 6, 1912). 493–495.

Cole, John N. "The Issue at Lawrence—The Manufacturers' Point of View," *Outlook*, 100 (February 24, 1912), 405–406.

"Commission on Industrial Relations," *Survey*, 29 (December 28, 1912), 381–382.

"The Compromises of the Socialist Convention," *Independent*, 72 (May 30, 1912), 1181–1182.

Comyn, Stella. "The Futility of Investigations," *Mother Earth*, 9 (February 1915), 376–379.

Conboy, Sara A. "Report on United Textile Workers of America," in "Labor's Progress—Onward and Upward: A Symposium," *American Federationist*, 23 (September 1916), 761–802.

"The Conviction of Alexander Scott," *International Socialist Review*, 14 (July 1913), 10–11.

"Cultivated Agitator," *Harper's Weekly*, 58 (March 28, 1914), 20.

Current Literature, 52 (April 1912), 380–388.

Current Opinion, 55 (August 1913), 80–81.

"Danger Ahead!" *New Review*, 1 (August 1913), 673–680.

Daniel DeLeon, The Man and His Works: A Symposium. New York: National Executive Committee of the Socialist Labor Party, 1934.

Debs, Eugene V. "Danger Ahead," *International Socialist Review*, 11 (January 1911), 413–415.

———. "The Industrial Convention," *International Socialist Review*, 6 (August 1905), 85–86.

———. "A Plea for Solidarity," *International Socialist Review*, 14 (March 1914), 534–538.

———. "Sound Socialist Tactics," *International Socialist Review*, 12 (February 1912), 481–486.

———. "This Is Our Year," *International Socialist Review*, 13 (July 1912), 16–18.

Deland, Lorin F. "The Lawrence Strike: A Study," *Atlantic Monthly*, 109 (May 1912), 694–705.

Delaney, Ed, and Rice, M. T. *The Bloodstained Trail: A History of Militant Labor in the United States.* Seattle: The Industrial Worker, 1927.

"Democracy on Trial," *New Review*, 1 (July 1913), 609–615.

"Developments at Lawrence," *Survey*, 27 (February 10, 1912), 1725–1726.

"Direct Action as a Weapon," *Independent*, 74 (January 9, 1913), 70–71.

"Does the I.W.W. Spell Social Revolution?" *Current Literature*, 52 (April 1912), 380–388.

Dosch, Arno. "What the I.W.W. Is," *The World's Work*, 26 (August 1913), 406–420.

"Double Labor War at Paterson, New Jersey," *Outlook*, 104 (May 3, 1913), 11.

"Dramatizing the Paterson Strike," *Survey*, 30 (May 31, 1913), 316.

Duchez, Louis. "The Strikes in Pennsylvania," *International Socialist Review*, 10 (September 1909), 193–203.

———. "Victory at McKees Rocks," *International Socialist Review*, 10 (October 1909), 289–300.

Duff, Hezekiah N. "The I.W.W.'s: What They Are and What They Are Trying To Do," *Square Deal*, 10 (May 1912), 297–310.

———. "What of the Year 1913?" *Square Deal*, 11 (January 1913), 485–489.

Dunbar, Robin Ernest. "A Conflict among Leaders," *International Socialist Review*, 10 (August 1909), 149–151.

Duncan, James. "Victory at McKees Rocks, *American Federationist*, 16 (October 1909), 877.

Dunn, Robert W. "Unionism in the Textile Industry," *American Labor Year Book, 1921–1922.* (New York: Rand School of Social Science, 1922), 155–162.

Dunn, Robert W., and Hardy, Jack. *Labor and Textiles.* New York: International Publishers Co., 1931.

Easley, Ralph M. "The Two Irreconcilable Foes of the Civic Federation," *The National Civic Federation Review*, 3 (November 15, 1909), 7–10.

Eastman, Max. "The Great American Scapegoat," *New Review*, 2 (August 1914), 465–470.

———. *Heroes I Have Known.* New York: Simon and Schuster, 1942.

———. *Reflections on the Failure of Socialism.* New York: Devin-Adair, 1962.

Ebert, Justus. *The I.W.W. in Theory and Practice.* Chicago: I.W.W. Publishing Bureau, 1920.

———. *The Trial of a New Society.* Cleveland: I.W.W. Publishing Bureau, 1913.

"E. G. Flynn: Labor Leader," *Outlook*, 111 (December 15, 1915), 905.

"The Embargo on Strike Children," *Survey*, 27 (March 2, 1912), 1822.

"End of the Paterson Strike," *Outlook*, 104 (August 9, 1913), 780.

Ettor, Joseph J. "I.W.W. vs. A.F. of L.," *New Review*, 2 (May 1914), 275–285.

———. "A Retrospect of Ten Years of the I.W.W.," *Solidarity*, August 14, 1915.

"Ettor and Giovannitti Must Be Saved," *International Socialist Review*, 13 (July 1912), 19.

"Ettor in Jail: Strike Goes On," *Survey*, 27 (February 10, 1912), 1726–1727.

Ettor and Giovannitti Before the Jury at Salem, Massachusetts, November 23, 1912. Chicago: I.W.W., n.d.

Fitch, John. "The I.W.W.: An Outlaw Organization," *Survey*, 30 (June 7, 1913), 355–362.

———. "The Paterson Silk Strike: A Year After," *Survey*, 32 (June 27, 1914), 339–340.

Flynn, Elizabeth Gurley. "Contract Slavery in the Paterson Silk Mills," *The Pageant of the Paterson Strike* (New York: Success Press, 1913), 29–31.

———. *Debs, Haywood, Ruthenberg.* New York: Workers Library Publishers, 1939.

_____. "The Fight for Free Speech in Spokane," *International Socialist Review*, 10 (December 1909), 483–488.

_____. "Figures and Facts," *The Pageant of the Paterson Strike* (New York: Success Press, 1913), 15, 19–23.

_____. *Sabotage*. Chicago: I.W.W. Publishing Bureau, 1916.

_____. "The Shame of Spokane," *International Socialist Review*, 10 (January 1910), 610–619.

Ford, James. "The Co-Operative Franco-Belge of Lawrence," *Survey*, 28 (April 6, 1912), 68–70.

Fosdick, Harry Emerson. "After the Strike—In Lawrence," *Outlook*, 101 (June 15, 1912), 340–346.

Foster, William Z. *The Bankruptcy of the American Labor Movement*. New York: Trade Union Educational League, 1922.

_____. *From Bryan to Stalin*. New York: International Publishers Co., 1937.

_____. *History of the Communist Party of the United States*. New York: International Publishers Co., 1952.

_____. *Misleaders of Labor*. New York: Trade Union Educational League, 1927.

Fraina, Louis C. "Daniel DeLeon," *New Review*, 2 (July 1914), 390–399.

"Free Speech on Trial," *The Masses*, 5 (November 1913), 14.

"Freedom of Press at Issue in Paterson," *Survey*, 30 (June 14, 1913), 368.

Giovannitti, Arturo M. "Syndicalism—The Creed of Force," *Independent*, 76 (October 30, 1913), 209–211.

"Glorious Paterson," *International Socialist Review*, 14 (December 1913), 355–357.

Golden, John. "Scientific Management in the Textile Industry," *American Federationist*, 18 (August 1911), 603–604.

Goldman, Emma. "Intellectual Proletarians," *Mother Earth*, 8 (February 1914), 363–370.

_____. "Syndicalism: In Theory and Practice," *Mother Earth*, 7 (January 1913), 373–378.

Gompers, Samuel. "A.F. of L. Political Policy," *American Federationist*, 17 (March 1910), 224–225.

_____. "Debs—The Apostle of Failure," *American Federationist*, 15 (September 1908), 736–740.

_____. "Destruction the Avowed Purpose of the I.W.W.," *American Federationist*, 20 (July 1913), 533–537.

_____. "Immigration—Up To Congress," *American Federationist*, 18 (January 1911), 17–21.

_____. "The I.W.W. Strikes," *American Federationist*, 20 (August 1913), 622–624.

_____. *Labor and the Employer*. New York: E. P. Dutton & Co., 1920.

_____. "Labor's Struggle for the Right to Organize," *Outlook*, 100 (February 4, 1911), 267–270.

_____. "Lawrence," *American Federationist*, 19 (April 1912), 281–293.

_____. "Organized Labor and the National Civic Federation," *American Federationist*, 18 (March 1911), 181–191.

———. "Those 'World Redeemers' at Chicago—Their Plight," *American Federationist*, 12 (August 1905), 514–516.

———. "'Tis Treason, Gentlemen,'" *American Federationist*, 12 (June 1905), 358–361.

———. "Trade Unions To Be Smashed Again," *American Federationist*, 12 (March 1905), 139–141.

———. "Trade Unions To Be Smashed Again—No. 2," *American Federationist*, 12 (April 1905), 214–217.

———. "Upton Sinclair's Mental Marksmanship," *American Federationist*, 21 (April 1914), 293–302.

Gordon, F. G. R. "A Labor Man's Story of the Paterson Strike," *National Civic Federation Review*, 4 (December 1, 1913), 16–17.

Hallowell, Robert. "John Reed," *New Republic*, 24 (November 17, 1920), 298–299.

"Have They Lost?" *Square Deal*, 13 (September 1913), 190.

Hayes, Max S. "The Rochester Convention of the A.F. of L.," *New Review*, 1 (January 4, 1913), 21–23.

Haywood, William D. "An Appeal for Industrial Solidarity," *International Socialist Review*, 14 (March 1914), 544–546.

———. "The Fighting I.W.W.," *International Socialist Review*, 13 (September 1912), 246–247.

———. *The General Strike*. Chicago: I.W.W. Publishing Bureau, n.d.

———. "On the Paterson Picket Line," *International Socialist Review*, 13 (June 1913), 847–851.

———. "On the Picket Line at Little Falls, New York," *International Socialist Review*, 13 (January 1913), 519–523.

———. "The Rip in the Silk Industry," *International Socialist Review*, 13 (May 1913), 783–788.

———. "Smoothing Out the Wrinkles in Silk," *The Pageant of the Paterson Strike*. (New York: Success Press, 1913), 22–27.

———. "When the Kiddies Came Home," *International Socialist Review*, 12 (May 1912), 716–717.

"Haywood and the I.W.W.," *International Socialist Review*, 14 (November 1913), 277.

"Haywood's Battle in Paterson," *Literary Digest*, 46 (May 10, 1913), 1043–1044.

Heaton, James P. "The Legal Aftermath of the Lawrence Strike," *Survey*, 28 (July 6, 1912), 503–510.

———. "The Salem Trial," *Survey*, 29 (December 7, 1912), 301–304.

Hopkins, M. A. "International Hotel Workers' Strike," *Collier's*, 49 (June 1, 1912), 27.

Hovey, Carl. "Haywood and Haywoodism," *Metropolitan Magazine*, 37 (June 1912), 17–19, 49.

Hoxie, Robert F. *Trade Unionism in the United States*. New York: D. Appleton and Co., 1920.

———. "The Truth about the I.W.W.," *Journal of Political Economy*, 21 (November 1913), 785–797.

Hunter, Robert. *Labor in Politics*. Chicago: The Socialist Party, 1915.

"Industrial Commission Is Announced by President Taft," *The Square Deal*, 11 (January 1913), 519–522.

"The Industrial Committee," *The Masses*, 8 (January 1916), 8.

"Industrial Relations," *The Masses*, 7 (October-November 1915), 21.

"Industrial Relations Commission," *Survey*, 30 (July 5, 1913), 452–453.

"Industrial Relations Statistics Or A Program?" *Survey*, 31 (November 8, 1913), 152–153.

"Industrial Workers," *Independent*, 72 (May 9, 1912), 1020–1021.

"Industrial Workers of the World," *International Socialist Review*, 10 (October 1909), 359–360.

"Industrial Workers of the World Make Confession," *Square Deal*, 13 (October 1913), 236–238.

"Investigation of the Paterson Troubles Urged," *Survey*, 30 (June 14, 1913), 368.

"I.W.W. and Revolution," *Review of Reviews*, 48 (September 1913), 370–371.

"I.W.W. Followers Are Now Object of the A.F. of L. Agitators," *Square Deal*, 11 (October 1912), 245–249.

"I.W.W. Leaders Must Disgorge," *Square Deal*, 15 (November 1914), 376–377.

"I.W.W. Pageant," *Outlook*, 104 (June 21, 1913), 352–353.

"I.W.W. Suffers," *Square Deal*, 12 (May 1913), 282–283.

The I.W.W.—What It Is and What It Is Not. Chicago: I.W.W. Publishing Bureau, n.d.

"I.W.W. Wins in New Jersey," *International Socialist Review*, 13 (June 1913), 888.

Jones, Ellis O. "The Parlor Socialists," *International Socialist Review*, 8 (October 1907), 204–212.

Kellogg, Paul U. "The Constructive Work before the Industrial Relations Committee," *Survey*, 30 (August 2, 1913), 571–574.

_____. "The Industrial Relations Commission," *Survey*, 29 (December 28, 1912), 385–386.

_____. "The McKee's Rocks Strike," *Survey*, 22 (August 7, 1909), 656–665.

Kennedy, John Curtis. "Socialistic Tendencies in American Trade Unions," *Journal of Political Economy*, 15 (October 1907), 470–488.

Kinkead, W. L. "Paterson Strike," *Survey*, 30 (May 31, 1913), 315–316.

Koettgen, Ewald. "I.W.W. Convention," *International Socialist Review*, 14 (November 1913), 275–276.

_____. "Making Silk," *International Socialist Review*, 14 (March 1914), 551–556.

_____. "No Grievances at All!" *The Pageant of the Paterson Strike*. (New York: Success Press, 1913), 9–11.

_____. *One Big Union in the Textile Industry*. Cleveland: I.W.W. Publicity Bureau, 1914.

"Labor Theories and a Labor War," *Outlook*, 104 (June 7, 1913), 275–278.

"Labor and the Law," *Nation*, 96 (May 22, 1913), 515–516.

Laidler, Harry W. *Boycotts and the Labor Struggle*. New York: John Lane, 1913.

"Larger Meaning of the Lawrence Strike," *Current Literature*, 52 (April 1912), 383.

"Last Week in Lawrence," *Survey*, 42 (May 10, 1919), 250–251.

Lauck, W. Jett. "The Hope of the American Wage-Earner," *North American Review*, 198 (July 1913), 18–26.

――――. "The Lesson from Lawrence," *North American Review*, 195 (May 1912), 665–672.

――――. "The Significance of the Situation at Lawrence," *Survey*, 27 (February 17, 1912), 1772–1774.

Laut, Agnes C. "Revolution Yawns," *Technical World Magazine*, 18 (October 1912), 124–144.

"Lawrence and the Industrial Workers of the World," *Survey*, 28 (April 6, 1912), 79–80.

"Lawrence Once More in the Foreground," *Survey*, 28 (September 7, 1912), 693–694.

"The Lawrence Settlement," *Survey*, 27 (March 23, 1912), 1949–1950.

"The Lawrence Strike," *Survey*, 42 (April 12, 1919), 82–83.

"The Lawrence Strike: A Poll of the Press," *Outlook*, 100 (February 17, 1912), 356–358.

"The Lawrence Strike: A Review," *Outlook*, 100 (March 9, 1912), 531-536.

"Lawrence Strike Raises a Big Question in Immigration," *Square Deal*, 10 (April 1912), 263–268.

"The Lawrence Strikers Win," *Survey*, 42 (May 31, 1919), 368.

"The Lesson of Lawrence," *The Masses*, 3 (April 1912), 3.

"Let Us Recall the Recall," *New Review*, 1 (April 12, 1913), 450–452.

Leupp, Constance D. "The Lawrence Strike Hearings," *Survey*, 27 (March 23, 1912), 1953–1954.

Levine, Louis. "The Development of Syndicalism in America," *Political Science Quarterly*, 28 (September 1913), 451–479.

――――. "The Philosophy of the Labor Struggles of To-Day," *Forum*, 47 (May 1912), 577–588.

Lippmann, Walter. "The I.W.W.: Insurrection Or Revolution?" *New Review*, 1 (August 1913), 701–706.

――――. "Legendary John Reed," *New Republic*, 1 (December 26, 1914), 15–16.

Lovejoy, Owen R. "The Right of Free Speech in Lawrence," *Survey*, 27 (March 9, 1912), 1904–1905.

Lusk, Hugh H. "Industrial War," *Forum*, 48 (November 1912), 553–564.

MacDonald, J. Ramsey. *Syndicalism*. London: Constable & Co., 1912.

McGowan, Kenneth. "Giovannitti: Poet of the Wop," *Forum*, 52 (October 1914), 609–611.

McGregor, Hugh. "Words of Warning," *American Federationist*, 12 (June 1905), 354–355.

"McKee's Rocks Strikers Win," *Survey*, 22 (September 11, 1909), 795.

Mann, Thomas. "A Plea for Solidarity," *International Socialist Review*, 14 (January 1914), 392–394.

Mannheimer, Leo. "Darkest New Jersey," *Independent*, 74 (May 29, 1913), 1190–1192.

Marcy, Leslie H. "800 Per Cent and the Akron Strike," *International Socialist Review*, 13 (April 1913), 711–724.

Marcy, Leslie H., and Boyd, Frederick S. "One Big Union Wins," *International Socialist Review*, 12 (April 1912), 613–630.

Marcy, Mary E. "The Battle for Bread at Lawrence," *International Socialist Review*, 12 (March 1912), 533–543.

————. "The Paterson Strike," *International Socialist Review*, 14 (October 1913), 177–178.

Martin, John. "Industrial Revolt at Lawrence," *Independent*, 72 (March 7, 1912), 491–495.

Mason, Gregory. "Industrial War in Paterson," *Outlook*, 104 (June 17, 1913), 283–287.

Montgomery, James. "The Lawrence Strike and the Literary Test," *New Review*, 1 (March 22, 1913), 376–381.

"Movement Under Way for Industrial Commission," *Survey*, 27 (March 2, 1912), 1821.

"The National Socialist Convention of 1912," *International Socialist Review*, 12 (June 1912), 807–828.

"The National Trades' and Workers' Association," *Square Deal*, 7 (October 1910), 193–201.

"A Needless Labor War," *Outlook*, 100 (January 27, 1912), 151–152.

"New Jersey's Journalistic Perils," *Literary Digest*, 46 (June 21, 1913), 1366–1367.

"A New Jersey Weaver, a Budget and a Gospel of Revolution," *Survey*, 28 (May 18, 1912), 289–291.

"New Labor Movement," *Literary Digest*, 44 (April 6, 1912), 677–678.

"New York a Prey to Strikes," *Outlook*, 103 (January 18, 1913), 102–103.

Oneal, James. *Sabotage or Socialism vs. Syndicalism*. St. Louis: The Rip-Saw Publishing Co., 1913.

O'Sullivan, Mary K. "The Labor War at Lawrence," *Survey*, 28 (April 6, 1912), 72–74.

"The Pageant As a Form of Propaganda," *Current Opinion*, 55 (July 1913), 32.

"Pageant of the Paterson Strike," *Survey*, 30 (June 28, 1913), 418.

Palmer, Lewis E. "A Strike for Four Loaves of Bread," *Survey*, 27 (February 3, 1912), 1690–1697.

Palmer, R. "Degrees of Redness," *Independent*, 76 (December 4, 1913), 460–461.

Pannekoek, Anton. "Socialism and Labor Unionism," *New Review*, 1 (July 1913), 615–662.

"Pat Quinlan," *The Masses*, 6 (April 1915), 16.

"Paterson," *New Review*, 1 (June 1913), 545–547.

"Paterson Convictions Again Set Aside," *Survey*, 31 (November 22, 1913), 191–192.

"Paterson and the I.W.W.," *Harper's Weekly*, 57 (June 14, 1913), 4

"Paterson Strike," *Independent*, 74 (May 29, 1913), 1172.

"Paterson Strike," *International Socialist Review*, 14 (September 1913), 177–178.

"Paterson Strike Leaders in Jersey Prison," *Survey*, 30 (April 3, 1913), 387.

"The Paterson Strike Is Leaderless," *Square Deal*, 13 (August 1913), 94.

"The Paterson Strike Pageant," *Independent*, 74 (June 19, 1913), 1406–1407.

"Peace in Paterson," *Survey*, 42 (August 23, 1919), 751.

Pease, Frank C. "I.W.W. and Revolution," *Forum*, 50 (August 1913), 153–168.

Perry, Grover H. *The Revolutionary I.W.W.* Cleveland: I.W.W. Publishing Bureau, 1916.

"Poet of the I.W.W.," *Outlook*, 104 (July 5, 1913), 504–506.

"Portrait," *Current Literature*, 52 (April 1912), 381.

"Possible Paterson," *Outlook*, 104 (June 14, 1913), 318–321.

Potter, Grace. "Strike of Brooklyn Shoe Workers," *International Socialist Review*, 11 (April 1911), 602–606.

Pratt, William Merriam. "The Lawrence Revolution," *New England Magazine*, 46 (March 1912), 7–16.

"Preaching Sabotage," *Square Deal*, 13 (November 1913), 382.

Priddy, Al. "Controlling the Passions of Men—In Lawrence," *Outlook*, 102 (October 19, 1912), 343–345.

Quinlan, Patrick. "Glorious Paterson," *International Socialist Review*, 14 (December 1913), 355–357.

———. "The Paterson Strike and After," *New Review*, 2 (January 1914), 26–33.

———. "Silk, Starvation and Solidarity," *Appeal to Reason*, August 16, 1913.

———. "The Trenton Penitentiary," *New Republic*, 9 (January 13, 1917), 292–295.

"Recall of Haywood," *Independent*, 74 (March 6, 1913), 490.

"Recall the Recall," *New Review*, 1 (April 12, 1913), 451–452.

Reitman, Ben L. "Impressions of the Chicago Convention," *Mother Earth*, 8 (October 1913), 239–242.

Reed, John. "Almost Thirty," *New Republic*, 86 (April 15-April 29, 1936), 267–270, 332–336.

———. "Sheriff Radcliff's Hotel," *Metropolitan Magazine*, 38 (September 1913), 14–15, 59–60.

———. "War in Paterson," *The Masses*, 4 (June 1913), 14–17.

"Revolutionary Unionism," *International Socialist Review*, 10 (September 1909), 266–268.

"The Rioting at McKee's Rocks," *Survey*, 22 (August 28, 1909), 719.

Rotzel, Harvell L. "The Lawrence Textile Strike," *American Labor Year Book*, 3 (1919–1920) 172–173.

Rowell, Wilbur E. "The Lawrence Strike," *Survey*, 27 (March 23, 1912), 1958–1960.

"Rumored Split in the Ranks of the Workers of the World," *Square Deal*, 11 (August 1912), 65–68.

Russell, Phillips, "The Acquittal of Ettor and Giovannitti," *International Socialist Review*, 13 (January 1913), 556–557.

———. "The Arrest of Haywood and Lessig," *International Socialist Review*, 13 (May 1913), 789–792.

———. "Lawrence and the Industrial Workers of the World," *Survey*, 28 (April 6, 1912), 79–80.

———. "Living on Determination in Paterson," *International Socialist Review*, 14 (August 1913), 100–101.

———. "The Second Battle of Lawrence," *International Socialist Review*, 13 (November 1912), 417–423.

_____. "Strike at Little Falls," *International Socialist Review*, 13 (December 1912), 455–460.

_____. "Strike Tactics," *New Review*, 1 (March 29, 1913), 405–409.

_____. "The World's Greatest Labor Play: The Paterson Strike Pageant," *International Socialist Review*, 14 (July 1913), 7–9.

St. John, Vincent. *The I.W.W.: Its History, Structure and Methods*. Chicago: I.W.W. Publishing Bureau, 1914.

"Salem Trial of the Lawrence Case," *Outlook*, 102 (December 7, 1912), 739–740.

Sanger, Margaret H. "The Paterson Strike," *Revolutionary Almanac, 1914*. Hippolyte Havel, ed. (New York: The Rabelais Press, 1914), 47–49.

Sawyer, Roland D. "What Threatens Ettor and Giovannitti," *International Socialist Review*, 13 (August 1912), 114–115.

Scanlon, Michael A. "What Lawrence Really Did," *Square Deal*, 11 (December 1912), 437–440.

Scott, Alexander. "What the Reds Are Doing in Paterson," *International Socialist Review*, 13 (June 1913), 852–856.

Scudder, Vida D. "For Justice Sake," *Survey*, 28 (April 6, 1912), 77–79.

"Security and Justice," *Harper's Weekly*, 60 (March 20, 1915), 267.

"Silencing Industrial Workers," *Literary Digest*, 44 (April 20, 1912), 800.

Simons, Algie M. "The Chicago Conference of Industrial Unions," *International Socialist Review*, 5 (February 1905), 496–499.

_____. "Industrial Workers of the World," *International Socialist Review*, 6 (August 1905), 65–76.

_____. "Socialism in the Present Campaign," *International Socialist Review*, 7 (October 1906), 241–243.

"Situation in Lawrence," *Outlook*, 102 (October 12, 1912), 286–287.

"Situation at McKee's Rocks," *Survey*, 22 (August 21, 1909), 693.

Smith, Rufus D. "Some Phases of the McKee's Rocks Strike," *Survey*, 23 (October 2, 1909), 38–45.

"Social Significance of Arturo Giovannitti," *Current Opinion*, 54 (January 1913), 24–26.

"Social War in New Jersey," *Current Opinion*, 55 (August 1913), 80–81.

"Socialism and Syndicalism," *Nation*, 94 (May 30, 1912), 533–534.

"Socialist Degeneration," *New Republic*, 1 (December 12, 1924), 10–11.

"Socialist Politics," *Nation*, 98 (February 12, 1924), 155–156.

"Socialists Rebuking Violence," *Literary Digest*, 44 (June 1, 1912), 1144–1145.

Spargo, John. *Syndicalism, Industrial Unionism, and Socialism*. New York: B. W. Huebsch, 1913.

"Statements by People Who Took Part," *Survey*, 28 (April 6, 1912), 75–77.

Stokes, Rose Pastor. "Paterson," *The Masses*, 5 (November 1913), 11.

Street, Julian. "A Soviet Saint," *Saturday Evening Post*, 203 (September 13, 1930), 8–9.

"The Strike of the New Jersey Silk Workers," *Survey*, 30 (April 19, 1913), 81–82.

"The Strike of the New Jersey Silk Weavers," *Survey*, 30 (May 31, 1913), 300.

Sumner, Mary Brown. "Broad-Silk Weavers of Paterson," *Survey*, 27 (March 16, 1912), 1932–1935.

_____. "Parting of the Ways in American Socialism," *Survey*, 29 (February 1, 1913), 623–630.

Thompson, Fred W. *The I.W.W.: Its First Fifty Years*. Chicago: I.W.W. Publishing Bureau, 1955.

_____. "The Way of the Wobbly," *Twenty-Five Years of Industrial Unionism*. (Chicago: I.W.W. Publishing Bureau, 1930.)

Tridon, Andre. "Haywood," *New Review*, 1 (May 1913), 502–506.

_____. *The New Unionism*. New York: B. W. Huebsch, 1913.

_____. "The Workers' Only Hope—Direct Action," *Independent*, 74 (January 9, 1913), 79–83.

"Two Hours, Reduced Wages, and a Strike," *Survey*, 27 (January 27, 1912), 1633–1634.

"Unemployment, an Illusive and Real Way Out," *American Federationist*, 21 (April 1914), 310–312.

"Violence and Democracy," *Outlook*, 100 (February 17, 1912), 352–353.

Vorse, Mary Heaton. "Elizabeth Gurley Flynn," *Nation*, 122 (February 17, 1926), 175–176.

_____. "The Trouble at Lawrence," *Harper's Weekly*, 56 (March 16, 1912), 10.

Walling, Anna Strunsky. "Giovannitti's Poems," *New Review*, 2 (May 1914), 288–292.

Weed, Inis, and Carey, Louis. "I Make Cheap Silk," *The Masses*, 5 (November 1913), 7.

Wetherell, Ellen. "Before Congress," *International Socialist Review*, 12 (March 1912), 631–632.

Weyl, Walter E. "It Is Time To Know," *Survey*, 28 (April 6, 1912), 65–67.

_____. "The Strikers at Lawrence," *Outlook*, 100 (February 10, 1912), 309–312.

"What Haywood Says on Political Action," *International Socialist Review*, 13 (February 1913), 622.

"What Is Hostility to Government?" *Outlook*, 104 (June 21, 1913), 351.

Wheeler, Robert J. "The Allentown Silk Dyers Strike," *International Socialist Review*, 13 (May 1913), 820–821.

Williams, Ben H. *Eleven Blind Leaders of "Practical Socialism" and "Revolutionary Tactics" from an I.W.W. Standpoint*. New Castle, Pa.: Press of the I.W.W. Publishing Bureau, 1911.

Wing, M. T. C. "The Flag at McKee's Rocks," *Survey*, 23 (October 2, 1909), 45–46.

Withington, Anne. "The Lawrence Strike," *Life and Labor*, 2 (March 1912), 73–77.

Woehlke, Walter V. "I.W.W.," *Outlook*, 101 (July 6, 1912), 531–536.

_____. "Terrorism in America," *Outlook*, 100 (February 17, 1912), 359–367.

Woods, Robert A. "The Breadth and Depth of the Lawrence Outcome," *Survey*, 28 (April 6, 1912), 67–68.

_____. "The Clod Stirs," *Survey*, 27 (March 16, 1912), 1929–1932.

"Work of the I.W.W. in Paterson," *Literary Digest*, 47 (August 9, 1913), 197–198.

"Workers of the World Now Run Affairs for New York Waiters," *Square Deal*, 12 (February 1913), 29–32.

"A Wave of Love in Henry Street," *Survey*, 30 (June 28, 1913), 427–428.

G. Unpublished Material

Beffel, John N. "Biographical Sketch of Joseph J. Ettor." Typescript, 1948. Labadie Collection, University of Michigan Library.

──────. "Patrick Quinlan." Typescript, n.d. Labadie Collection, University of Michigan Library.

Flynn, Elizabeth Gurley. "The Truth About the Paterson Strike." Typescript of the Speech Delivered at the New York Civic Club Forum, January 31, 1914. Labadie Collection, University of Michigan Library. Included in Joyce Kornbluh, ed., *Rebel Voices: An I.W.W. Anthology* (Ann Arbor: University of Michigan, 1964), pp. 215–226.

Gill, Patrick F., and Brennan, Redmond S. "Report on the Inferior Courts and Police of Paterson." Typescript, 1914. Paterson Free Public Library.

Inglis, Agnes. "Reminiscences." Typescript, July 19, 1926. Labadie Collection, University of Michigan Library.

II. SECONDARY SOURCES

A. Unpublished Monographs

Altarelli, Carlo C. "History and Present Conditions of the Italian Colony of Paterson, New Jersey." Unpublished M. A. Thesis. Columbia University, 1911.

Brooks, Robert R. R. "The United Textile Workers of America." Unpublished Ph.D. Dissertation. Yale University, 1935.

Carpenter, John A. "The Industrial Development of Paterson, New Jersey, 1792–1913." Unpublished Ph.D. Dissertation. Rutgers University, 1968.

Garber, Morris William. "The Silk Industry of Paterson, New Jersey, 1840–1913." Unpublished Ph.D. Dissertation. Rutgers University, 1968.

Liberman, Esther. "The Influence of Left-Wing Radicalism in the Paterson Silk Strikes of 1912–1913, and the Passaic Woolen Strike of 1925." Typescript in the Paterson Free Public Library, n.d.

Mooney, Martin C. "The Industrial Workers of the World and the Immigrants of Paterson and Passaic, New Jersey, 1907–1913." Unpublished M. A. Thesis. Seton Hall University, 1969.

Noble, Richard A. "The Relation of the Middle Classes and Local Government of Paterson, New Jersey, to the Labor Movement in the Paterson Silk Industry, 1877–1913." Unpublished Senior Thesis. Princeton University, n.d.

Tierney, Ruth. "The Decline of the Silk Industry in Paterson, New Jersey." Unpublished M. A. Thesis. Cornell University, 1938.

Wood, James E. "History of Labor in the Broad-Silk Industry of Paterson, New Jersey, 1879–1940." Unpublished Ph.D. Dissertation. University of California, 1942.

B. Published Monographs

Aaron, Daniel. *Writers on the Left.* New York: Harcourt, Brace & World, 1961.

Abrams, Richard. *Conservatism in a Progressive Era: Massachusetts Politics, 1900–1912.* Cambridge: Harvard University Press, 1964.

Adams, Graham. *Age of Industrial Violence, 1910–1915: The Activities and Findings of the United States Commission on Industrial Relations.* New York: Columbia University Press, 1966.

Allen, Franklin. *The Silk Industry of the World at the Opening of the Twentieth Century.* New York: Silk Association of America, 1904.

Bedford, Henry F. *Socialism and the Workers in Massachusetts, 1886–1912.* Amherst: University of Massachusetts Press, 1966.

Bloomfield, Maxwell H. *Alarms and Diversions: The American Mind Through American Magazines, 1900–1914.* The Hague, Netherlands: Mouton & Co., 1967.

Boone, Gladys. *The Women's Trade Union League in Great Britain and the United States of America.* New York: AMS Press, 1968.

Bremner, Robert H. *From The Depths: The Discovery of Poverty in America.* New York: New York University Press, 1956.

Brissenden, Paul F. *The I.W.W.: A Study of American Syndicalism.* New York: Russell & Russell, 1919.

Brooks, Van Wyck. *The Confident Years: 1885–1915.* New York: E. P. Dutton & Co., 1952.

Buhle, Mari Jo. *Women and American Socialism, 1870–1920.* Urbana: University of Illinois Press, 1981.

Cantor, Milton. *Max Eastman.* New York: Twayne Publishers, 1970.

Carlson, Peter. *Roughneck: The Life and Times of Big Bill Haywood.* New York: W. W. Norton & Co., 1983.

Chambers, Clark A. *Paul U. Kellogg and the Survey: Voices for Social Welfare and Social Justice.* Minneapolis: University of Minnesota Press, 1971.

Churchill, Allen. *The Improper Bohemians: A Re-creation of Greenwich Village in Its Heyday.* New York: E. P. Dutton & Co., 1959.

Clark, Victor S. *History of Manufactures in the United States.* 3 vols. New York: Carnegie Institution, 1929.

Cole, Donald B. *Immigrant City: Lawrence, Massachusetts, 1845–1921.* Chapel Hill: University of North Carolina Press, 1963.

Cole, G. D. H. *A History of Socialist Thought.* 3 vols. London: Macmillan & Co., 1956.

Commons, John R. et al. *History of Labor in the United States.* vol. 4. New York: Macmillan Co., 1921.

Conlin, Joseph R., ed. *The American Radical Press, 1880–1960.* Westport, Conn.: Greenwood Press, 1974.

———. *Big Bill Haywood and the Radical Union Movement.* Syracuse: Syracuse University Press, 1969.

———. *Bread and Roses Too, Studies of the Wobblies.* Westport, Conn.: Greenwood Press, 1969.

Cunningham, John T. *New Jersey — America's Main Road.* Garden City, N. Y.: Doubleday & Co., 1966.

Dick, William M. *Labor and Socialism in America: The Gompers Era.* Port Washington, N. Y.: Kennikat Press, 1972.

Dorgan, Maurice B. *History of Lawrence, Massachusetts.* Lawrence, Mass.: Privately Published, 1924.

Douglas, Emily Taft. *Margaret Sanger: Pioneer of the Future.* New York: Holt, Rinehart and Winston, 1970.

Drinnon, Richard. *Rebel In Paradise.* Chicago: University of Chicago Press, 1961.

Dubofsky, Melvyn. *We Shall Be All: A History of the I.W.W.* Chicago: Quadrangle Books, 1969.

Dulles, Foster Rhea. *Labor in America.* New York: Thomas Y. Crowell Co., 1955.

Egbert, Donald Drew, and Persons, Stow, eds. *Socialism and American Life.* 2 vols. Princeton: Princeton University Press, 1952.

Faulkner, Harold U. *The Quest For Social Justice, 1898–1914.* New York: Macmillan Co., 1931.

Fishbein, Leslie. *Rebels in Bohemia: The Radicals of the Masses, 1911–1917.* Chapel Hill: University of North Carolina Press, 1982.

Fine, Nathan. *Labor and Farmer Parties in the United States, 1828–1928.* New York: The Rand School of Social Science, 1928.

Foner, Philip S. *History of the Labor Movement in the United States,* vol. 4: *The Industrial Workers of the World, 1905–1917.* New York: International Publishers Co., 1965.

Gambs, John S. *The Decline of the I.W.W.* New York: Columbia University Press, 1932.

Gelb, Barbara. *So Short A Time: A Biography of John Reed and Louise Bryant.* New York: W. W. Norton & Co., 1973.

Gilbert, James B. *Writers and Partisans: A History of Literary Radicalism In America.* New York: John Wiley and Sons, 1968.

Ginger, Ray. *The Bending Cross—A Biography of Eugene Victor Debs.* New Brunswick: Rutgers University Press, 1949.

Gray, Madeline. *Margaret Sanger.* New York: Richard Marek Publishers, 1979.

Greaves, C. Desmond. *Liam Mellows and the Irish Rebellion.* London: Lawrence & Wishart, 1971.

——. *The Life and Times of James Connolly.* London: Lawrence & Wishart, 1961.

Green, Marguerite. *The National Civic Federation and the American Labor Movement, 1900–1925.* Washington: Catholic University Press, 1956.

Groat, George G. *An Introduction to the Study of Organized Labor in America.* New York: Macmillan Co., 1916.

Grover, David H. *Debaters and Dynamiters—The Story of the Haywood Trial.* Corvallis: Oregon State University Press, 1964.

Heusser, Albert H. *The History of the Silk Dyeing Industry in the United States.* Paterson: Silk Dyers Association of America, 1927.

Hicks, Granville. *John Reed: The Making of a Revolutionary.* New York: Macmillan Co., 1936.

Hiller, Ernest T. *The Strike: A Study in Collective Action.* Chicago: University of Chicago Press, 1928.

Hutchins, Grace. *Labor and Silk.* New York: International Publishers Co., 1929.

Jensen, Vernon H. *Heritage of Conflict.* Ithaca: Cornell University Press, 1950.

Joll, James. *The Anarchists.* Boston: Little, Brown and Co., 1964.

Kaplan, Justin. *Lincoln Steffens, A Biography.* New York: Simon and Schuster, 1974.

Karson, Marc. *American Labor Unions and Politics, 1900–1918.* Carbondale: Southern Illinois University Press, 1958.

Kaufman, Stuart Bruce. *Samuel Gompers and the Origins of the American Federation of Labor, 1848–1896.* Westport, Conn.: Greenwood Press, 1973.

Kipnis, Ira. *The American Socialist Movement, 1897–1912.* New York: Columbia University Press, 1952.

Kraditor, Aileen S. *The Radical Persuasion, 1890–1917.* Baton Rouge: Louisiana State University Press, 1981.

Kreuter, Kent and Gretchen. *An American Dissenter: The Life of Algie M. Simons, 1870–1950.* Lexington: University of Kentucky Press, 1969.

Lader, Lawrence. *The Margaret Sanger Story and the Fight For Birth Control.* Garden City, N. Y.: Doubleday & Co., 1955.

Larkin, Emmet. *James Larkin—Irish Labour Leader, 1876–1947.* Cambridge: The M.I.T. Press, 1965.

Lasch, Christopher. *The New Radicalism in America, 1889–1963: The Intellectual As a Social Type.* New York: Alfred A. Knopf, 1965.

Laslett, John H. M. *Labor and the Left: A Study of Socialist and Radical Influence in the American Labor Movement, 1881–1924.* New York: Basic Books, 1970.

Lens, Sidney. *The Labor Wars.* New York: Doubleday & Co., 1974.

————. *Radicalism in America.* New York: Thomas Y. Crowell Co., 1969.

Lorwin, Lewis L. *The American Federation of Labor.* Washington: The Brookings Institution, 1933.

Madison, Charles A. *American Labor Leaders.* New York: Ungar, 1962.

————. *Critics and Crusaders: A Century of American Protest.* New York: Henry Holt and Co., 1947.

Mandel, Bernard. *Samuel Gompers: A Biography.* Yellow Springs, Ohio: The Antioch Press, 1963.

Matsui, Shichiro. *The History of the Silk Industry in the United States.* New York: Howes Publishing Co., 1930.

May, Henry F. *The End of American Innocence.* New York: Alfred A. Knopf, 1959.

Miller, Sally M. *The Radical Immigrant.* New York: Twayne Publishers, 1974.

————. *Victor Berger and the Promise of Constructive Socialism: 1910–1920.* Westport, Conn.: Greenwood Press, 1973.

Morgan, H. Wayne. *Eugene V. Debs: Socialist for President, 1900–1924.* Syracuse: Syracuse University Press, 1962.

Nelson, William, and Shriner, Charles. *History of Paterson and Its Environs.* 3 vols. New York: Lewis Historical Publishing Co., 1920.

Newman, Philip C. *The Labor Legislation of New Jersey.* Washington: American Council on Public Affairs, 1943.

Nomad, Max. *Rebels and Renegades.* New York: Macmillan Co., 1932.

Norwood, Christopher. *About Paterson.* New York: E. P. Dutton, 1974.

O'Connor, Richard, and Walker, Dale L. *The Lost Revolutionary: A Biography of John Reed.* New York: Harcourt, Brace & World, 1967.

Parry, Albert. *Garrets and Pretenders, A History of Bohemianism in America.* New York: Dover Publications, 1960.

Perlman, Selig. *A Theory of the Labor Movement.* New York: Macmillan Co., 1928.

Perlman, Selig, and Taft, Philip. *History of Labor in the United States, 1896–1932.* John R. Commons et al., vol. 4: *Labor Movements.* New York: Macmillan Co., 1935.

Petersen, Arnold. *Daniel DeLeon: Social Architect.* 2 vols. New York: New York Labor News Company, 1953.

Pratt, Norma Fain. *Morris Hillquit.* Westport, Conn.: Greenwood Press, 1979.

Preston, William. *Aliens and Dissenters: Federal Suppression of Radicals, 1903–1933.* Cambridge: Harvard University Press, 1963.

Quint, Howard H. *The Forging of American Socialism: Origins of the Modern Movement.* Columbia: University of South Carolina Press, 1953.

Renshaw, Patrick. *The Wobblies: The Story of Syndicalism in the United States.* New York: Doubleday & Co., 1967.

Rideout, Walter B. *The Radical Novel in the United States, 1900–1954.* Cambridge: Harvard University Press, 1965.

Rogoff, Hillel. *An East Side Epic—The Life and Work of Meyer London.* New York: The Vanguard Press, 1930.

Rohan, Jack. *Yankee Arms Maker—The Incredible Career of Samuel Colt.* New York: Harper & Brothers, 1935.

Rosenblum, Gerald. *Immigrant Workers: Their Impact on American Labor Radicalism.* New York: Basic Books, 1973.

Rosenstone, Robert A. *Romantic Revolutionary: A Biography of John Reed.* New York: Alfred A. Knopf, 1975.

Saposs, David J. *Left Wing Unionism: A Study of Radical Politics and Tactics.* New York: International Publishers Co., 1926.

Savage, Marion D. *Industrial Unionism in America.* New York: The Ronald Press, 1922.

Schonbach, Morris. *Radicals and Visionaries: A History of Dissent in New Jersey.* Princeton: D. Van Nostrand Co., 1964.

Shannon, David A. *The Socialist Party of America.* New York: Macmillan Co., 1955.

Shriver, William P. *The Silk Workers of Paterson: A Pioneering Study.* New York: Board of National Missions, Presbyterian Church of U.S.A., 1929.

Taft, Philip. *Organized Labor in American History.* New York: Harper & Row, 1964.

Tax, Meredith. *The Rising of the Women: Feminist Solidarity and Class Conflict, 1880–1917.* New York: Monthly Review Press, 1980.

Troy, Leo. *Organized Labor in New Jersey.* New Brunswick: Rutgers University Press, 1965.

Tyler, Robert L. *Rebels of the Woods: The I.W.W. in the Pacific Northwest.* Eugene: University of Oregon Press, 1967.

Van Tine, Warren R. *The Making of the Labor Bureaucrat: Union Leadership in the United States, 1870–1920.* Amherst: University of Massachusetts Press, 1973.

Vecoli, Rudolph J. *The People of New Jersey.* Princeton: D. Van Nostrand Co., 1965.

Weinstein, James. *The Decline of Socialism in America, 1912–1925.* New York: Monthly Review Press, 1967.

Yellen, Samuel. *American Labor Struggles.* New York: S. A. Russell, 1936.

Yellowitz, Irwin. *Labor and the Progressive Movement in New York State, 1897–1916.* Ithaca: Cornell University Press, 1965.

Zaretz, Charles E. *Amalgamated Clothing Workers of America: A Study in Progressive Trades-Unionism.* New York: Ancon Publishing Co., 1934.

C. Articles

Allen, Harber. "The Flynn," *American Mercury,* 9 (December 1926), 426–433.

Bassett, Michael. "The Socialist Party Dilemma, 1912–1914," *Mid-America,* 47 (October 1965), 243–256.

Blum, Albert A. "Why Unions Grow," *Labor History,* 9 (Winter 1968), 39–72.

Brazier, Richard. "The Mass I.W.W. Trial of 1918: A Retrospect," *Labor History,* 7 (Spring 1966), 178–192.

Broyles, Glen J. "The Spokane Free Speech Fight, 1909–1910: A Study in I.W.W. Tactics," *Labor History,* 19 (Spring 1978), 238–252.

Camp, Helen C. "Elizabeth Gurley Flynn," *Notable American Women — The Modern Period* (Cambridge: Harvard University Press, 1980), 242–246.

Conlin, Joseph R. "The I.W.W. and the Question of Violence," *Wisconsin Magazine of History,* 51 (Spring 1968), 316–326.

———. "The I.W.W. and the Socialist Party," *Science and Society,* 31 (Winter 1967), 22–36.

Derber, Milton. "The Idea of Industrial Democracy in America, 1898–1915," *Labor History,* 7 (Fall 1966), 259–286.

Dubofsky, Melvyn. "Organized Labor and the Immigrant in New York City, 1900–1918," *Labor History,* 2 (Spring 1961), 182–201.

———. "The Origins of Western Working Class Radicalism, 1890–1905," *Labor History,* 7 (Spring 1966), 131–154.

———. "Success and Failure of Socialism in New York City, 1900–1918: A Case Study," *Labor History,* 9 (Fall 1968), 361–375.

Ebner, Michael H. "The Passaic Strike of 1912 and the Two I.W.W.s," *Labor History,* 11 (Fall 1970), 452–466.

Eulau, Heinz. "Mover and Shaker: Walter Lippmann As a Young Man," *Antioch Review,* 11 (September 1951), 291–312.

Fogelson, Nancy. "They Paved the Street with Silk: New Jersey Silk Workers, 1913–1924," *New Jersey History,* 97 (Autumn 1979), 133–148.

Fox, Richard W. "The Paradox of 'Progressive' Socialism: The Case of Morris Hillquit, 1901–1914," *American Quarterly,* 26 (May 1974), 127–140.

Glaser, William A. "Algie Martin Simons and Marxism in America," *Mississippi Valley Historical Review*, 41 (December 1954), 419–434.

Golin, Steve. "Defeat Becomes Disaster: The Paterson Strike of 1913 and the Decline of the I.W.W.," *Labor History*, 24 (Spring 1983), 223–248.

———. "The Paterson Pageant: Success or Failure?" *Socialist Review*, 69 (May-June 1983), 45–78.

Greenbaum, Fred. "The Social Ideas of Samuel Gompers," *Labor History*, 7 (Winter 1966), 35–61.

Gutman, Herbert G. "Class, Status and Community Power in Nineteenth-Century American Industrial Cities—Paterson, New Jersey: A Case Study," in Frederic C. Jaher, ed., *The Age of Industrialism: Essays in Social Structure and Cultural Values* (New York: Macmillan Co., 1968), 263–287.

———. "Industrial Invasion of the Village Green," *Transaction*, 3 (May-June 1966), 19–24.

Hollander, Jay Michael. "Prelude to a Strike," *New Jersey Historical Society Proceedings*, 79 (July 1961), 161–168.

Ingham, John N. "A Strike in the Progressive Era: McKees Rocks, 1909," *Pennsylvania Magazine*, 90 (July 1966), 353–377.

Kizer, B. H. "Elizabeth Gurley Flynn," *Pacific Northwest Quarterly*, 57 (July 1966), 110–112.

Laslett, John H. M. "Reflections on the Failure of Socialism in the American Federation of Labor," *Mississippi Valley Historical Review*, 50 (March 1964), 634–651.

———. "Socialism and the American Labor Movement: Some New Reflections," *Labor History*, 8 (Spring 1967), 136–155.

Levin, Howard. "Paterson Silk Workers' Strike," *King's Crown Essays*, 9 (Winter 1961–1962), 44–64.

Lynn, Kenneth S. "The Rebels of Greenwich Village," *Perspectives in American History*, 8 (1974), 335–377.

McKee, Don K. "Daniel DeLeon: A Reappraisal," *Labor History*, 1 (Fall 1960), 264–297.

Most, Mel. "The 1913 Silk Strike Terror—The Hoax That Killed Silk City," *Bergen Record* (September 30, 1973), 6–12.

Neufeld, Maurice. "The Historical Relationship of Liberals and Intellectuals to Organized Labor in the United States," *The Annals of the American Academy of Political and Social Science*, 350 (November 1963), 115–128.

Newman, Philip. "The First I.W.W. Invasion of New Jersey," *Proceedings of the New Jersey Historical Society*, 58 (October 1940), 268–283.

Nochlin, Linda. "The Paterson Strike Pageant of 1913," *Art in America*, 62 (May-June 1974), 64–68.

Osborne, James D. "Italian Immigrants and the Working Class in Paterson: The Strike of 1913 in Ethnic Perspective," in Paul A. Stellhorn, ed., *New Jersey's Ethnic Heritage* (Trenton: New Jersey Historical Commission, 1978), 11–34.

———. "Paterson: Immigrant Strikers and the War of 1913," Joseph R. Conlin, ed., *At the Point of Production: The Local History of the I.W.W.* (Westport, Conn.: Greenwood Press, 1981), 61–78.

Peck, Sidney M. "The Sociology of Unionism: An Appraisal," *American Journal of Economics and Sociology*, 25 (January 1966), 53–67.

Preston, William. "Shall This Be All? Historians Versus William D. Haywood, et. al.," *Labor History*, 12 (Summer 1971), 435–463.

Quint, Howard H. "Julius A. Wayland, Pioneer Socialist Propagandist," *Mississippi Valley Historical Review*, 35 (March 1949), 585–606.

Rischin, Moses. "From Gompers to Hillman: Labor Goes Middle Class," *Antioch Review*, 13 (June 1953), 191–201.

Seretan, L. Glen. "The Personal Style and Political Methods of Daniel DeLeon: A Reconsideration," *Labor History*, 14 (Spring 1973), 163–201.

Shannon, David A. "Rose Harriet Pastor Stokes," in *Notable American Women*, vol. 3 (Cambridge: Harvard University Press, 1971), 384–386.

Snyder, Robert E. "Women, Wobblies, and Workers' Rights: The 1912 Textile Strike in Little Falls, New York," *New York History*, 60 (January 1979), 29–57.

Taft, Philip. "The I.W.W. in the Grain Belt," *Labor History*, 1 (Winter 1960), 53–67.

Tobin, Eugene M. "Direct Action and Conscience: The 1913 Paterson Strike as Example of the Relationship Between Labor Radicals and Liberals," *Labor History*, 20 (Winter 1979), 73–88.

Tuchman, Barbara W. "The Anarchists," *Atlantic Monthly*, 211 (May 1963), 91–110.

Wakefield, Dan. "The Haunted Hall: I.W.W. at Fifty," *Dissent*, (Fall 1956), 414–419.

Weinstein, James. "Gompers and the New Liberalism, 1900–1909," *Studies on The Left*, 1 (Winter 1960), 5–27.

Wolman, Leo. "The Extent of Labor Organization in the United States in 1910," *Quarterly Journal of Economics*, 30 (May 1916), 602–624.

Zeiger, Robert H. "Robin Hood in the Silk City: The I.W.W. and the Paterson Silk Strike of 1913," *New Jersey Historical Society Proceedings*, 84 (July 1966), 182–195.

D. Works of Fiction

Bynner, Witter. *Cake*. New York: Alfred A. Knopf, 1926.

Churchill, Winston. *The Dwelling Place of Light*. New York: Macmillan Co., 1917.

Eastman, Max. *Venture*. New York: Albert & Charles Boni, 1927.

Kemp, Harry. *More Miles*. New York: Boni and Liveright, 1926.

Van Vechten, Carl. *Peter Whiffle*. New York: Alfred A. Knopf, 1922.

Index

A Note on the Author

Anne Huber Tripp is an associate professor of History at Oakland University in Rochester, Michigan. She received her bachelor's degree from Wheaton College in Massachusetts and her master's and doctorate from the University of Michigan, where she wrote her dissertation on the career of Ben Lindsey. *The I.W.W. and the Paterson Silk Strike of 1913* is her first book.